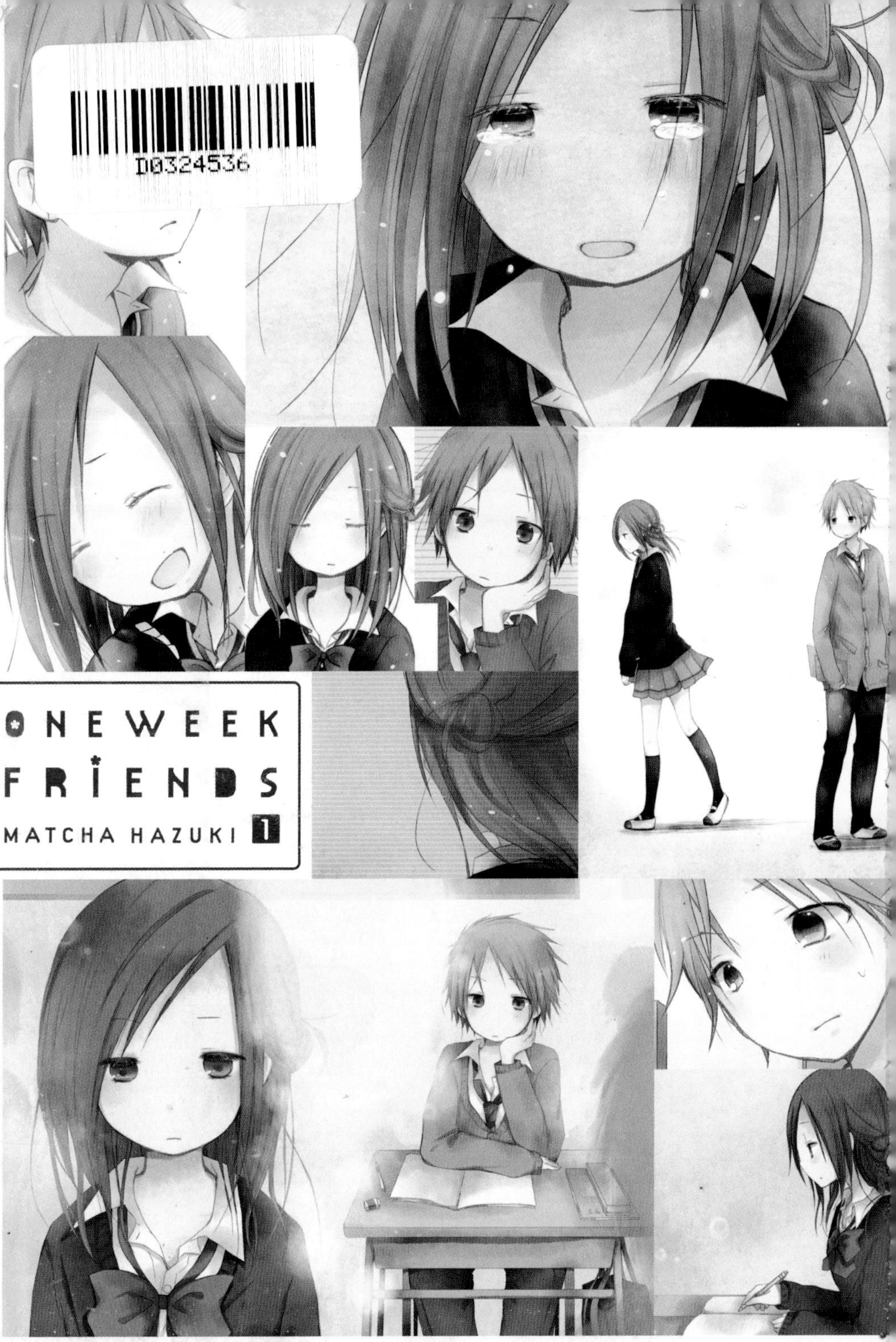

# ONE WEEK FRIENDS

MATCHA HAZUKI 1

# ONE WEEK FRIENDS 1

## Contents

Chapter 0  The Start of a Friendship     3

Chapter 1  Please Be My Friend          47

Chapter 2  A Day Out with a Friend       89

Chapter 3  Friend of a Friend          117

Bonus Skit                             151

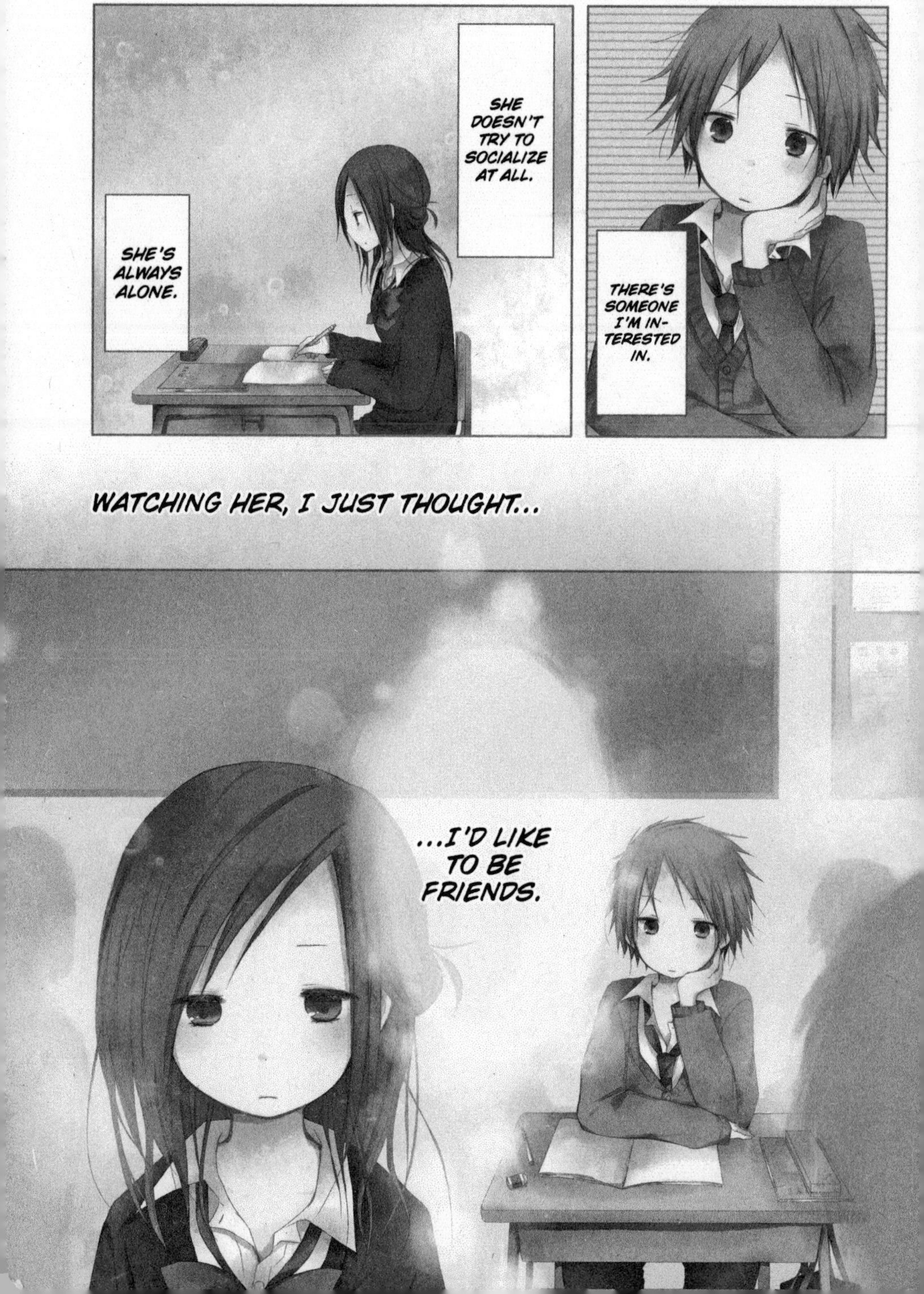
THERE'S SOMEONE I'M INTERESTED IN.
SHE DOESN'T TRY TO SOCIALIZE AT ALL.
SHE'S ALWAYS ALONE.
WATCHING HER, I JUST THOUGHT...
...I'D LIKE TO BE FRIENDS.

# CHAPTER 0
# THE START OF A FRIENDSHIP

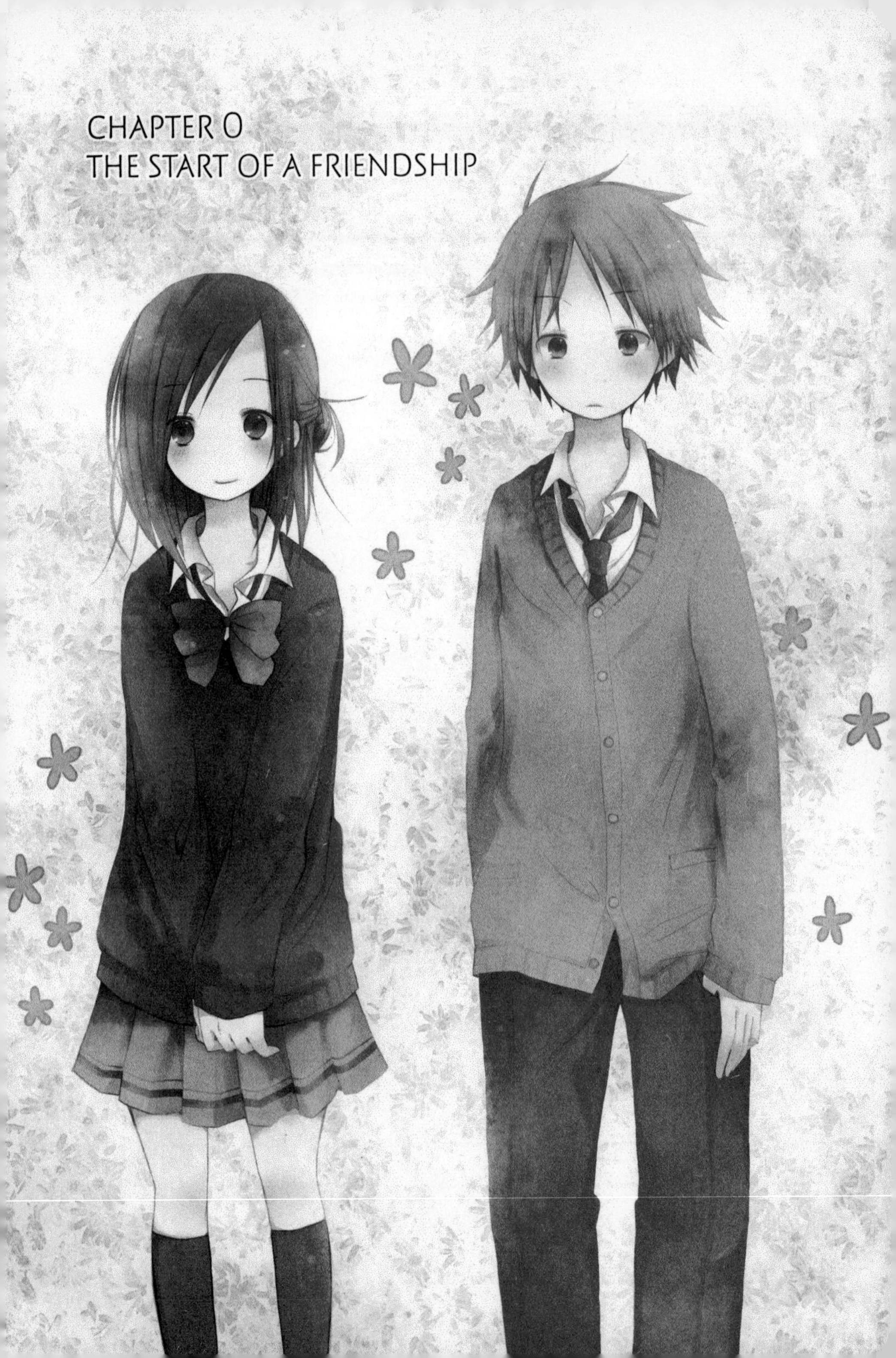

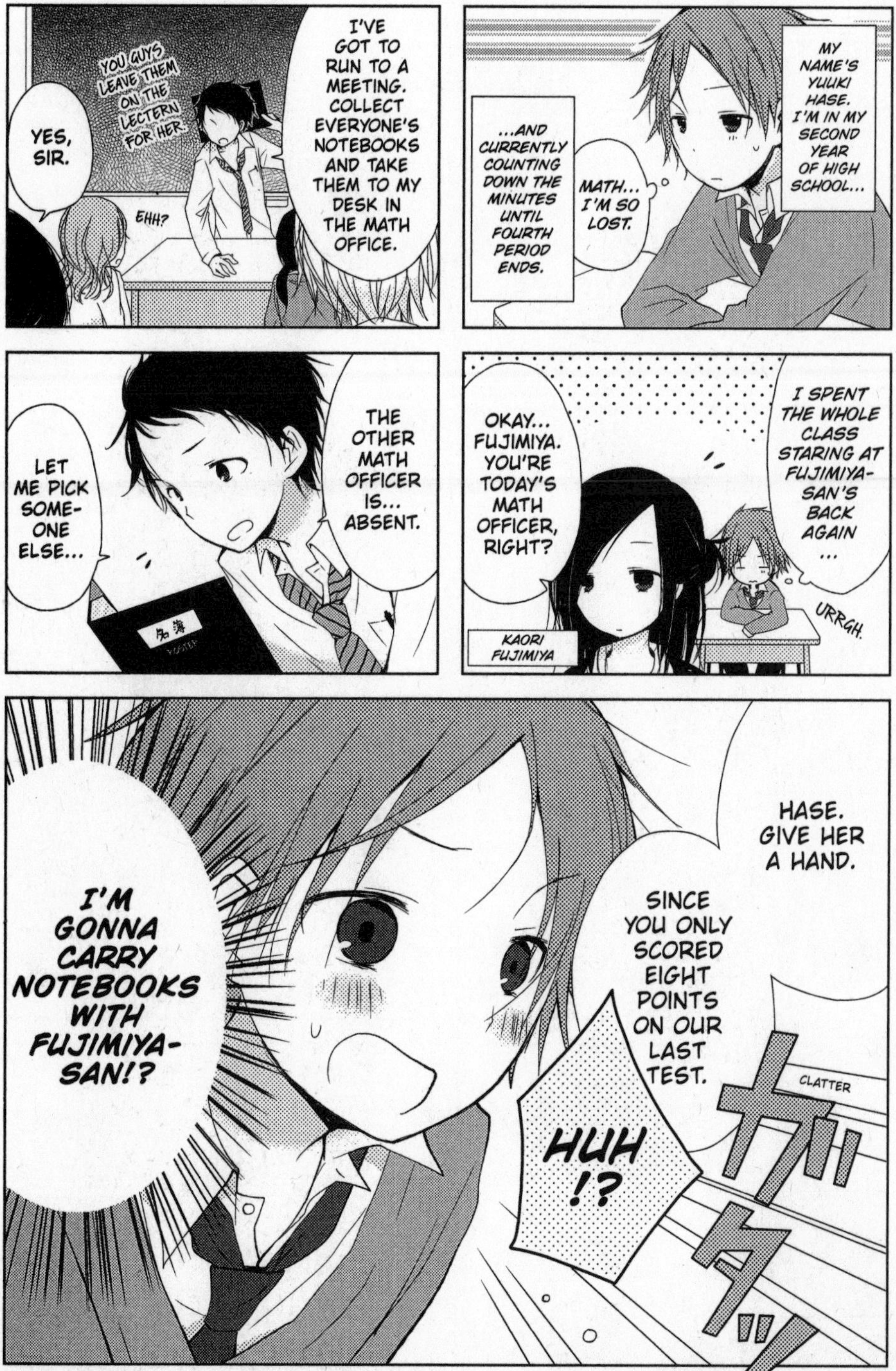
MY NAME'S YUUKI HASE. I'M IN MY SECOND YEAR OF HIGH SCHOOL...
...AND CURRENTLY COUNTING DOWN THE MINUTES UNTIL FOURTH PERIOD ENDS.
MATH... I'M SO LOST.
I'VE GOT TO RUN TO A MEETING. COLLECT EVERYONE'S NOTEBOOKS AND TAKE THEM TO MY DESK IN THE MATH OFFICE.
YOU GUYS LEAVE THEM ON THE LECTERN FOR HER.
EHH?
YES, SIR.
I SPENT THE WHOLE CLASS STARING AT FUJIMIYA-SAN'S BACK AGAIN...
URRGH.
OKAY... FUJIMIYA. YOU'RE TODAY'S MATH OFFICER, RIGHT?
KAORI FUJIMIYA
THE OTHER MATH OFFICER IS... ABSENT.
LET ME PICK SOME-ONE ELSE...
HASE. GIVE HER A HAND.
SINCE YOU ONLY SCORED EIGHT POINTS ON OUR LAST TEST.
CLATTER
HUH!?
I'M GONNA CARRY NOTEBOOKS WITH FUJIMIYA-SAN!?

## A CHANCE AND A FAIL

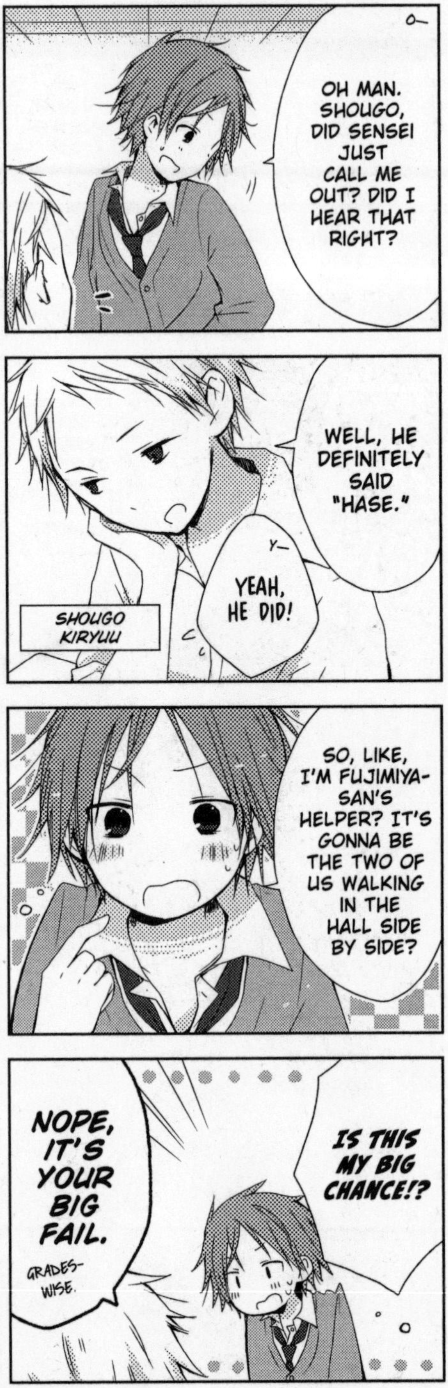
O—
OH MAN. SHOUGO, DID SENSEI JUST CALL ME OUT? DID I HEAR THAT RIGHT?
WELL, HE DEFINITELY SAID "HASE."
Y— YEAH, HE DID!
SHOUGO KIRYUU
SO, LIKE, I'M FUJIMIYA-SAN'S HELPER? IT'S GONNA BE THE TWO OF US WALKING IN THE HALL SIDE BY SIDE?
IS THIS MY BIG CHANCE!?
NOPE, IT'S YOUR BIG FAIL.
GRADES-WISE.

## WEIRD TASTE?

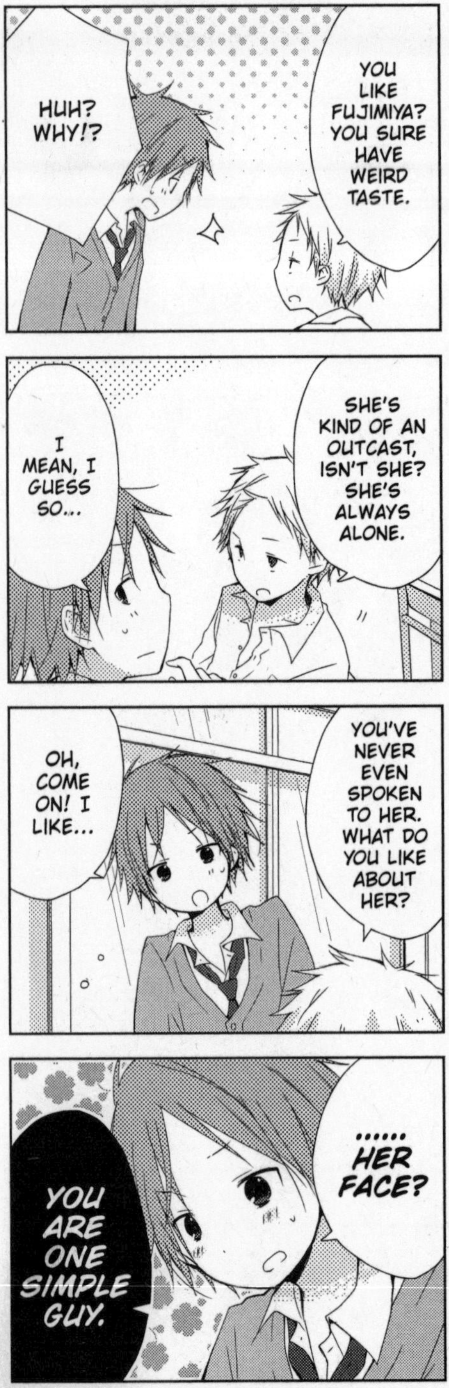
YOU LIKE FUJIMIYA? YOU SURE HAVE WEIRD TASTE.
HUH? WHY!?
SHE'S KIND OF AN OUTCAST, ISN'T SHE? SHE'S ALWAYS ALONE.
I MEAN, I GUESS SO...
YOU'VE NEVER EVEN SPOKEN TO HER. WHAT DO YOU LIKE ABOUT HER?
OH, COME ON! I LIKE...
......HER FACE?
YOU ARE ONE SIMPLE GUY.

## LACKING FORTITUDE

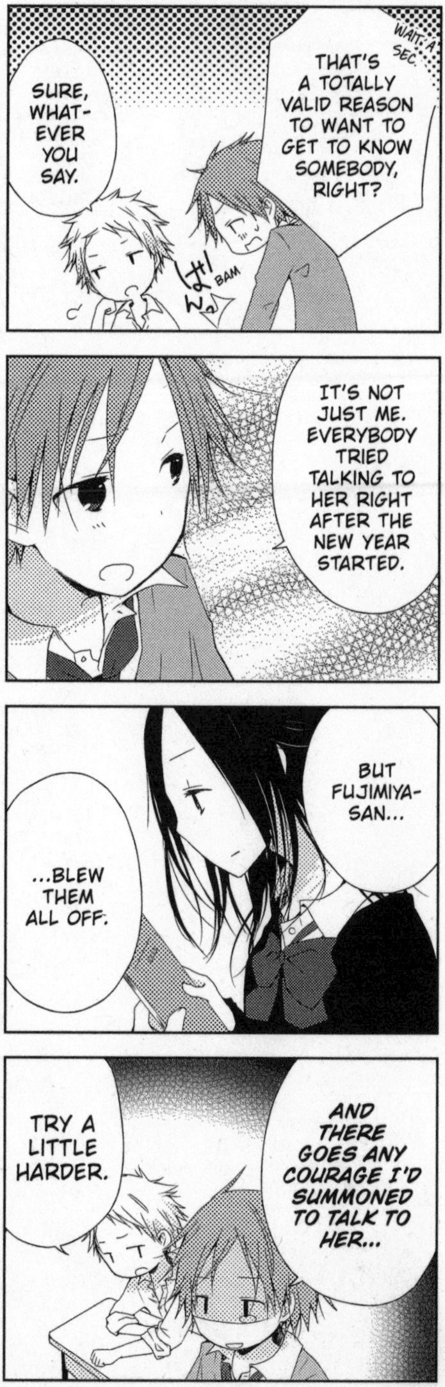
WAIT A SEC.
THAT'S A TOTALLY VALID REASON TO WANT TO GET TO KNOW SOMEBODY, RIGHT?
SURE, WHATEVER YOU SAY.
BAM
IT'S NOT JUST ME. EVERYBODY TRIED TALKING TO HER RIGHT AFTER THE NEW YEAR STARTED.
BUT FUJIMIYA-SAN...
...BLEW THEM ALL OFF.
AND THERE GOES ANY COURAGE I'D SUMMONED TO TALK TO HER...
TRY A LITTLE HARDER.

## TYPICAL DAY

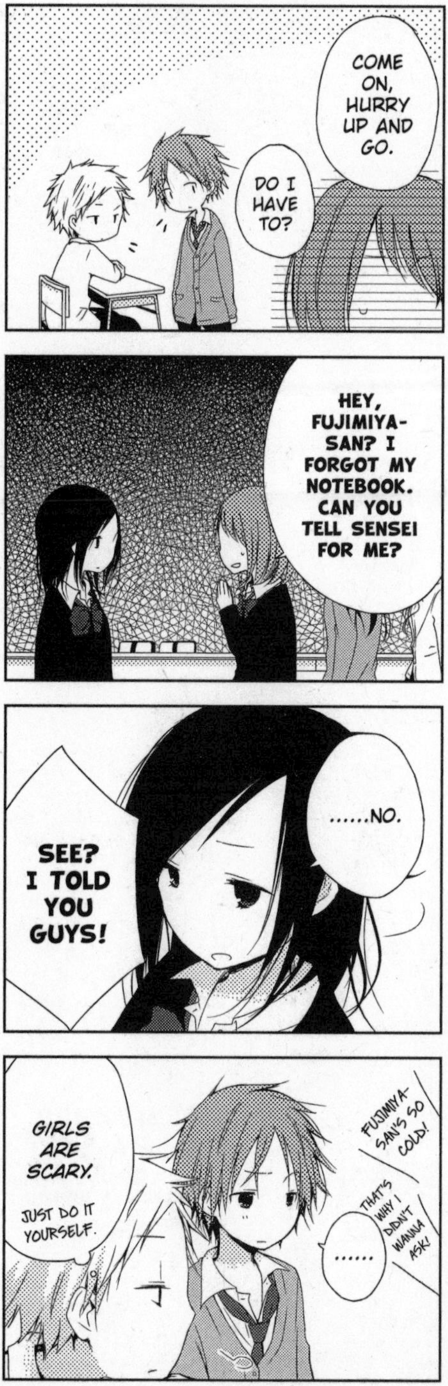
COME ON, HURRY UP AND GO.
DO I HAVE TO?
HEY, FUJIMIYA-SAN? I FORGOT MY NOTEBOOK. CAN YOU TELL SENSEI FOR ME?
......NO.
SEE? I TOLD YOU GUYS!
FUJIMIYA-SAN'S SO COLD!
THAT'S WHY I DIDN'T WANNA ASK!
......
GIRLS ARE SCARY.
JUST DO IT YOURSELF.

## WHAT'S MISSING

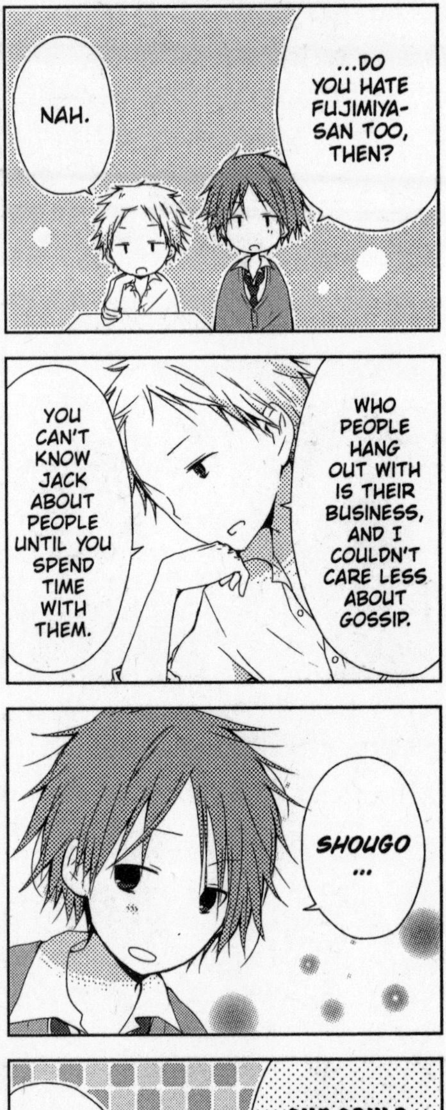
...DO YOU HATE FUJIMIYA-SAN TOO, THEN?
NAH.
WHO PEOPLE HANG OUT WITH IS THEIR BUSINESS, AND I COULDN'T CARE LESS ABOUT GOSSIP.
YOU CAN'T KNOW JACK ABOUT PEOPLE UNTIL YOU SPEND TIME WITH THEM.
SHOUGO ...
SHE COULD STAND TO SMILE A LITTLE MORE THOUGH.
LIKE YOU'RE ONE TO TALK.

## LOYAL TO HUNGER

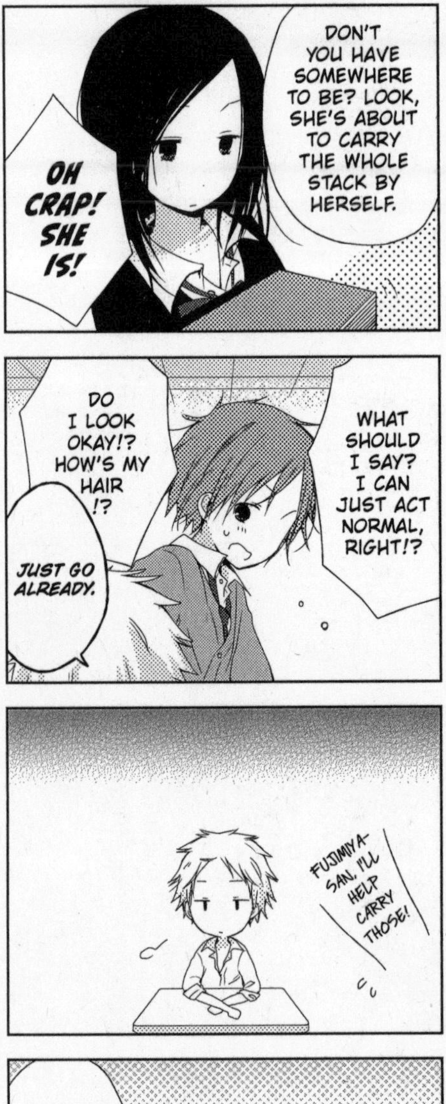
DON'T YOU HAVE SOMEWHERE TO BE? LOOK, SHE'S ABOUT TO CARRY THE WHOLE STACK BY HERSELF.
OH CRAP! SHE IS!
WHAT SHOULD I SAY? I CAN JUST ACT NORMAL, RIGHT!?
DO I LOOK OKAY!? HOW'S MY HAIR !?
JUST GO ALREADY.
FUJIMIYA-SAN, I'LL HELP CARRY THOSE!
I'M NOT WAITING. FOOD AND THEN SLEEP...
RUSTLE
RUSTLE

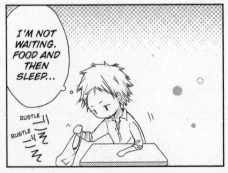

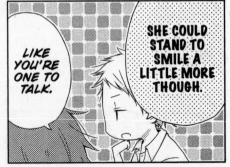

## BADUM BADUM

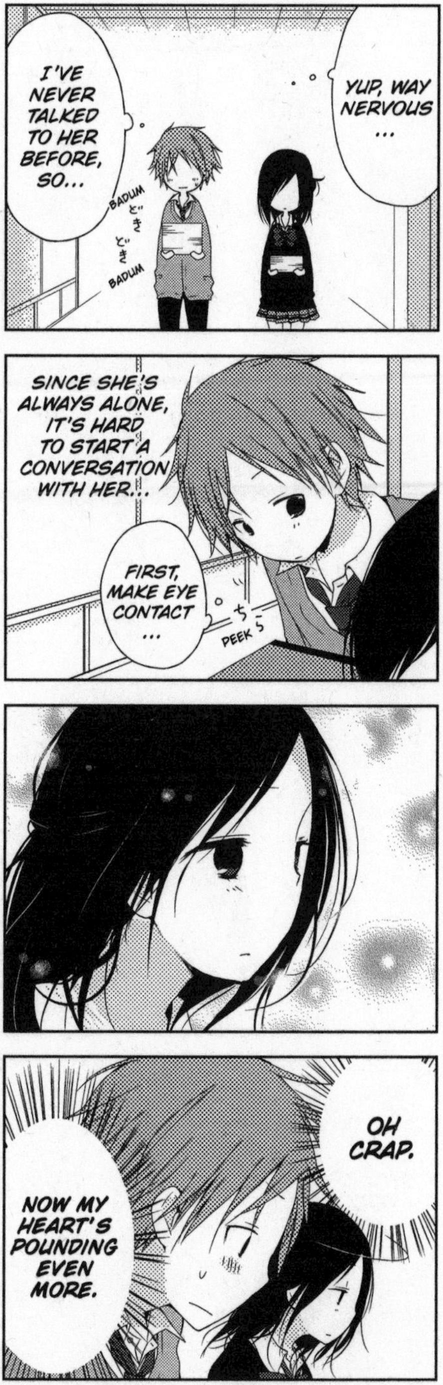
YUP, WAY NERVOUS ...
I'VE NEVER TALKED TO HER BEFORE, SO...
BADUM どき どき BADUM
SINCE SHE'S ALWAYS ALONE, IT'S HARD TO START A CONVERSATION WITH HER...
FIRST, MAKE EYE CONTACT ...
ちら PEEK
OH CRAP.
NOW MY HEART'S POUNDING EVEN MORE.

## HANG IN THERE, ME

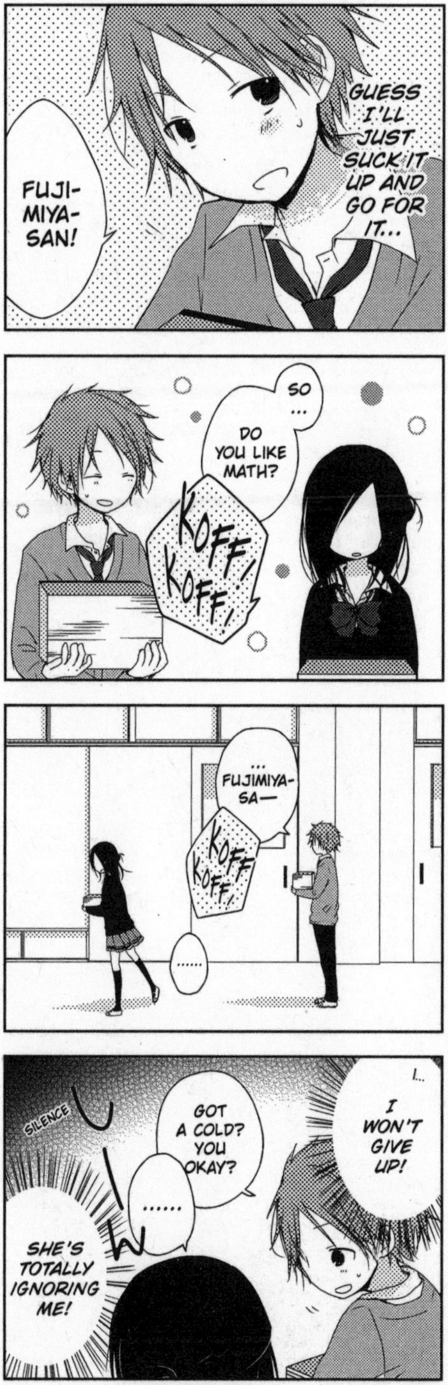
GUESS I'LL JUST SUCK IT UP AND GO FOR IT...
FUJI-MIYA-SAN!
SO ...
DO YOU LIKE MATH?
KOFF! KOFF!
... FUJIMIYA-SA—
KOFF KOFF!
......
I... I WON'T GIVE UP!
GOT A COLD? YOU OKAY?
......
SILENCE
SHE'S TOTALLY IGNORING ME!

## NOTEBOOK DELIVERY: DONE

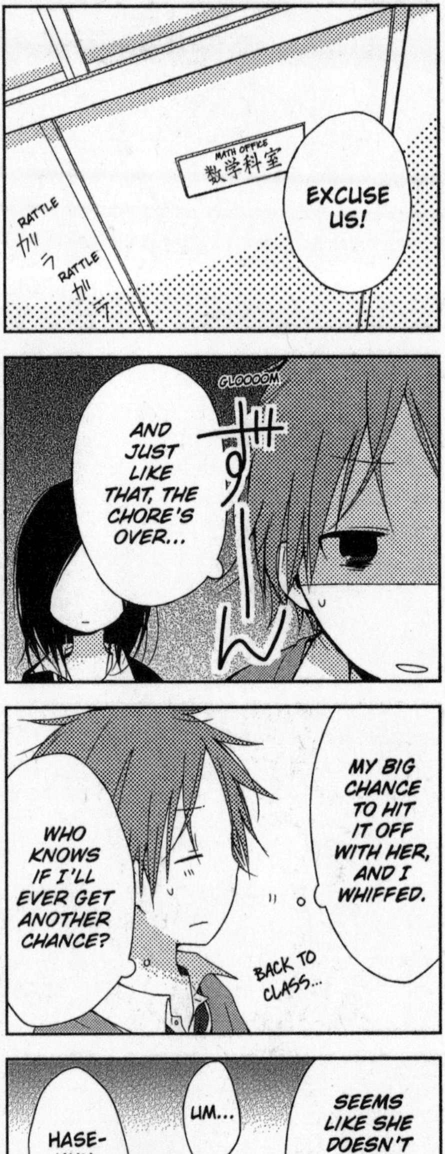
EXCUSE US!
MATH OFFICE
数学科室
RATTLE
RATTLE
GLOOOOM
AND JUST LIKE THAT, THE CHORE'S OVER...
MY BIG CHANCE TO HIT IT OFF WITH HER, AND I WHIFFED.
WHO KNOWS IF I'LL EVER GET ANOTHER CHANCE?
BACK TO CLASS...
SEEMS LIKE SHE DOESN'T LIKE ME ANYWAY, SO I GUESS THAT'S THAT...
UM...
HASE-KUN.
...YEAH-HUH!?

## OH MY GOD

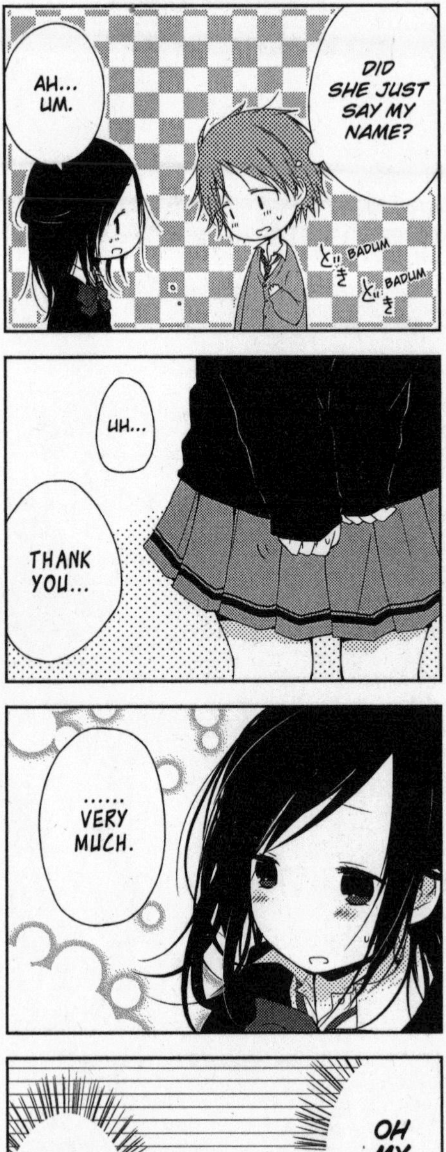
DID SHE JUST SAY MY NAME?
AH... UM.
BADUM
BADUM
UH...
THANK YOU...
...... VERY MUCH.
OH MY GOD.
SHE'S TOO CUTE!

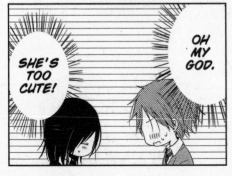

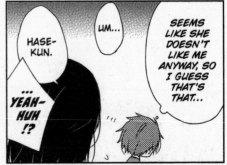

BE BOLD

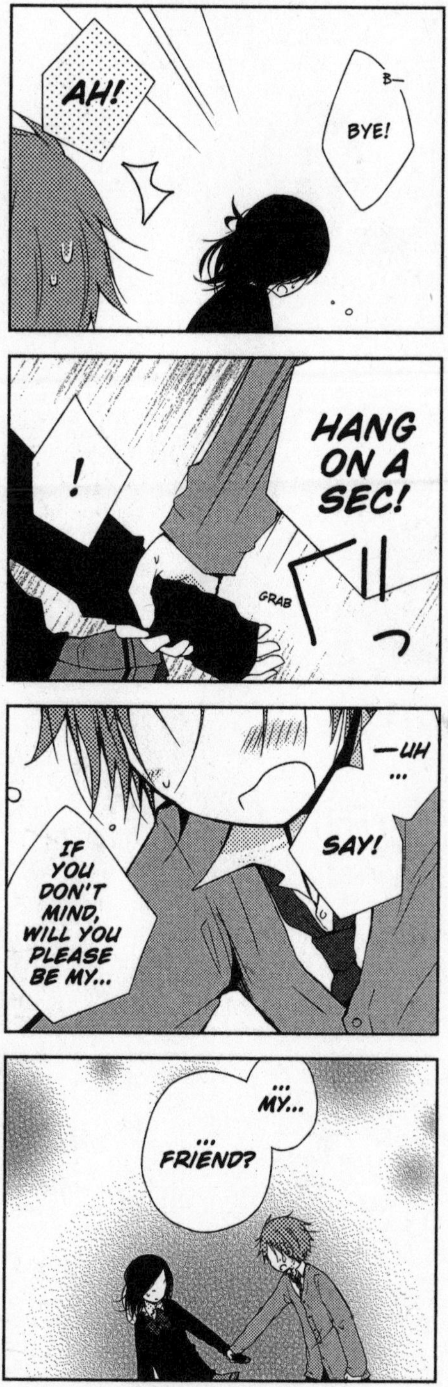
B— BYE!
AH!
HANG ON A SEC!
GRAB
!
—UH ... SAY!
IF YOU DON'T MIND, WILL YOU PLEASE BE MY...
... MY... ... FRIEND?

WHY?

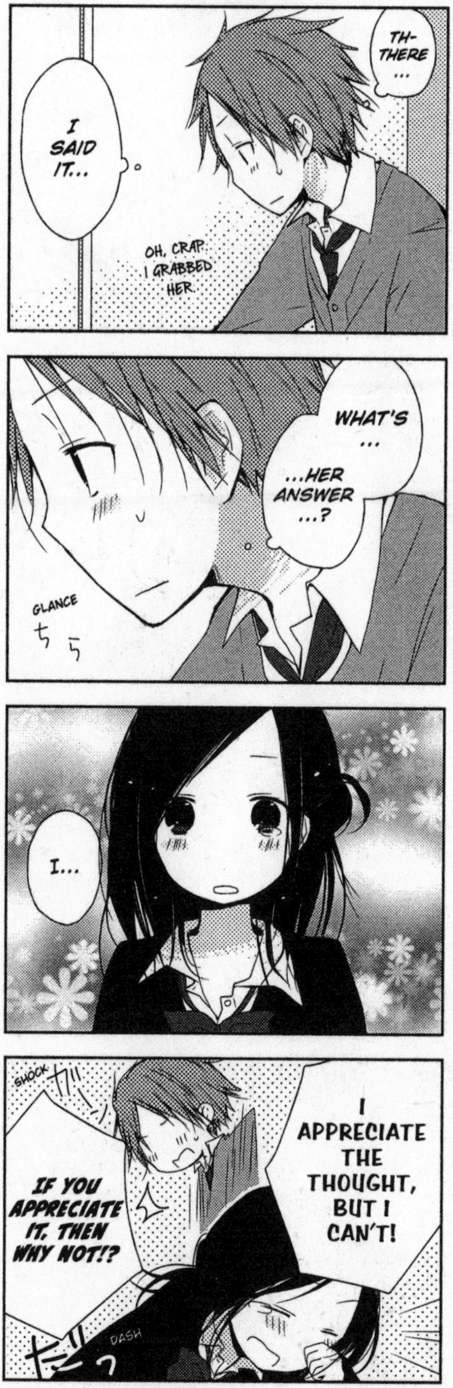
TH-THERE ...
I SAID IT...
OH, CRAP. I GRABBED HER.
WHAT'S ... ...HER ANSWER ...?
GLANCE
I...
SHOCK
I APPRECIATE THE THOUGHT, BUT I CAN'T!
IF YOU APPRECIATE IT, THEN WHY NOT!?
DASH

## A LITTLE SYMPATHY

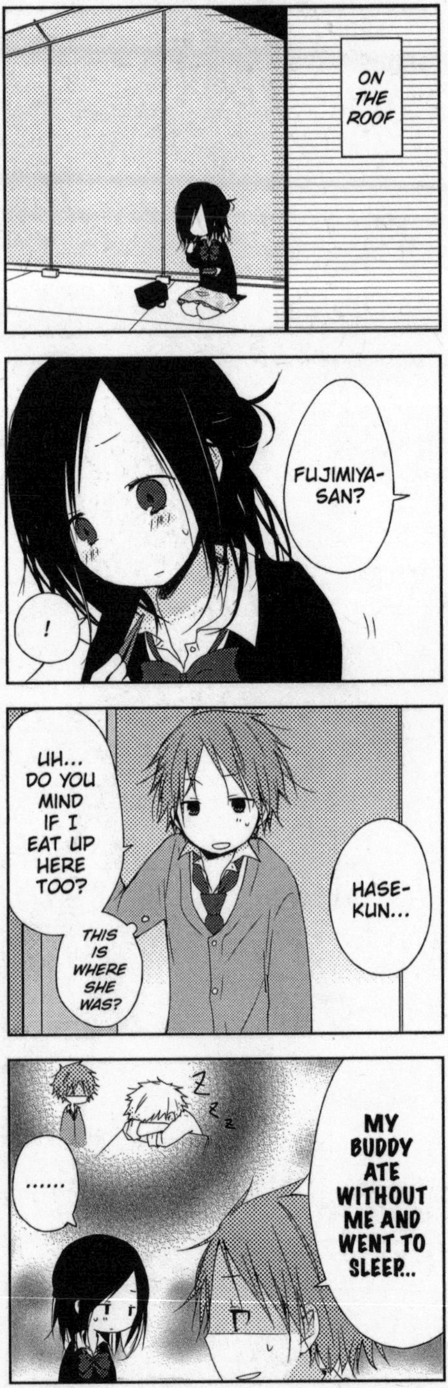
ON THE ROOF
FUJIMIYA-SAN?
!
HASE-KUN...
UH... DO YOU MIND IF I EAT UP HERE TOO?
THIS IS WHERE SHE WAS?
MY BUDDY ATE WITHOUT ME AND WENT TO SLEEP...
......

## THE REASON

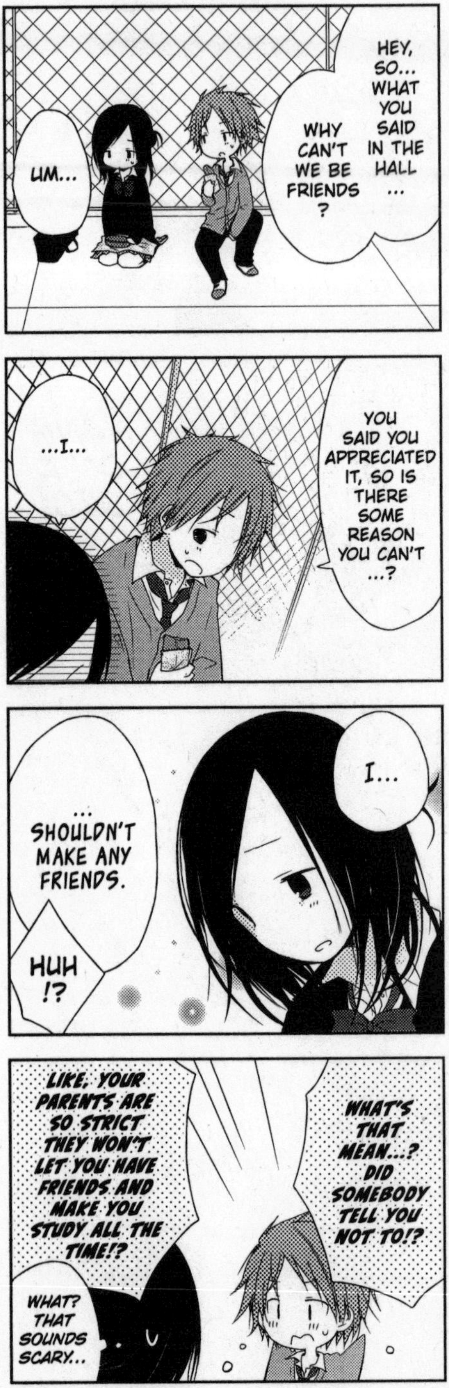
HEY, SO... WHAT YOU SAID IN THE HALL...
WHY CAN'T WE BE FRIENDS?
UM...
YOU SAID YOU APPRECIATED IT, SO IS THERE SOME REASON YOU CAN'T...?
...I...
I...
...SHOULDN'T MAKE ANY FRIENDS.
HUH!?
WHAT'S THAT MEAN...? DID SOMEBODY TELL YOU NOT TO!?
LIKE, YOUR PARENTS ARE SO STRICT THEY WON'T LET YOU HAVE FRIENDS AND MAKE YOU STUDY ALL THE TIME!?
WHAT? THAT SOUNDS SCARY...

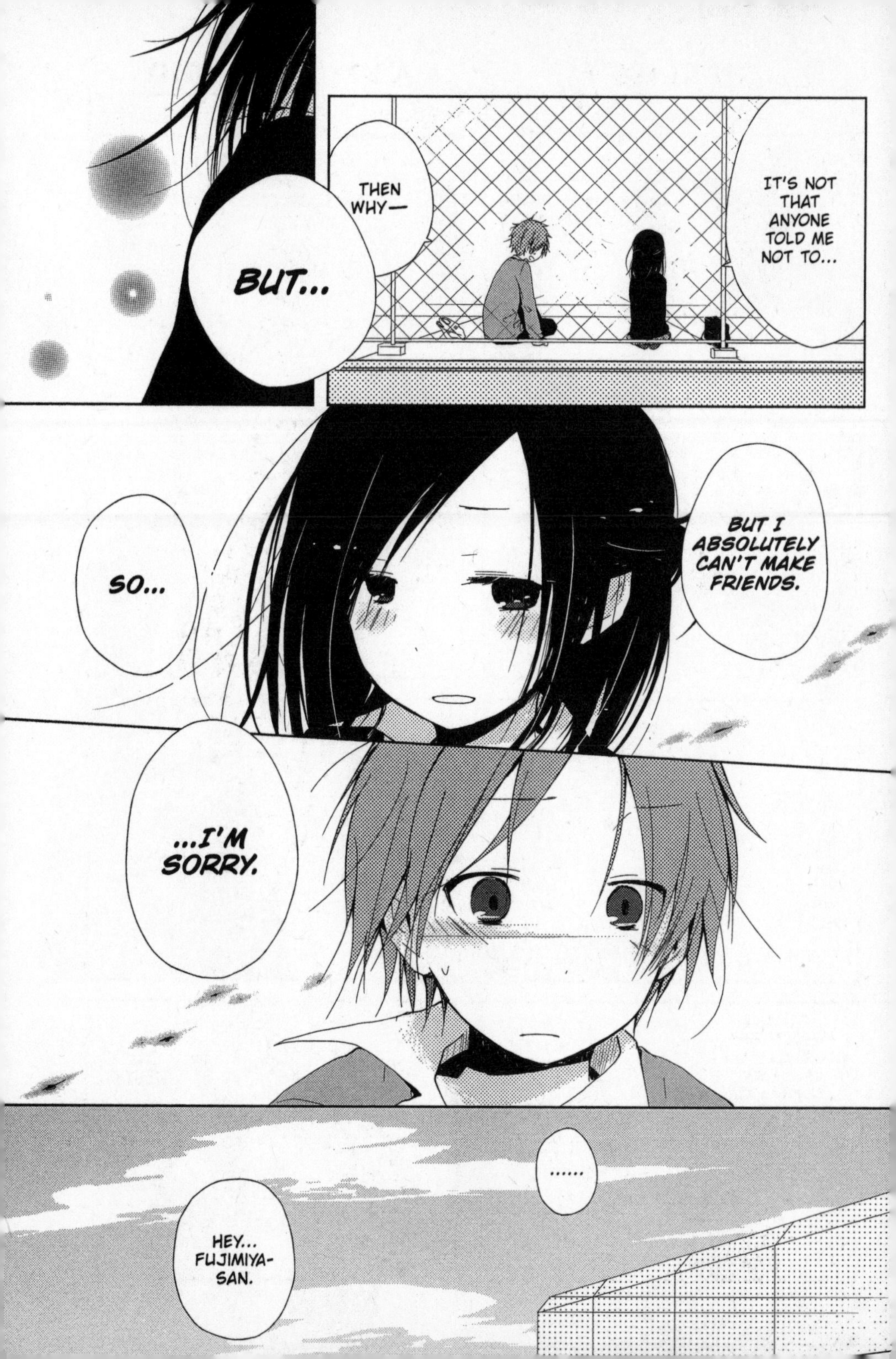
IT'S NOT THAT ANYONE TOLD ME NOT TO...
THEN WHY—
BUT...
BUT I ABSOLUTELY CAN'T MAKE FRIENDS.
SO...
...I'M SORRY.
......
HEY... FUJIMIYA-SAN.

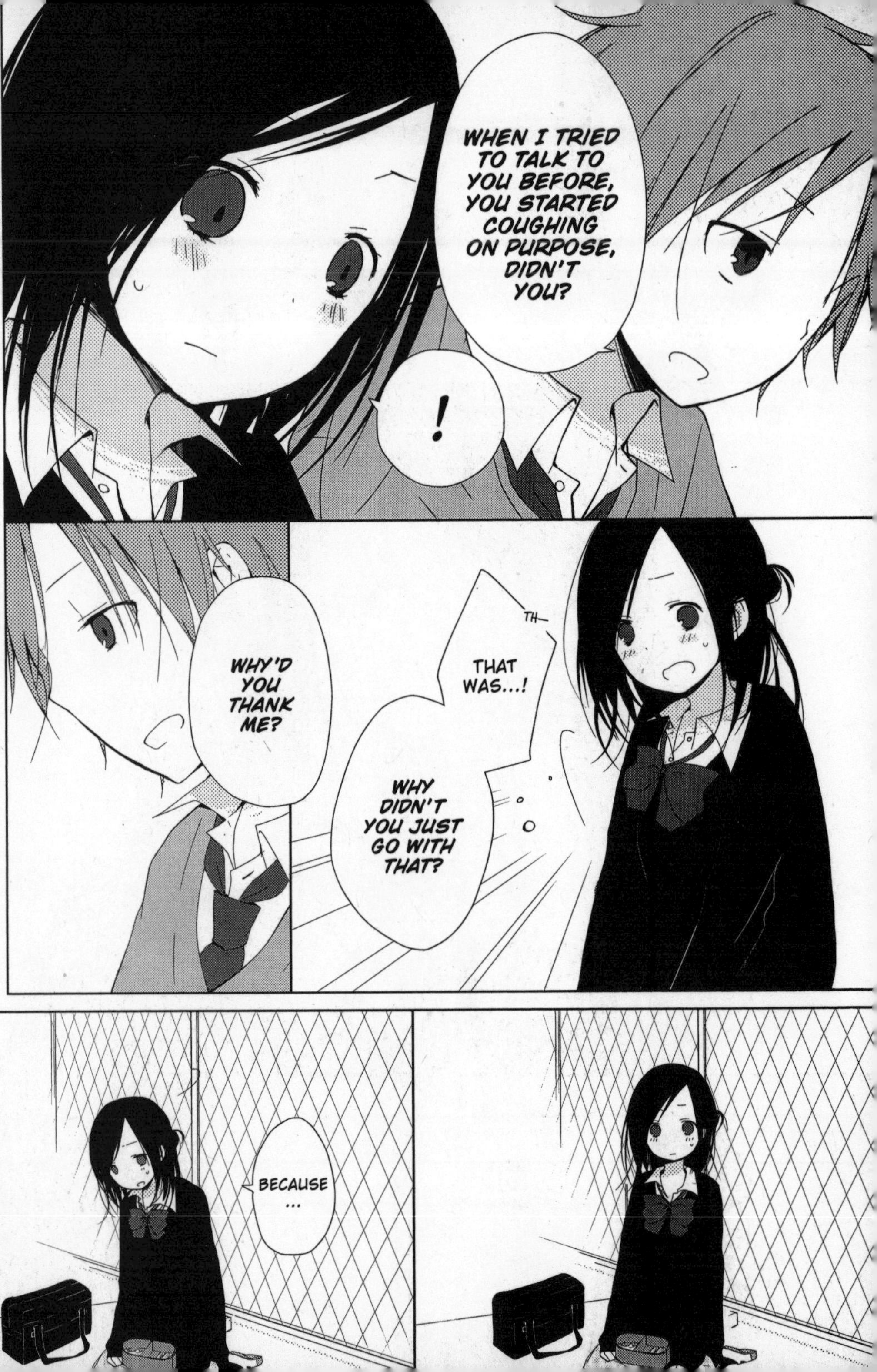
WHEN I TRIED TO TALK TO YOU BEFORE, YOU STARTED COUGHING ON PURPOSE, DIDN'T YOU?
!
TH—
THAT WAS...!
WHY DIDN'T YOU JUST GO WITH THAT?
WHY'D YOU THANK ME?
BECAUSE ...

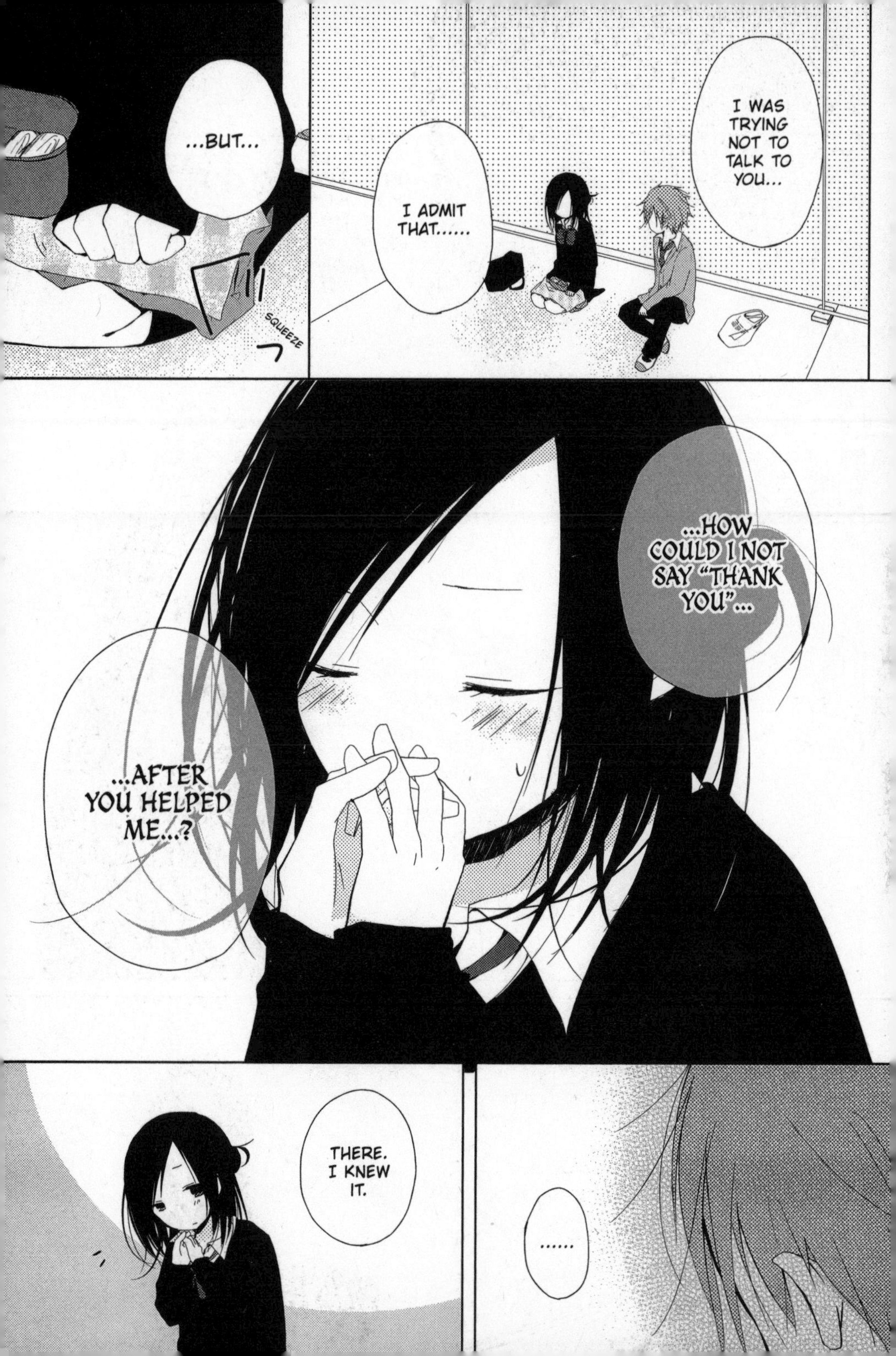
I WAS TRYING NOT TO TALK TO YOU...
I ADMIT THAT......
...BUT...
SQUEEZE
...HOW COULD I NOT SAY "THANK YOU"...
...AFTER YOU HELPED ME...?
......
THERE. I KNEW IT.

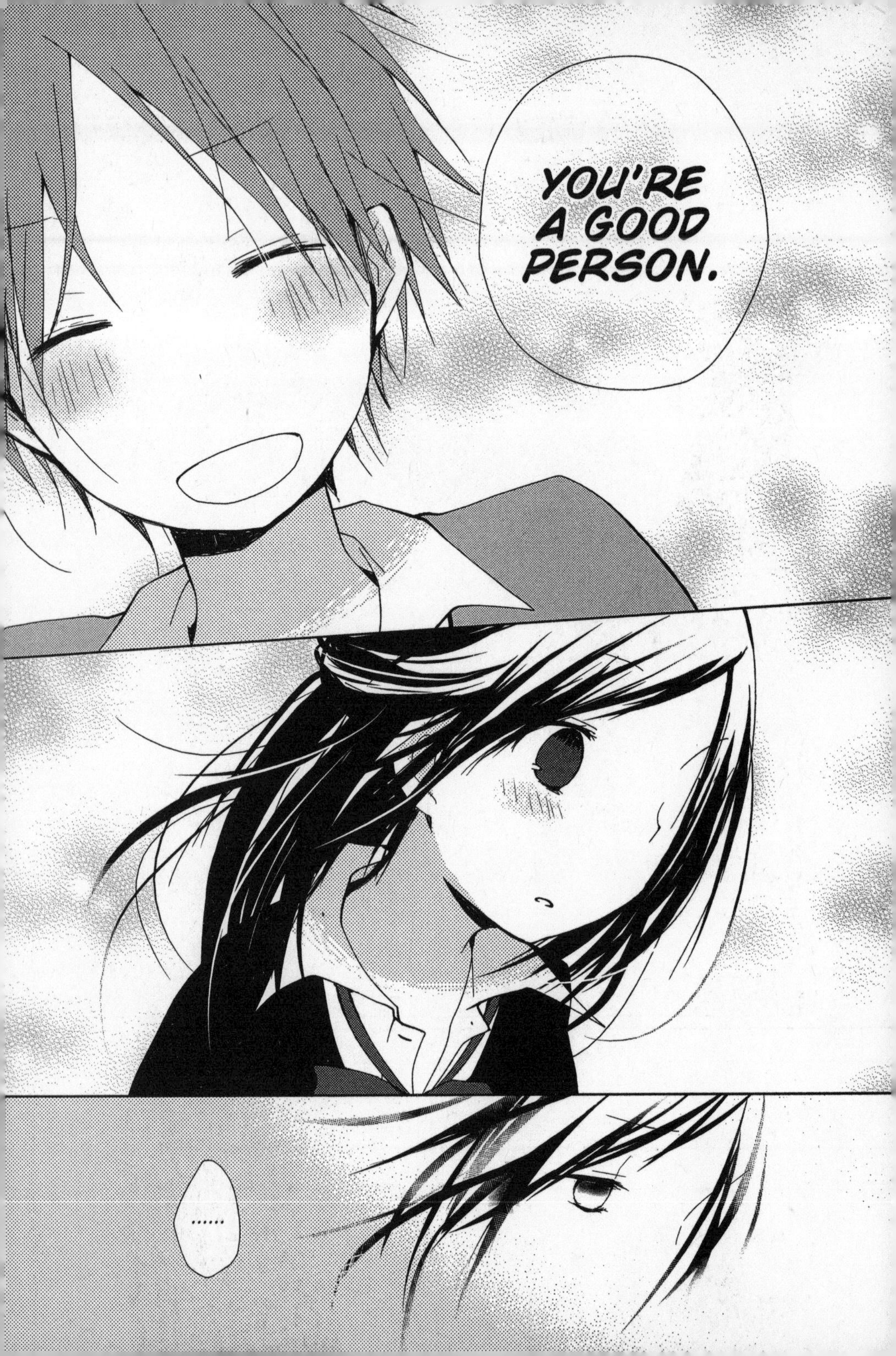
YOU'RE A GOOD PERSON.
......

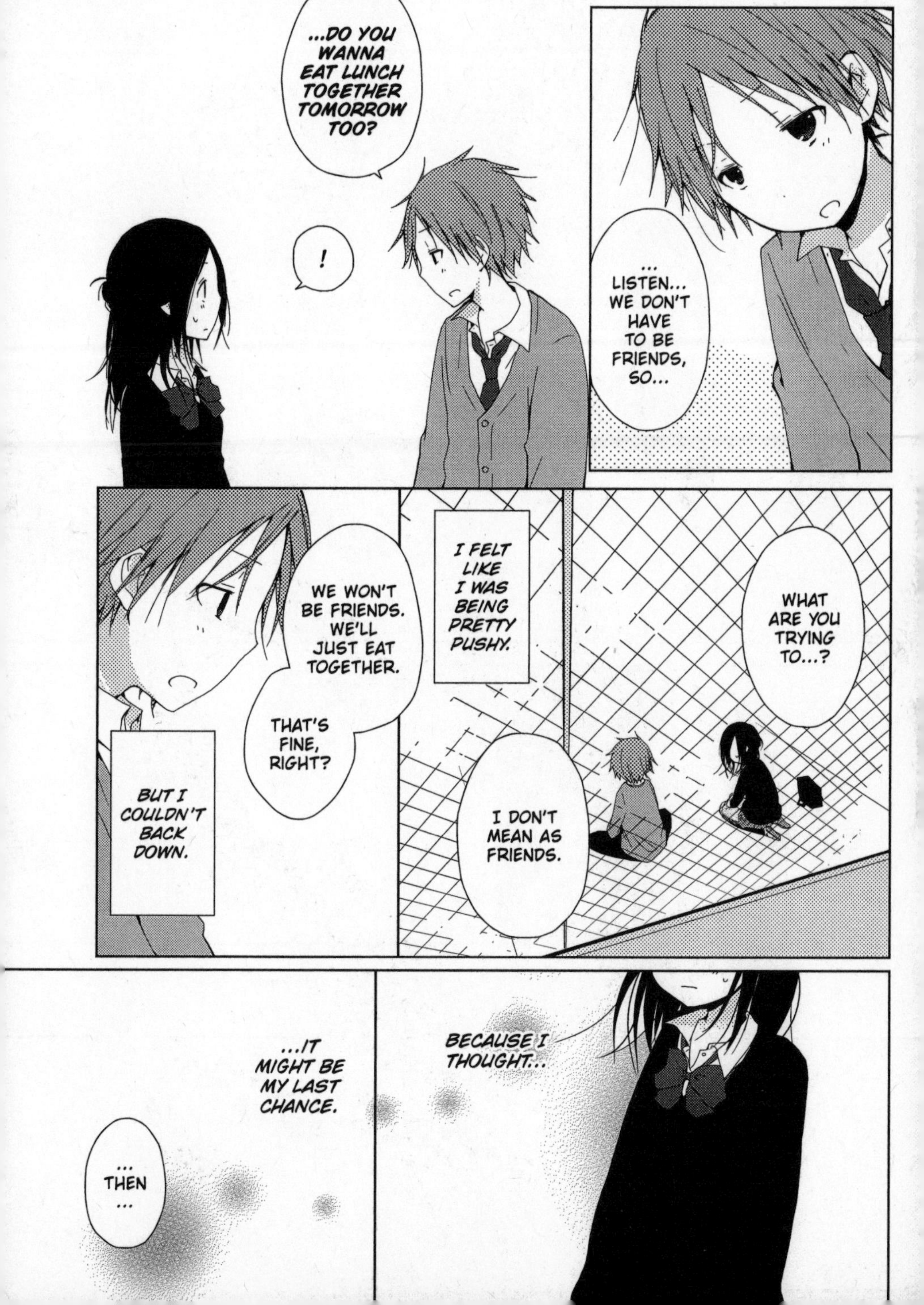
...LISTEN... WE DON'T HAVE TO BE FRIENDS, SO...
...DO YOU WANNA EAT LUNCH TOGETHER TOMORROW TOO?
!
WHAT ARE YOU TRYING TO...?
I DON'T MEAN AS FRIENDS.
I FELT LIKE I WAS BEING PRETTY PUSHY.
WE WON'T BE FRIENDS. WE'LL JUST EAT TOGETHER.
THAT'S FINE, RIGHT?
BUT I COULDN'T BACK DOWN.
BECAUSE I THOUGHT...
...IT MIGHT BE MY LAST CHANCE.
...THEN...

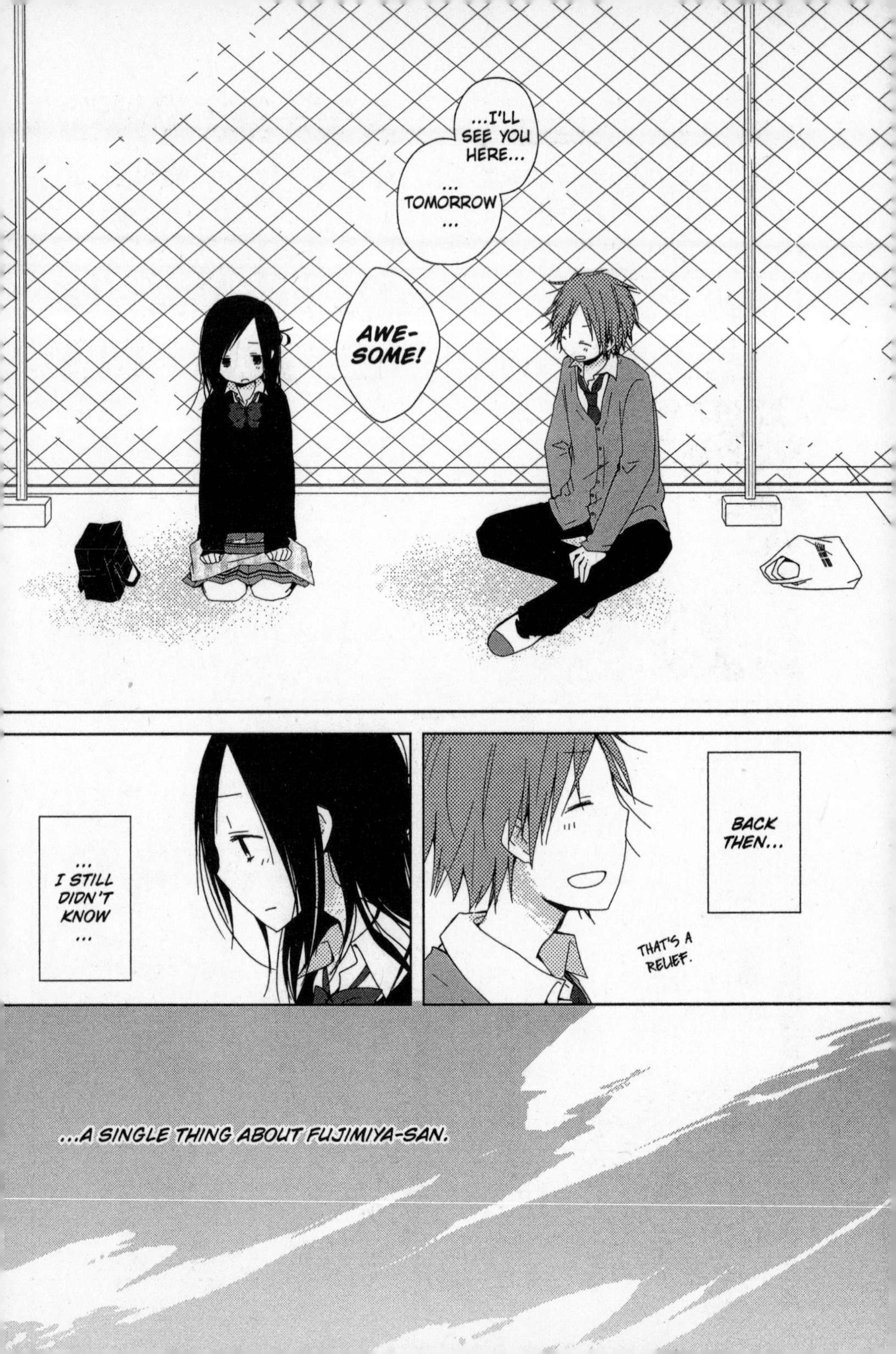
...I'LL SEE YOU HERE...
...TOMORROW...
AWE-SOME!
BACK THEN...
THAT'S A RELIEF.
...I STILL DIDN'T KNOW...
...A SINGLE THING ABOUT FUJIMIYA-SAN.

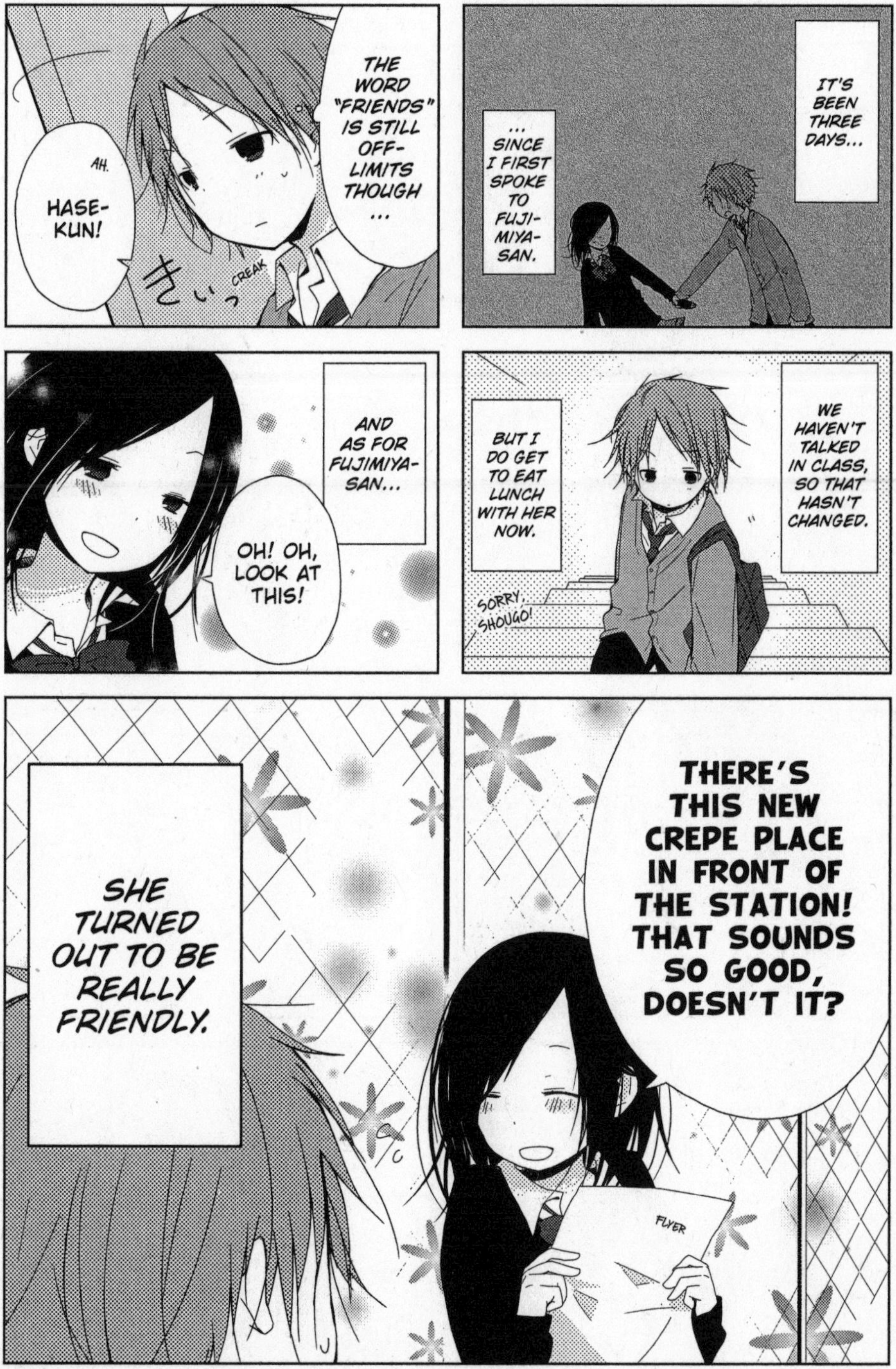
IT'S BEEN THREE DAYS...
...SINCE I FIRST SPOKE TO FUJIMIYA-SAN.
THE WORD "FRIENDS" IS STILL OFF-LIMITS THOUGH...
AH.
HASE-KUN!
きぃっ
CREAK
WE HAVEN'T TALKED IN CLASS, SO THAT HASN'T CHANGED.
BUT I DO GET TO EAT LUNCH WITH HER NOW.
SORRY, SHOUGO!
AND AS FOR FUJIMIYA-SAN...
OH! OH, LOOK AT THIS!
THERE'S THIS NEW CREPE PLACE IN FRONT OF THE STATION! THAT SOUNDS SO GOOD, DOESN'T IT?
FLYER
SHE TURNED OUT TO BE REALLY FRIENDLY.

LOOKS LIKE THIS

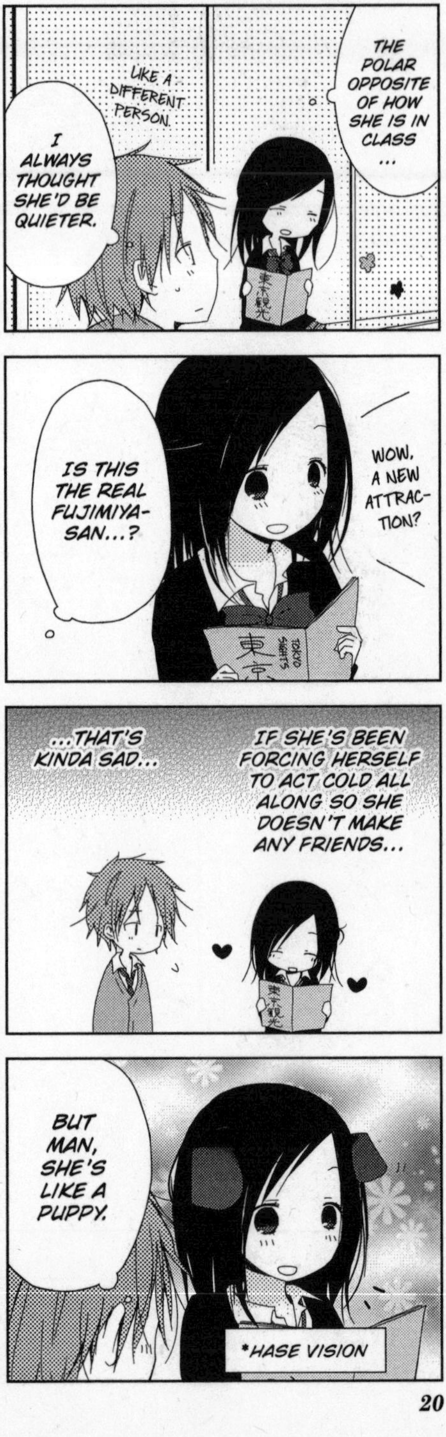
THE POLAR OPPOSITE OF HOW SHE IS IN CLASS ...
LIKE A DIFFERENT PERSON.
I ALWAYS THOUGHT SHE'D BE QUIETER.
WOW, A NEW ATTRACTION?
IS THIS THE REAL FUJIMIYA-SAN...?
TOKYO SIGHTS
IF SHE'S BEEN FORCING HERSELF TO ACT COLD ALL ALONG SO SHE DOESN'T MAKE ANY FRIENDS...
...THAT'S KINDA SAD...
BUT MAN, SHE'S LIKE A PUPPY.
*HASE VISION

SHOCK

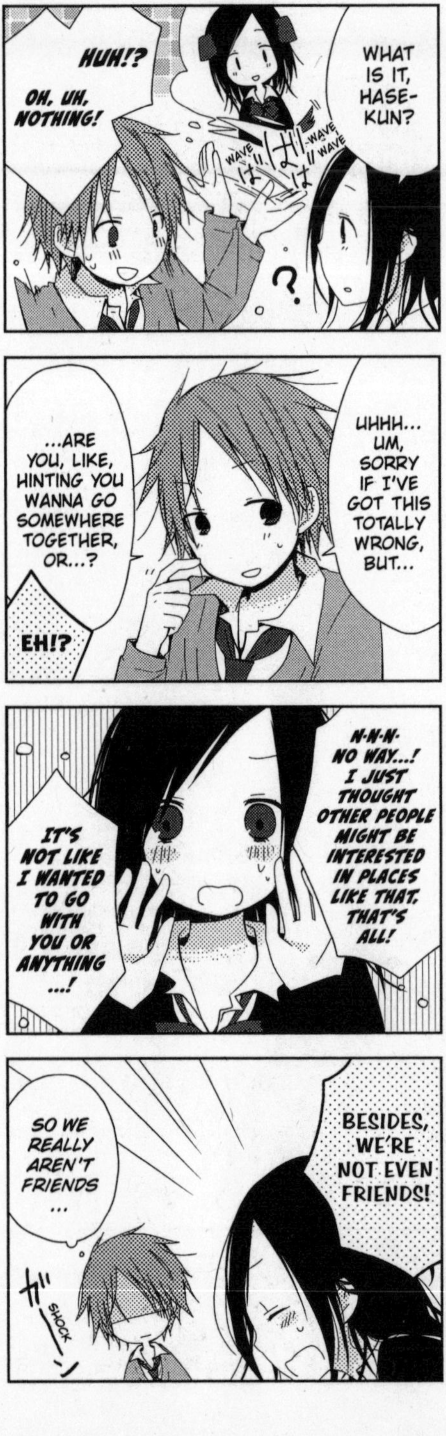
WHAT IS IT, HASE-KUN?
WAVE WAVE WAVE
HUH!?
OH, UH, NOTHING!
?
UHHH... UM, SORRY IF I'VE GOT THIS TOTALLY WRONG, BUT...
...ARE YOU, LIKE, HINTING YOU WANNA GO SOMEWHERE TOGETHER, OR...?
EH!?
N-N-N-NO WAY...! I JUST THOUGHT OTHER PEOPLE MIGHT BE INTERESTED IN PLACES LIKE THAT. THAT'S ALL!
IT'S NOT LIKE I WANTED TO GO WITH YOU OR ANYTHING ...!
BESIDES, WE'RE NOT EVEN FRIENDS!
SO WE REALLY AREN'T FRIENDS ...
SHOCK

## WHAT'S A FRIEND?

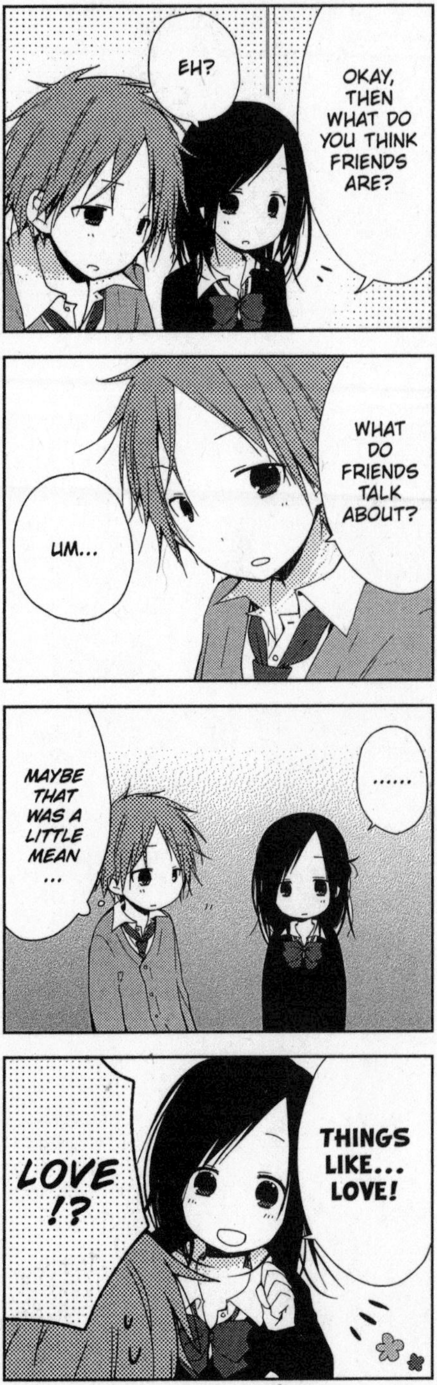
OKAY, THEN WHAT DO YOU THINK FRIENDS ARE?
EH?
WHAT DO FRIENDS TALK ABOUT?
UM...
......
MAYBE THAT WAS A LITTLE MEAN...
THINGS LIKE... LOVE!
LOVE!?

## DECISION

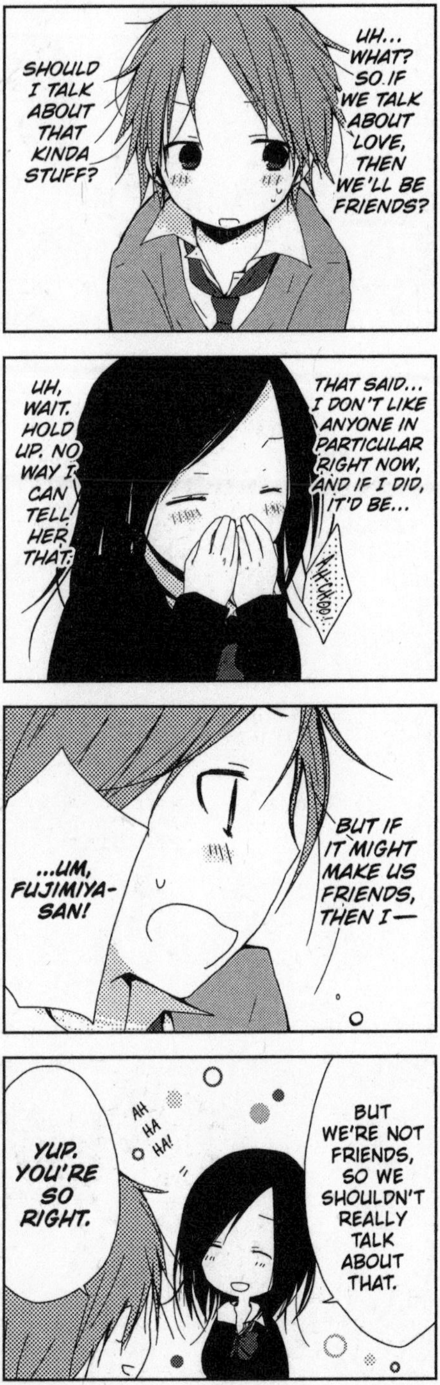
UH... WHAT? SO IF WE TALK ABOUT LOVE, THEN WE'LL BE FRIENDS?
SHOULD I TALK ABOUT THAT KINDA STUFF?
THAT SAID... I DON'T LIKE ANYONE IN PARTICULAR RIGHT NOW, AND IF I DID, IT'D BE...
AH-CHOO!
UH, WAIT. HOLD UP. NO WAY I CAN TELL HER THAT.
BUT IF IT MIGHT MAKE US FRIENDS, THEN I—
...UM, FUJIMIYA-SAN!
BUT WE'RE NOT FRIENDS, SO WE SHOULDN'T REALLY TALK ABOUT THAT.
AH HA HA!
YUP. YOU'RE SO RIGHT.

## LUNCH BREAK CLASSIC

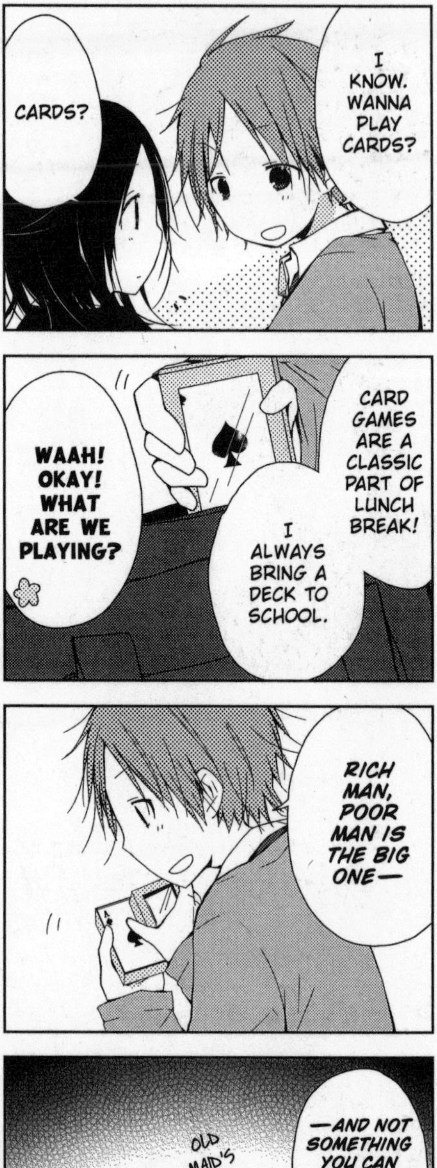
I KNOW. WANNA PLAY CARDS?
CARDS?
CARD GAMES ARE A CLASSIC PART OF LUNCH BREAK!
I ALWAYS BRING A DECK TO SCHOOL.
WAAH! OKAY! WHAT ARE WE PLAYING?
RICH MAN, POOR MAN IS THE BIG ONE—
—AND NOT SOMETHING YOU CAN PLAY WITH TWO PEOPLE...
OLD MAID'S OUT TOO...

## CONCENTRATION

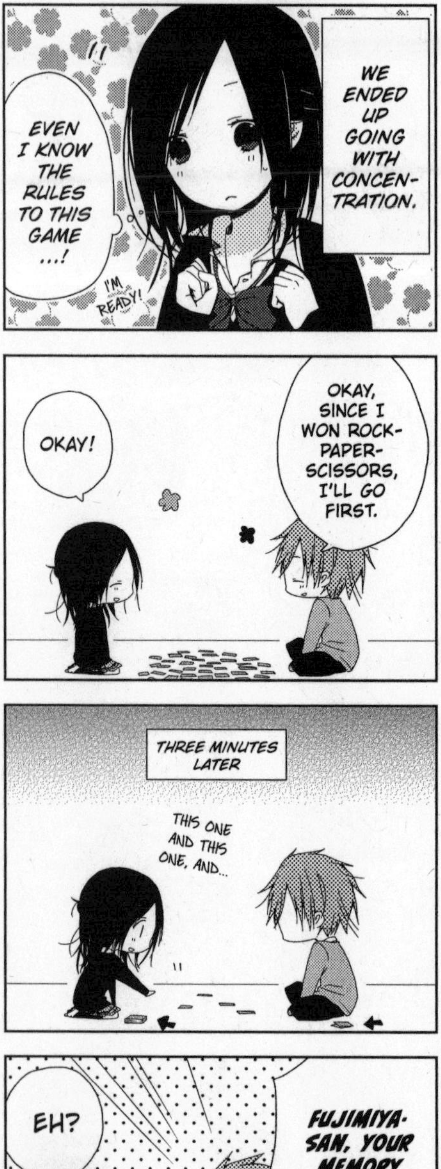
WE ENDED UP GOING WITH CONCEN-TRATION.
EVEN I KNOW THE RULES TO THIS GAME ...!
I'M READY!
OKAY, SINCE I WON ROCK-PAPER-SCISSORS, I'LL GO FIRST.
OKAY!
THREE MINUTES LATER
THIS ONE AND THIS ONE, AND...
FUJIMIYA-SAN, YOUR MEMORY IS CRAZY GOOD!!
GRAWR
EH?

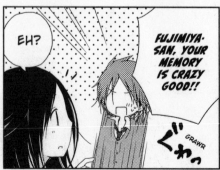

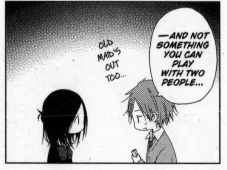

## WEAK (IN MORE WAYS THAN ONE)

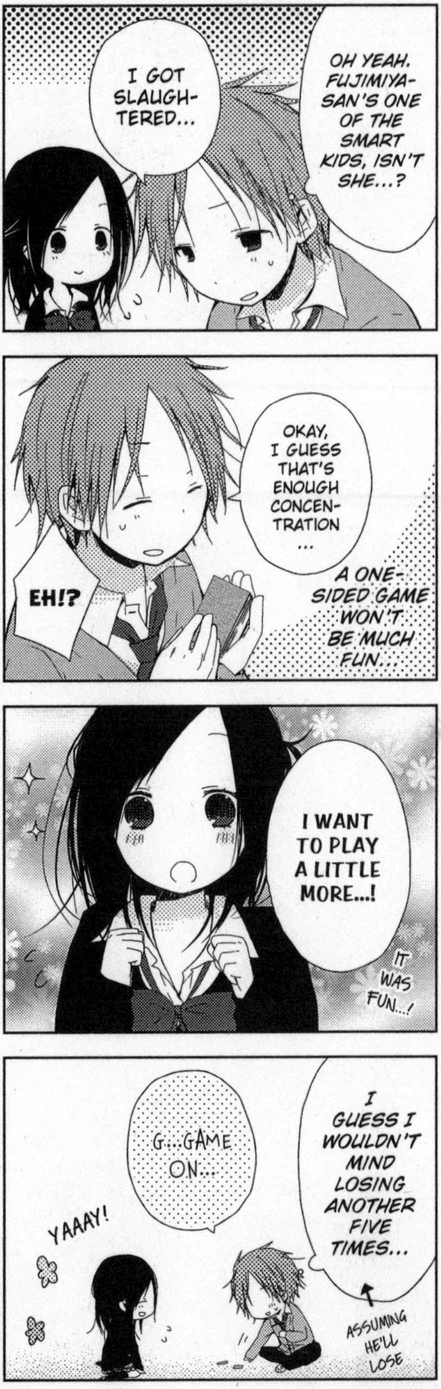
OH YEAH. FUJIMIYA-SAN'S ONE OF THE SMART KIDS, ISN'T SHE...?
I GOT SLAUGHTERED...
OKAY, I GUESS THAT'S ENOUGH CONCENTRATION ...
A ONE-SIDED GAME WON'T BE MUCH FUN...
EH!?
I WANT TO PLAY A LITTLE MORE...!
IT WAS FUN...!
I GUESS I WOULDN'T MIND LOSING ANOTHER FIVE TIMES...
ASSUMING HE'LL LOSE
G...GAME ON...
YAAAY!

## MEMORY

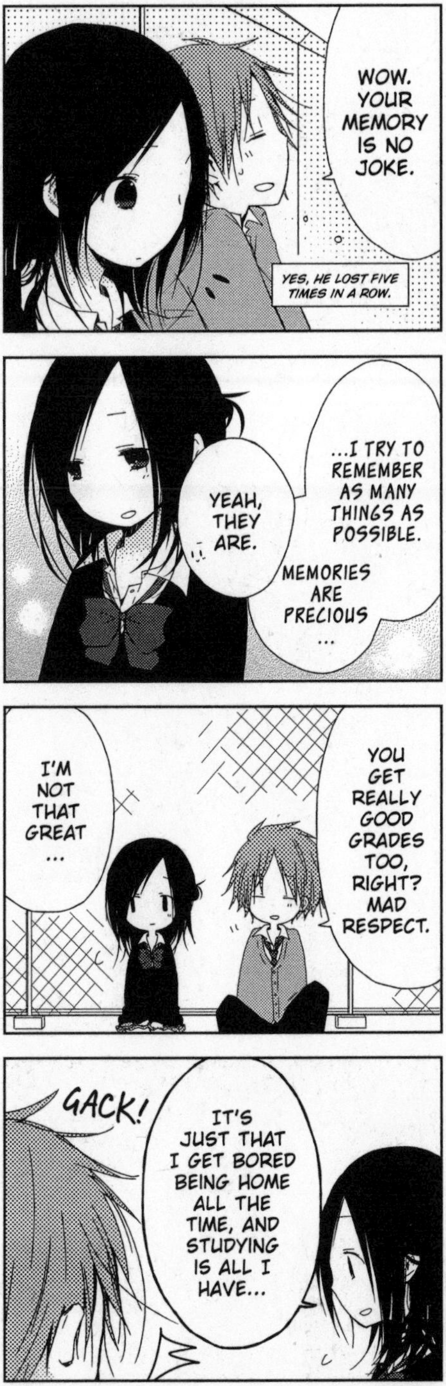
WOW. YOUR MEMORY IS NO JOKE.
YES, HE LOST FIVE TIMES IN A ROW.
...I TRY TO REMEMBER AS MANY THINGS AS POSSIBLE.
MEMORIES ARE PRECIOUS ...
YEAH, THEY ARE.
YOU GET REALLY GOOD GRADES TOO, RIGHT? MAD RESPECT.
I'M NOT THAT GREAT ...
IT'S JUST THAT I GET BORED BEING HOME ALL THE TIME, AND STUDYING IS ALL I HAVE...
GACK!

## A LITTLE SURPRISING

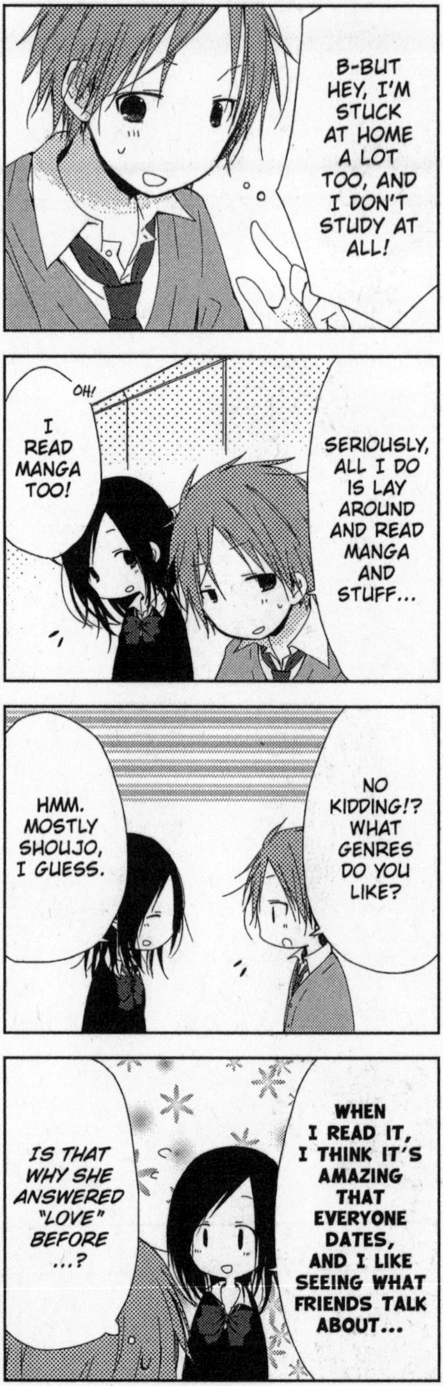
B-BUT HEY, I'M STUCK AT HOME A LOT TOO, AND I DON'T STUDY AT ALL!
SERIOUSLY, ALL I DO IS LAY AROUND AND READ MANGA AND STUFF...
OH!
I READ MANGA TOO!
NO KIDDING!? WHAT GENRES DO YOU LIKE?
HMM. MOSTLY SHOUJO, I GUESS.
WHEN I READ IT, I THINK IT'S AMAZING THAT EVERYONE DATES, AND I LIKE SEEING WHAT FRIENDS TALK ABOUT...
IS THAT WHY SHE ANSWERED "LOVE" BEFORE ...?

## SUDDENLY

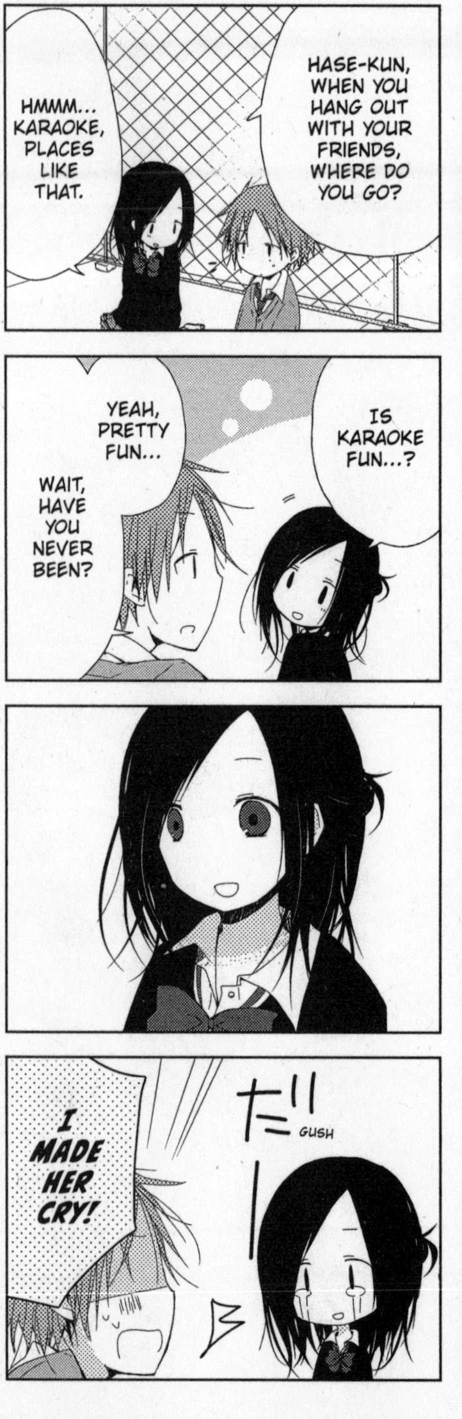
HASE-KUN, WHEN YOU HANG OUT WITH YOUR FRIENDS, WHERE DO YOU GO?
HMMM... KARAOKE, PLACES LIKE THAT.
IS KARAOKE FUN...?
YEAH, PRETTY FUN...
WAIT, HAVE YOU NEVER BEEN?
GUSH
I MADE HER CRY!

## WITH ALL ONE'S MIGHT

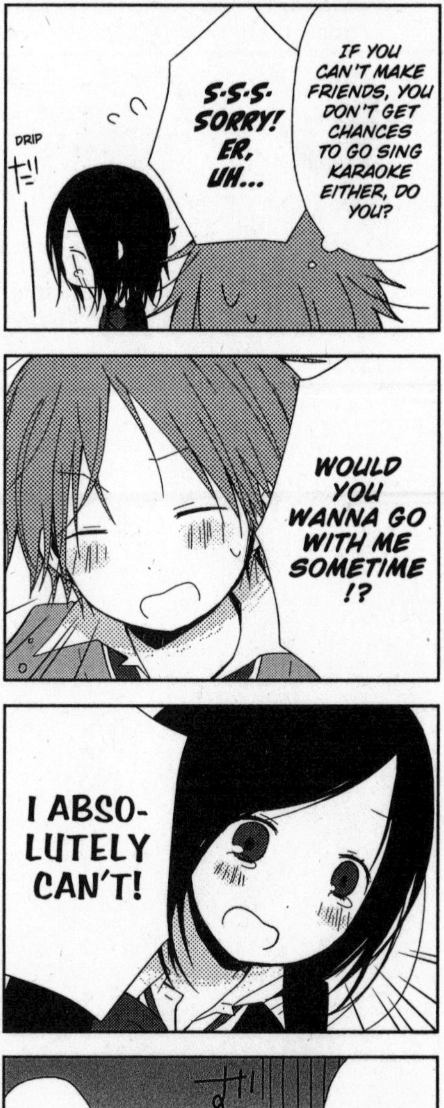
IF YOU CAN'T MAKE FRIENDS, YOU DON'T GET CHANCES TO GO SING KARAOKE EITHER, DO YOU?
S-S-S-SORRY! ER, UH...
DRIP
WOULD YOU WANNA GO WITH ME SOMETIME!?
I ABSOLUTELY CAN'T!
SHOT ME DOWN WITH ALL HER MIGHT...
GLOOM
S... SORRY ......

## ONE DAY

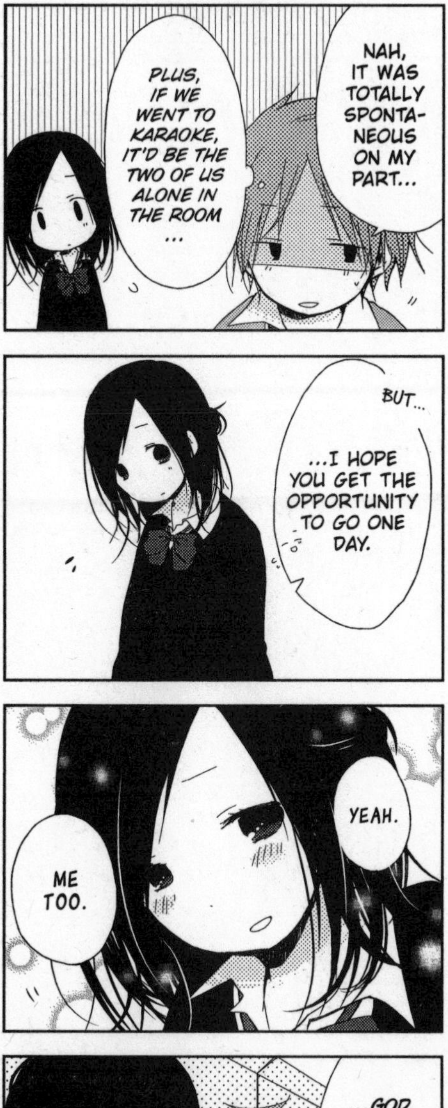
NAH, IT WAS TOTALLY SPONTANEOUS ON MY PART...
PLUS, IF WE WENT TO KARAOKE, IT'D BE THE TWO OF US ALONE IN THE ROOM ...
BUT...
...I HOPE YOU GET THE OPPORTUNITY TO GO ONE DAY.
YEAH.
ME TOO.
...GOD, SHE REALLY IS CUTE.

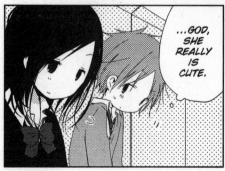

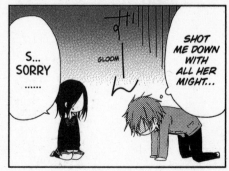

## TOMORROW

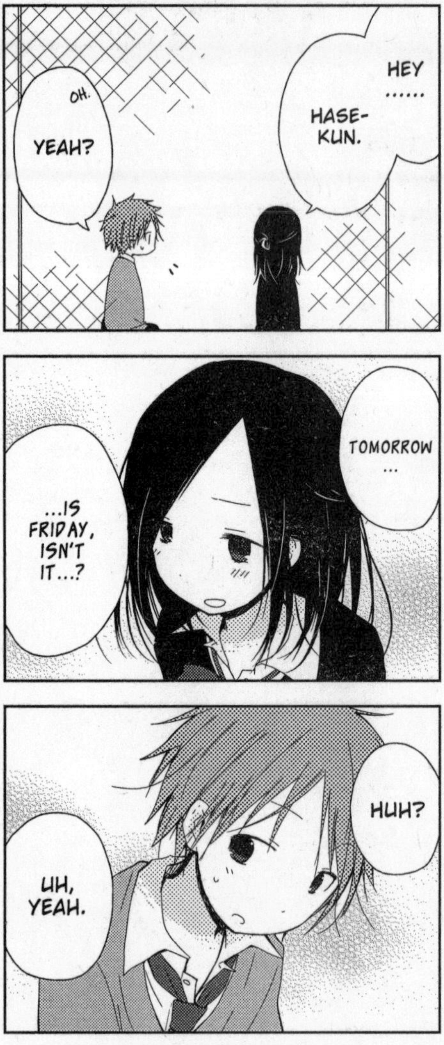
HEY ...... HASE-KUN.
OH. YEAH?
TOMORROW ...
...IS FRIDAY, ISN'T IT...?
HUH?
UH, YEAH.
IS THERE A TV SHOW SHE WANTS TO CATCH ...?
?

## ON THE WAY HOME

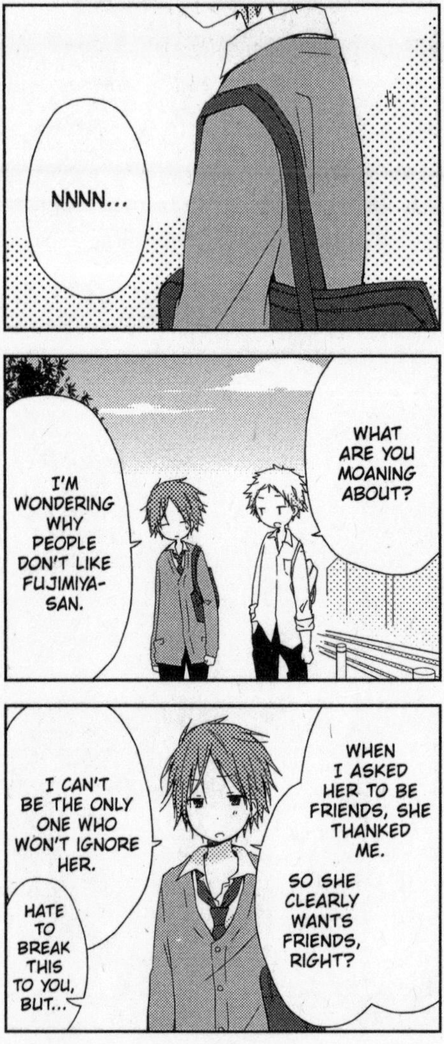
NNNN...
WHAT ARE YOU MOANING ABOUT?
I'M WONDERING WHY PEOPLE DON'T LIKE FUJIMIYA-SAN.
WHEN I ASKED HER TO BE FRIENDS, SHE THANKED ME.
SO SHE CLEARLY WANTS FRIENDS, RIGHT?
I CAN'T BE THE ONLY ONE WHO WON'T IGNORE HER.
HATE TO BREAK THIS TO YOU, BUT...
...PEOPLE DON'T NORMALLY OUTRIGHT ASK SOMEBODY TO BE THEIR FRIEND.
LIKE YOU'RE ASKING THEM OUT
O-OH...!

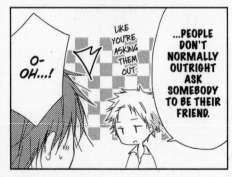

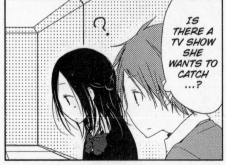

## POINT-BLANK

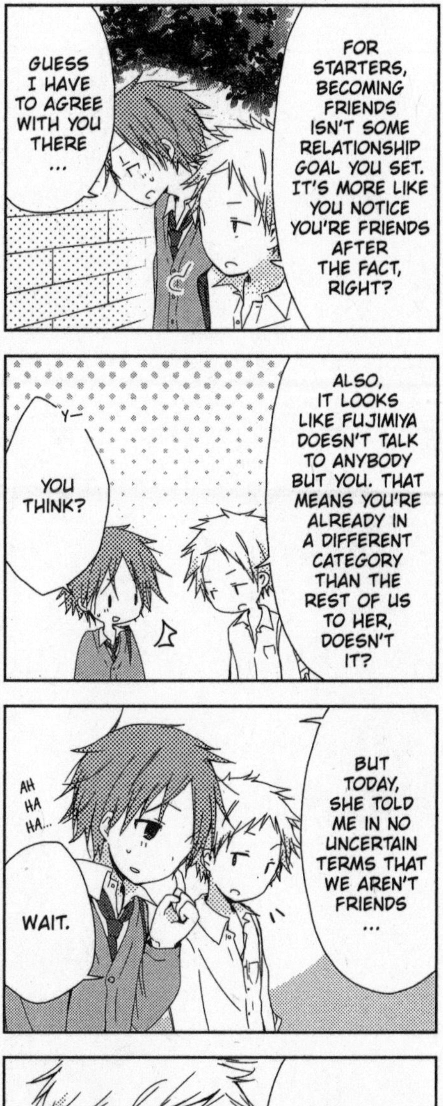
FOR STARTERS, BECOMING FRIENDS ISN'T SOME RELATIONSHIP GOAL YOU SET. IT'S MORE LIKE YOU NOTICE YOU'RE FRIENDS AFTER THE FACT, RIGHT?
GUESS I HAVE TO AGREE WITH YOU THERE ...
ALSO, IT LOOKS LIKE FUJIMIYA DOESN'T TALK TO ANYBODY BUT YOU. THAT MEANS YOU'RE ALREADY IN A DIFFERENT CATEGORY THAN THE REST OF US TO HER, DOESN'T IT?
Y— YOU THINK?
BUT TODAY, SHE TOLD ME IN NO UNCERTAIN TERMS THAT WE AREN'T FRIENDS ...
AH HA HA...
WAIT.
ARE YOU SURE SHE DOESN'T HATE YOUR GUTS?
PLAIN AND SIMPLE.
YOU'RE REALLY GONNA SAY THAT!?

## I'LL KEEP TRYING

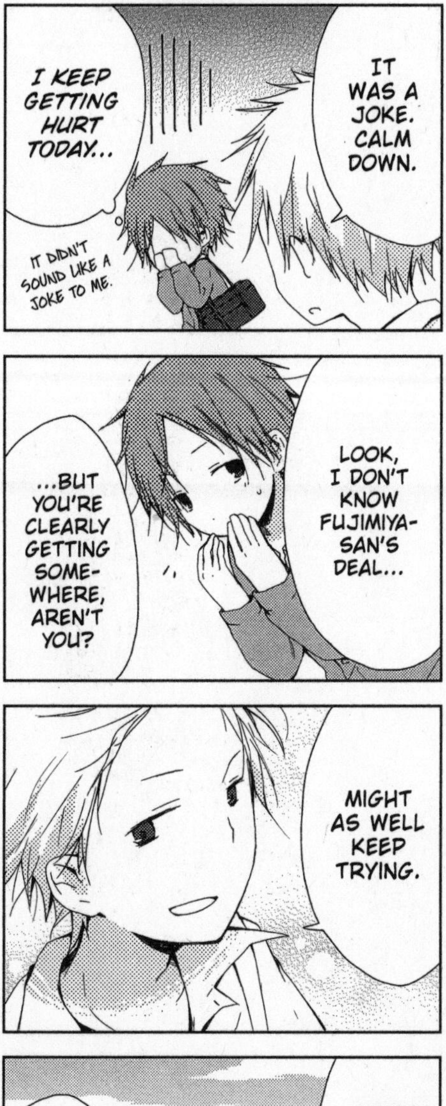
IT WAS A JOKE. CALM DOWN.
I KEEP GETTING HURT TODAY...
IT DIDN'T SOUND LIKE A JOKE TO ME.
LOOK, I DON'T KNOW FUJIMIYA-SAN'S DEAL...
...BUT YOU'RE CLEARLY GETTING SOME-WHERE, AREN'T YOU?
MIGHT AS WELL KEEP TRYING.
SINCE YOU SMILED, I FEEL LIKE I CAN KEEP GOING!
YEAAAAH!
WHAT THE HECK?

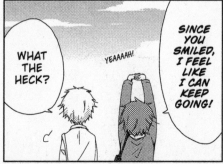

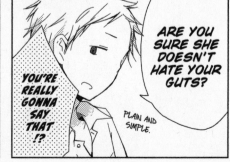

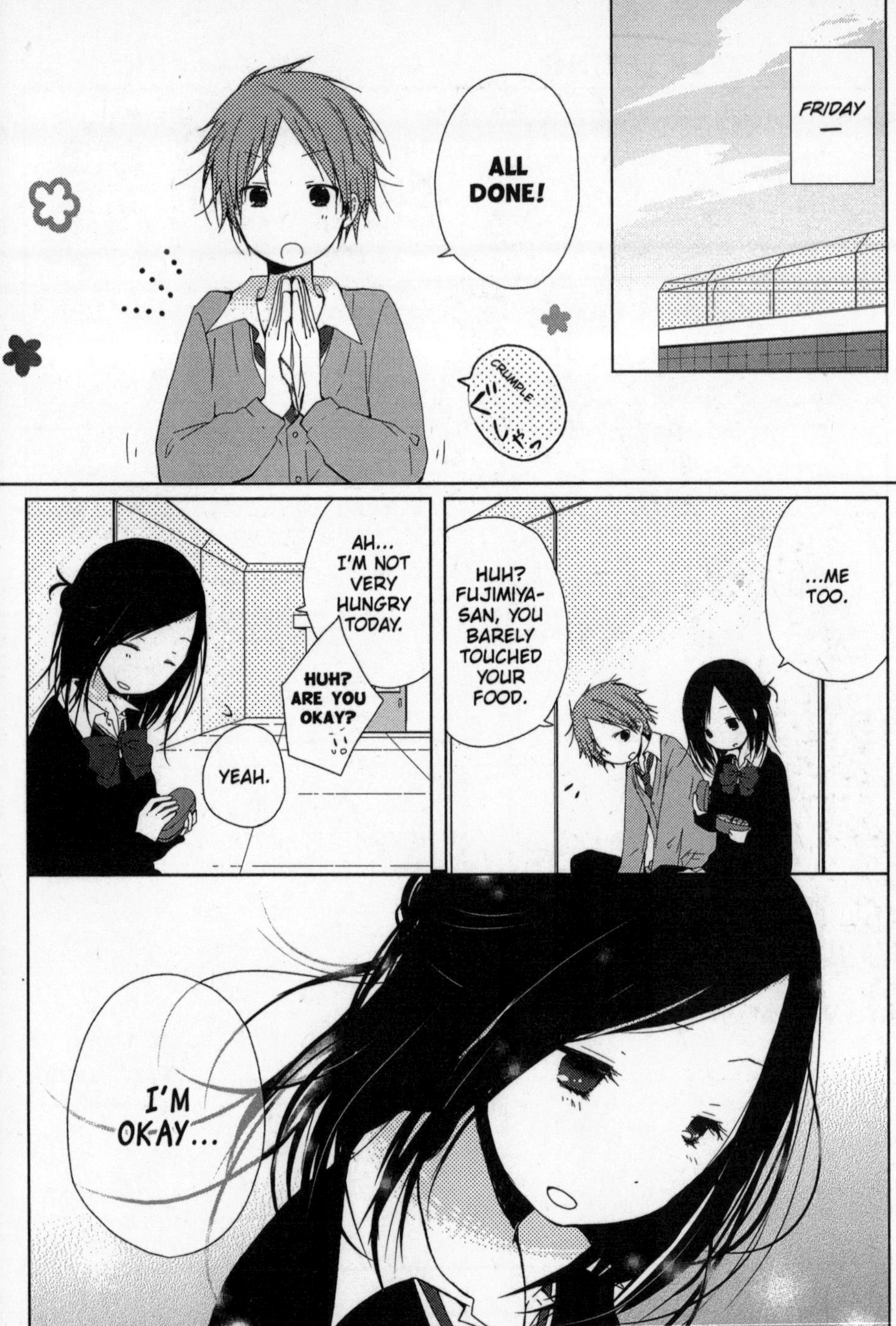
FRIDAY —
ALL DONE!
CRUMPLE
HUH? FUJIMIYA-SAN, YOU BARELY TOUCHED YOUR FOOD.
...ME TOO.
AH... I'M NOT VERY HUNGRY TODAY.
HUH? ARE YOU OKAY?
YEAH.
I'M OKAY...

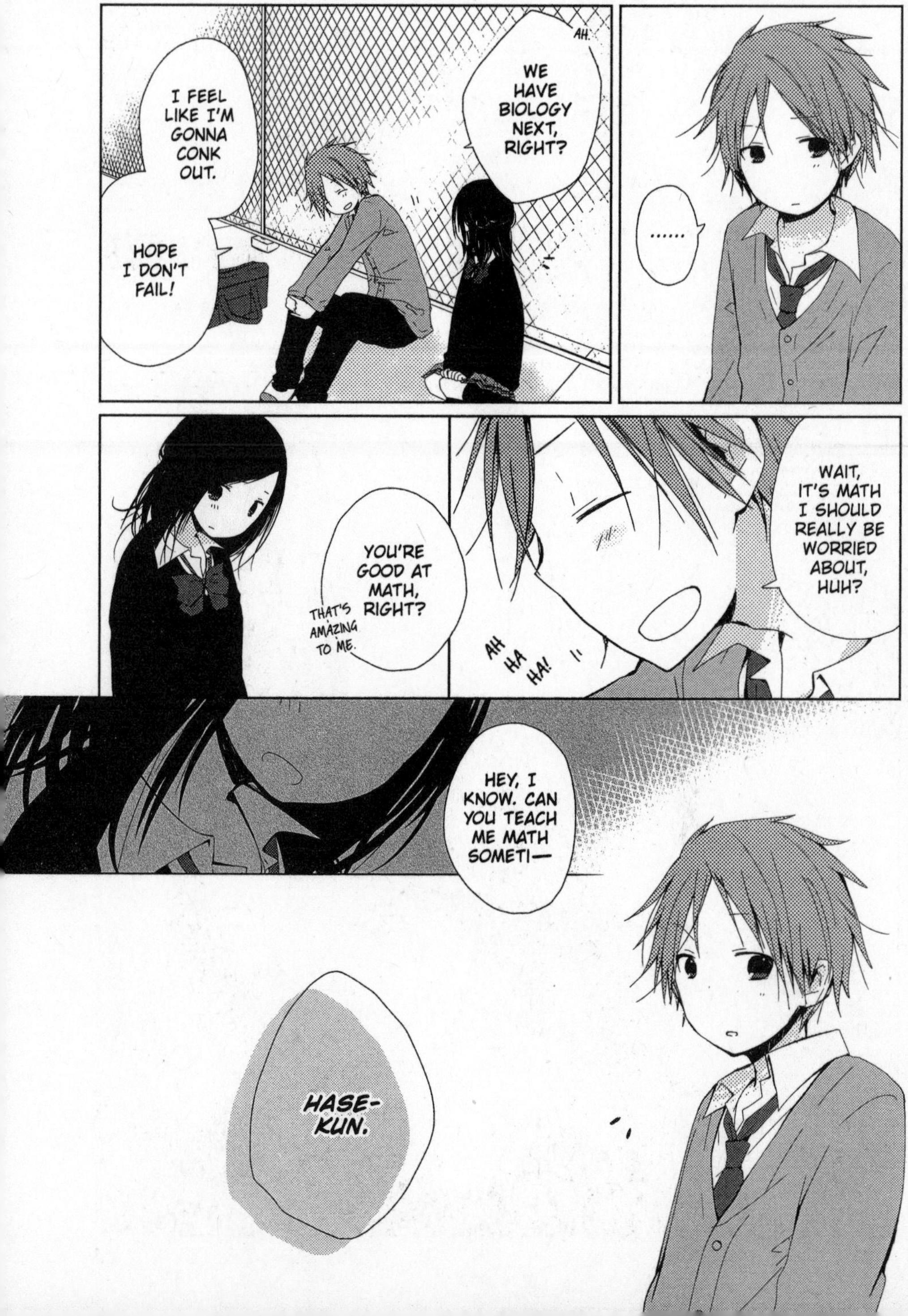
......
AH.
WE HAVE BIOLOGY NEXT, RIGHT?
I FEEL LIKE I'M GONNA CONK OUT.
HOPE I DON'T FAIL!
WAIT, IT'S MATH I SHOULD REALLY BE WORRIED ABOUT, HUH?
AH HA HA!
YOU'RE GOOD AT MATH, RIGHT?
THAT'S AMAZING TO ME.
HEY, I KNOW. CAN YOU TEACH ME MATH SOMETI—
HASE-KUN.

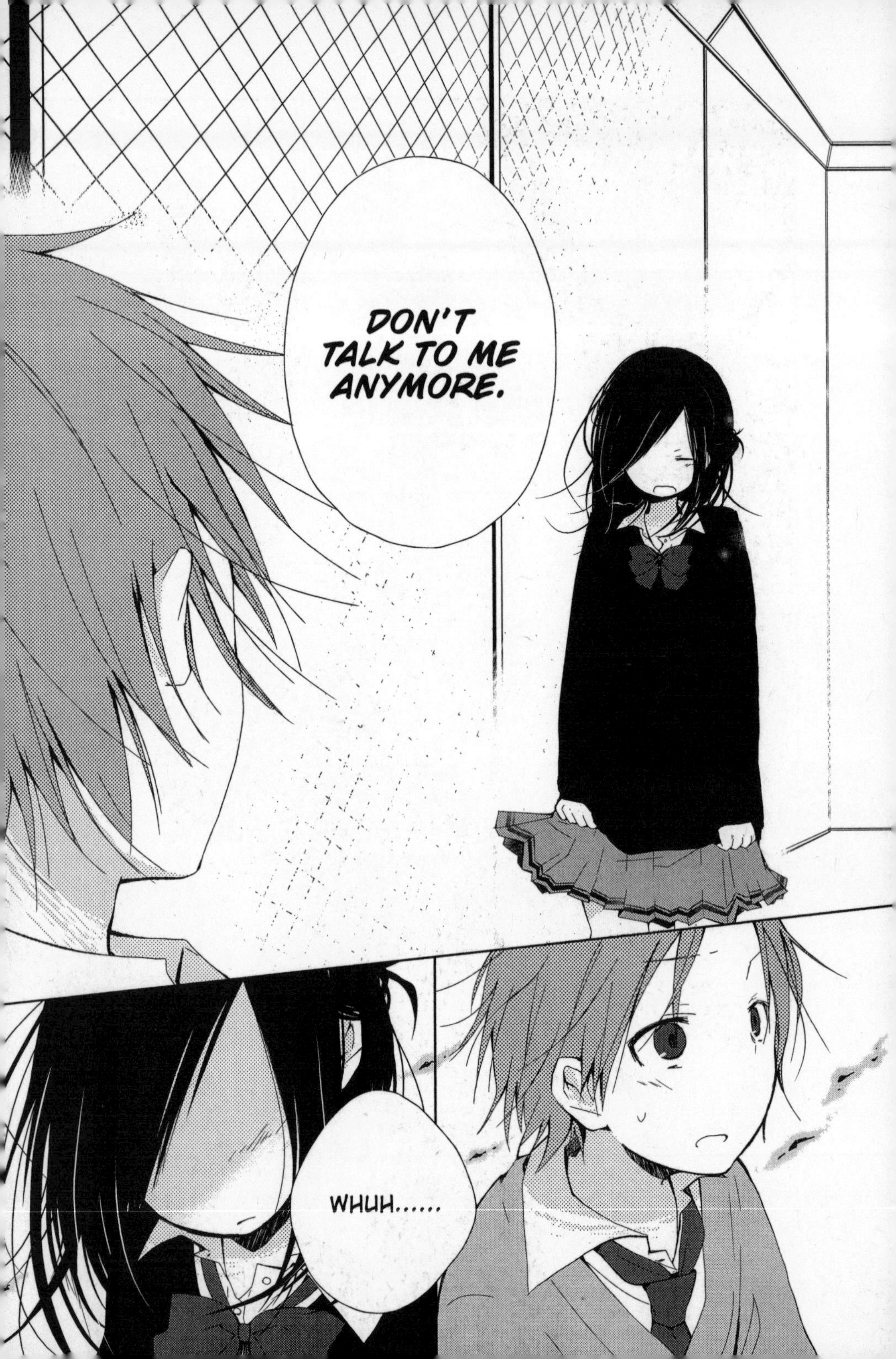
DON'T TALK TO ME ANYMORE.
WHUH......

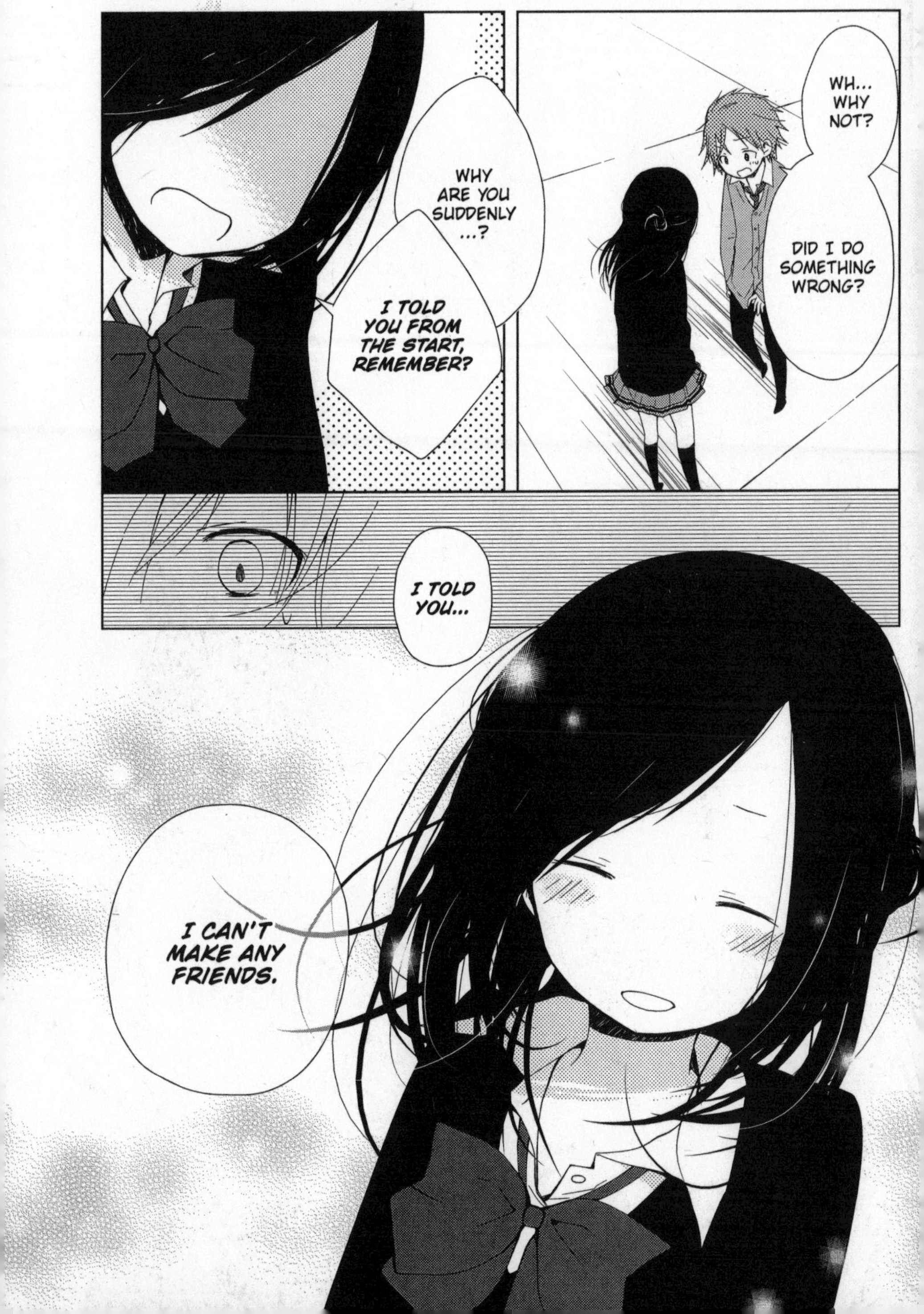
WH... WHY NOT?
DID I DO SOMETHING WRONG?
WHY ARE YOU SUDDENLY ...?
I TOLD YOU FROM THE START, REMEMBER?
I TOLD YOU...
I CAN'T MAKE ANY FRIENDS.

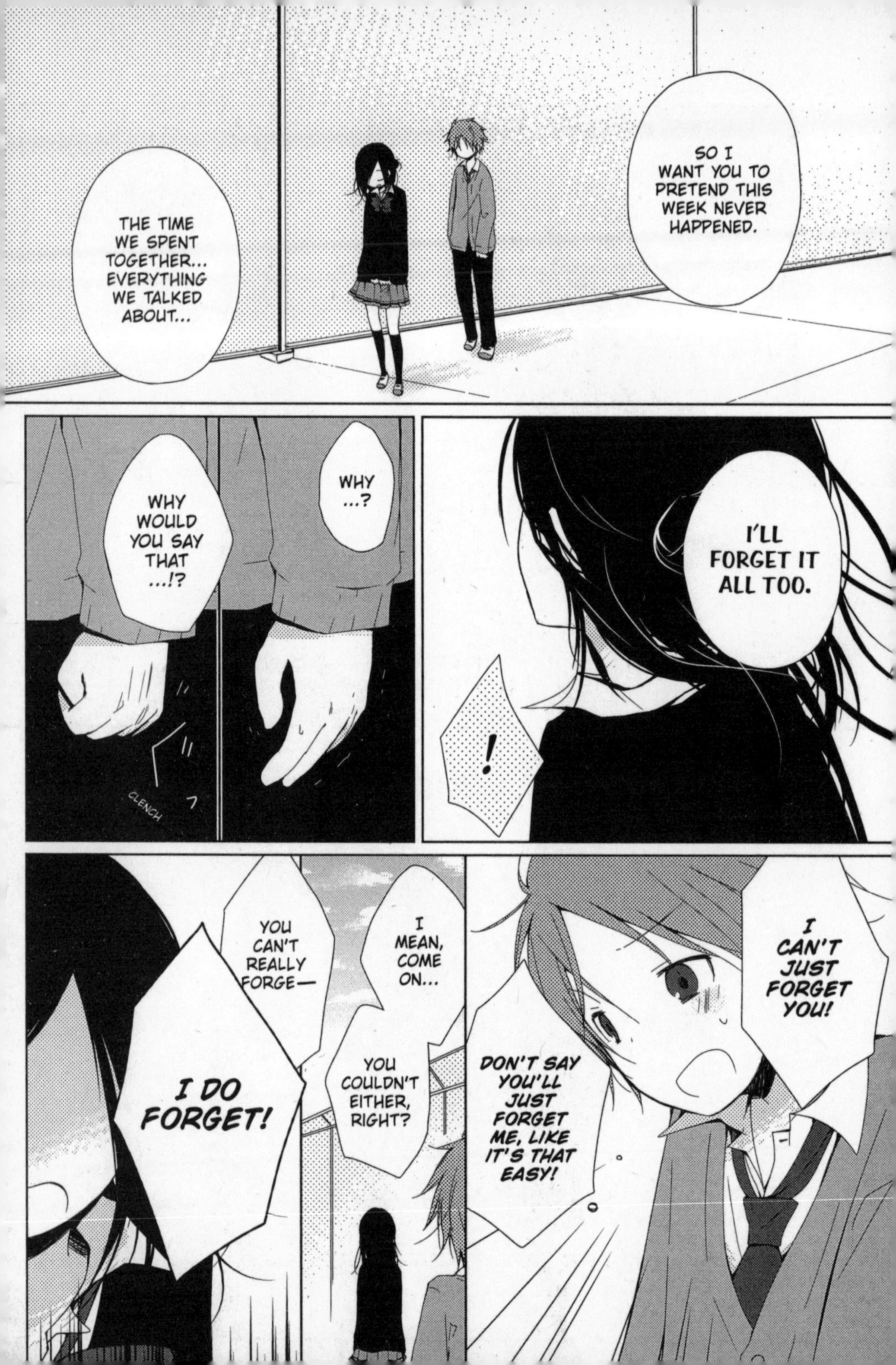
SO I WANT YOU TO PRETEND THIS WEEK NEVER HAPPENED.
THE TIME WE SPENT TOGETHER... EVERYTHING WE TALKED ABOUT...
I'LL FORGET IT ALL TOO.
!
WHY ...?
WHY WOULD YOU SAY THAT ...!?
CLENCH
I CAN'T JUST FORGET YOU!
DON'T SAY YOU'LL JUST FORGET ME, LIKE IT'S THAT EASY!
I MEAN, COME ON...
YOU COULDN'T EITHER, RIGHT?
YOU CAN'T REALLY FORGE—
I DO FORGET!

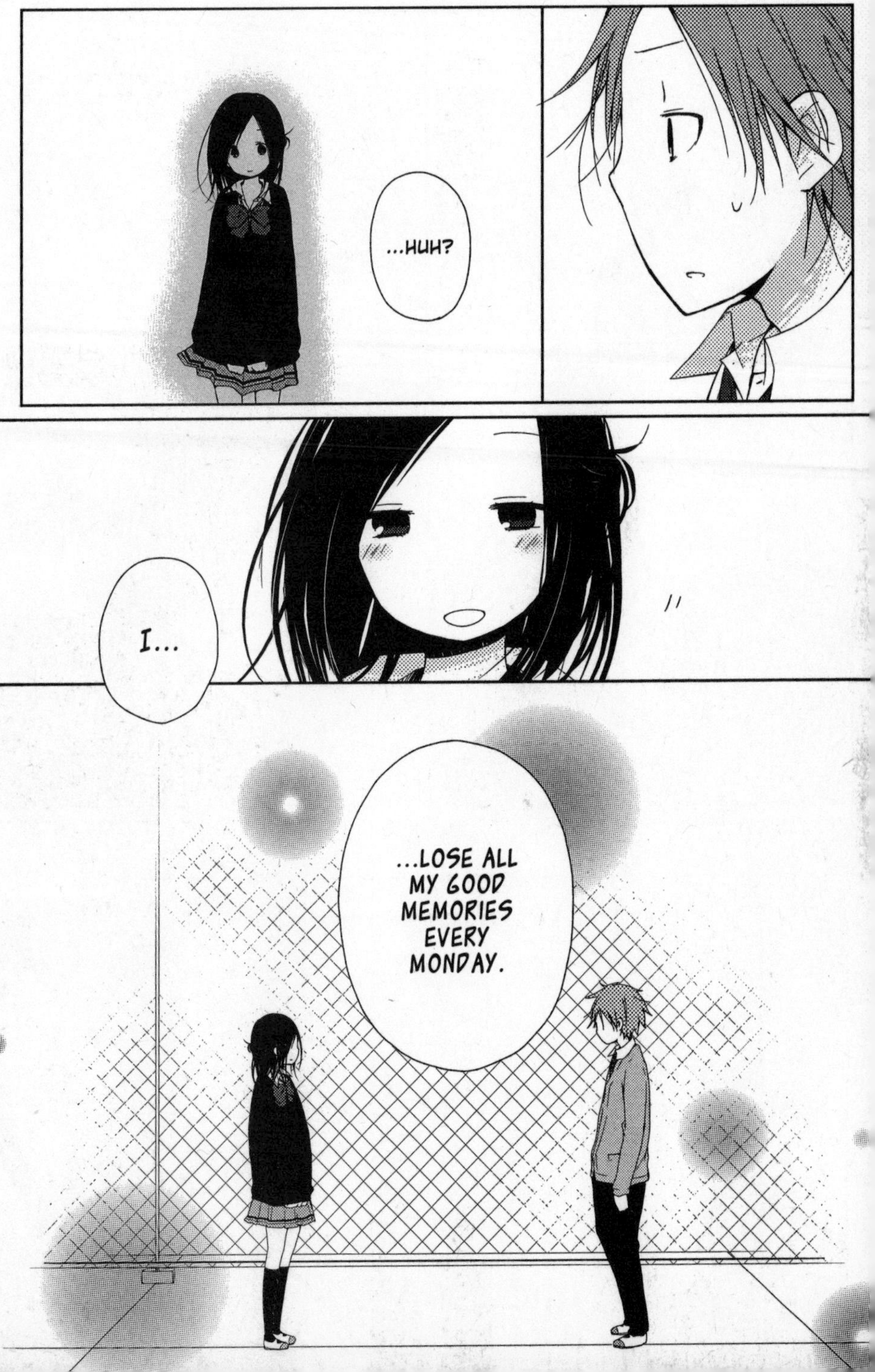
...HUH?
I...
...LOSE ALL MY GOOD MEMORIES EVERY MONDAY.

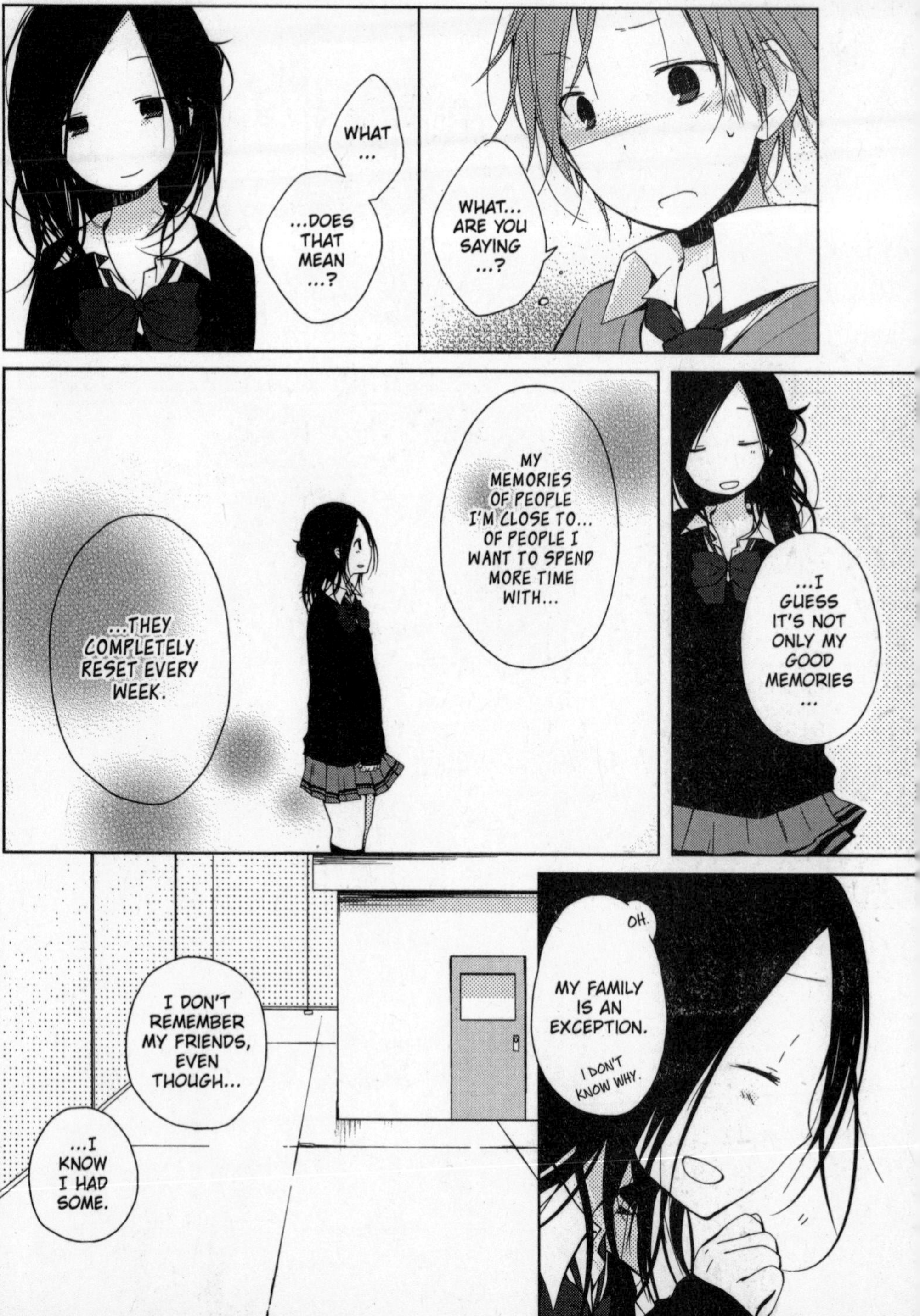
WHAT... ARE YOU SAYING ...?
WHAT ...
...DOES THAT MEAN ...?
...I GUESS IT'S NOT ONLY MY GOOD MEMORIES ...
MY MEMORIES OF PEOPLE I'M CLOSE TO... OF PEOPLE I WANT TO SPEND MORE TIME WITH...
...THEY COMPLETELY RESET EVERY WEEK.
OH.
MY FAMILY IS AN EXCEPTION.
I DON'T KNOW WHY.
I DON'T REMEMBER MY FRIENDS, EVEN THOUGH...
...I KNOW I HAD SOME.

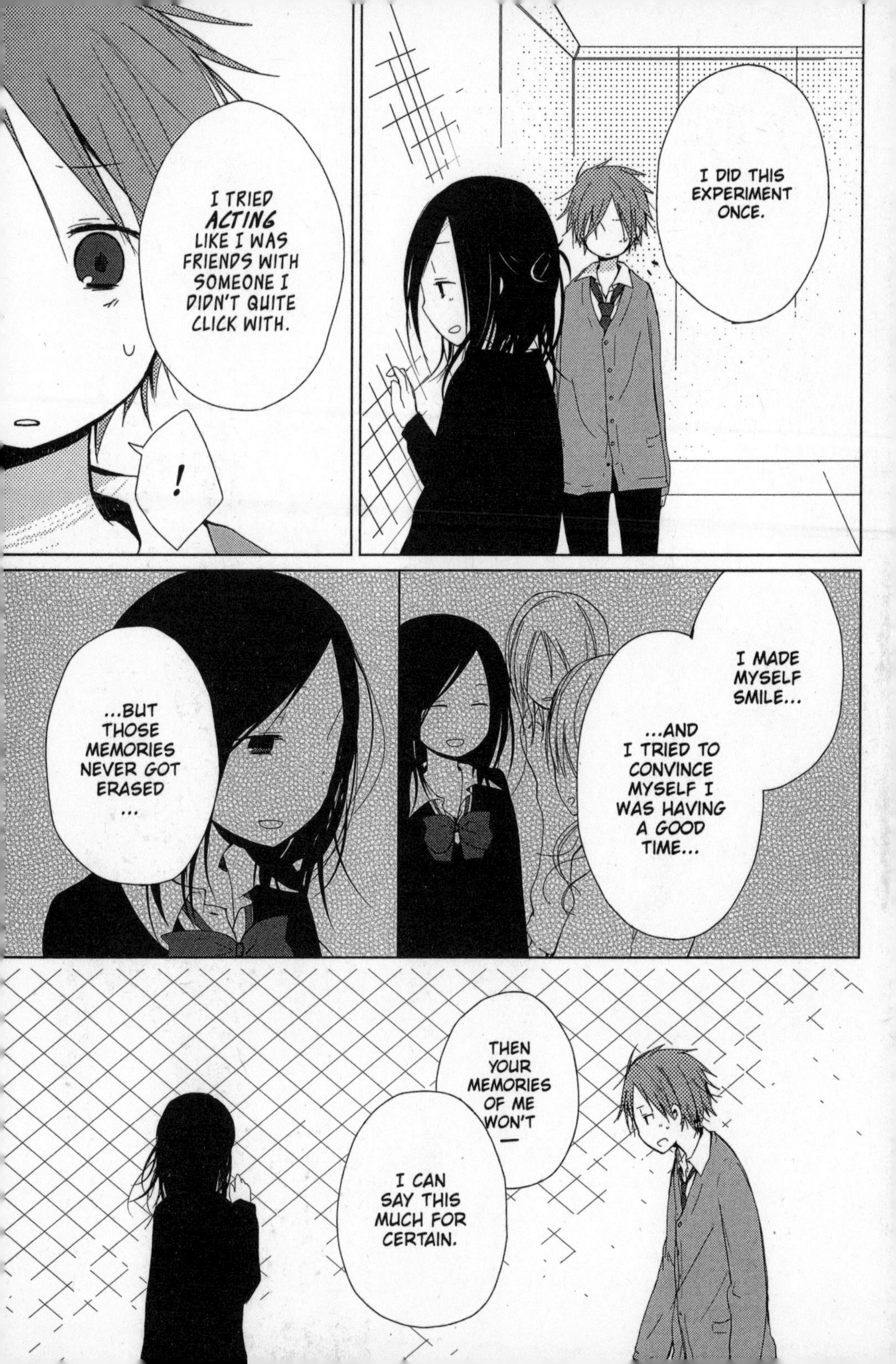
I DID THIS EXPERIMENT ONCE.
I TRIED ACTING LIKE I WAS FRIENDS WITH SOMEONE I DIDN'T QUITE CLICK WITH.
!
I MADE MYSELF SMILE...
...AND I TRIED TO CONVINCE MYSELF I WAS HAVING A GOOD TIME...
...BUT THOSE MEMORIES NEVER GOT ERASED...
THEN YOUR MEMORIES OF ME WON'T—
I CAN SAY THIS MUCH FOR CERTAIN.

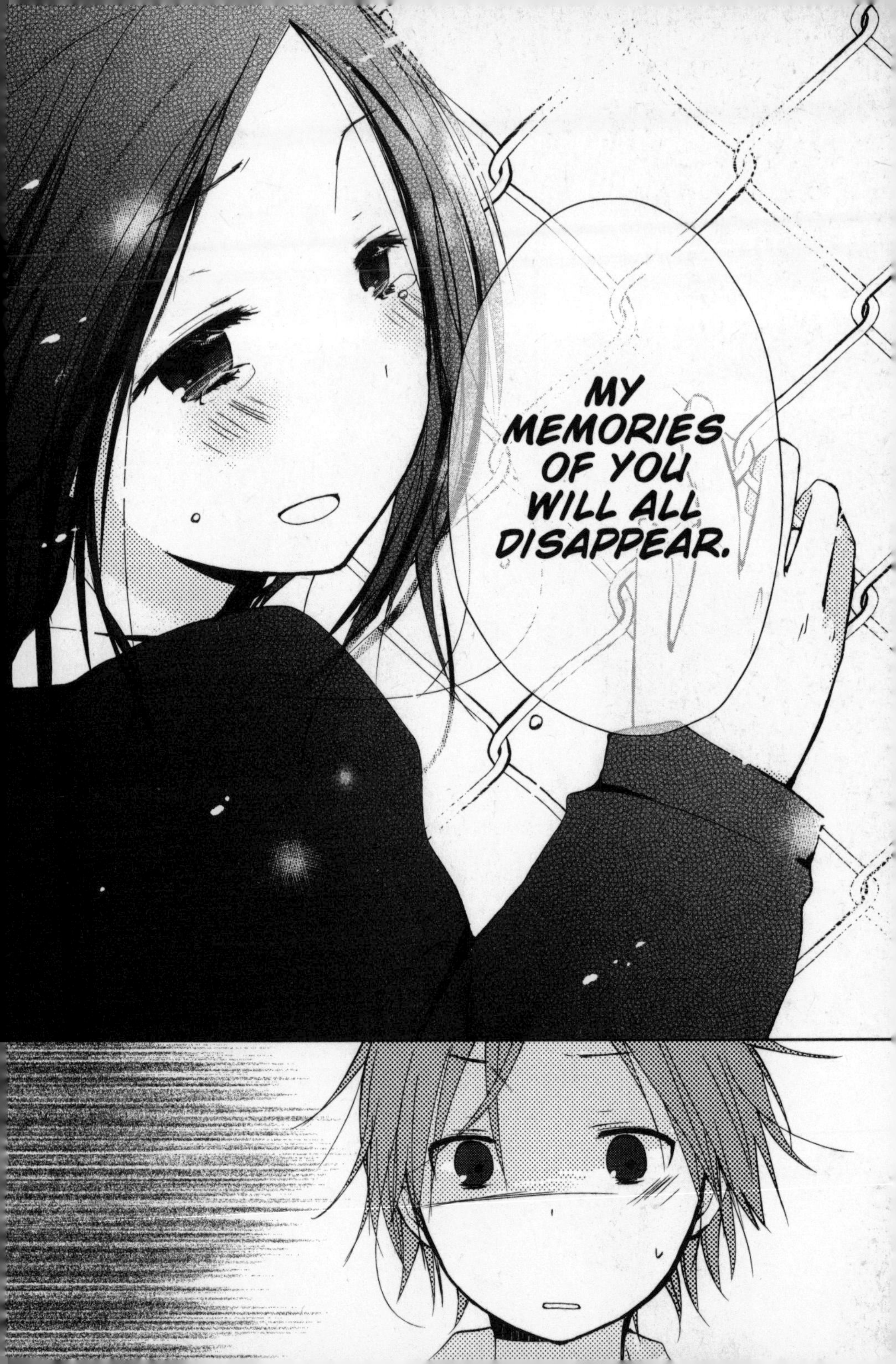
MY MEMORIES OF YOU WILL ALL DISAPPEAR.

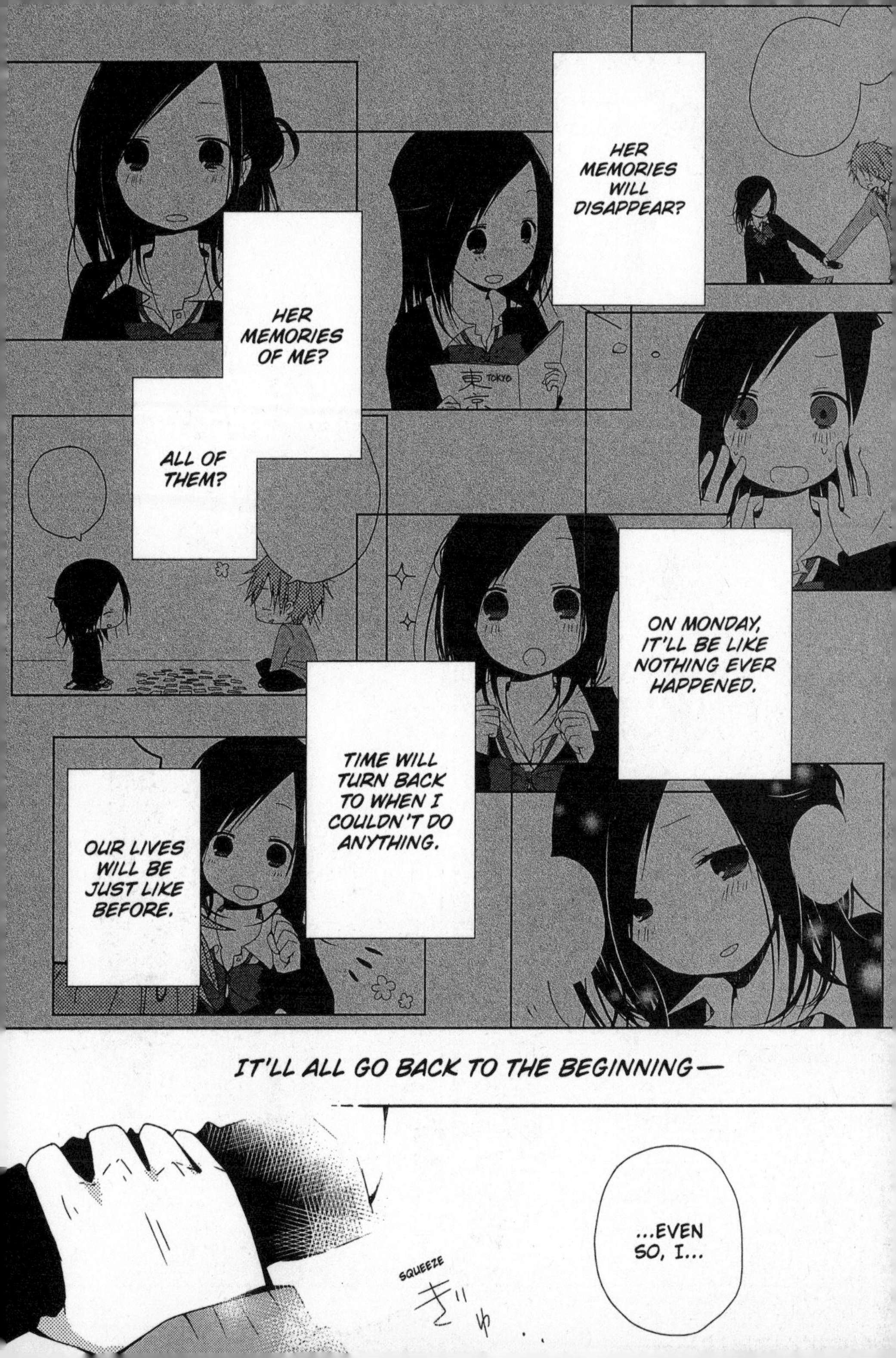

HER MEMORIES WILL DISAPPEAR?
TOKYO
HER MEMORIES OF ME?
ALL OF THEM?
ON MONDAY, IT'LL BE LIKE NOTHING EVER HAPPENED.
TIME WILL TURN BACK TO WHEN I COULDN'T DO ANYTHING.
OUR LIVES WILL BE JUST LIKE BEFORE.
IT'LL ALL GO BACK TO THE BEGINNING—
...EVEN SO, I...
SQUEEZE

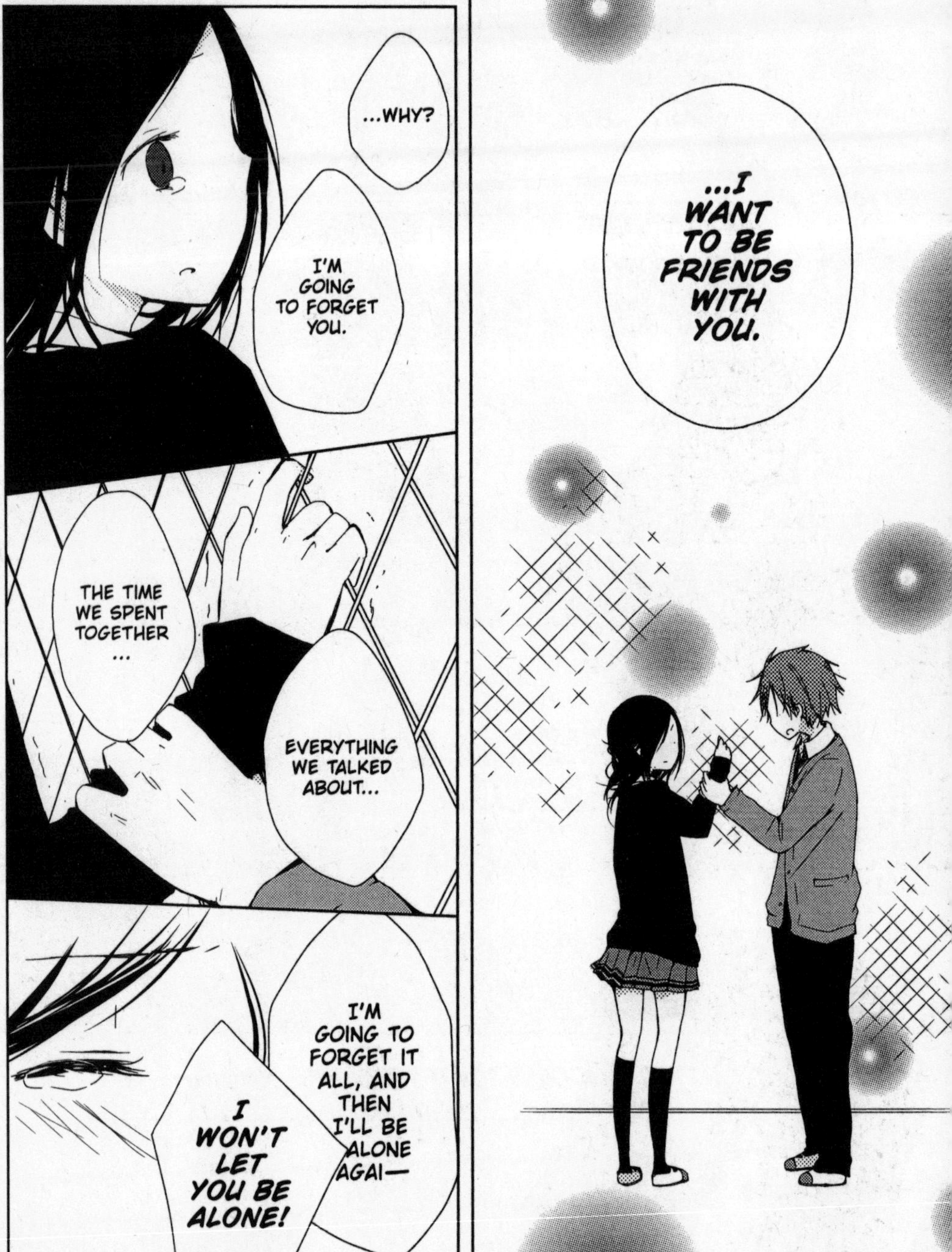
...I WANT TO BE FRIENDS WITH YOU.
...WHY?
I'M GOING TO FORGET YOU.
THE TIME WE SPENT TOGETHER ...
EVERYTHING WE TALKED ABOUT...
I'M GOING TO FORGET IT ALL, AND THEN I'LL BE ALONE AGAI—
I WON'T LET YOU BE ALONE!

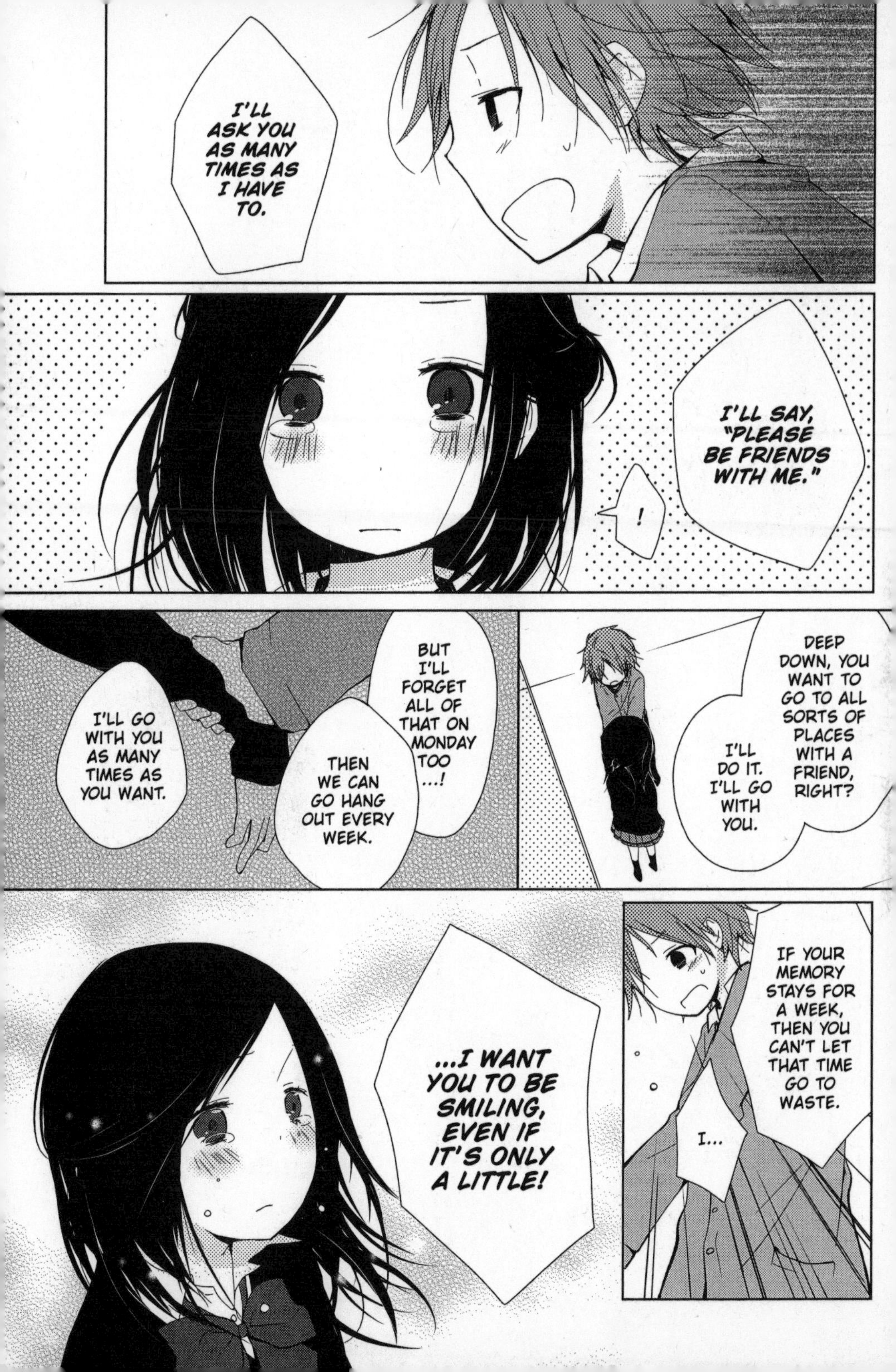
I'LL ASK YOU AS MANY TIMES AS I HAVE TO.
I'LL SAY, "PLEASE BE FRIENDS WITH ME."
!
DEEP DOWN, YOU WANT TO GO TO ALL SORTS OF PLACES WITH A FRIEND, RIGHT?
I'LL DO IT. I'LL GO WITH YOU.
BUT I'LL FORGET ALL OF THAT ON MONDAY TOO ...!
THEN WE CAN GO HANG OUT EVERY WEEK.
I'LL GO WITH YOU AS MANY TIMES AS YOU WANT.
IF YOUR MEMORY STAYS FOR A WEEK, THEN YOU CAN'T LET THAT TIME GO TO WASTE.
I...
...I WANT YOU TO BE SMILING, EVEN IF IT'S ONLY A LITTLE!

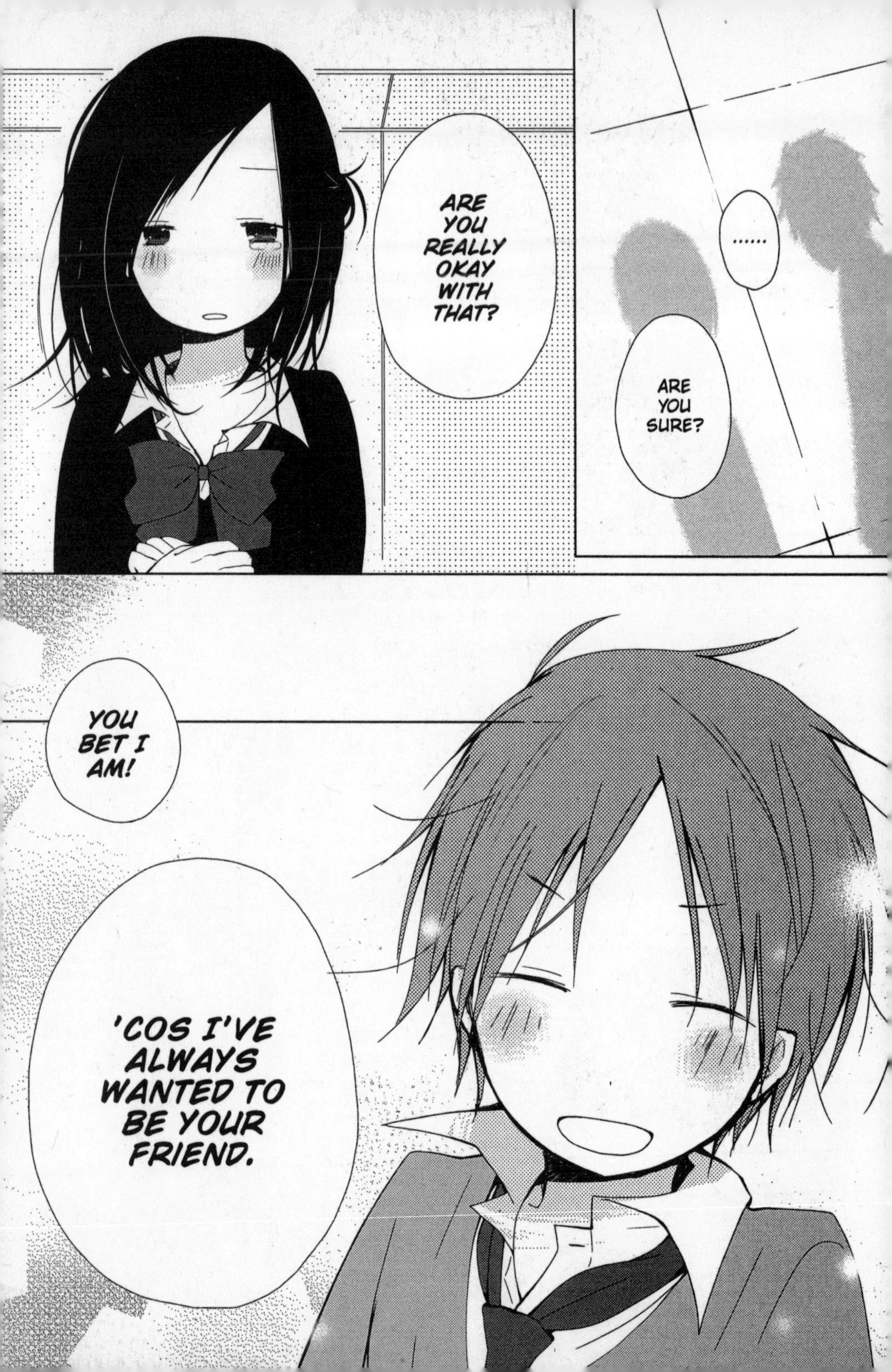
......
ARE YOU SURE?
ARE YOU REALLY OKAY WITH THAT?
YOU BET I AM!
'COS I'VE ALWAYS WANTED TO BE YOUR FRIEND.

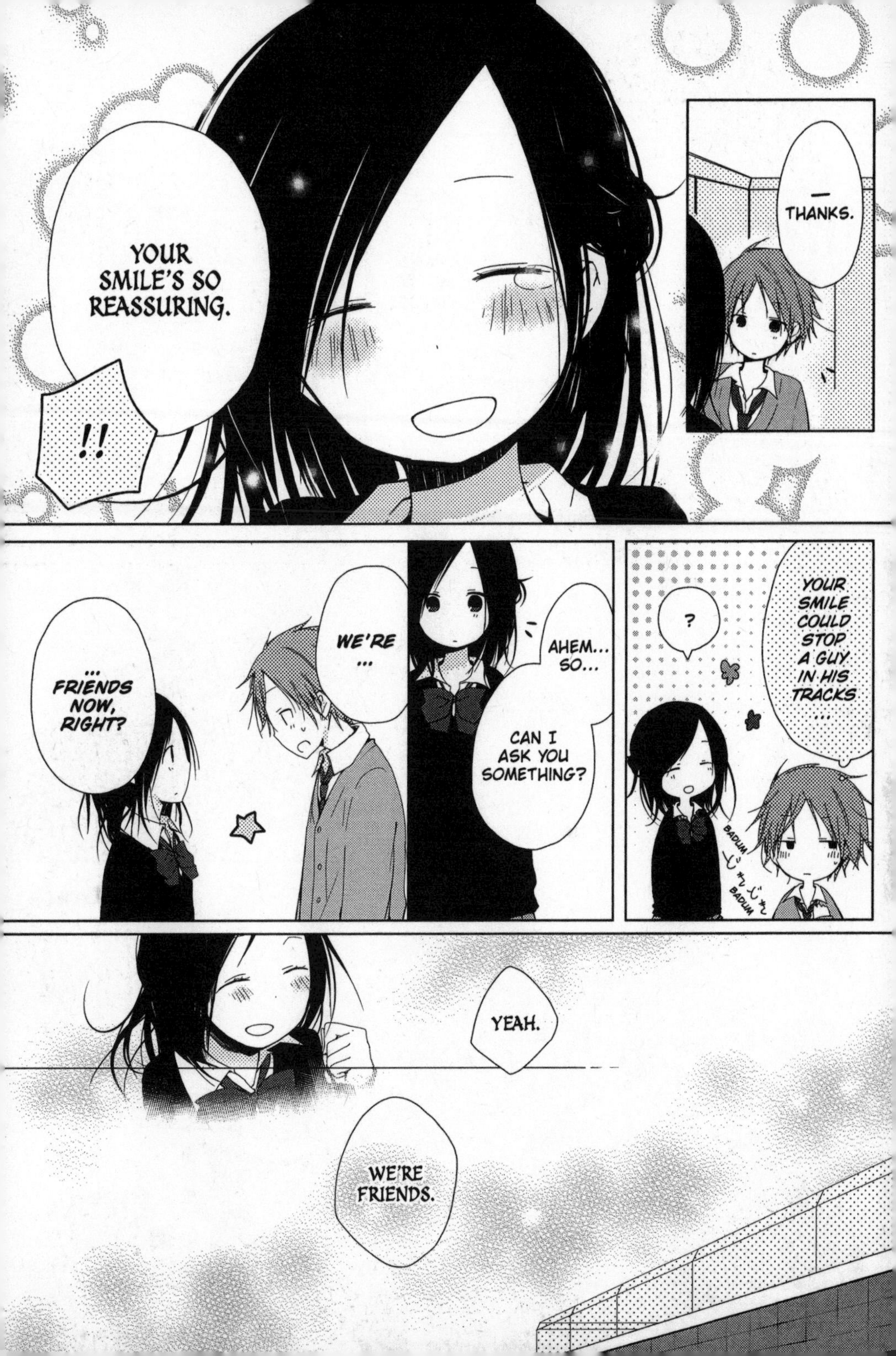
— THANKS.
YOUR SMILE'S SO REASSURING.
!!
YOUR SMILE COULD STOP A GUY IN HIS TRACKS...
?
BADUM
BADUM
AHEM... SO...
CAN I ASK YOU SOMETHING?
WE'RE ...
... FRIENDS NOW, RIGHT?
YEAH.
WE'RE FRIENDS.

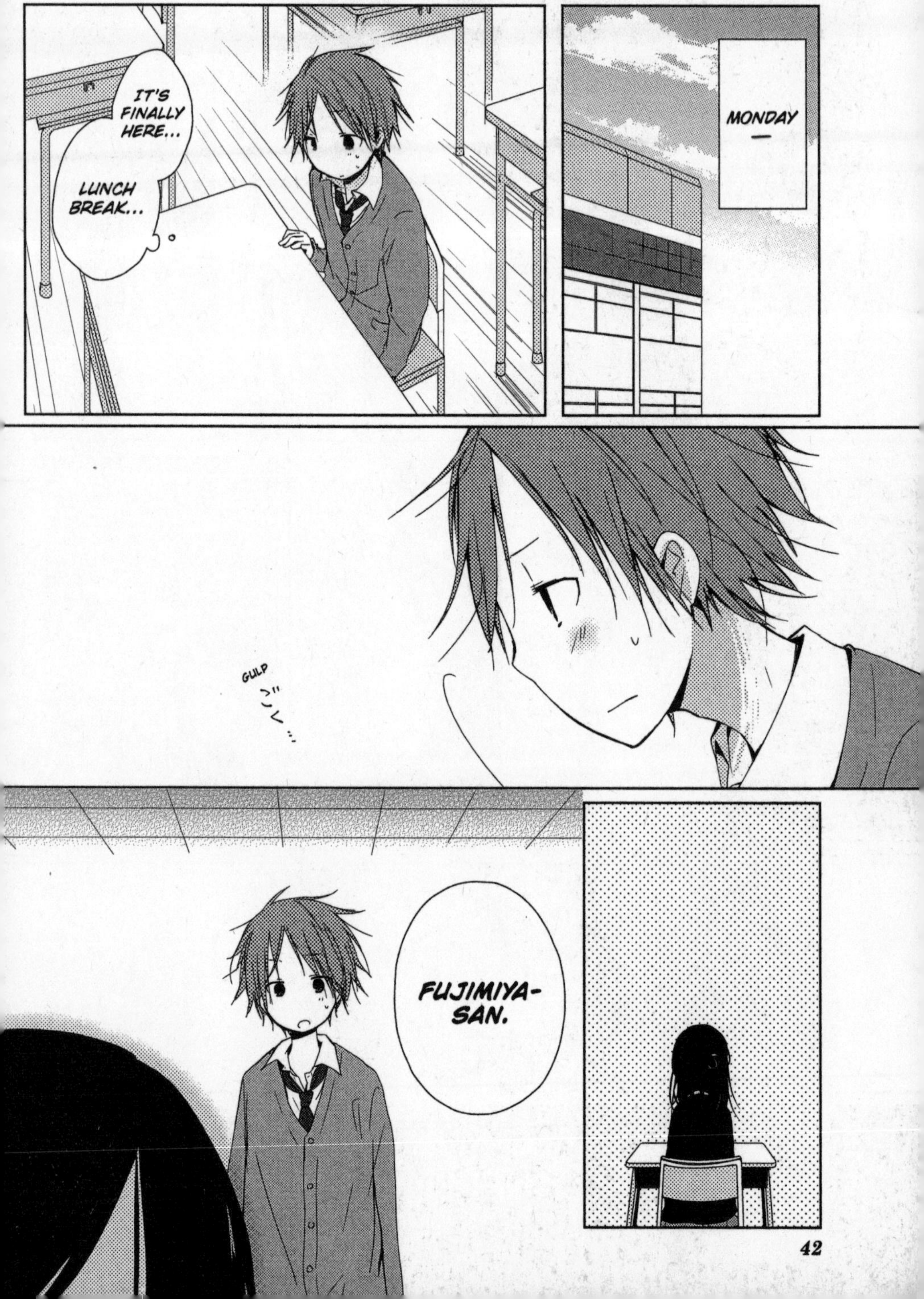
MONDAY —
IT'S FINALLY HERE...
LUNCH BREAK...
GULP
ごく…
FUJIMIYA-SAN.

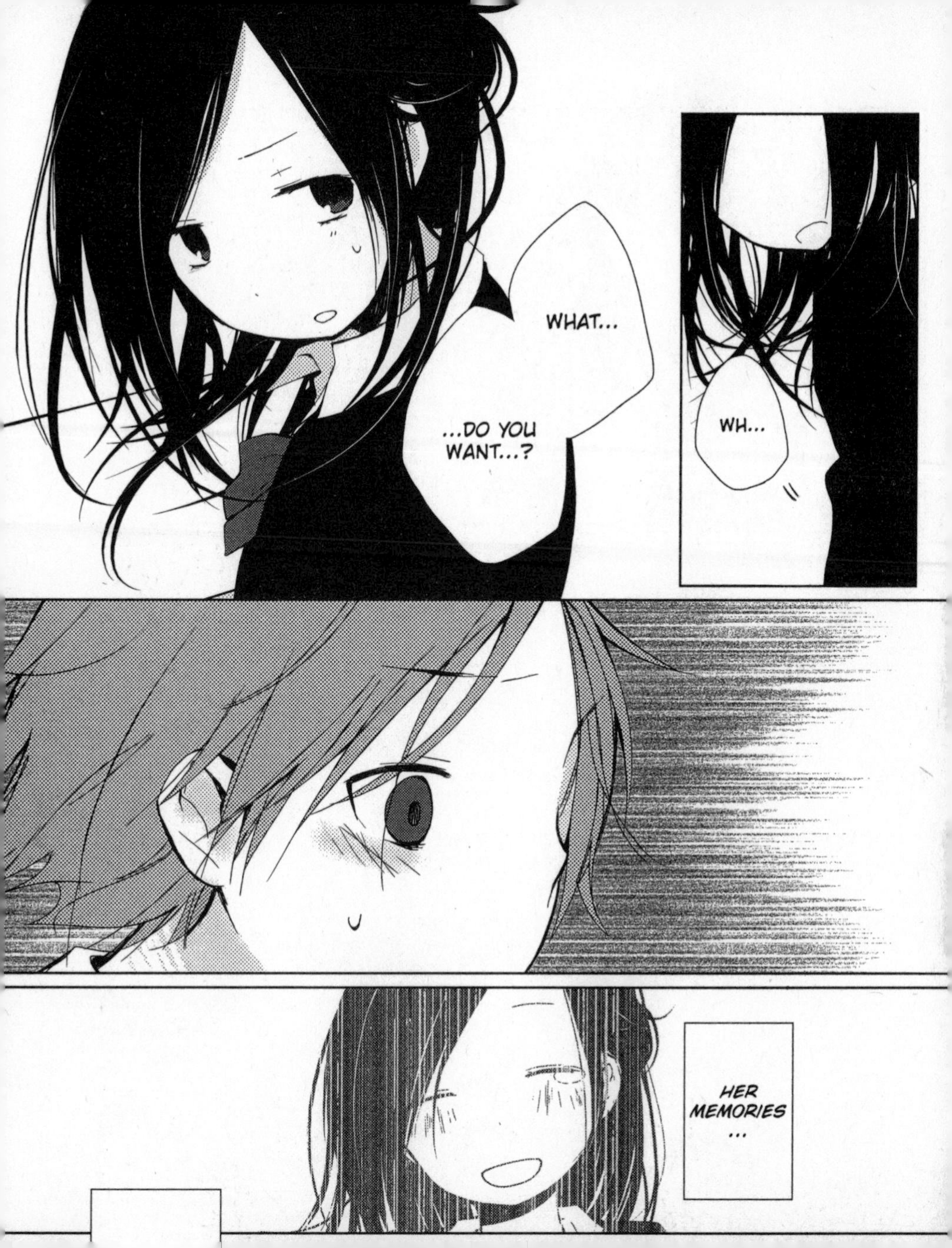
WH...
WHAT...
...DO YOU WANT...?
HER MEMORIES ...

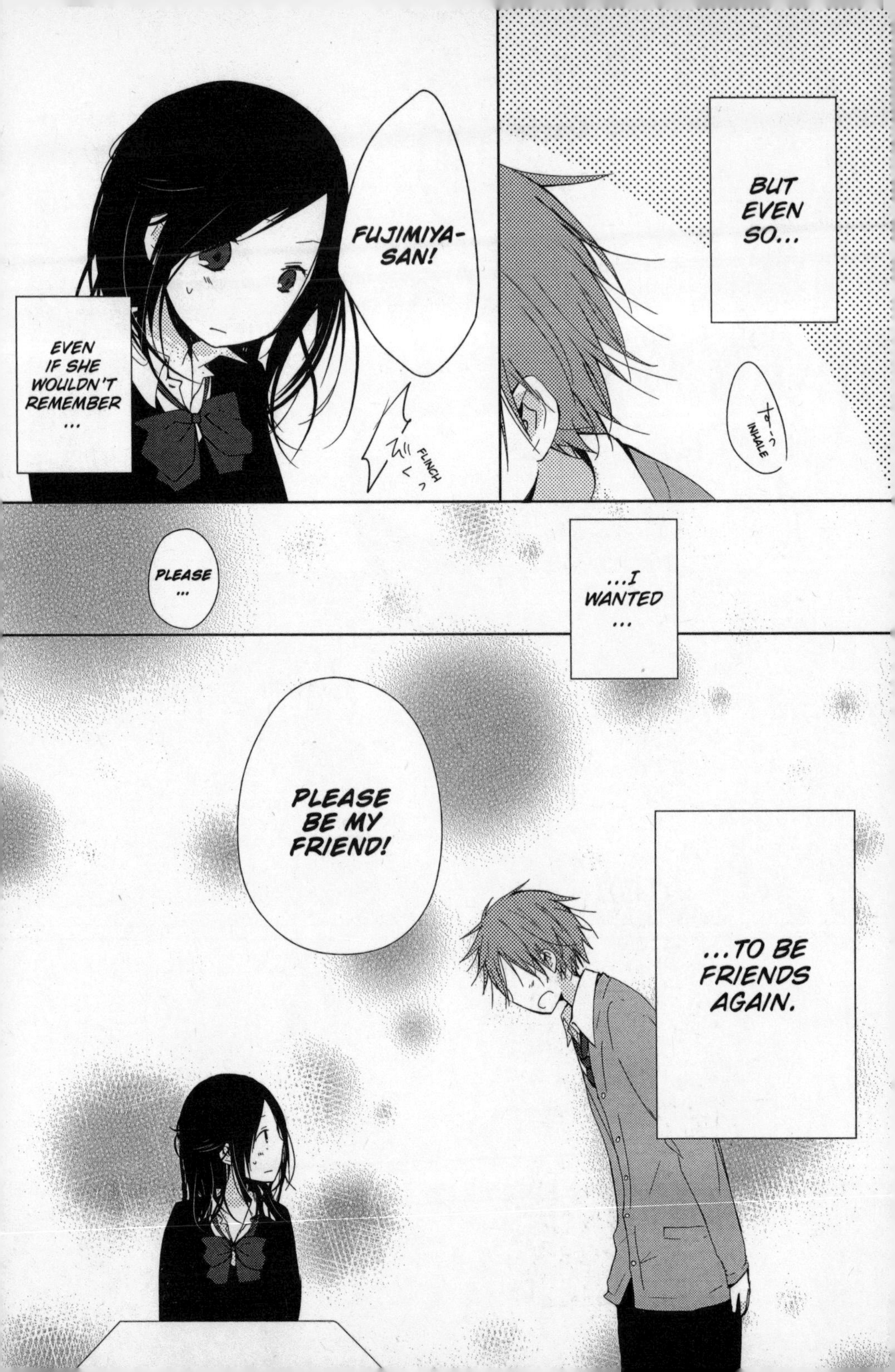

BUT EVEN SO...
INHALE
FUJIMIYA-SAN!
EVEN IF SHE WOULDN'T REMEMBER...
FLINCH
...I WANTED...
PLEASE...
...TO BE FRIENDS AGAIN.
PLEASE BE MY FRIEND!

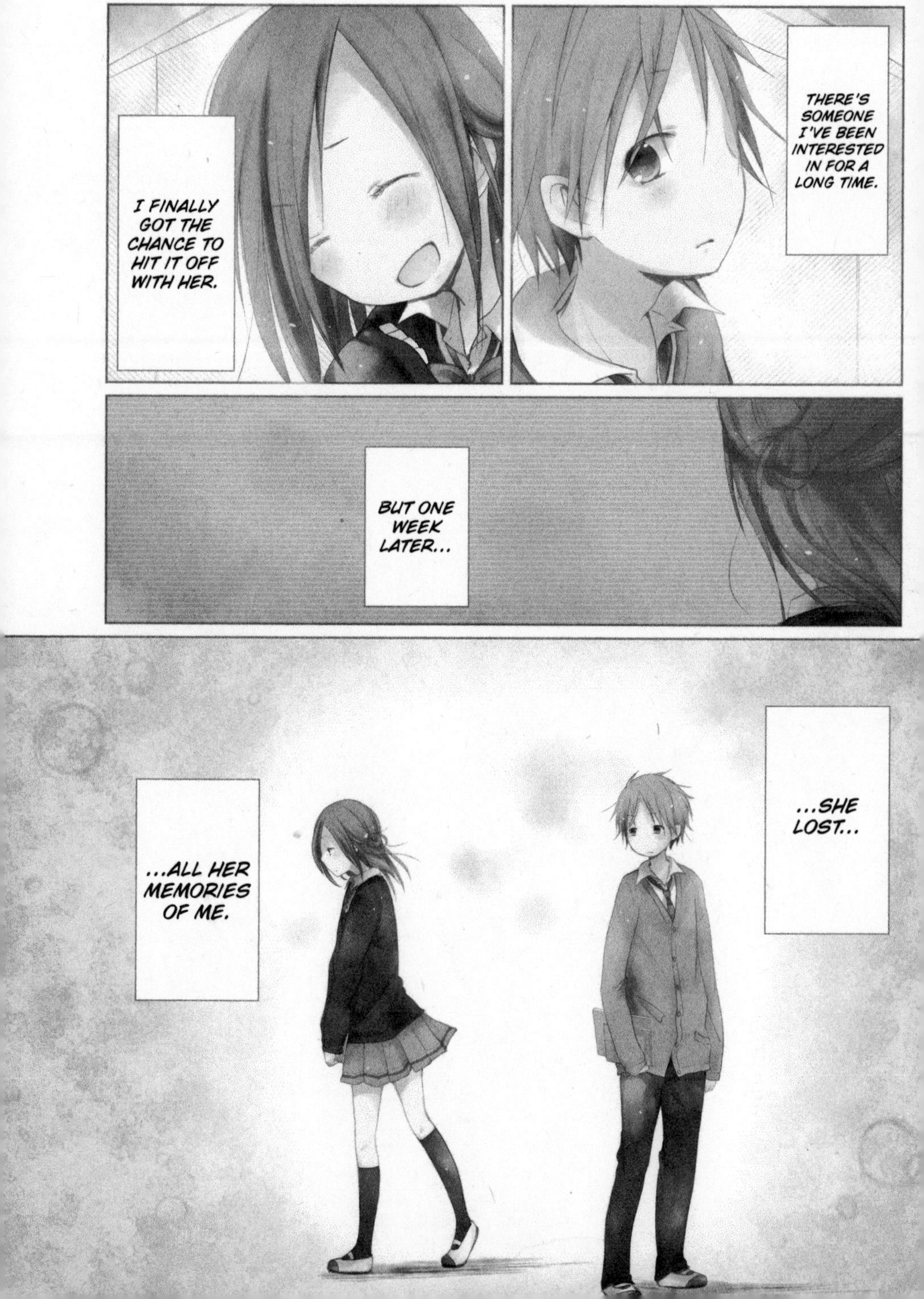
THERE'S SOMEONE I'VE BEEN INTERESTED IN FOR A LONG TIME.
I FINALLY GOT THE CHANCE TO HIT IT OFF WITH HER.
BUT ONE WEEK LATER...
...SHE LOST...
...ALL HER MEMORIES OF ME.

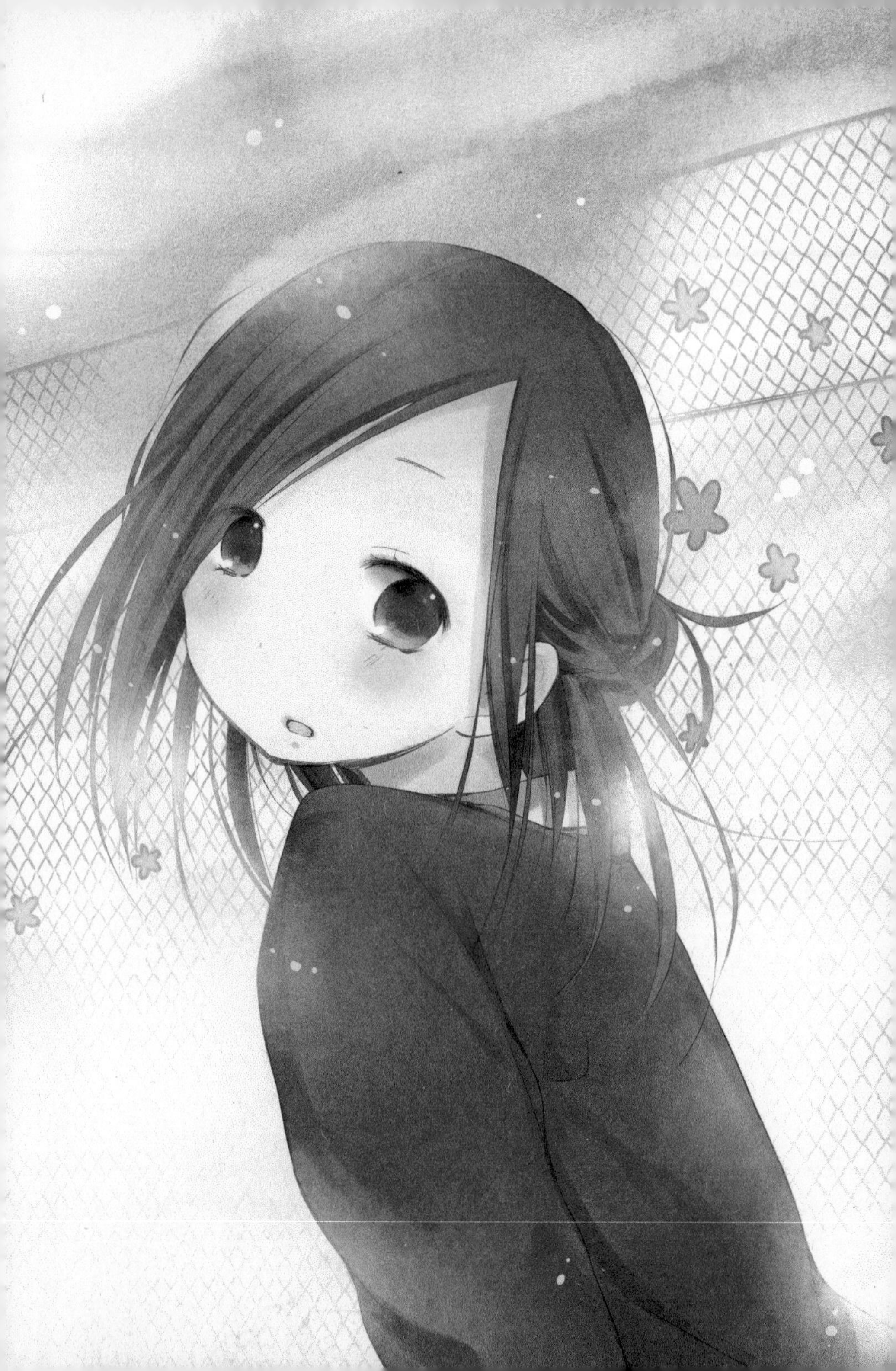

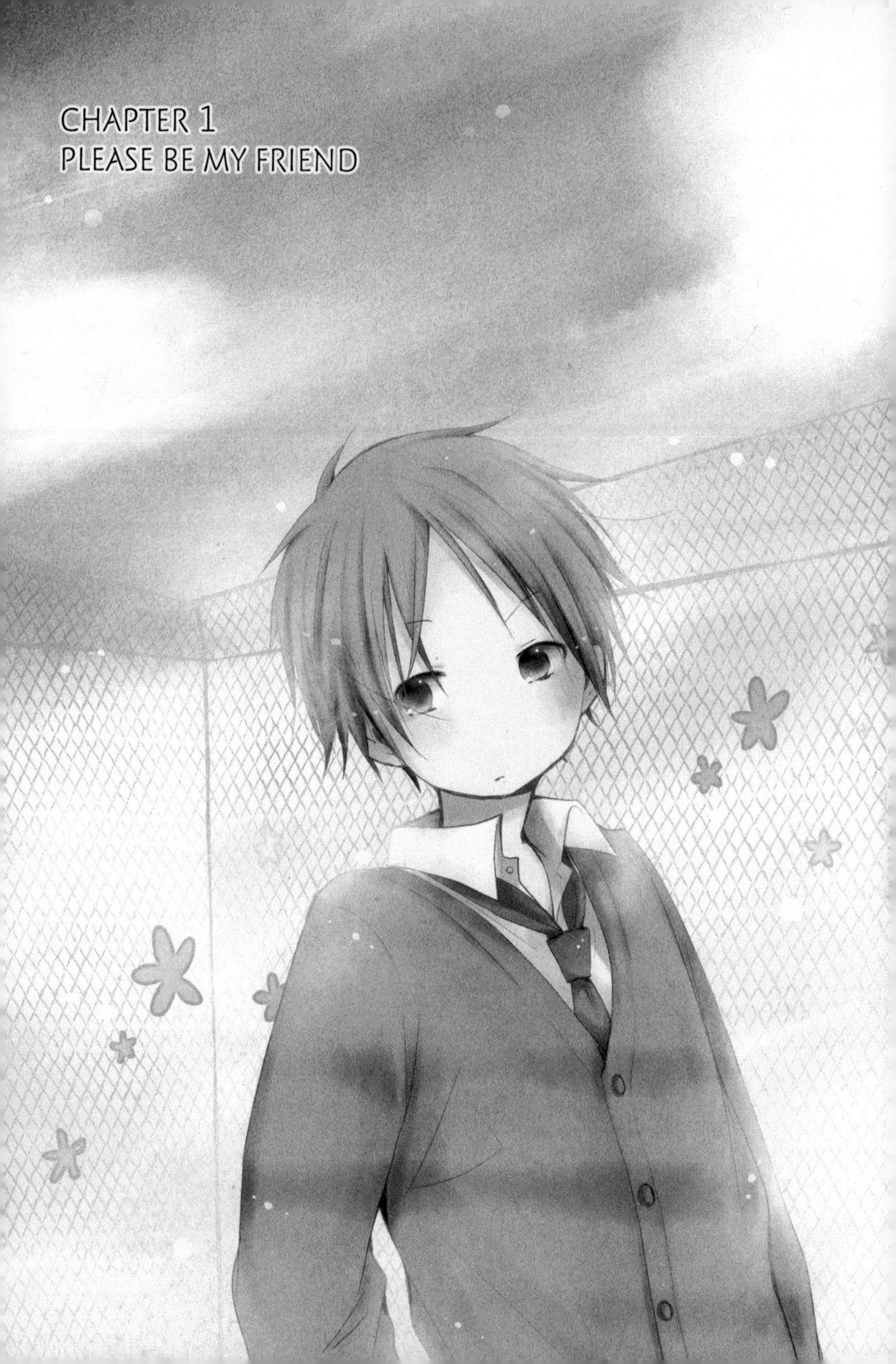
CHAPTER 1
PLEASE BE MY FRIEND

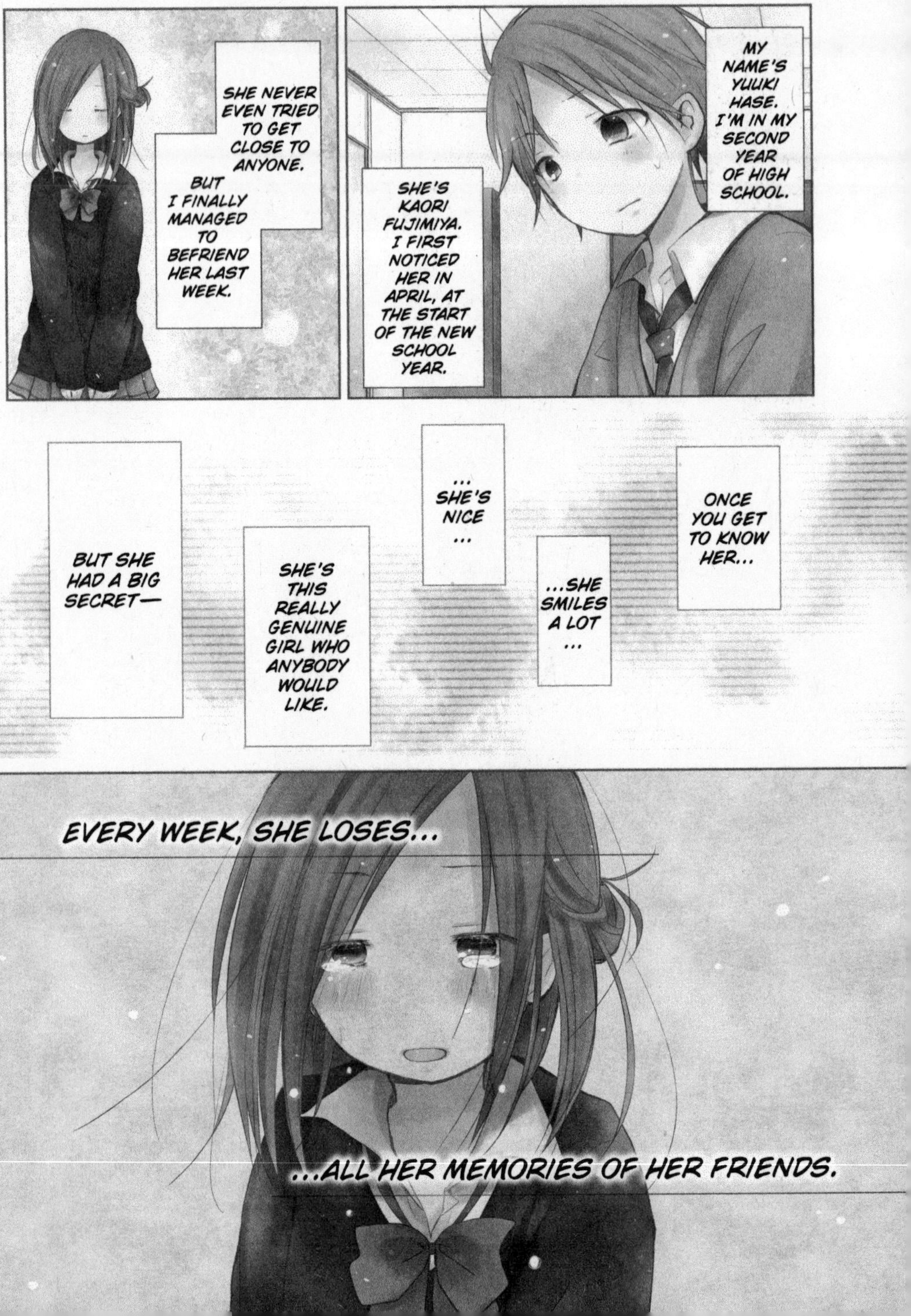
MY NAME'S YUUKI HASE. I'M IN MY SECOND YEAR OF HIGH SCHOOL.
SHE'S KAORI FUJIMIYA. I FIRST NOTICED HER IN APRIL, AT THE START OF THE NEW SCHOOL YEAR.
SHE NEVER EVEN TRIED TO GET CLOSE TO ANYONE.
BUT I FINALLY MANAGED TO BEFRIEND HER LAST WEEK.
ONCE YOU GET TO KNOW HER...
...SHE SMILES A LOT ...
... SHE'S NICE ...
SHE'S THIS REALLY GENUINE GIRL WHO ANYBODY WOULD LIKE.
BUT SHE HAD A BIG SECRET—
EVERY WEEK, SHE LOSES...
...ALL HER MEMORIES OF HER FRIENDS.

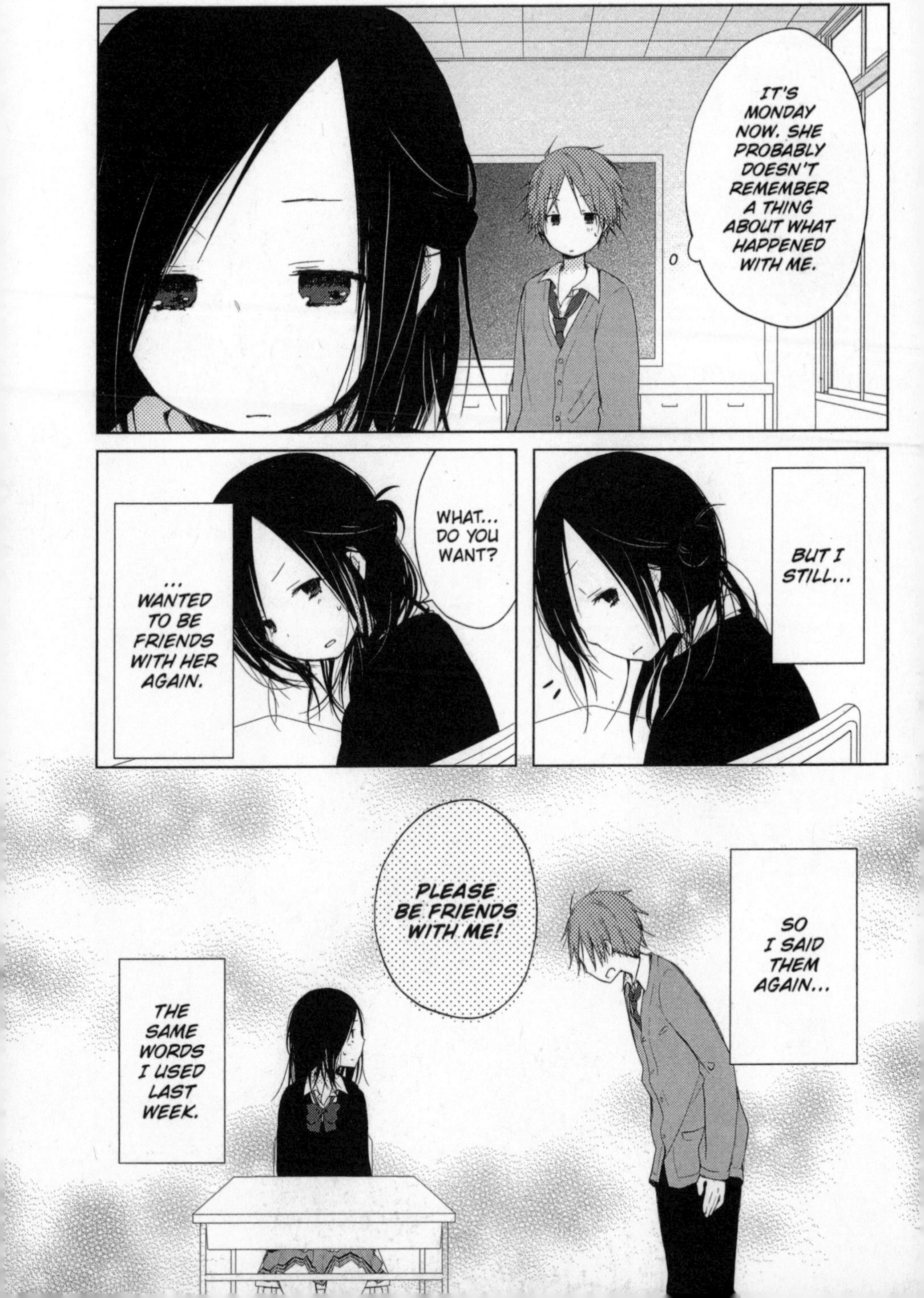
IT'S MONDAY NOW. SHE PROBABLY DOESN'T REMEMBER A THING ABOUT WHAT HAPPENED WITH ME.
BUT I STILL...
WHAT... DO YOU WANT?
...WANTED TO BE FRIENDS WITH HER AGAIN.
SO I SAID THEM AGAIN...
PLEASE BE FRIENDS WITH ME!
THE SAME WORDS I USED LAST WEEK.

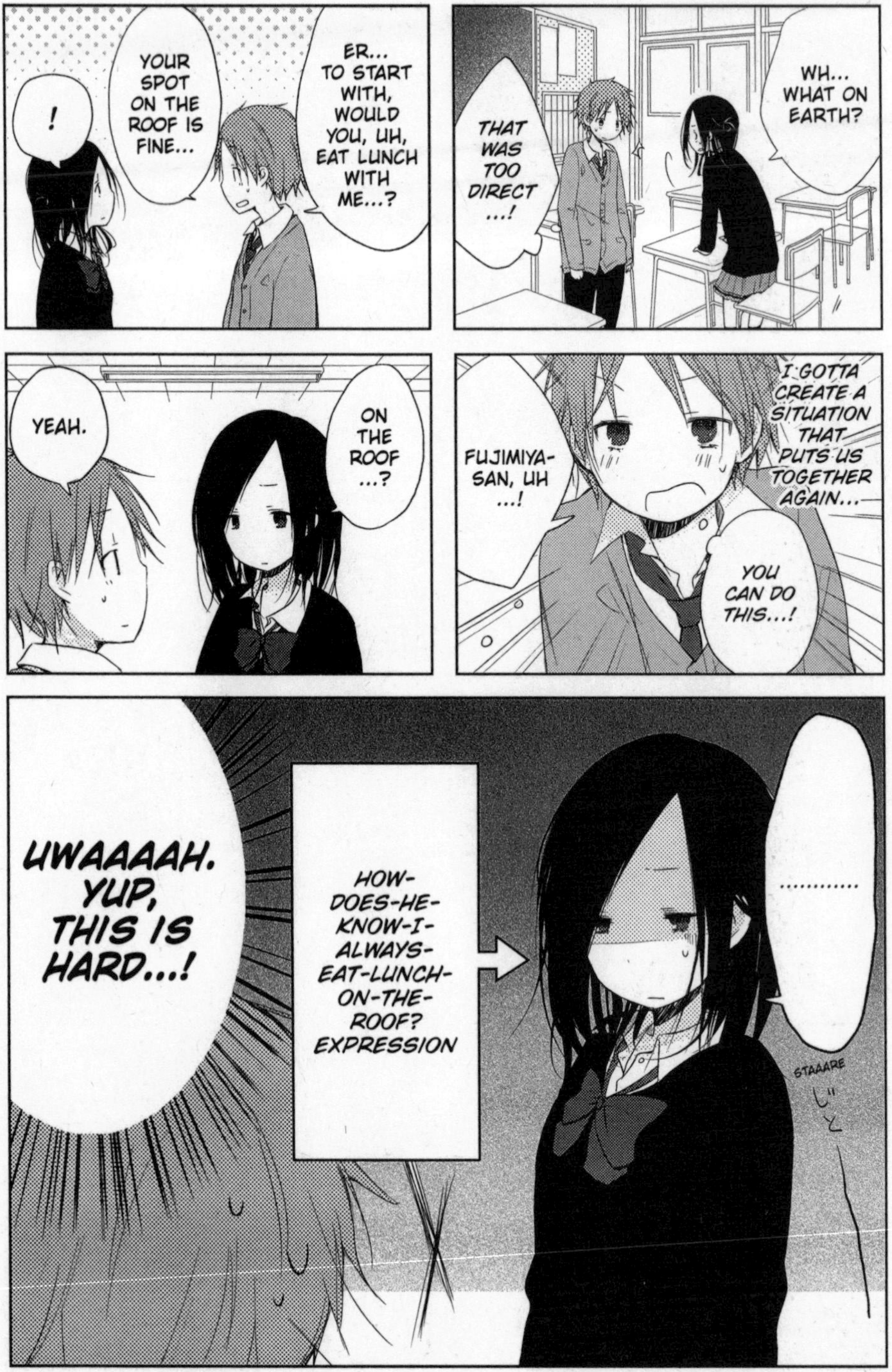
WH... WHAT ON EARTH?
THAT WAS TOO DIRECT ...!
ER... TO START WITH, WOULD YOU, UH, EAT LUNCH WITH ME...?
YOUR SPOT ON THE ROOF IS FINE...
!
I GOTTA CREATE A SITUATION THAT PUTS US TOGETHER AGAIN...
FUJIMIYA-SAN, UH ...!
YOU CAN DO THIS...!
ON THE ROOF ...?
YEAH.
............
STAAARE
じーっ
HOW-DOES-HE-KNOW-I-ALWAYS-EAT-LUNCH-ON-THE-ROOF? EXPRESSION
UWAAAAH. YUP, THIS IS HARD...!

## HARSH REALITY

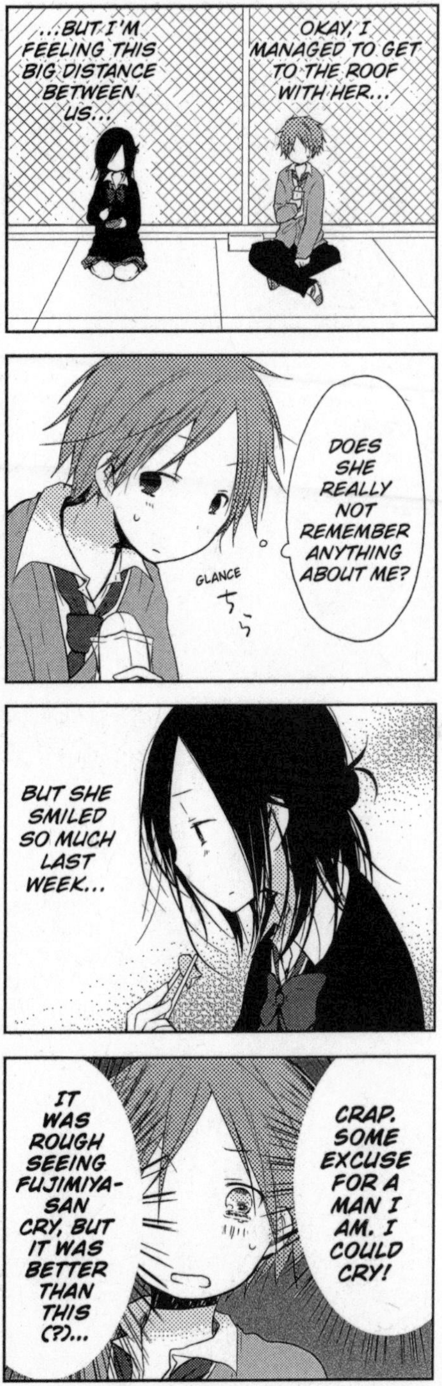
OKAY, I MANAGED TO GET TO THE ROOF WITH HER...
...BUT I'M FEELING THIS BIG DISTANCE BETWEEN US...
DOES SHE REALLY NOT REMEMBER ANYTHING ABOUT ME?
GLANCE
ちら
BUT SHE SMILED SO MUCH LAST WEEK...
CRAP. SOME EXCUSE FOR A MAN I AM. I COULD CRY!
IT WAS ROUGH SEEING FUJIMIYA-SAN CRY, BUT IT WAS BETTER THAN THIS (?)...

## SURPRISINGLY

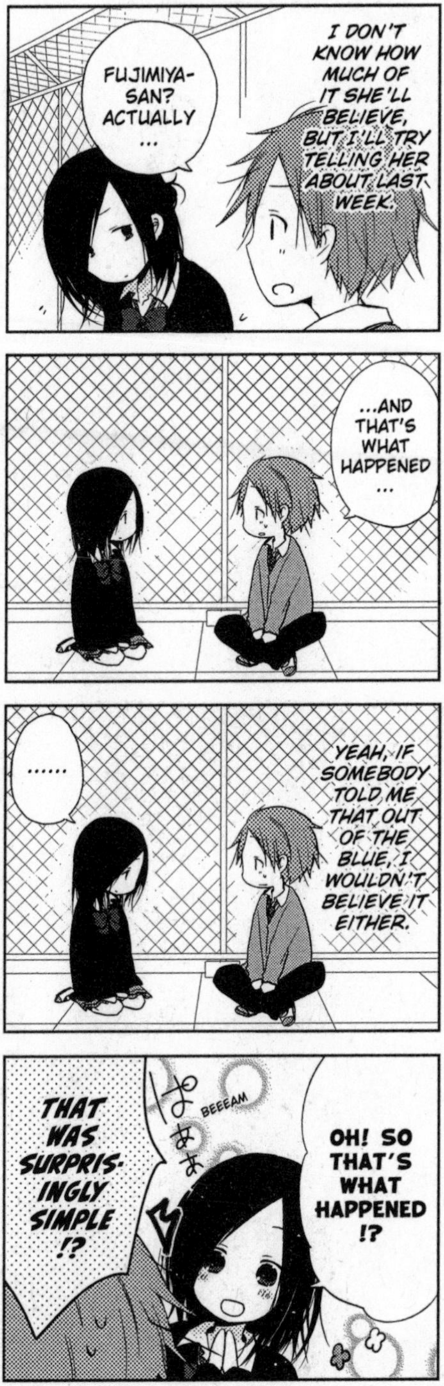
I DON'T KNOW HOW MUCH OF IT SHE'LL BELIEVE, BUT I'LL TRY TELLING HER ABOUT LAST WEEK.
FUJIMIYA-SAN? ACTUALLY...
...AND THAT'S WHAT HAPPENED...
YEAH, IF SOMEBODY TOLD ME THAT OUT OF THE BLUE, I WOULDN'T BELIEVE IT EITHER.
......
OH! SO THAT'S WHAT HAPPENED!?
BEEEAM
THAT WAS SURPRISINGLY SIMPLE!?

## CAN'T HOLD IT IN

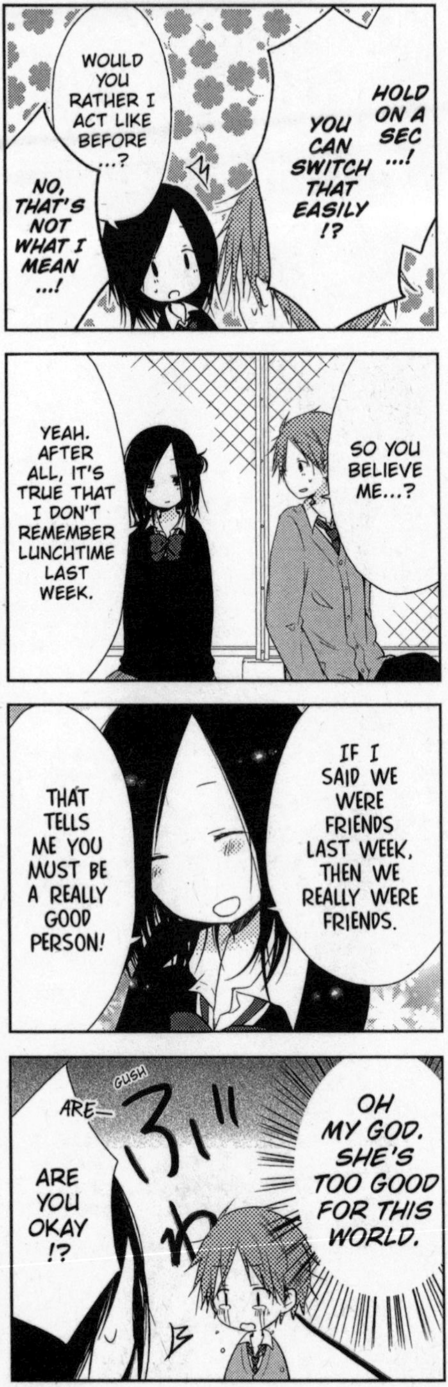
HOLD ON A SEC ...!
YOU CAN SWITCH THAT EASILY !?
WOULD YOU RATHER I ACT LIKE BEFORE ...?
NO, THAT'S NOT WHAT I MEAN ...!
SO YOU BELIEVE ME...?
YEAH. AFTER ALL, IT'S TRUE THAT I DON'T REMEMBER LUNCHTIME LAST WEEK.
IF I SAID WE WERE FRIENDS LAST WEEK, THEN WE REALLY WERE FRIENDS.
THAT TELLS ME YOU MUST BE A REALLY GOOD PERSON!
OH MY GOD. SHE'S TOO GOOD FOR THIS WORLD.
GUSH
ARE—
ARE YOU OKAY !?

## WE'RE FRIENDS, BUT—

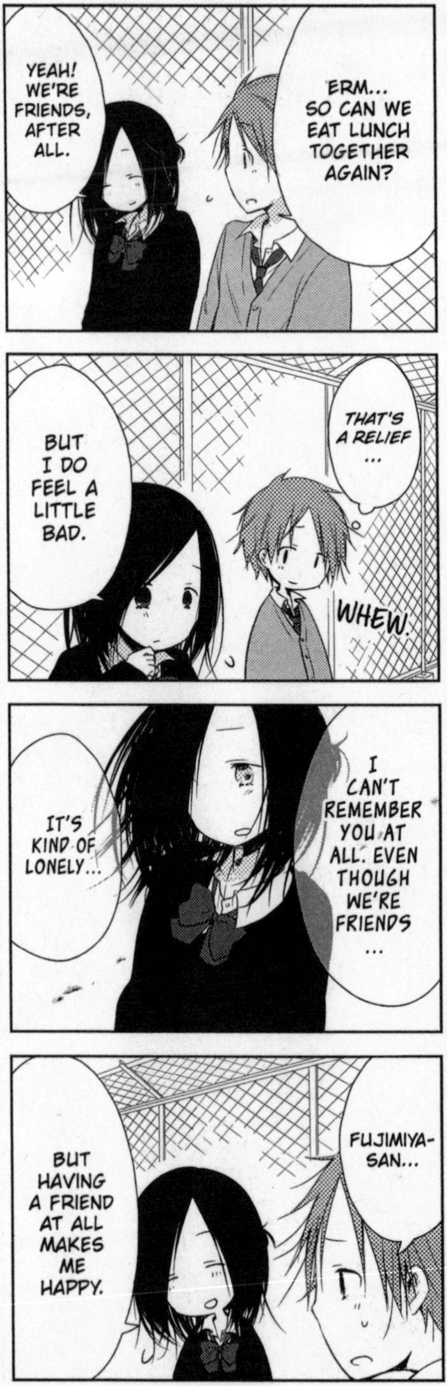
ERM... SO CAN WE EAT LUNCH TOGETHER AGAIN?
YEAH! WE'RE FRIENDS, AFTER ALL.
THAT'S A RELIEF ...
WHEW.
BUT I DO FEEL A LITTLE BAD.
I CAN'T REMEMBER YOU AT ALL. EVEN THOUGH WE'RE FRIENDS ...
IT'S KIND OF LONELY...
FUJIMIYA-SAN...
BUT HAVING A FRIEND AT ALL MAKES ME HAPPY.

## MEMORY SUBSTITUTE

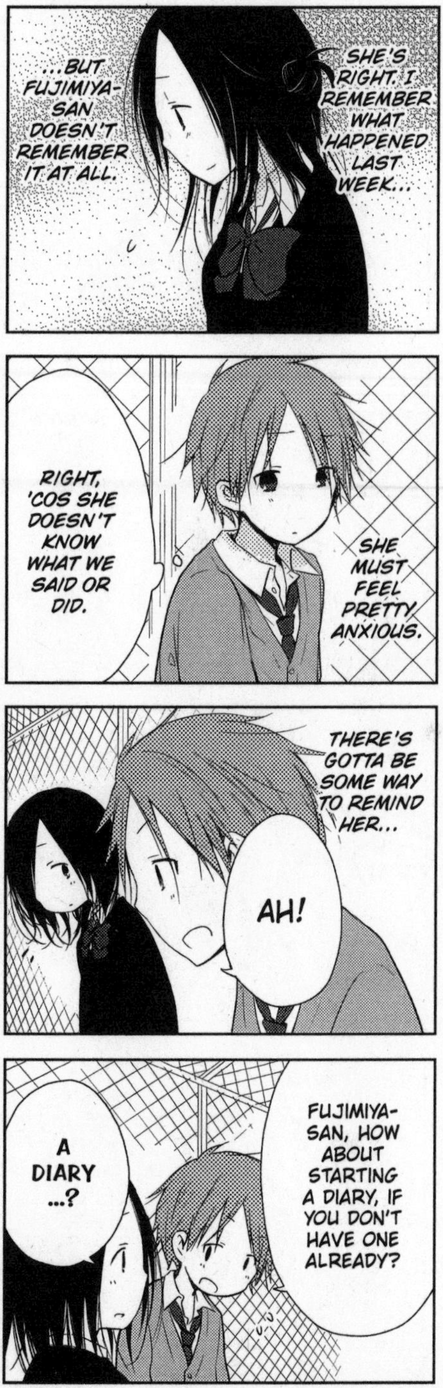
SHE'S RIGHT. I REMEMBER WHAT HAPPENED LAST WEEK...
...BUT FUJIMIYA-SAN DOESN'T REMEMBER IT AT ALL.
SHE MUST FEEL PRETTY ANXIOUS.
RIGHT, 'COS SHE DOESN'T KNOW WHAT WE SAID OR DID.
THERE'S GOTTA BE SOME WAY TO REMIND HER...
AH!
FUJIMIYA-SAN, HOW ABOUT STARTING A DIARY, IF YOU DON'T HAVE ONE ALREADY?
A DIARY ...?

## DIARY

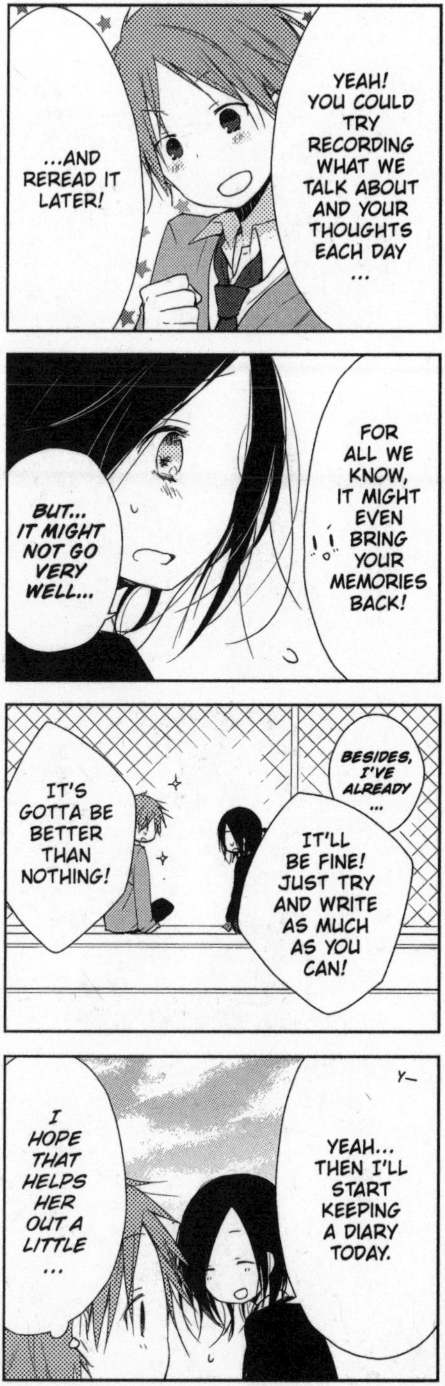
YEAH! YOU COULD TRY RECORDING WHAT WE TALK ABOUT AND YOUR THOUGHTS EACH DAY ...
...AND REREAD IT LATER!
FOR ALL WE KNOW, IT MIGHT EVEN BRING YOUR MEMORIES BACK!
BUT... IT MIGHT NOT GO VERY WELL...
BESIDES, I'VE ALREADY ...
IT'LL BE FINE! JUST TRY AND WRITE AS MUCH AS YOU CAN!
IT'S GOTTA BE BETTER THAN NOTHING!
Y—
YEAH... THEN I'LL START KEEPING A DIARY TODAY.
I HOPE THAT HELPS HER OUT A LITTLE ...

## MATH TALK

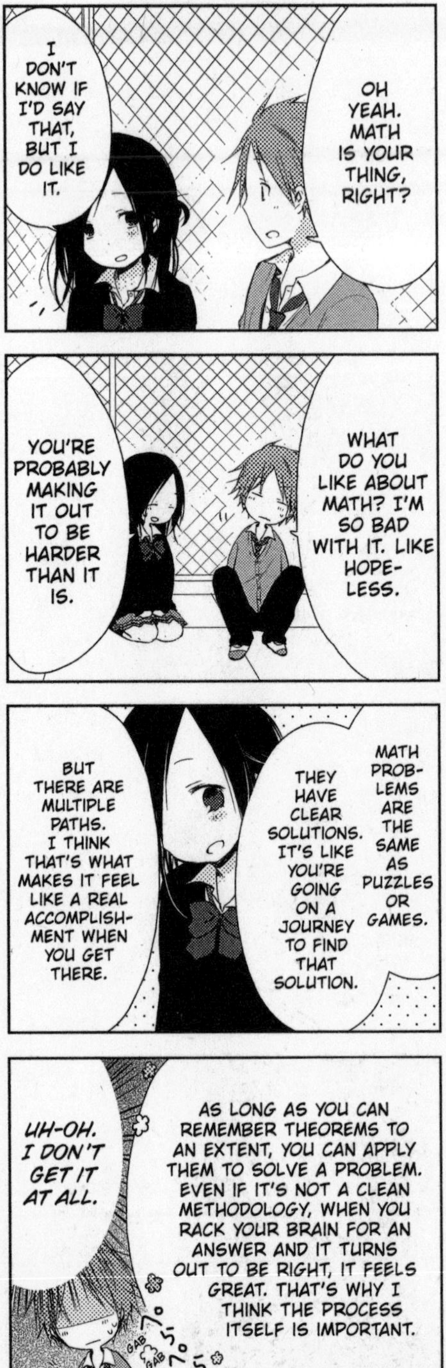
OH YEAH. MATH IS YOUR THING, RIGHT?
I DON'T KNOW IF I'D SAY THAT, BUT I DO LIKE IT.
WHAT DO YOU LIKE ABOUT MATH? I'M SO BAD WITH IT. LIKE HOPE-LESS.
YOU'RE PROBABLY MAKING IT OUT TO BE HARDER THAN IT IS.
MATH PROB-LEMS ARE THE SAME AS PUZZLES OR GAMES.
THEY HAVE CLEAR SOLUTIONS. IT'S LIKE YOU'RE GOING ON A JOURNEY TO FIND THAT SOLUTION.
BUT THERE ARE MULTIPLE PATHS. I THINK THAT'S WHAT MAKES IT FEEL LIKE A REAL ACCOMPLISH-MENT WHEN YOU GET THERE.
AS LONG AS YOU CAN REMEMBER THEOREMS TO AN EXTENT, YOU CAN APPLY THEM TO SOLVE A PROBLEM. EVEN IF IT'S NOT A CLEAN METHODOLOGY, WHEN YOU RACK YOUR BRAIN FOR AN ANSWER AND IT TURNS OUT TO BE RIGHT, IT FEELS GREAT. THAT'S WHY I THINK THE PROCESS ITSELF IS IMPORTANT.
UH-OH. I DON'T GET IT AT ALL.
GAB GAB

## EMBARRASSING

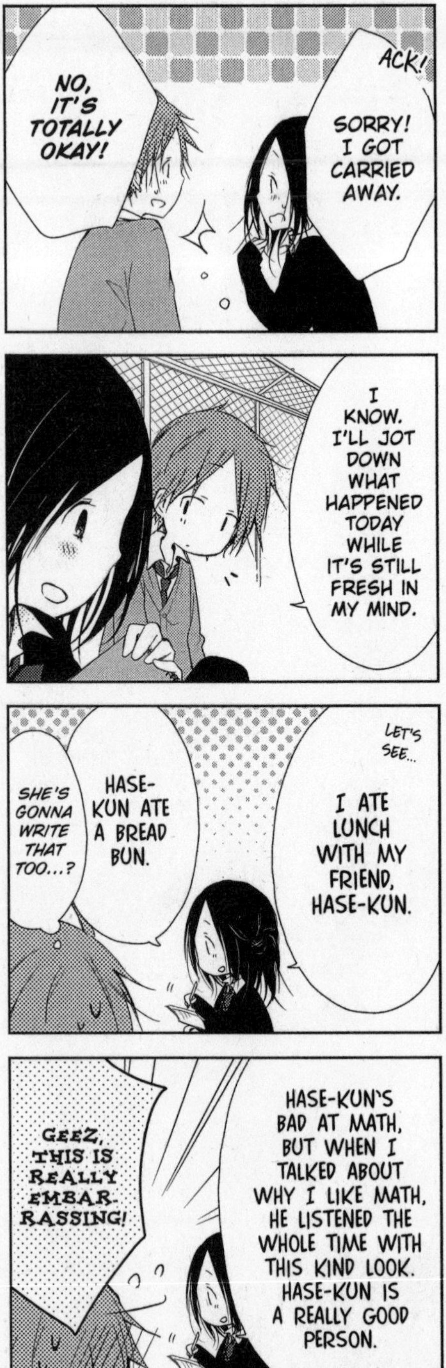
ACK!
SORRY! I GOT CARRIED AWAY.
NO, IT'S TOTALLY OKAY!
I KNOW. I'LL JOT DOWN WHAT HAPPENED TODAY WHILE IT'S STILL FRESH IN MY MIND.
LET'S SEE...
I ATE LUNCH WITH MY FRIEND, HASE-KUN.
HASE-KUN ATE A BREAD BUN.
SHE'S GONNA WRITE THAT TOO...?
HASE-KUN'S BAD AT MATH, BUT WHEN I TALKED ABOUT WHY I LIKE MATH, HE LISTENED THE WHOLE TIME WITH THIS KIND LOOK. HASE-KUN IS A REALLY GOOD PERSON.
GEEZ, THIS IS REALLY EMBAR-RASSING!

FRIDAY

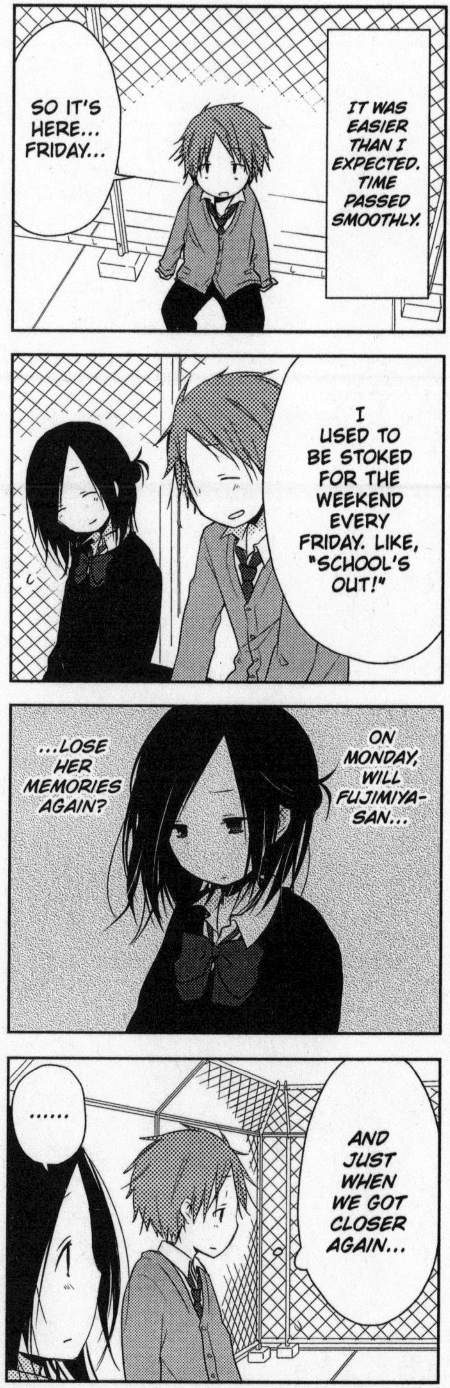
IT WAS EASIER THAN I EXPECTED. TIME PASSED SMOOTHLY.
SO IT'S HERE... FRIDAY...
I USED TO BE STOKED FOR THE WEEKEND EVERY FRIDAY. LIKE, "SCHOOL'S OUT!"
ON MONDAY, WILL FUJIMIYA-SAN...
...LOSE HER MEMORIES AGAIN?
AND JUST WHEN WE GOT CLOSER AGAIN...
......

IT'S OKAY

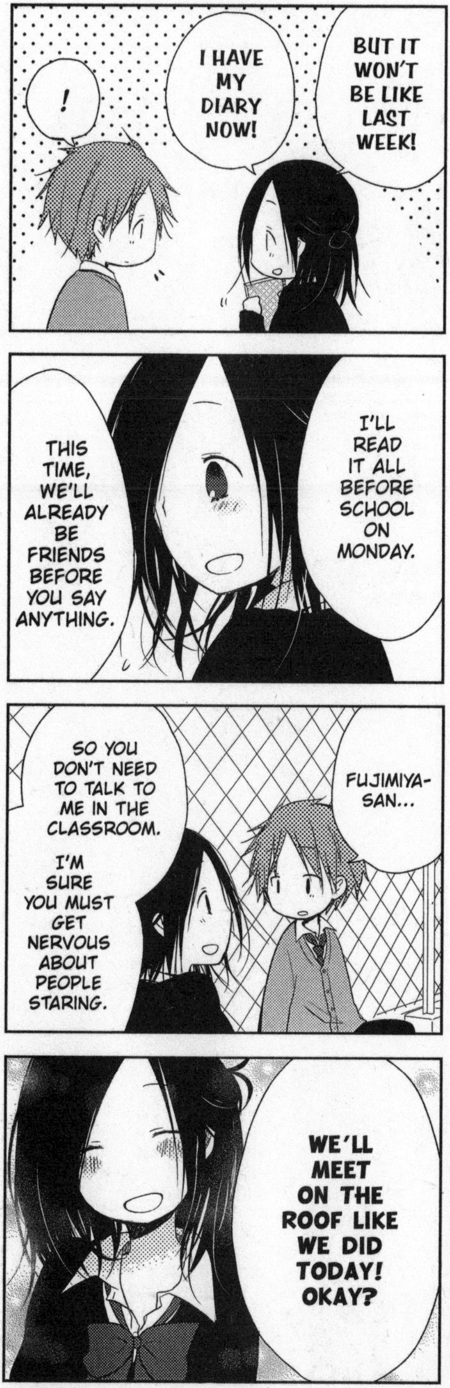
BUT IT WON'T BE LIKE LAST WEEK!
I HAVE MY DIARY NOW!
!
I'LL READ IT ALL BEFORE SCHOOL ON MONDAY.
THIS TIME, WE'LL ALREADY BE FRIENDS BEFORE YOU SAY ANYTHING.
FUJIMIYA-SAN...
SO YOU DON'T NEED TO TALK TO ME IN THE CLASSROOM.
I'M SURE YOU MUST GET NERVOUS ABOUT PEOPLE STARING.
WE'LL MEET ON THE ROOF LIKE WE DID TODAY! OKAY?

## SCARY

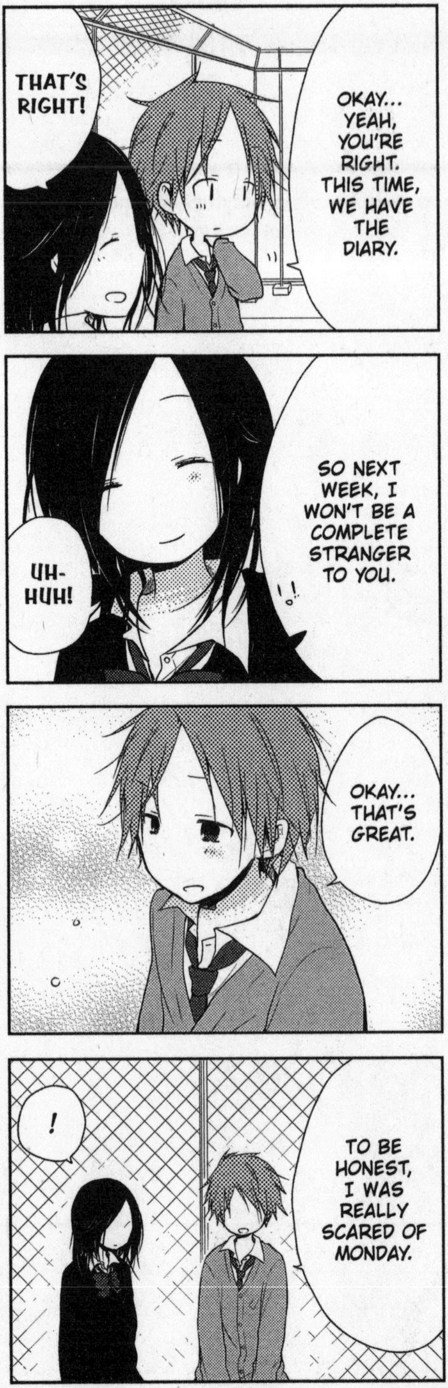
OKAY... YEAH, YOU'RE RIGHT. THIS TIME, WE HAVE THE DIARY.
THAT'S RIGHT!
SO NEXT WEEK, I WON'T BE A COMPLETE STRANGER TO YOU.
UH-HUH!
OKAY... THAT'S GREAT.
TO BE HONEST, I WAS REALLY SCARED OF MONDAY.
!

## WITH A DIARY...

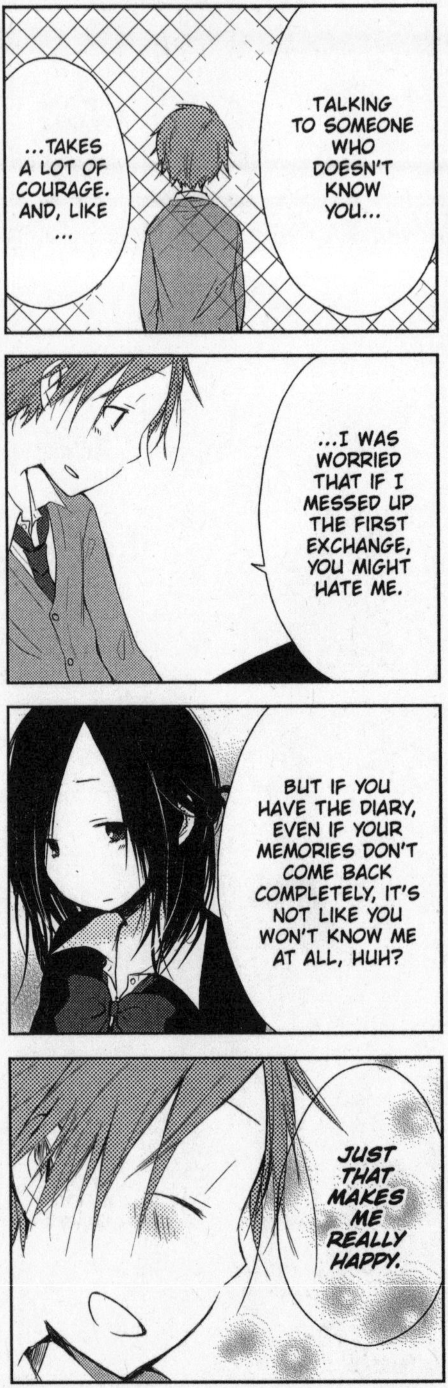
TALKING TO SOMEONE WHO DOESN'T KNOW YOU...
...TAKES A LOT OF COURAGE. AND, LIKE ...
...I WAS WORRIED THAT IF I MESSED UP THE FIRST EXCHANGE, YOU MIGHT HATE ME.
BUT IF YOU HAVE THE DIARY, EVEN IF YOUR MEMORIES DON'T COME BACK COMPLETELY, IT'S NOT LIKE YOU WON'T KNOW ME AT ALL, HUH?
JUST THAT MAKES ME REALLY HAPPY.

## POSITIVE

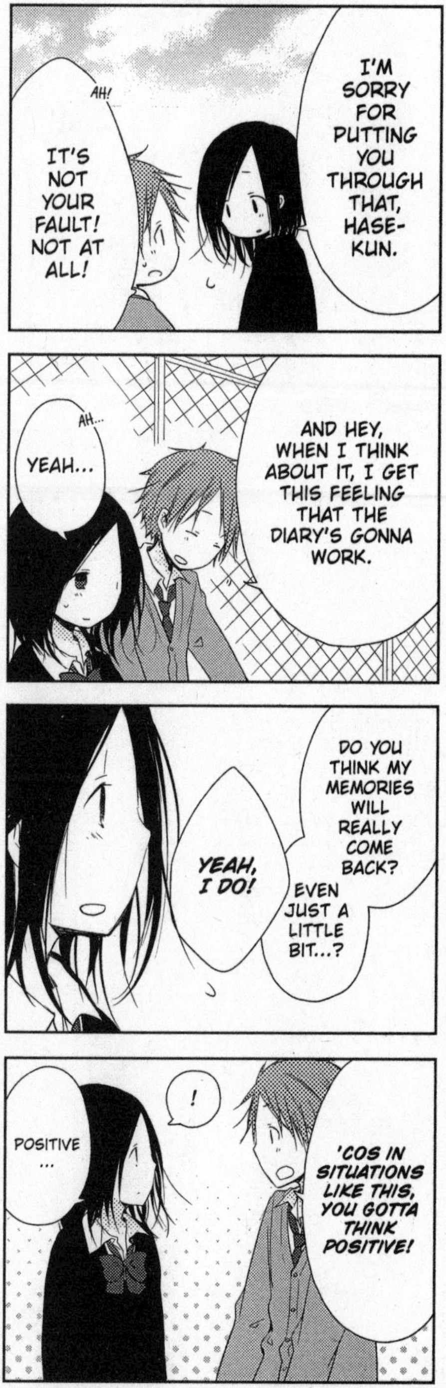
I'M SORRY FOR PUTTING YOU THROUGH THAT, HASE-KUN.
AH!
IT'S NOT YOUR FAULT! NOT AT ALL!
AND HEY, WHEN I THINK ABOUT IT, I GET THIS FEELING THAT THE DIARY'S GONNA WORK.
AH...
YEAH...
DO YOU THINK MY MEMORIES WILL REALLY COME BACK?
EVEN JUST A LITTLE BIT...?
YEAH, I DO!
'COS IN SITUATIONS LIKE THIS, YOU GOTTA THINK POSITIVE!
!
POSITIVE ...

## FOR SURE

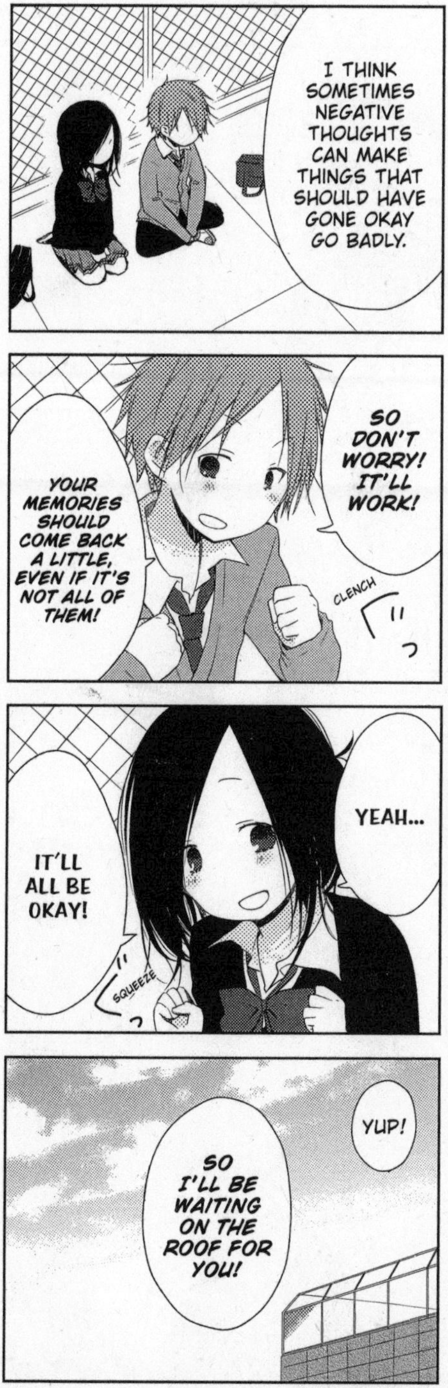
I THINK SOMETIMES NEGATIVE THOUGHTS CAN MAKE THINGS THAT SHOULD HAVE GONE OKAY GO BADLY.
SO DON'T WORRY! IT'LL WORK!
CLENCH
YOUR MEMORIES SHOULD COME BACK A LITTLE, EVEN IF IT'S NOT ALL OF THEM!
YEAH...
IT'LL ALL BE OKAY!
SQUEEZE
YUP!
SO I'LL BE WAITING ON THE ROOF FOR YOU!

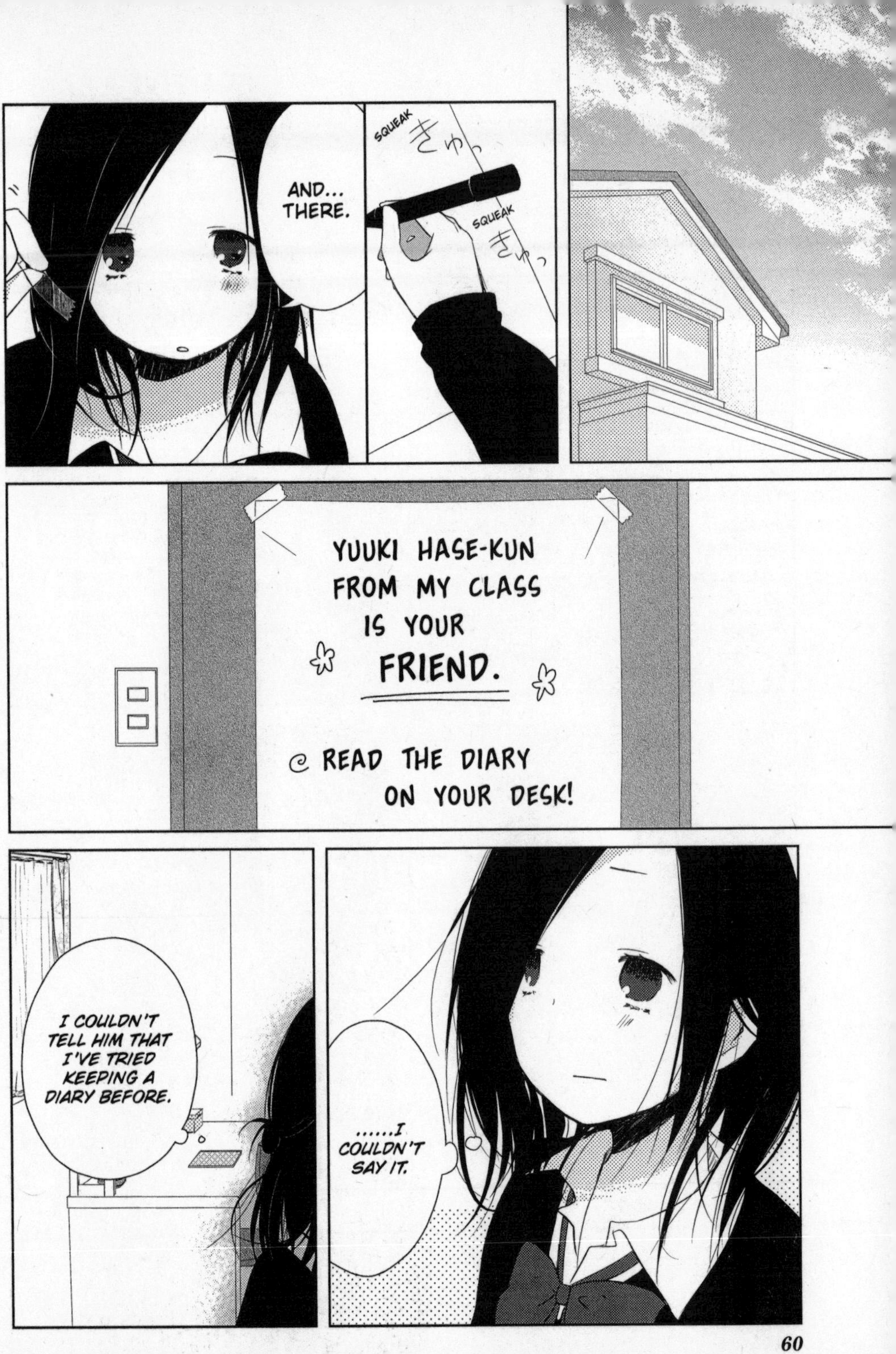
SQUEAK
きゅっ
SQUEAK
きゅっ
AND... THERE.
YUUKI HASE-KUN FROM MY CLASS IS YOUR FRIEND.
READ THE DIARY ON YOUR DESK!
......I COULDN'T SAY IT.
I COULDN'T TELL HIM THAT I'VE TRIED KEEPING A DIARY BEFORE.

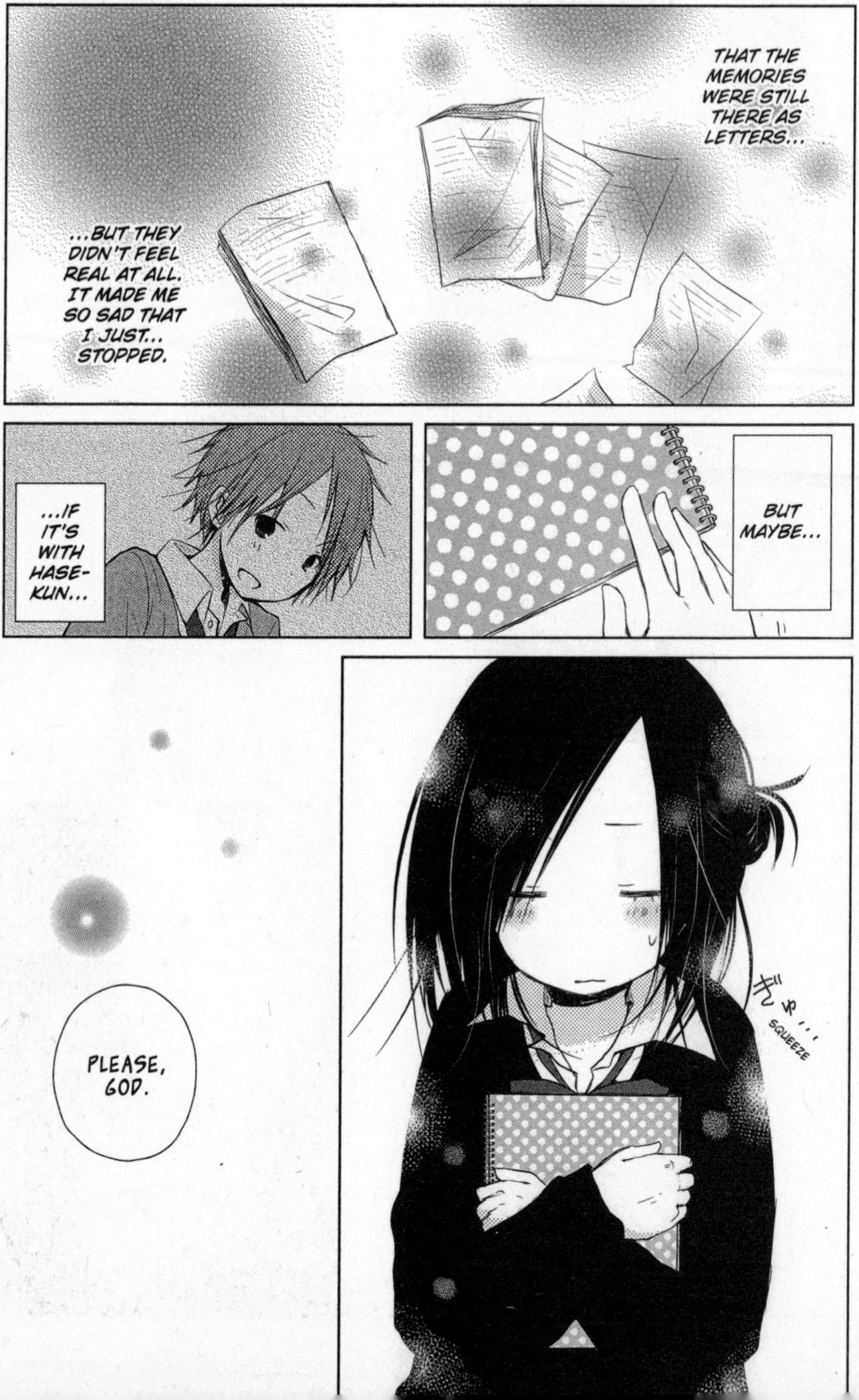
THAT THE MEMORIES WERE STILL THERE AS LETTERS...
...BUT THEY DIDN'T FEEL REAL AT ALL. IT MADE ME SO SAD THAT I JUST... STOPPED.
BUT MAYBE...
...IF IT'S WITH HASE-KUN...
ぎゅ...
SQUEEZE
PLEASE, GOD.

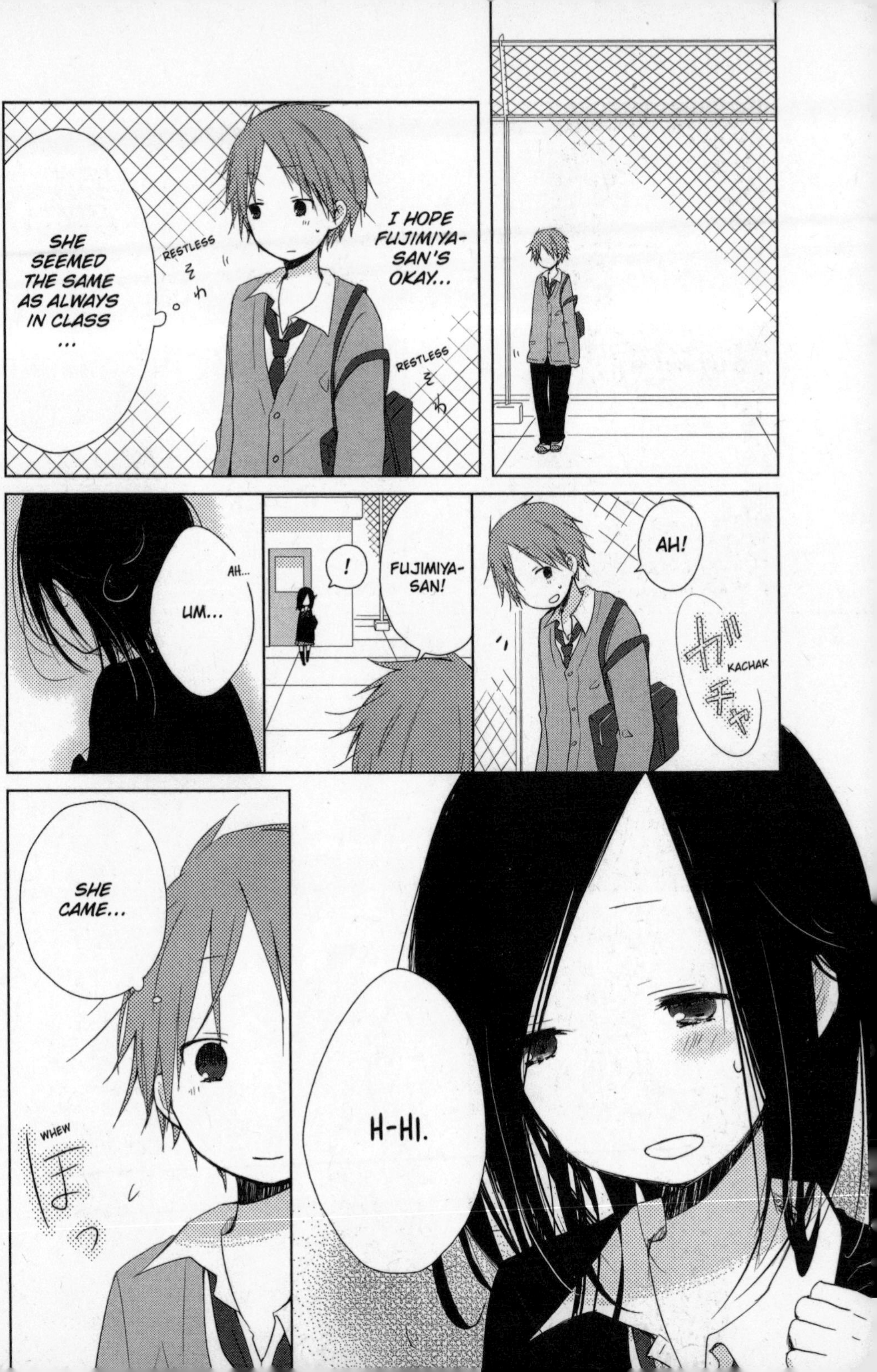
I HOPE FUJIMIYA-SAN'S OKAY...
RESTLESS
RESTLESS
SHE SEEMED THE SAME AS ALWAYS IN CLASS ...
AH!
KACHAK
FUJIMIYA-SAN!
!
AH...
UM...
H-HI.
SHE CAME...
WHEW

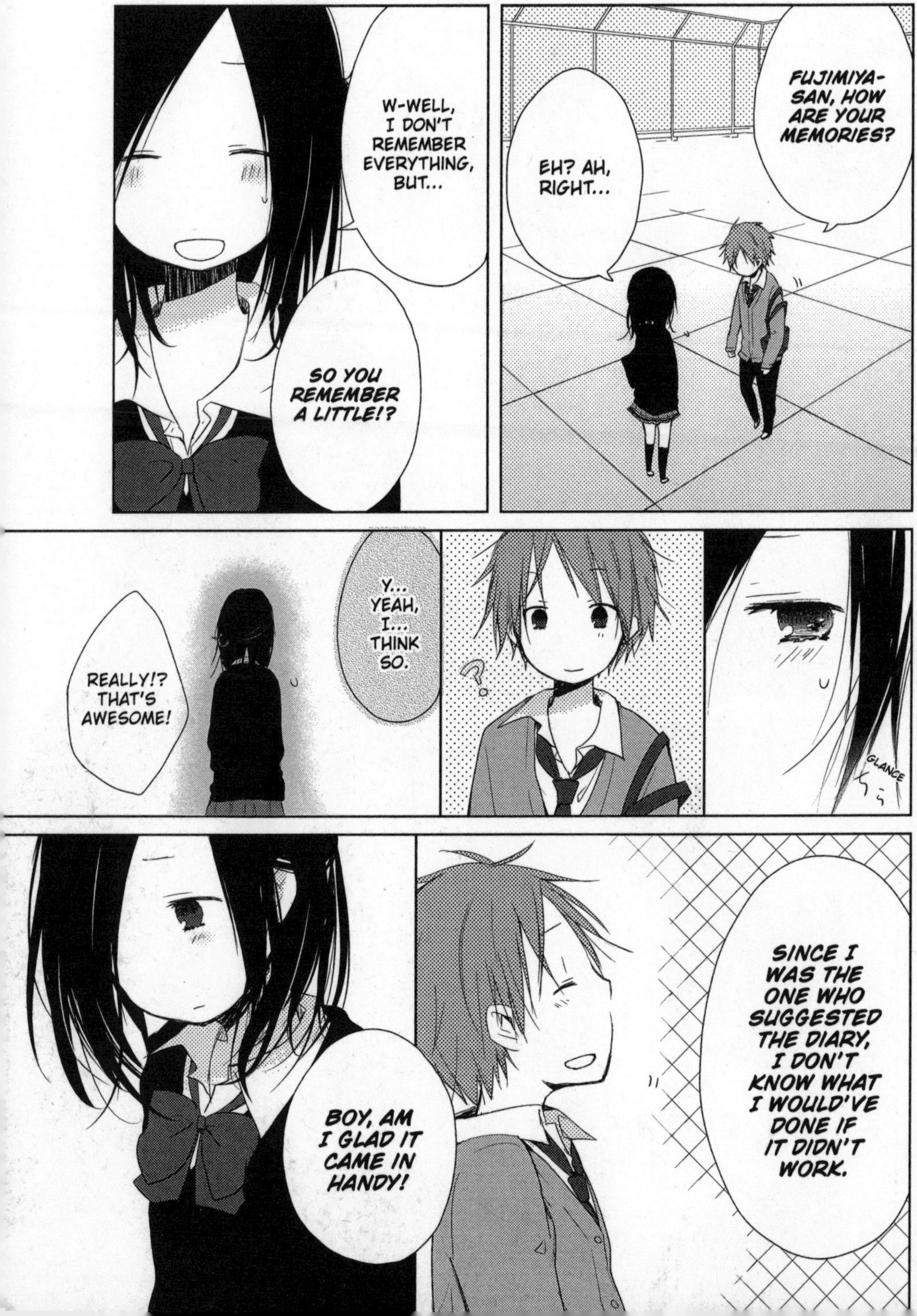
FUJIMIYA-SAN, HOW ARE YOUR MEMORIES?
EH? AH, RIGHT...
W-WELL, I DON'T REMEMBER EVERYTHING, BUT...
SO YOU REMEMBER A LITTLE!?
GLANCE
Y... YEAH, I... THINK SO.
REALLY!? THAT'S AWESOME!
SINCE I WAS THE ONE WHO SUGGESTED THE DIARY, I DON'T KNOW WHAT I WOULD'VE DONE IF IT DIDN'T WORK.
BOY, AM I GLAD IT CAME IN HANDY!

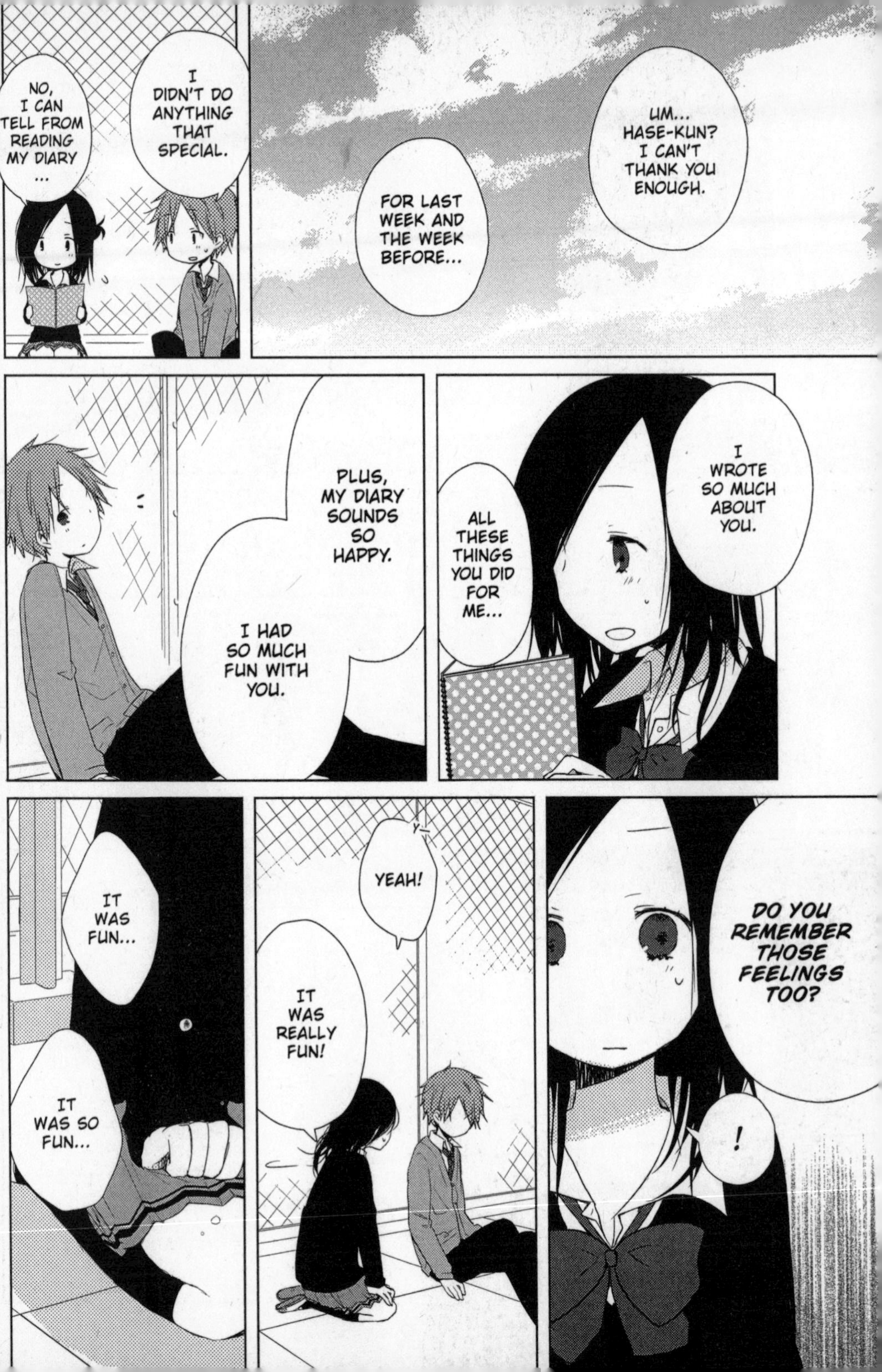
UM... HASE-KUN? I CAN'T THANK YOU ENOUGH.
FOR LAST WEEK AND THE WEEK BEFORE...
I DIDN'T DO ANYTHING THAT SPECIAL.
NO, I CAN TELL FROM READING MY DIARY ...
I WROTE SO MUCH ABOUT YOU.
ALL THESE THINGS YOU DID FOR ME...
PLUS, MY DIARY SOUNDS SO HAPPY.
I HAD SO MUCH FUN WITH YOU.
DO YOU REMEMBER THOSE FEELINGS TOO?
!
Y—
YEAH!
IT WAS REALLY FUN!
IT WAS FUN...
IT WAS SO FUN...

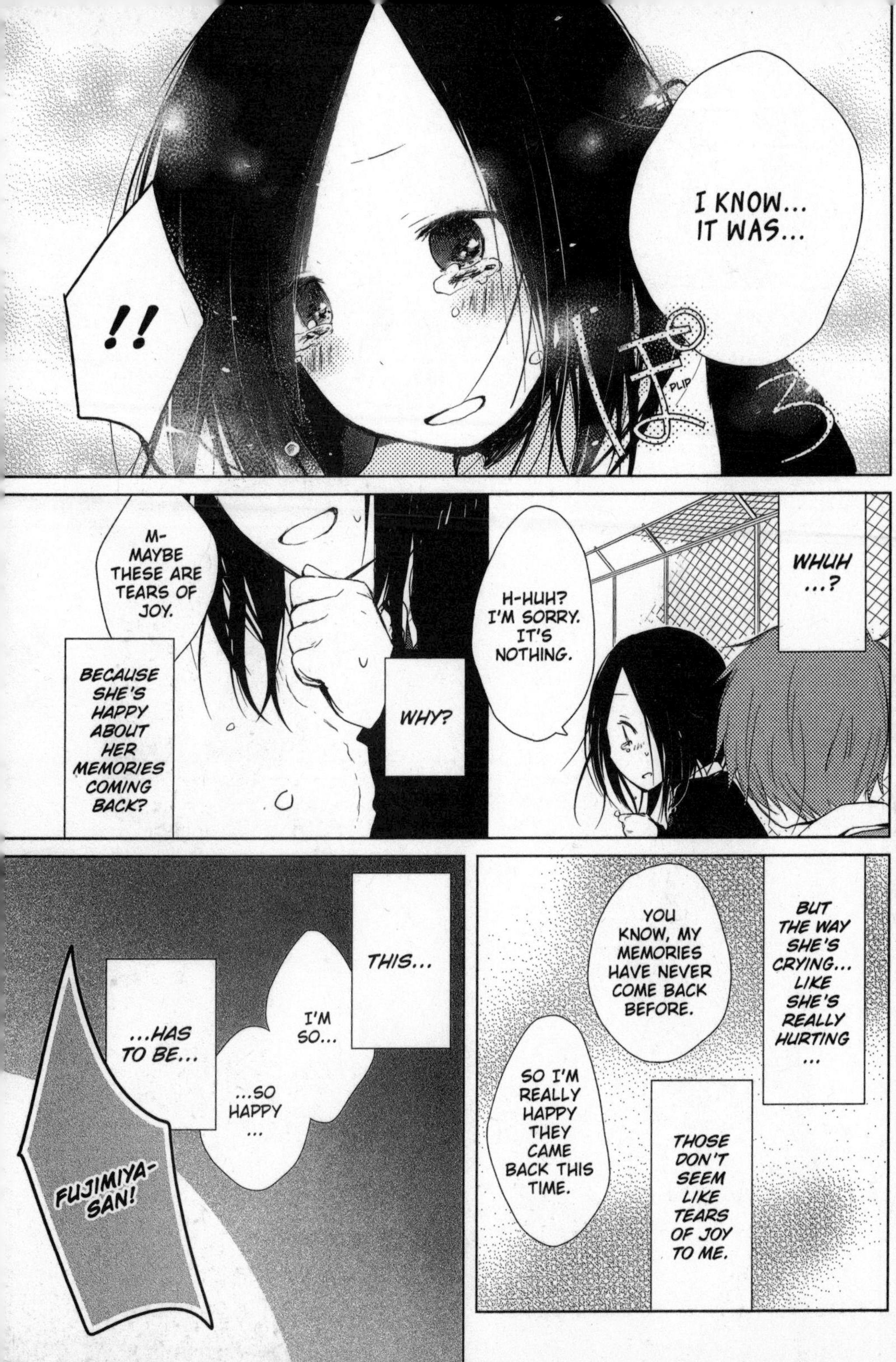
I KNOW... IT WAS...
PLIP
!!
WHUH ...?
H-HUH? I'M SORRY. IT'S NOTHING.
M-MAYBE THESE ARE TEARS OF JOY.
WHY?
BECAUSE SHE'S HAPPY ABOUT HER MEMORIES COMING BACK?
BUT THE WAY SHE'S CRYING... LIKE SHE'S REALLY HURTING...
YOU KNOW, MY MEMORIES HAVE NEVER COME BACK BEFORE.
SO I'M REALLY HAPPY THEY CAME BACK THIS TIME.
THOSE DON'T SEEM LIKE TEARS OF JOY TO ME.
THIS...
I'M SO...
...HAS TO BE...
...SO HAPPY...
FUJIMIYA-SAN!

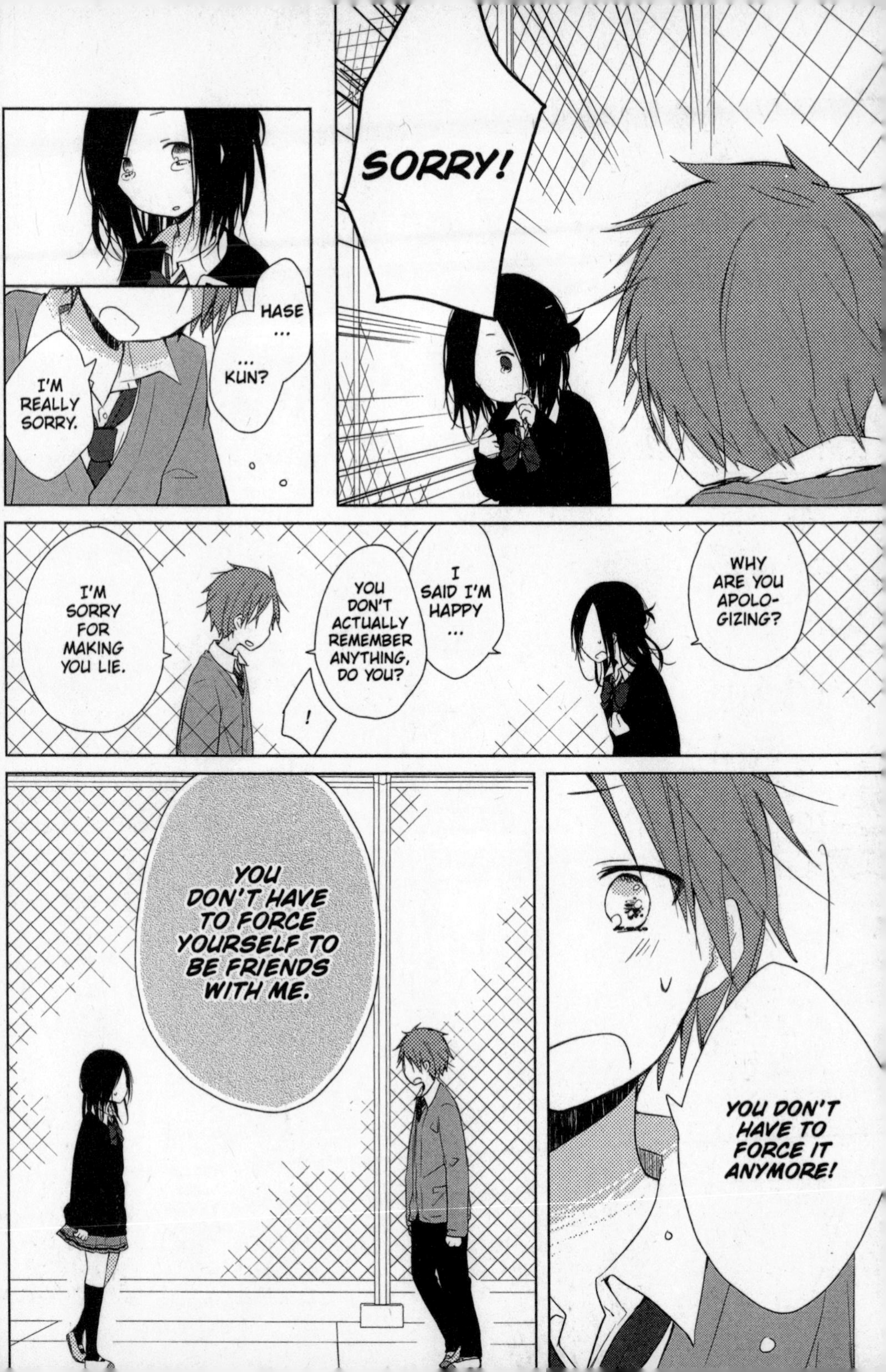
SORRY!
HASE... ...KUN?
I'M REALLY SORRY.
WHY ARE YOU APOLOGIZING?
I SAID I'M HAPPY...
YOU DON'T ACTUALLY REMEMBER ANYTHING, DO YOU?
!
I'M SORRY FOR MAKING YOU LIE.
YOU DON'T HAVE TO FORCE IT ANYMORE!
YOU DON'T HAVE TO FORCE YOURSELF TO BE FRIENDS WITH ME.

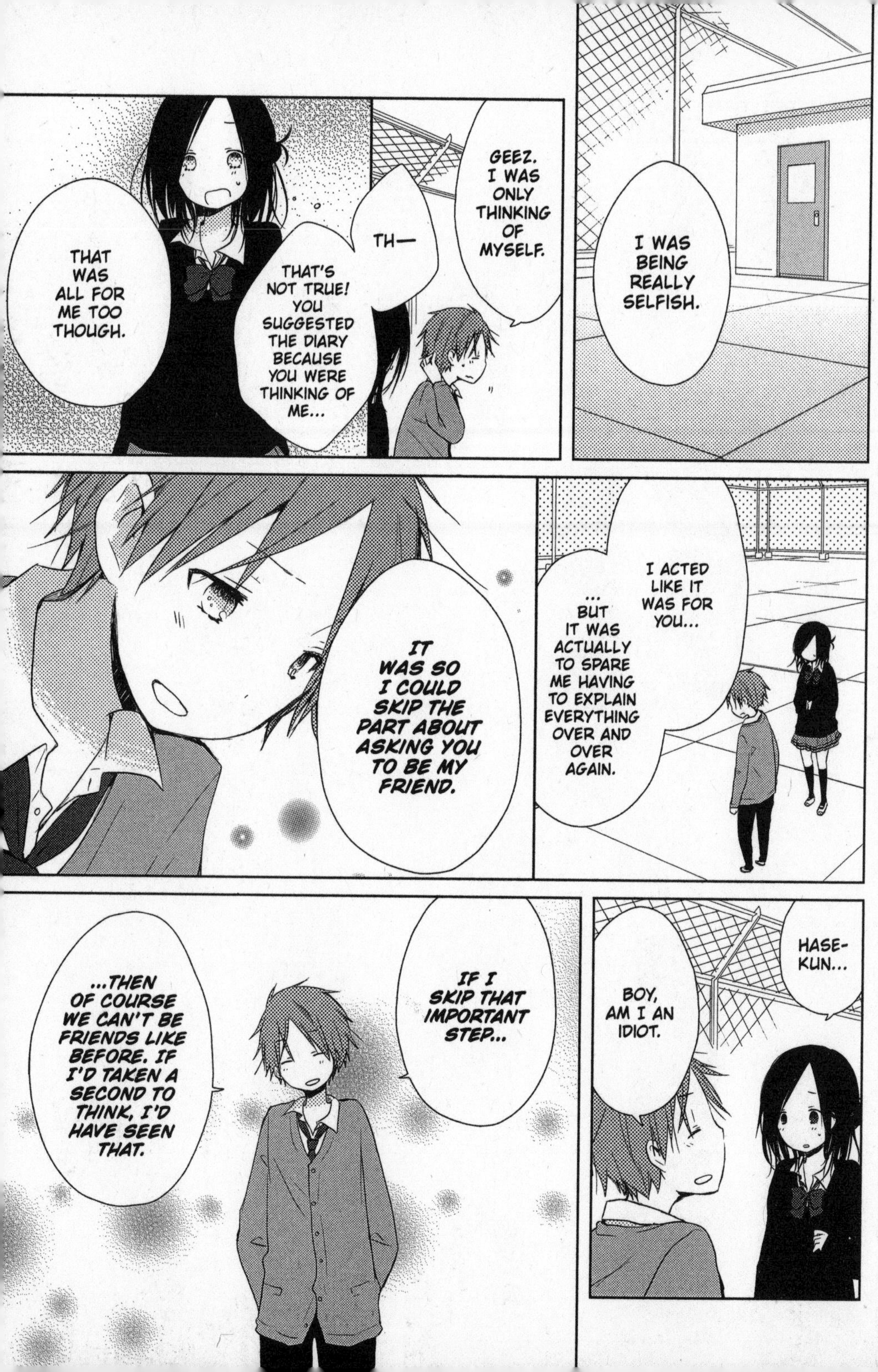
I WAS BEING REALLY SELFISH.
GEEZ. I WAS ONLY THINKING OF MYSELF.
TH—
THAT'S NOT TRUE! YOU SUGGESTED THE DIARY BECAUSE YOU WERE THINKING OF ME...
THAT WAS ALL FOR ME TOO THOUGH.
I ACTED LIKE IT WAS FOR YOU...
...BUT IT WAS ACTUALLY TO SPARE ME HAVING TO EXPLAIN EVERYTHING OVER AND OVER AGAIN.
IT WAS SO I COULD SKIP THE PART ABOUT ASKING YOU TO BE MY FRIEND.
HASE-KUN...
BOY, AM I AN IDIOT.
IF I SKIP THAT IMPORTANT STEP...
...THEN OF COURSE WE CAN'T BE FRIENDS LIKE BEFORE. IF I'D TAKEN A SECOND TO THINK, I'D HAVE SEEN THAT.

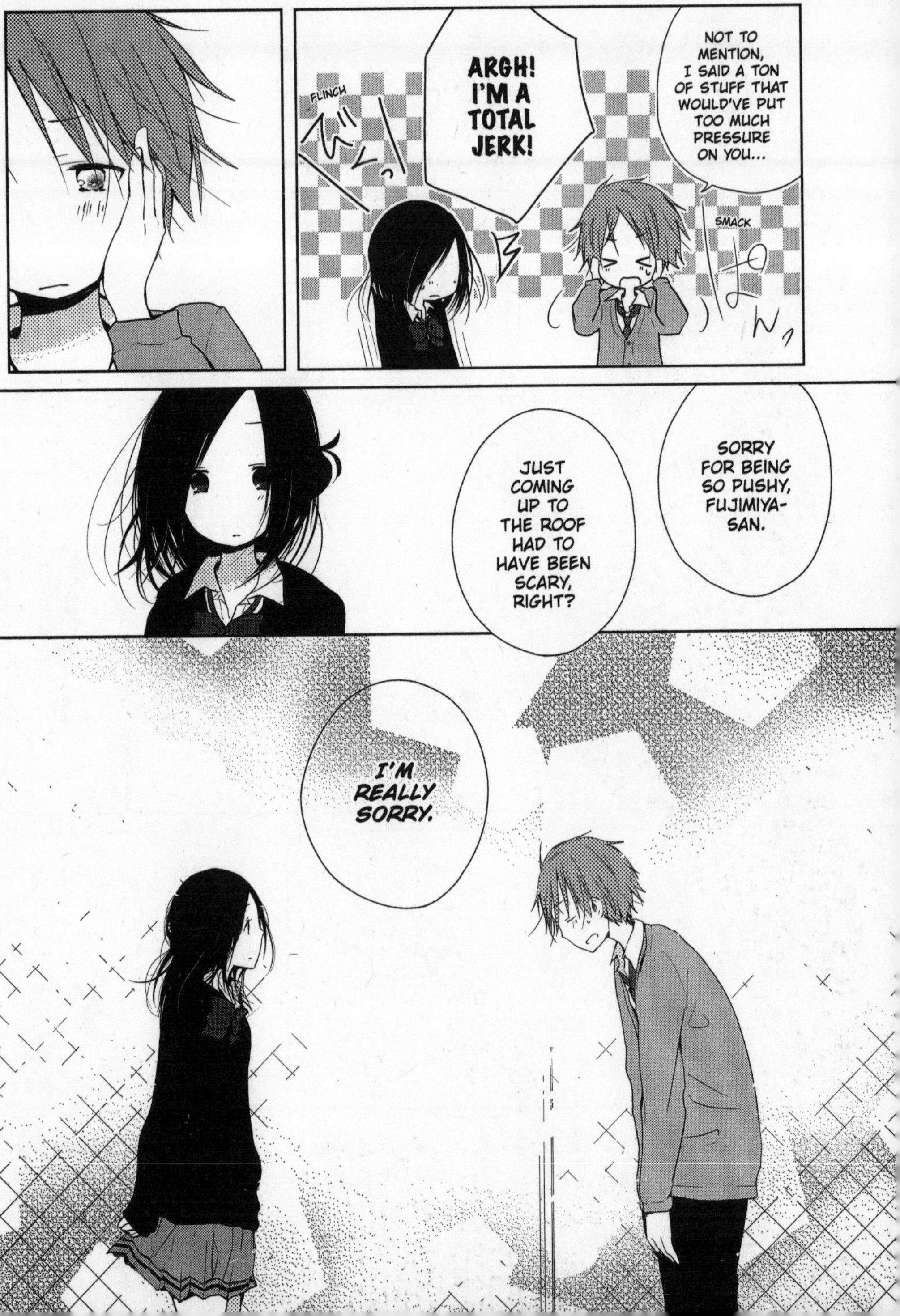
NOT TO MENTION, I SAID A TON OF STUFF THAT WOULD'VE PUT TOO MUCH PRESSURE ON YOU...
ARGH! I'M A TOTAL JERK!
SMACK
FLINCH
SORRY FOR BEING SO PUSHY, FUJIMIYA-SAN.
JUST COMING UP TO THE ROOF HAD TO HAVE BEEN SCARY, RIGHT?
I'M REALLY SORRY.

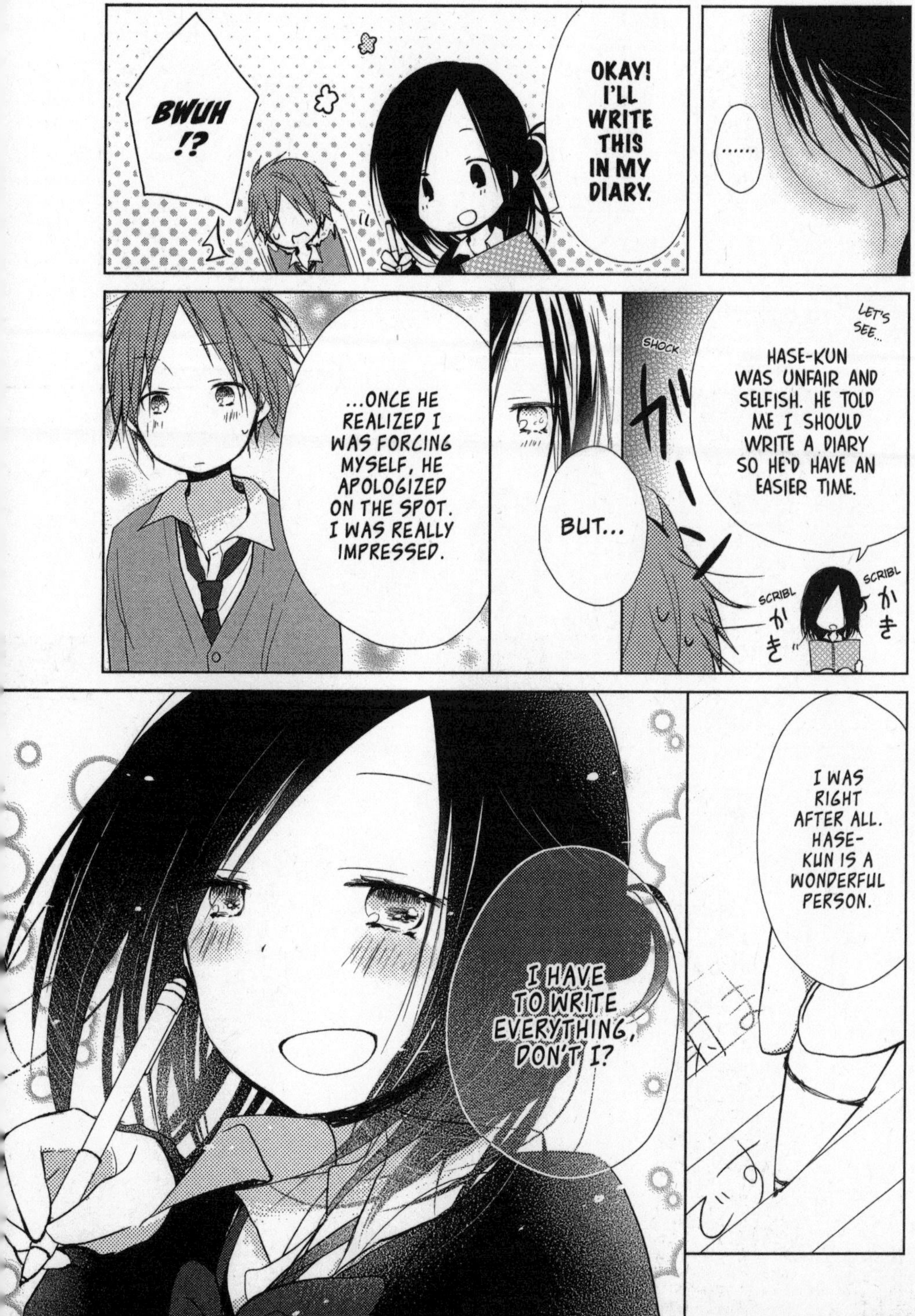
......
OKAY! I'LL WRITE THIS IN MY DIARY.
BWUH !?
LET'S SEE...
HASE-KUN WAS UNFAIR AND SELFISH. HE TOLD ME I SHOULD WRITE A DIARY SO HE'D HAVE AN EASIER TIME.
SCRIBL かき
SCRIBL かき
SHOCK ガーン
BUT...
...ONCE HE REALIZED I WAS FORCING MYSELF, HE APOLOGIZED ON THE SPOT. I WAS REALLY IMPRESSED.
I WAS RIGHT AFTER ALL. HASE-KUN IS A WONDERFUL PERSON.
I HAVE TO WRITE EVERYTHING, DON'T I?

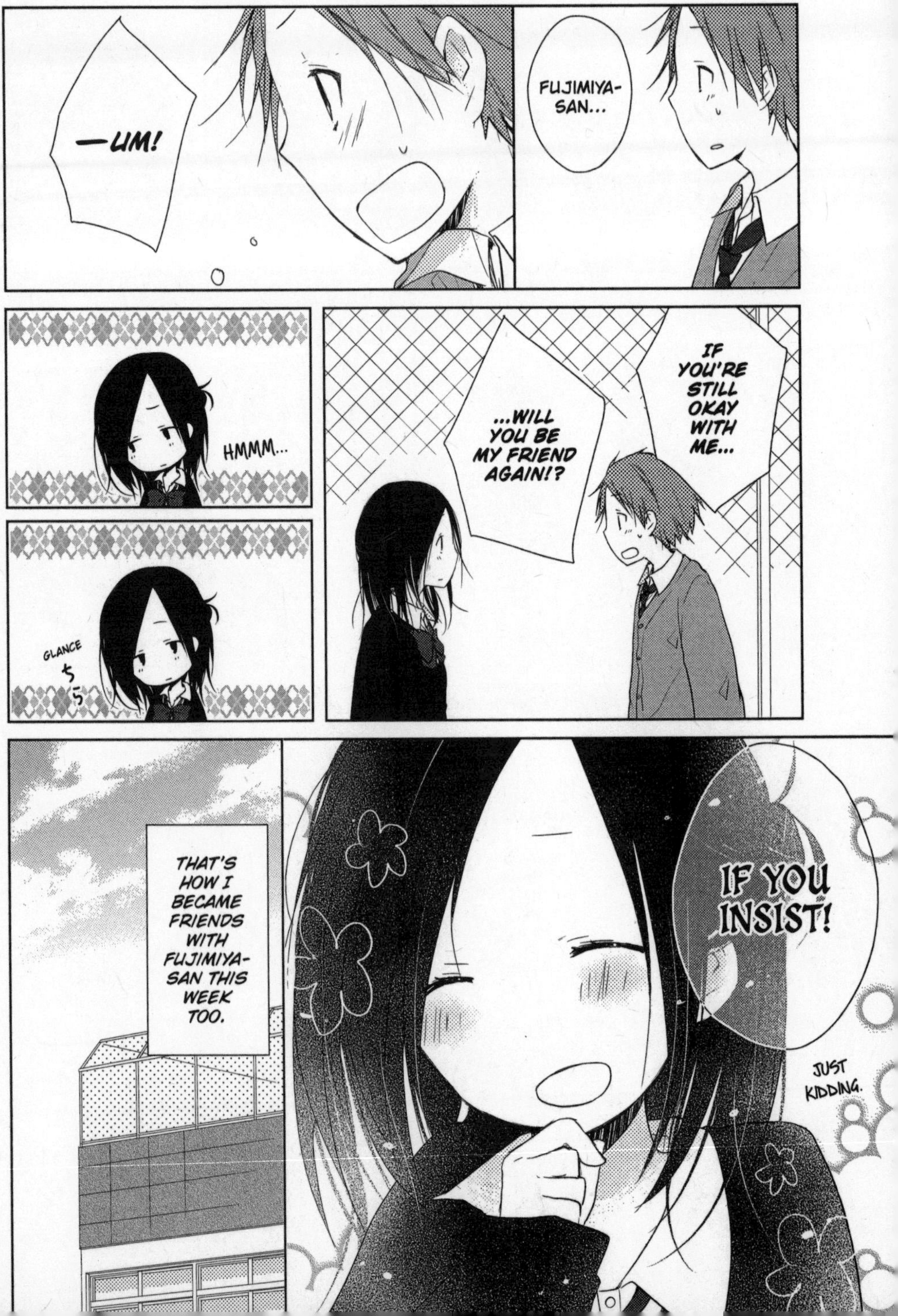
FUJIMIYA-SAN...
—UM!
IF YOU'RE STILL OKAY WITH ME...
...WILL YOU BE MY FRIEND AGAIN!?
HMMM...
GLANCE
ちら
IF YOU INSIST!
JUST KIDDING.
THAT'S HOW I BECAME FRIENDS WITH FUJIMIYA-SAN THIS WEEK TOO.

# ONE WEEK FRIENDS

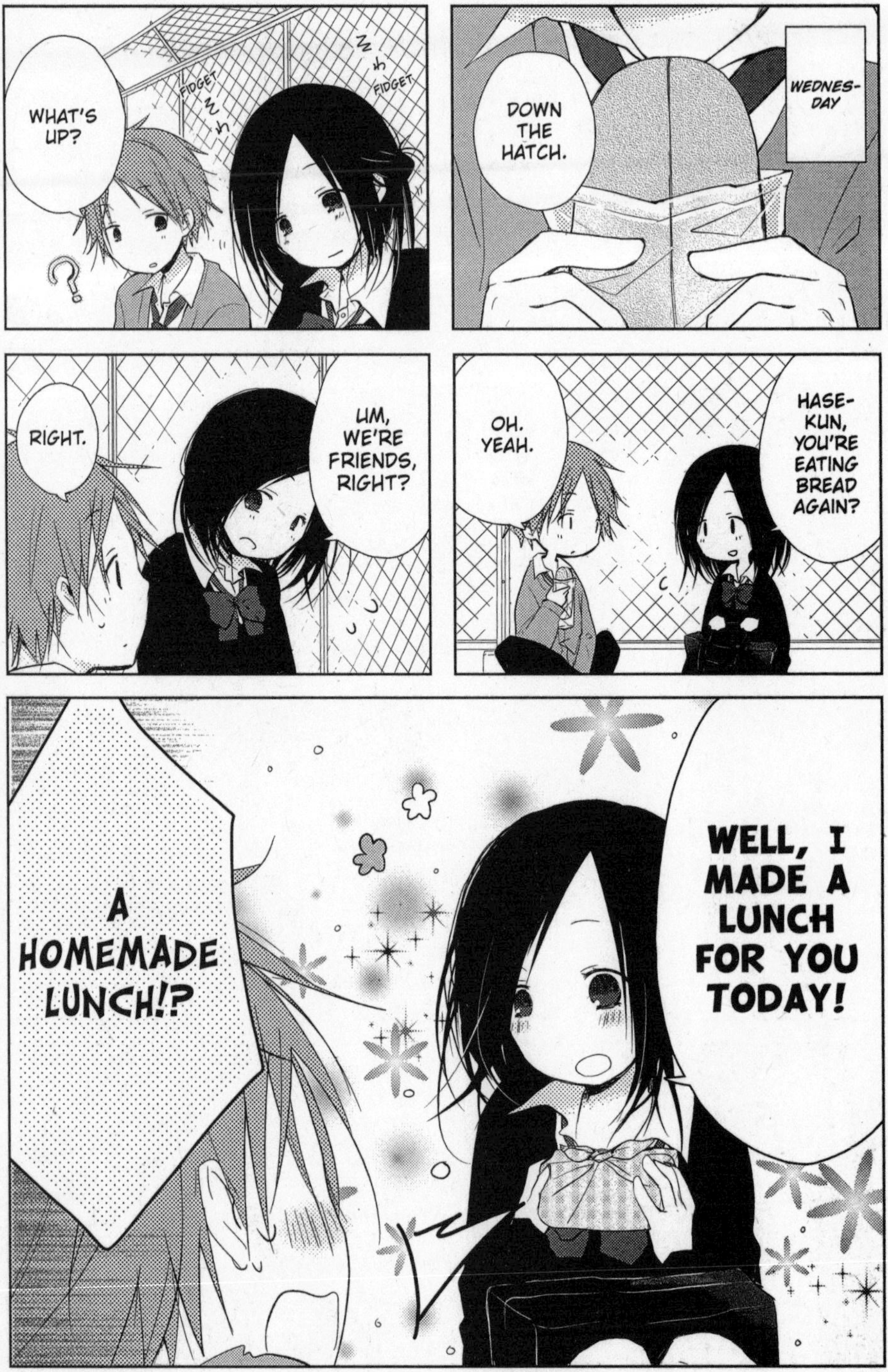
WEDNES-DAY
DOWN THE HATCH.
FIDGET
FIDGET
WHAT'S UP?
HASE-KUN, YOU'RE EATING BREAD AGAIN?
OH. YEAH.
UM, WE'RE FRIENDS, RIGHT?
RIGHT.
WELL, I MADE A LUNCH FOR YOU TODAY!
A HOMEMADE LUNCH!?

## MANGA-LIKE TURN OF EVENTS

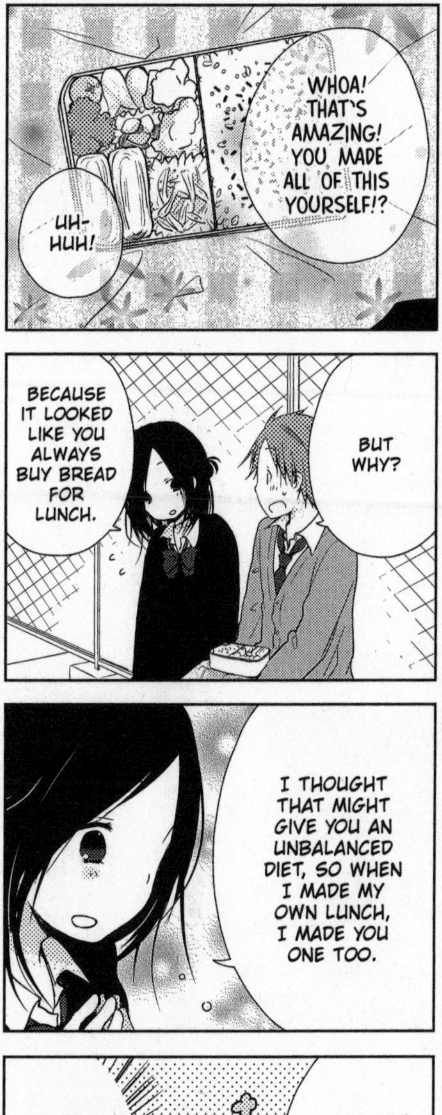
WHOA! THAT'S AMAZING! YOU MADE ALL OF THIS YOURSELF!?
UH-HUH!
BUT WHY?
BECAUSE IT LOOKED LIKE YOU ALWAYS BUY BREAD FOR LUNCH.
I THOUGHT THAT MIGHT GIVE YOU AN UNBALANCED DIET, SO WHEN I MADE MY OWN LUNCH, I MADE YOU ONE TOO.
FRIENDS DO THIS ALL THE TIME, RIGHT? I'VE SEEN IT IN MANGA!
YOUR KNOWLEDGE IS UNBALANCED. BUT GOOD JOB, MANGA!

## FRIED EGG

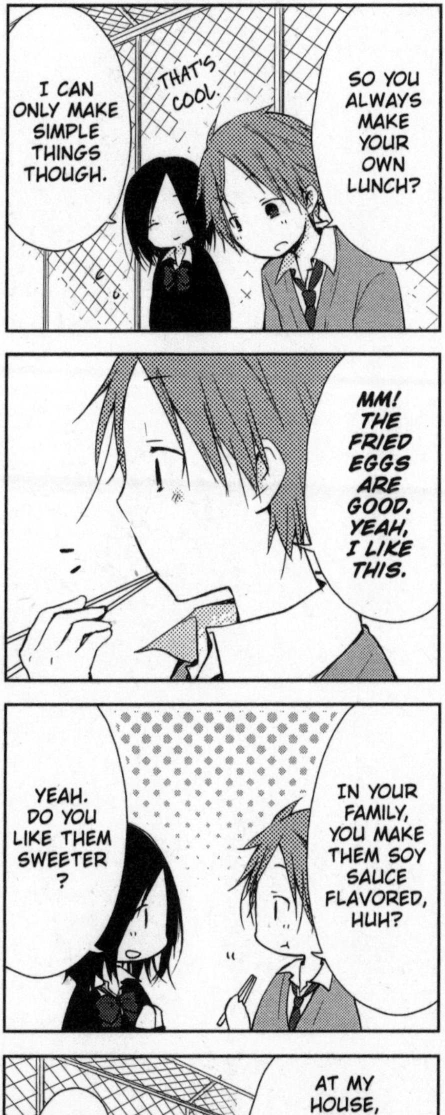
SO YOU ALWAYS MAKE YOUR OWN LUNCH?
THAT'S COOL.
I CAN ONLY MAKE SIMPLE THINGS THOUGH.
MM! THE FRIED EGGS ARE GOOD. YEAH, I LIKE THIS.
IN YOUR FAMILY, YOU MAKE THEM SOY SAUCE FLAVORED, HUH?
YEAH. DO YOU LIKE THEM SWEETER?
AT MY HOUSE, THEY'RE EXTRA-SWEET, SO THAT'S WHAT I'M USED TO...BUT IT'S GOOD THIS WAY TOO!
......

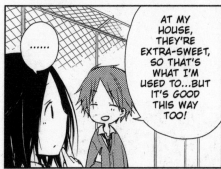

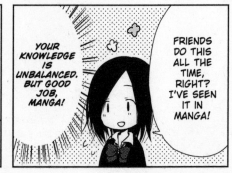

## COOKING

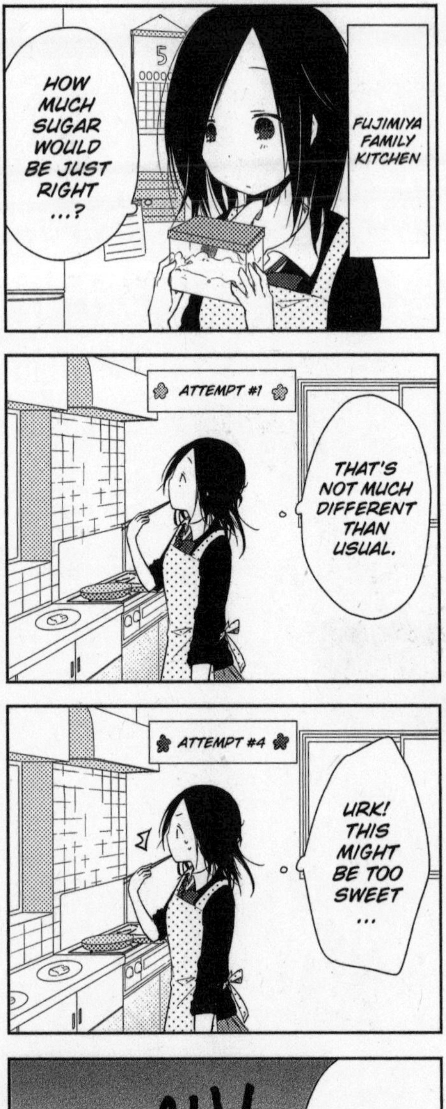
FUJIMIYA FAMILY KITCHEN
HOW MUCH SUGAR WOULD BE JUST RIGHT ...?
ATTEMPT #1
THAT'S NOT MUCH DIFFERENT THAN USUAL.
ATTEMPT #4
URK! THIS MIGHT BE TOO SWEET ...
KAORI? HOW MANY FRIED EGGS ARE YOU GOING TO MAKE?
MOM
AH!
すら—
CLUTTERED

## WHAT'S BEST

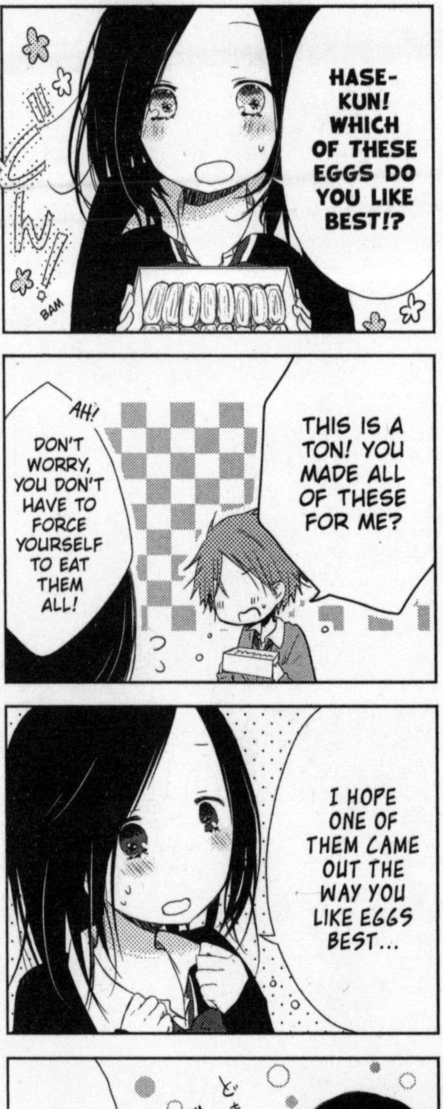
HASE-KUN! WHICH OF THESE EGGS DO YOU LIKE BEST!?
BAM
THIS IS A TON! YOU MADE ALL OF THESE FOR ME?
AH! DON'T WORRY, YOU DON'T HAVE TO FORCE YOURSELF TO EAT THEM ALL!
I HOPE ONE OF THEM CAME OUT THE WAY YOU LIKE EGGS BEST...
どき BADUM どき BADUM
WHOA. SHOULD I BE THIS HAPPY?
TASTE IS THE LAST THING ON HIS MIND

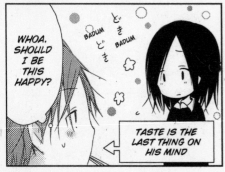

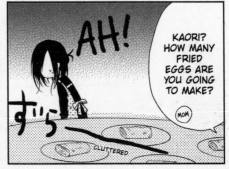

## TO BEGIN WITH

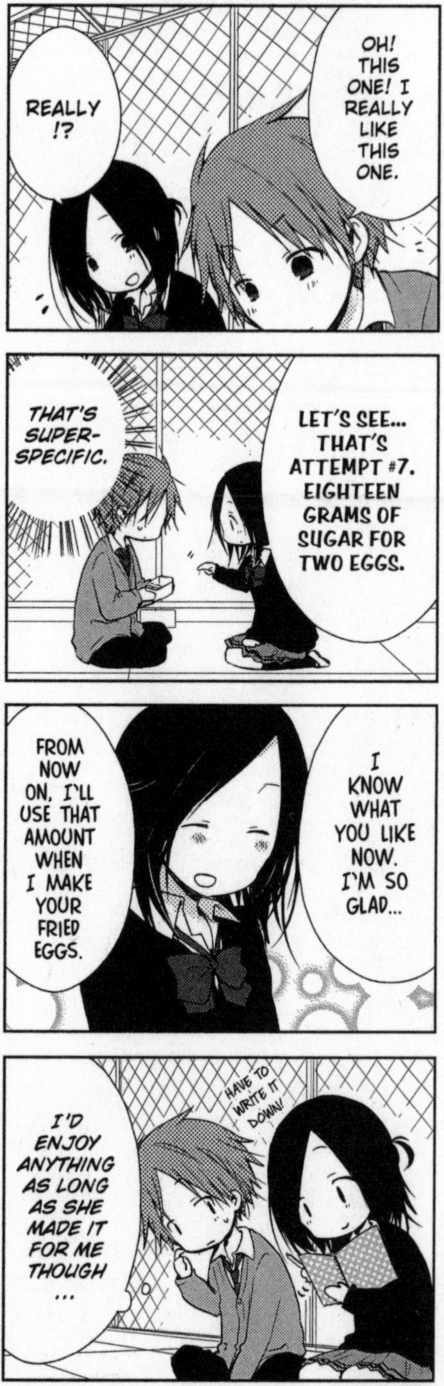
OH! THIS ONE! I REALLY LIKE THIS ONE.
REALLY !?
LET'S SEE... THAT'S ATTEMPT #7. EIGHTEEN GRAMS OF SUGAR FOR TWO EGGS.
THAT'S SUPER-SPECIFIC.
I KNOW WHAT YOU LIKE NOW. I'M SO GLAD...
FROM NOW ON, I'LL USE THAT AMOUNT WHEN I MAKE YOUR FRIED EGGS.
HAVE TO WRITE IT DOWN!
I'D ENJOY ANYTHING AS LONG AS SHE MADE IT FOR ME THOUGH ...

## PRUDENCE

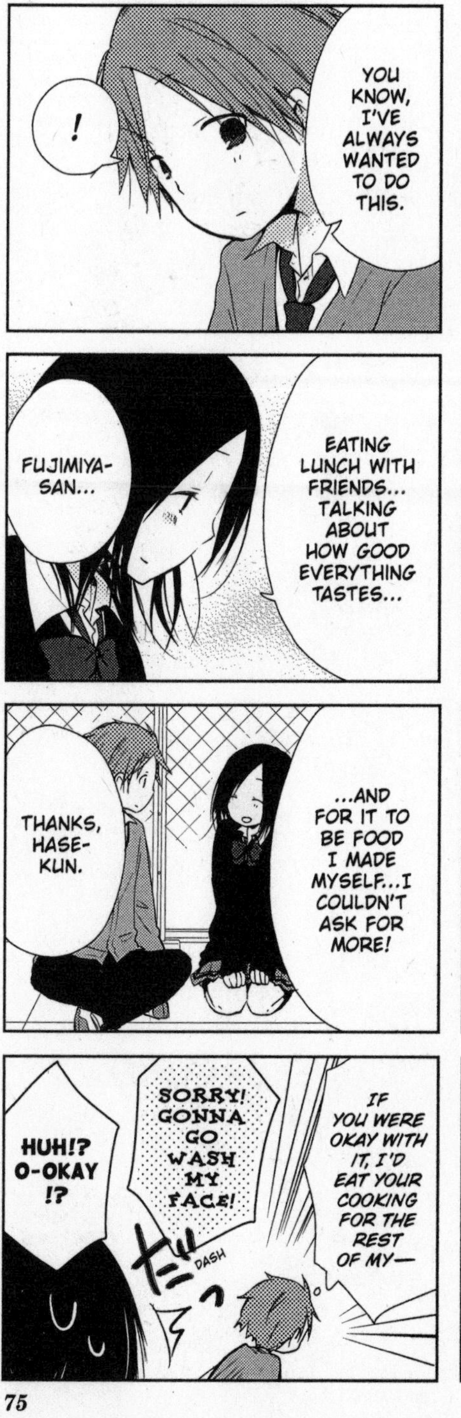
YOU KNOW, I'VE ALWAYS WANTED TO DO THIS.
!
EATING LUNCH WITH FRIENDS... TALKING ABOUT HOW GOOD EVERYTHING TASTES...
FUJIMIYA-SAN...
...AND FOR IT TO BE FOOD I MADE MYSELF...I COULDN'T ASK FOR MORE!
THANKS, HASE-KUN.
IF YOU WERE OKAY WITH IT, I'D EAT YOUR COOKING FOR THE REST OF MY—
SORRY! GONNA GO WASH MY FACE!
DASH
HUH!? O-OKAY !?

# SHOUGO KIRYUU IN THE BATHROOM

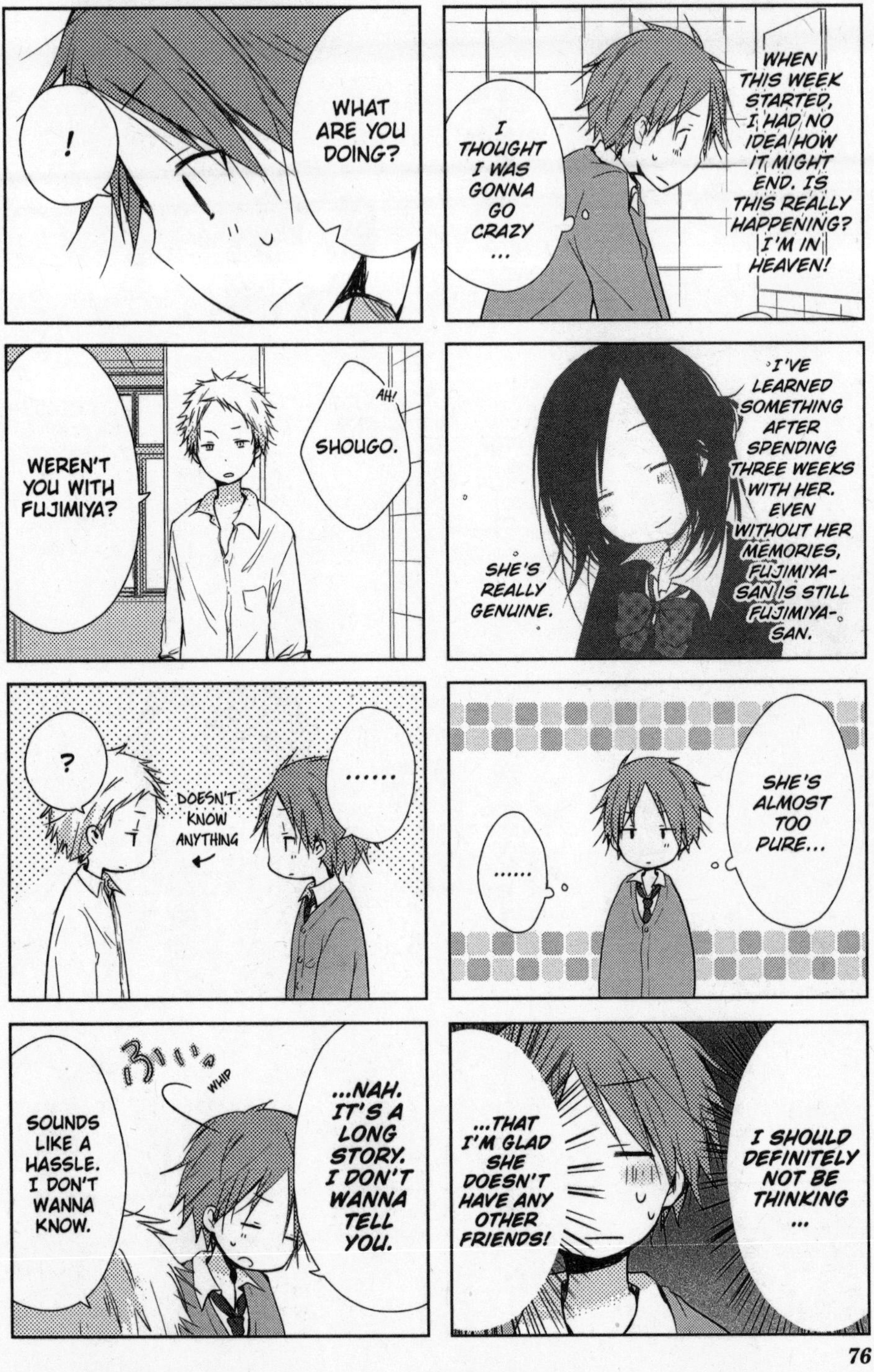

WHEN THIS WEEK STARTED, I HAD NO IDEA HOW IT MIGHT END. IS THIS REALLY HAPPENING? I'M IN HEAVEN!
I THOUGHT I WAS GONNA GO CRAZY ...
I'VE LEARNED SOMETHING AFTER SPENDING THREE WEEKS WITH HER. EVEN WITHOUT HER MEMORIES, FUJIMIYA-SAN IS STILL FUJIMIYA-SAN.
SHE'S REALLY GENUINE.
SHE'S ALMOST TOO PURE...
......
I SHOULD DEFINITELY NOT BE THINKING ...
...THAT I'M GLAD SHE DOESN'T HAVE ANY OTHER FRIENDS!
WHAT ARE YOU DOING?
!
AH!
SHOUGO.
WEREN'T YOU WITH FUJIMIYA?
......
DOESN'T KNOW ANYTHING
?
...NAH. IT'S A LONG STORY. I DON'T WANNA TELL YOU.
WHIP
SOUNDS LIKE A HASSLE. I DON'T WANNA KNOW.

## I WAS WATCHING

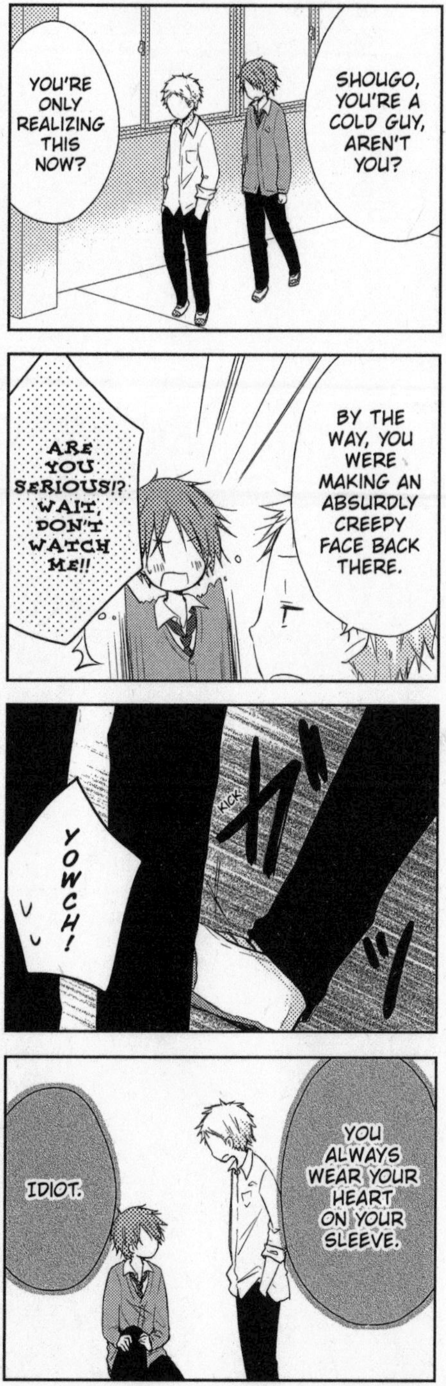
SHOUGO, YOU'RE A COLD GUY, AREN'T YOU?
YOU'RE ONLY REALIZING THIS NOW?
BY THE WAY, YOU WERE MAKING AN ABSURDLY CREEPY FACE BACK THERE.
ARE YOU SERIOUS!? WAIT, DON'T WATCH ME!!
KICK
YOWCH!
YOU ALWAYS WEAR YOUR HEART ON YOUR SLEEVE.
IDIOT.

## SENSING SOMETHING

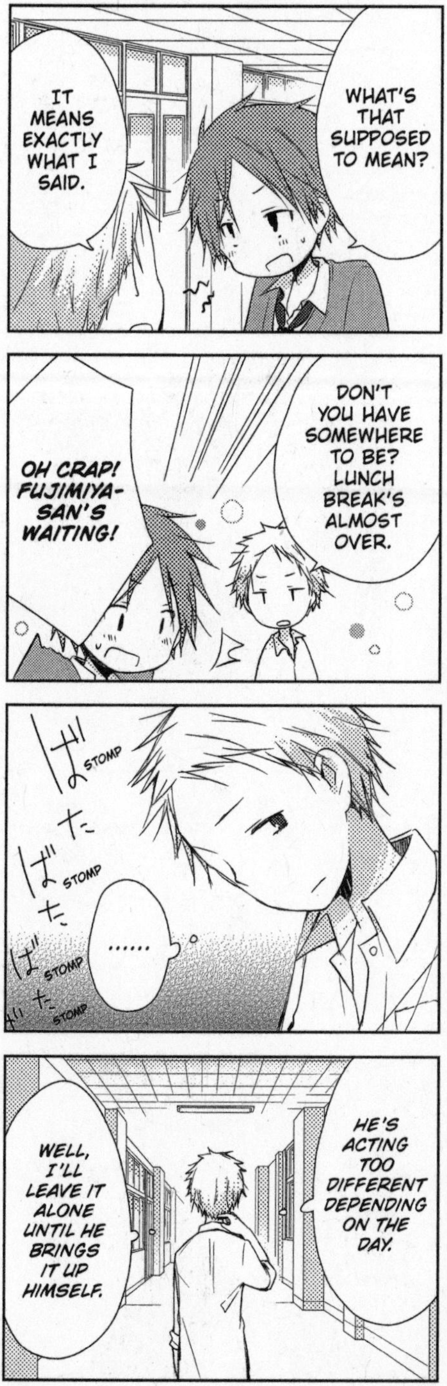
WHAT'S THAT SUPPOSED TO MEAN?
IT MEANS EXACTLY WHAT I SAID.
DON'T YOU HAVE SOMEWHERE TO BE? LUNCH BREAK'S ALMOST OVER.
OH CRAP! FUJIMIYA-SAN'S WAITING!
STOMP
STOMP
STOMP
STOMP
......
HE'S ACTING TOO DIFFERENT DEPENDING ON THE DAY.
WELL, I'LL LEAVE IT ALONE UNTIL HE BRINGS IT UP HIMSELF.

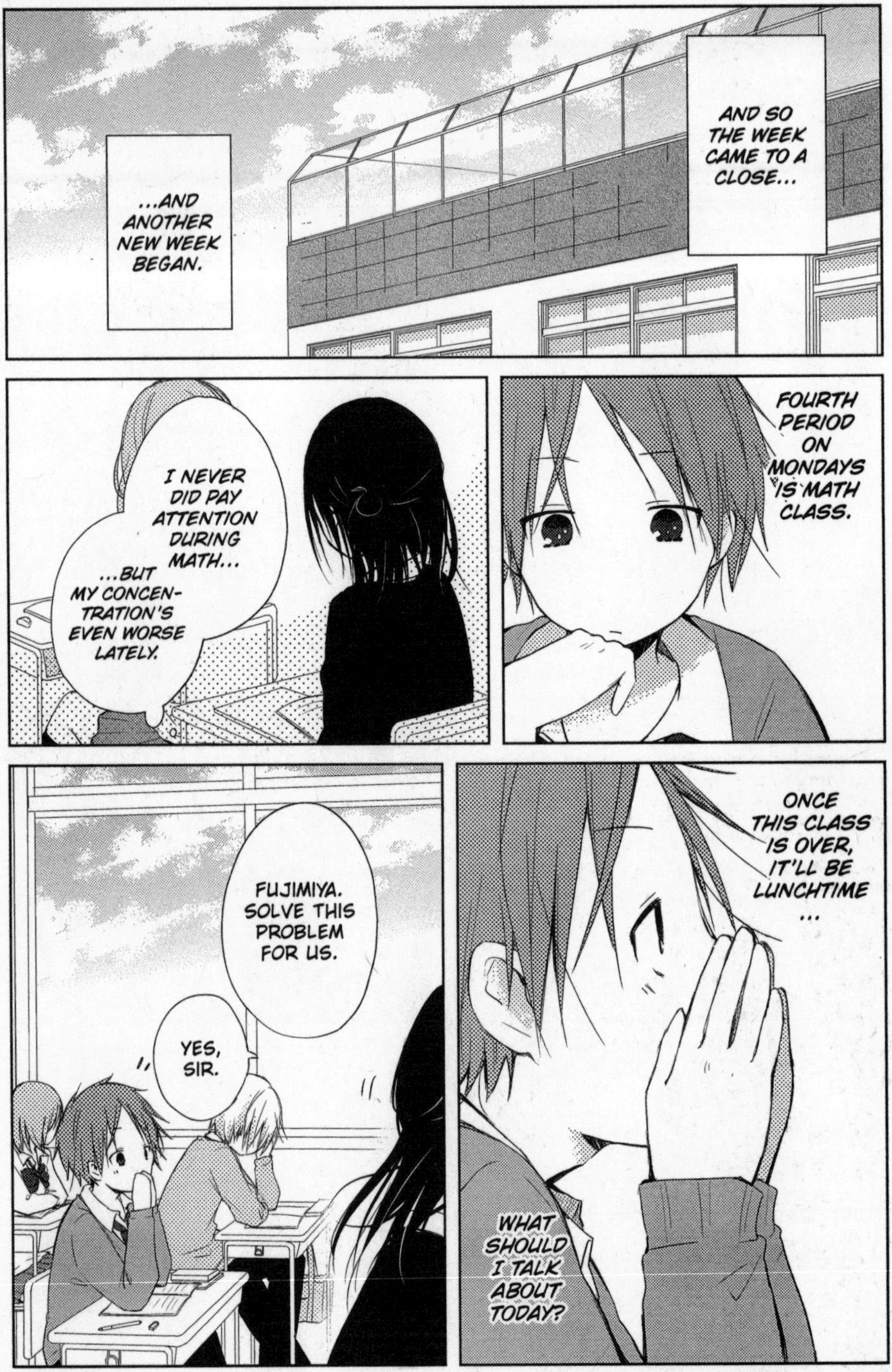
AND SO THE WEEK CAME TO A CLOSE...
...AND ANOTHER NEW WEEK BEGAN.
FOURTH PERIOD ON MONDAYS IS MATH CLASS.
I NEVER DID PAY ATTENTION DURING MATH...
...BUT MY CONCENTRATION'S EVEN WORSE LATELY.
ONCE THIS CLASS IS OVER, IT'LL BE LUNCHTIME...
WHAT SHOULD I TALK ABOUT TODAY?
FUJIMIYA. SOLVE THIS PROBLEM FOR US.
YES, SIR.

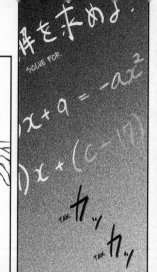

THAT'S A MATH WHIZ FOR YOU. SHE'S SOLVING IT WITHOUT A SECOND'S HESITATION.

SHE DOESN'T EVEN HAVE TO LOOK AT THE TEXTBOOK...

I'LL BREAK THE ICE WITH HER ONCE CLASS IS OVER.

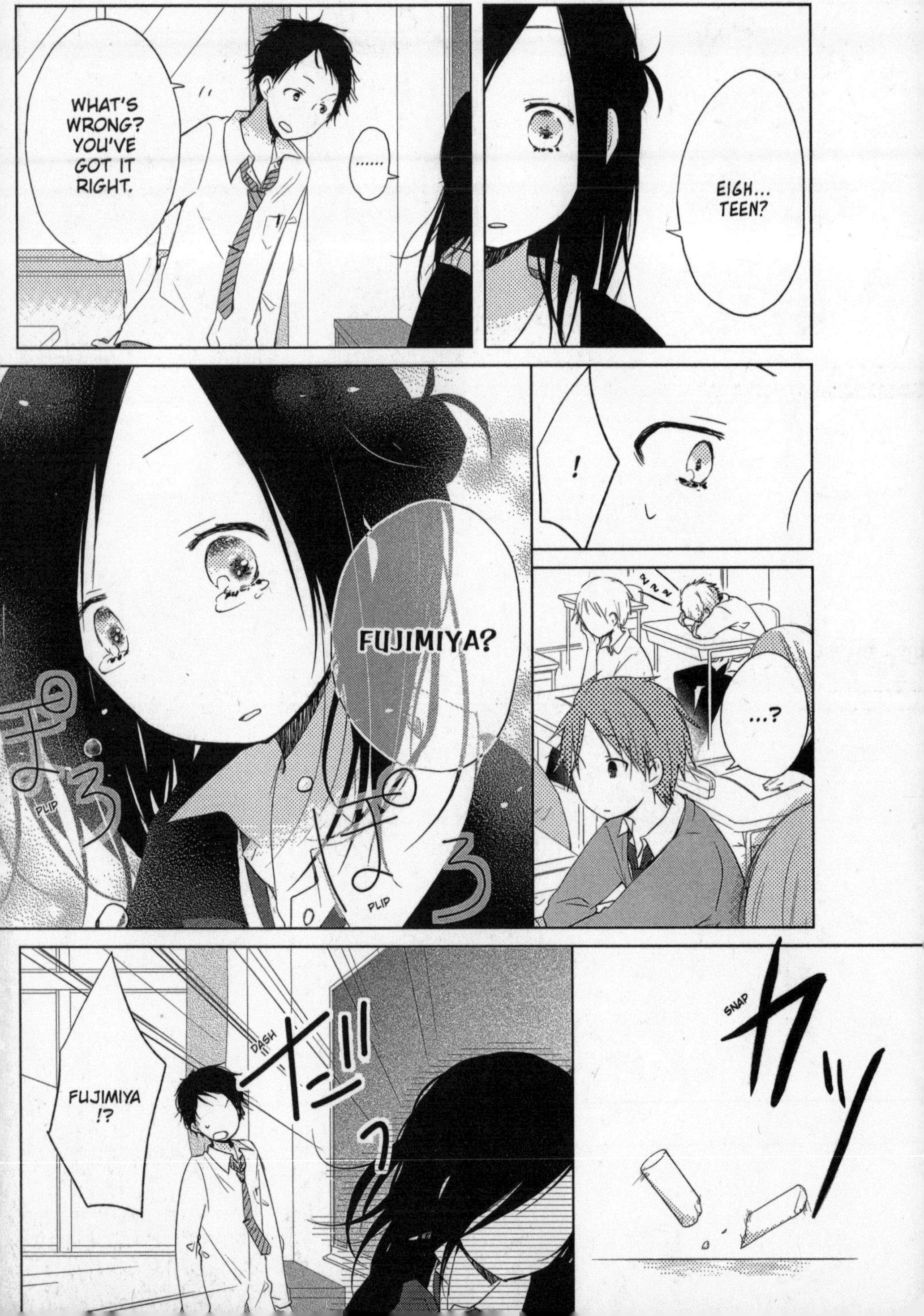
EIGH... TEEN?
WHAT'S WRONG? YOU'VE GOT IT RIGHT.
......
!
...?
FUJIMIYA?
PLIP
PLIP
SNAP
DASH
FUJIMIYA !?

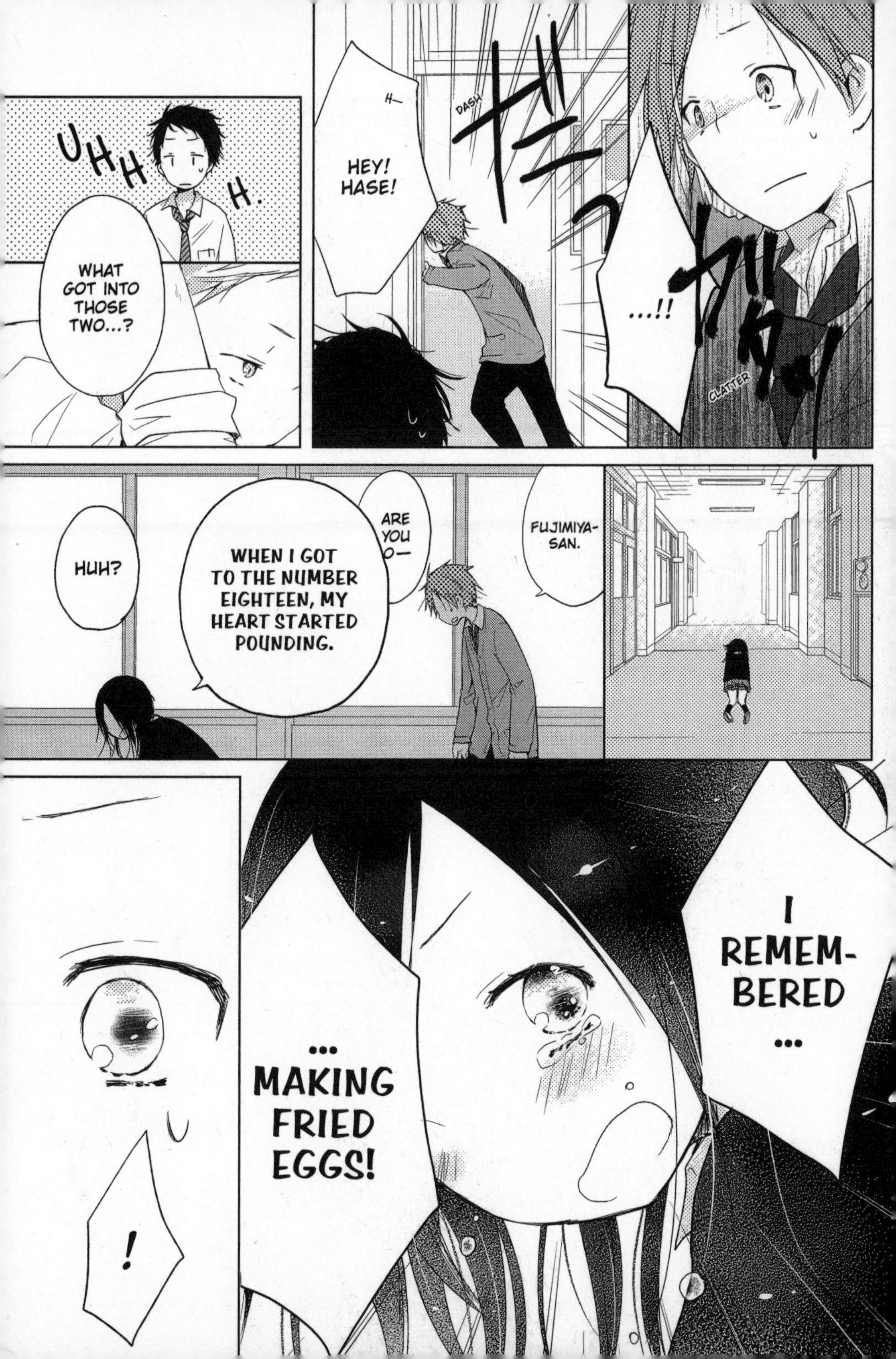
...!!
CLATTER
DASH
H— HEY! HASE!
UHHH H.
WHAT GOT INTO THOSE TWO...?
FUJIMIYA-SAN.
ARE YOU O—
WHEN I GOT TO THE NUMBER EIGHTEEN, MY HEART STARTED POUNDING.
HUH?
I REMEMBERED...
...MAKING FRIED EGGS!
!

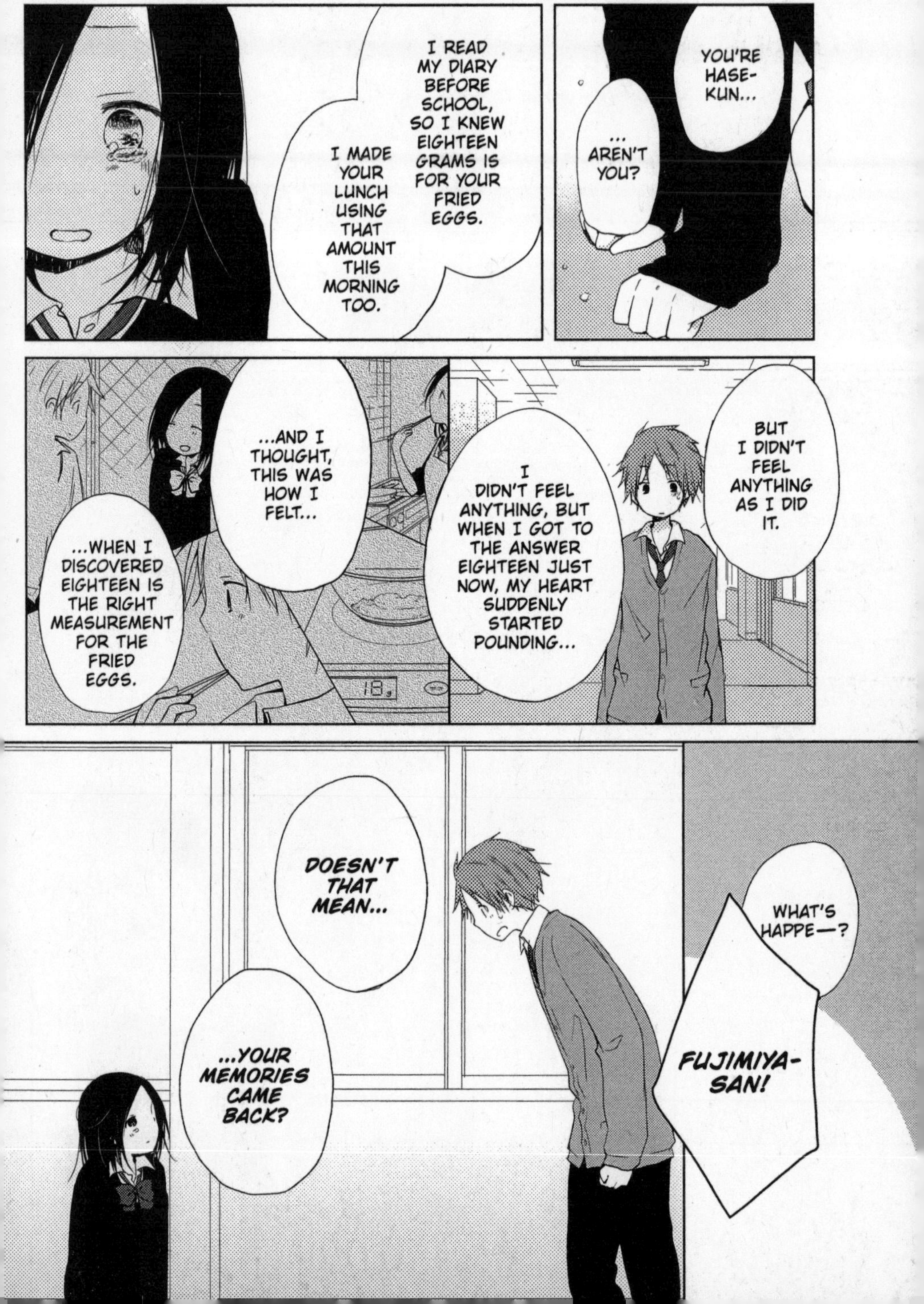
YOU'RE HASE-KUN...
...AREN'T YOU?
I READ MY DIARY BEFORE SCHOOL, SO I KNEW EIGHTEEN GRAMS IS FOR YOUR FRIED EGGS.
I MADE YOUR LUNCH USING THAT AMOUNT THIS MORNING TOO.
BUT I DIDN'T FEEL ANYTHING AS I DID IT.
I DIDN'T FEEL ANYTHING, BUT WHEN I GOT TO THE ANSWER EIGHTEEN JUST NOW, MY HEART SUDDENLY STARTED POUNDING...
...AND I THOUGHT, THIS WAS HOW I FELT...
...WHEN I DISCOVERED EIGHTEEN IS THE RIGHT MEASUREMENT FOR THE FRIED EGGS.
18g
WHAT'S HAPPE—?
FUJIMIYA-SAN!
DOESN'T THAT MEAN...
...YOUR MEMORIES CAME BACK?

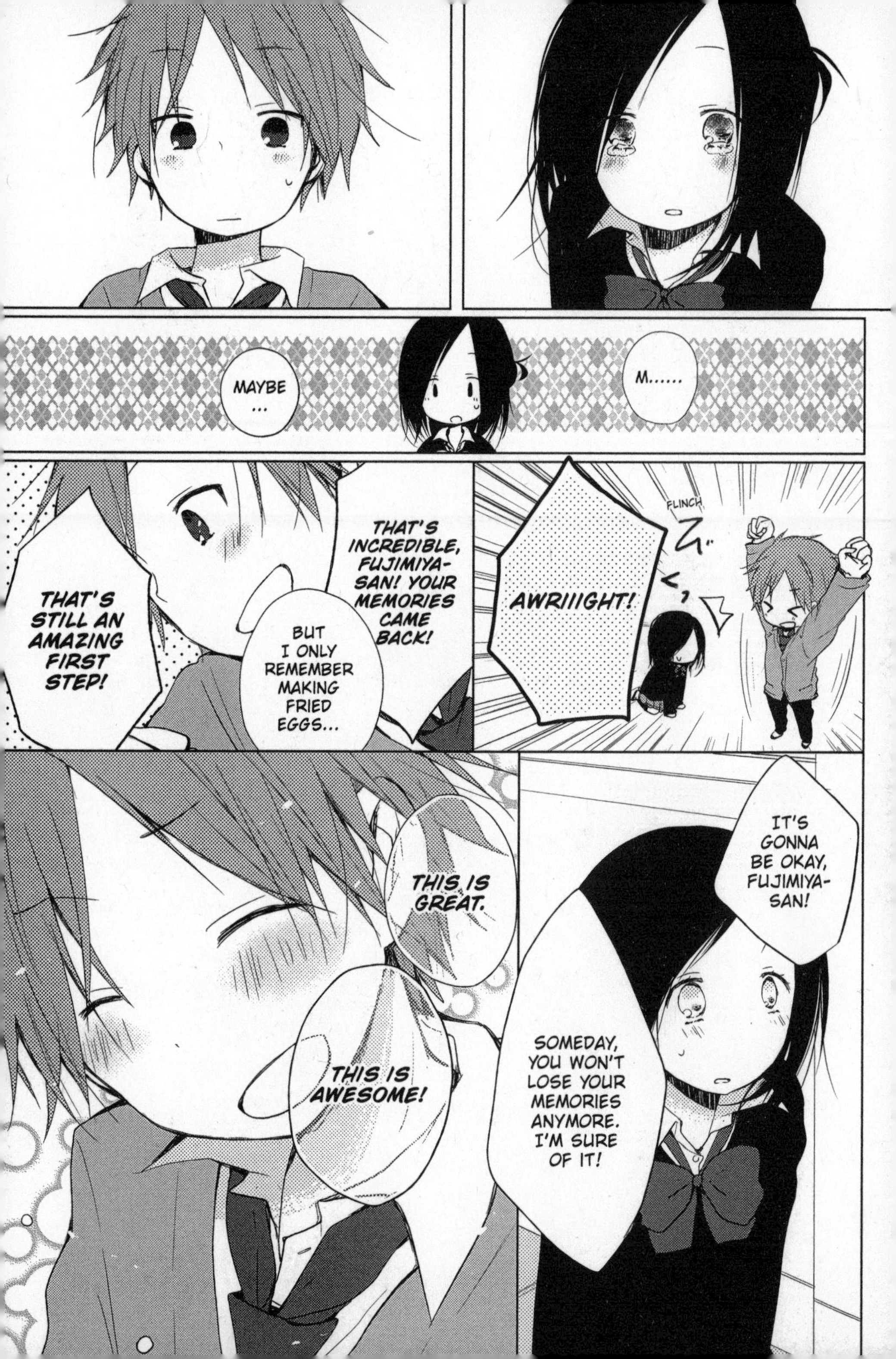
M......
MAYBE ...
FLINCH
AWRIIIGHT!
THAT'S INCREDIBLE, FUJIMIYA-SAN! YOUR MEMORIES CAME BACK!
BUT I ONLY REMEMBER MAKING FRIED EGGS...
THAT'S STILL AN AMAZING FIRST STEP!
IT'S GONNA BE OKAY, FUJIMIYA-SAN!
SOMEDAY, YOU WON'T LOSE YOUR MEMORIES ANYMORE. I'M SURE OF IT!
THIS IS GREAT.
THIS IS AWESOME!

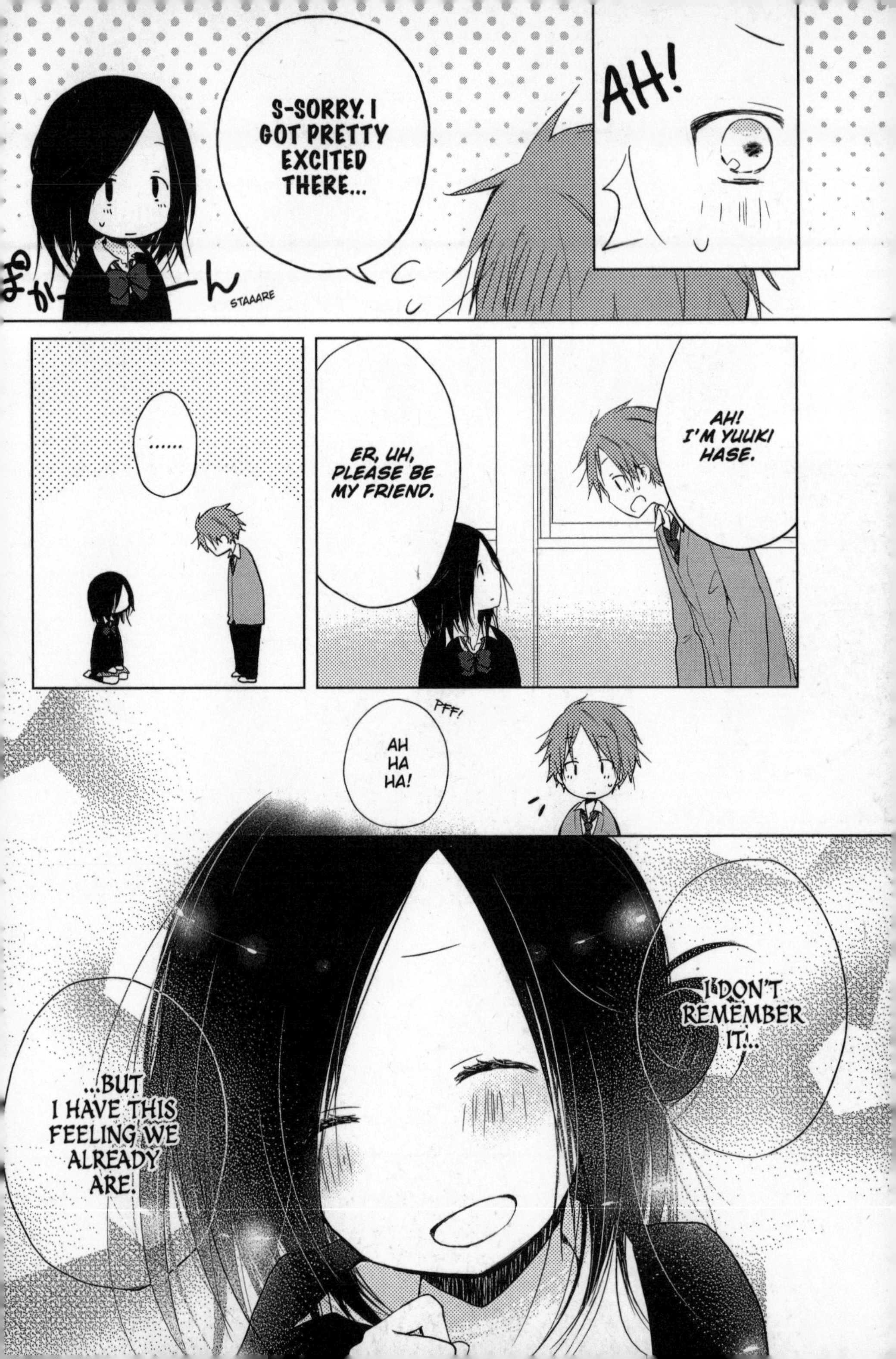
AH!
S-SORRY. I GOT PRETTY EXCITED THERE...
ぽかーん
STAAARE
AH! I'M YUUKI HASE.
ER, UH, PLEASE BE MY FRIEND.
......
PFF!
AH HA HA!
I DON'T REMEMBER IT...
...BUT I HAVE THIS FEELING WE ALREADY ARE.

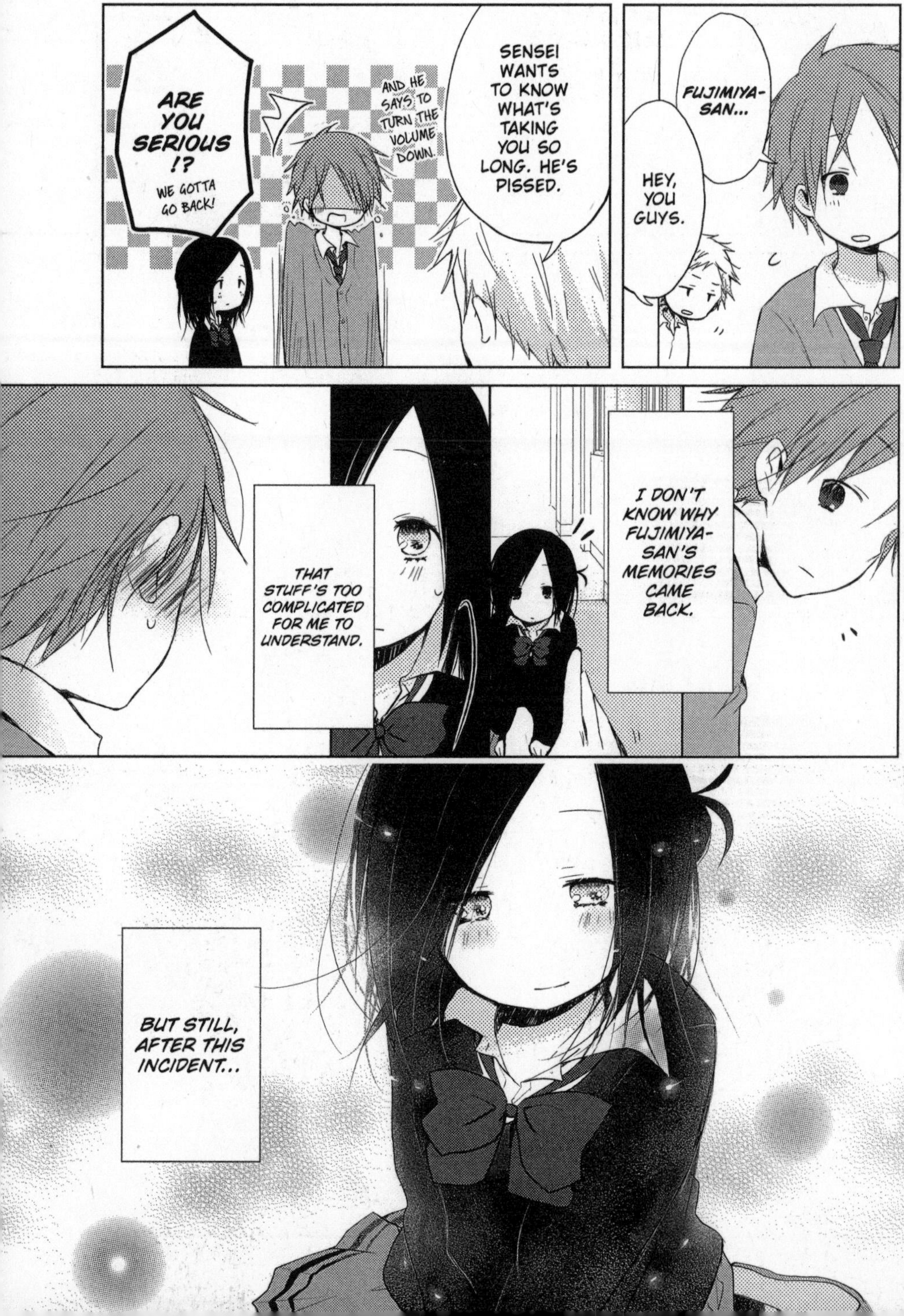
FUJIMIYA-SAN...
HEY, YOU GUYS.
SENSEI WANTS TO KNOW WHAT'S TAKING YOU SO LONG. HE'S PISSED.
AND HE SAYS TO TURN THE VOLUME DOWN.
ARE YOU SERIOUS!?
WE GOTTA GO BACK!
I DON'T KNOW WHY FUJIMIYA-SAN'S MEMORIES CAME BACK.
THAT STUFF'S TOO COMPLICATED FOR ME TO UNDERSTAND.
BUT STILL, AFTER THIS INCIDENT...

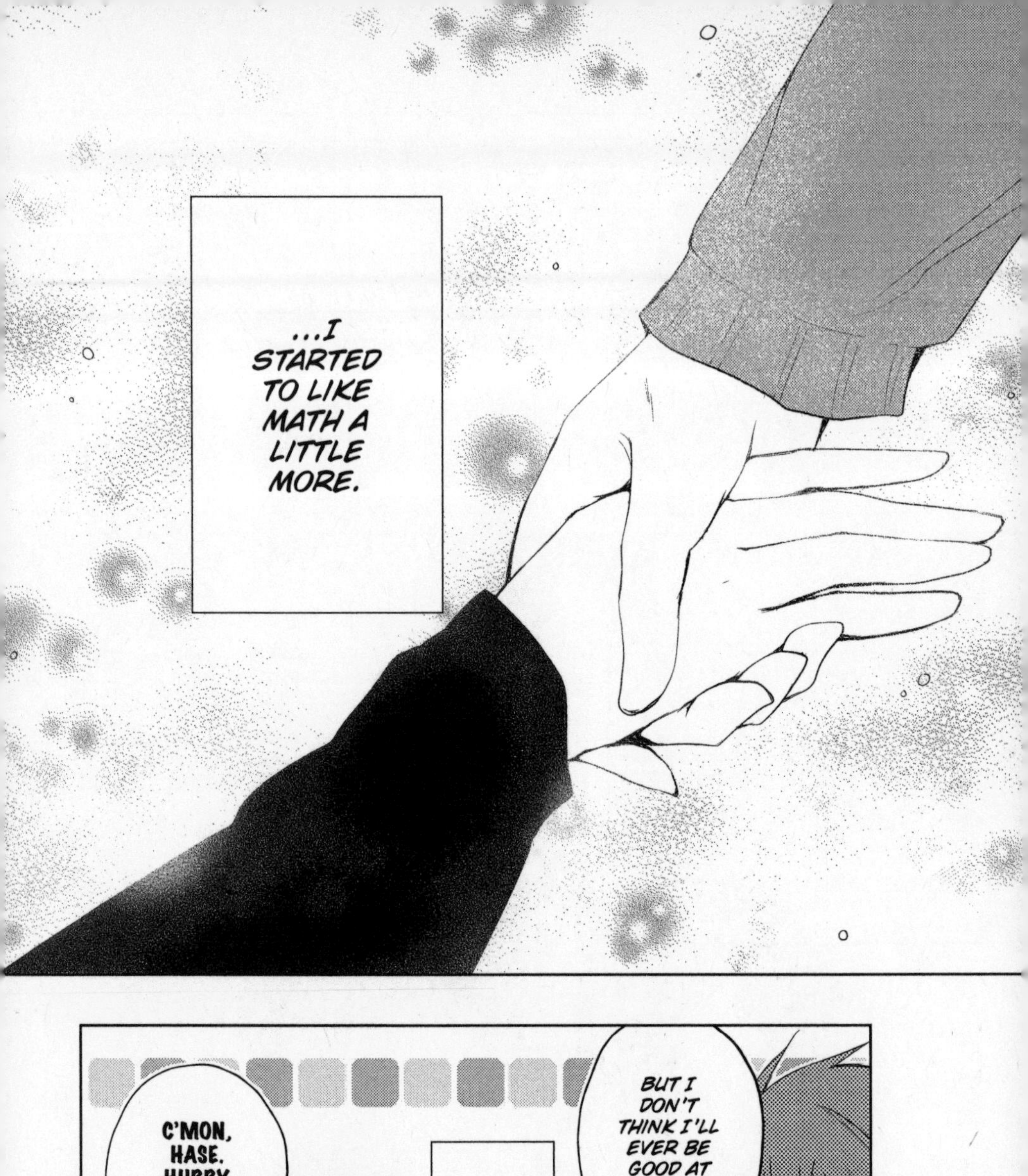
...I STARTED TO LIKE MATH A LITTLE MORE.

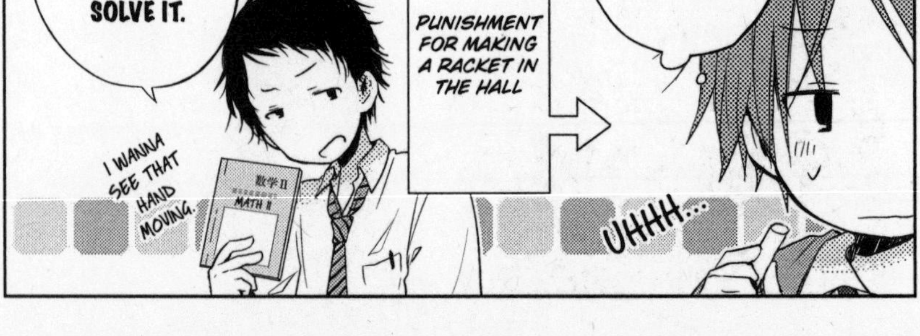
BUT I DON'T THINK I'LL EVER BE GOOD AT IT. NOPE.
UHHH...
PUNISHMENT FOR MAKING A RACKET IN THE HALL
C'MON, HASE. HURRY UP AND SOLVE IT.
I WANNA SEE THAT HAND MOVING.
数学II
MATH II

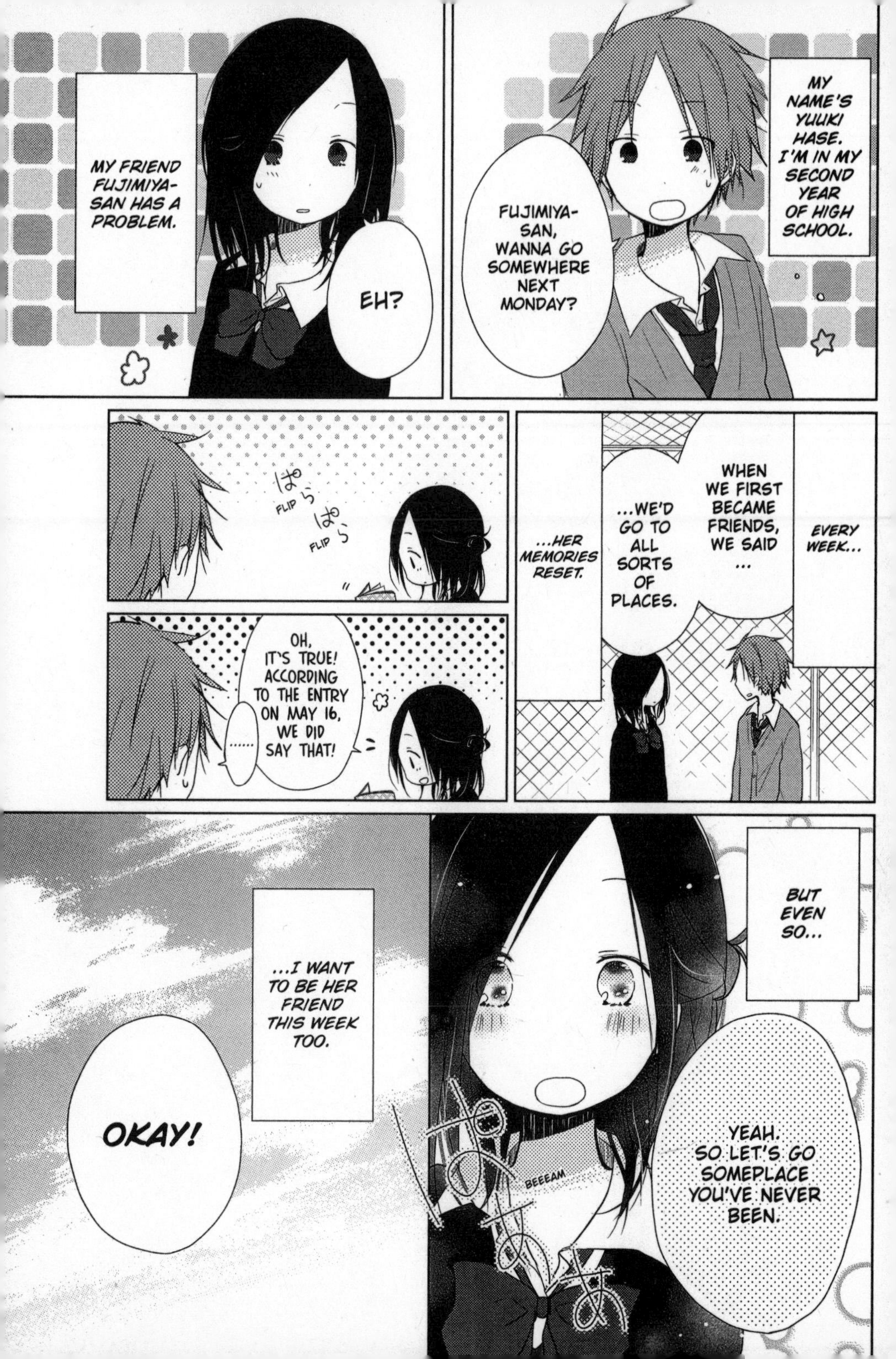
MY NAME'S YUUKI HASE. I'M IN MY SECOND YEAR OF HIGH SCHOOL.
FUJIMIYA-SAN, WANNA GO SOMEWHERE NEXT MONDAY?
MY FRIEND FUJIMIYA-SAN HAS A PROBLEM.
EH?
EVERY WEEK...
WHEN WE FIRST BECAME FRIENDS, WE SAID ...
...WE'D GO TO ALL SORTS OF PLACES.
...HER MEMORIES RESET.
ぱら FLIP
ぱら FLIP
OH, IT'S TRUE! ACCORDING TO THE ENTRY ON MAY 16, WE DID SAY THAT!
......
BUT EVEN SO...
YEAH. SO LET'S GO SOMEPLACE YOU'VE NEVER BEEN.
BEEEAM
...I WANT TO BE HER FRIEND THIS WEEK TOO.
OKAY!

# CHAPTER 2
# A DAY OUT WITH A FRIEND

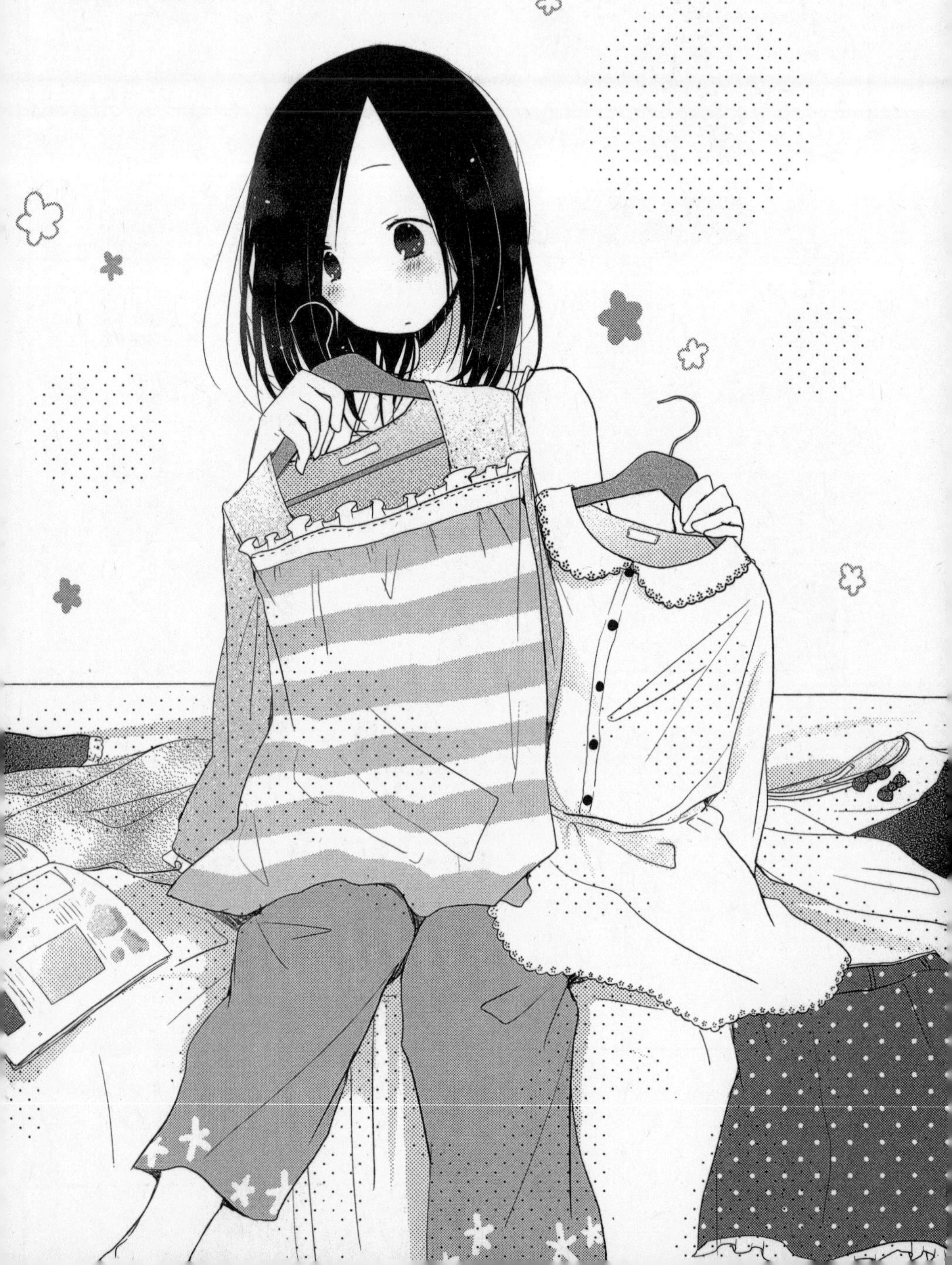

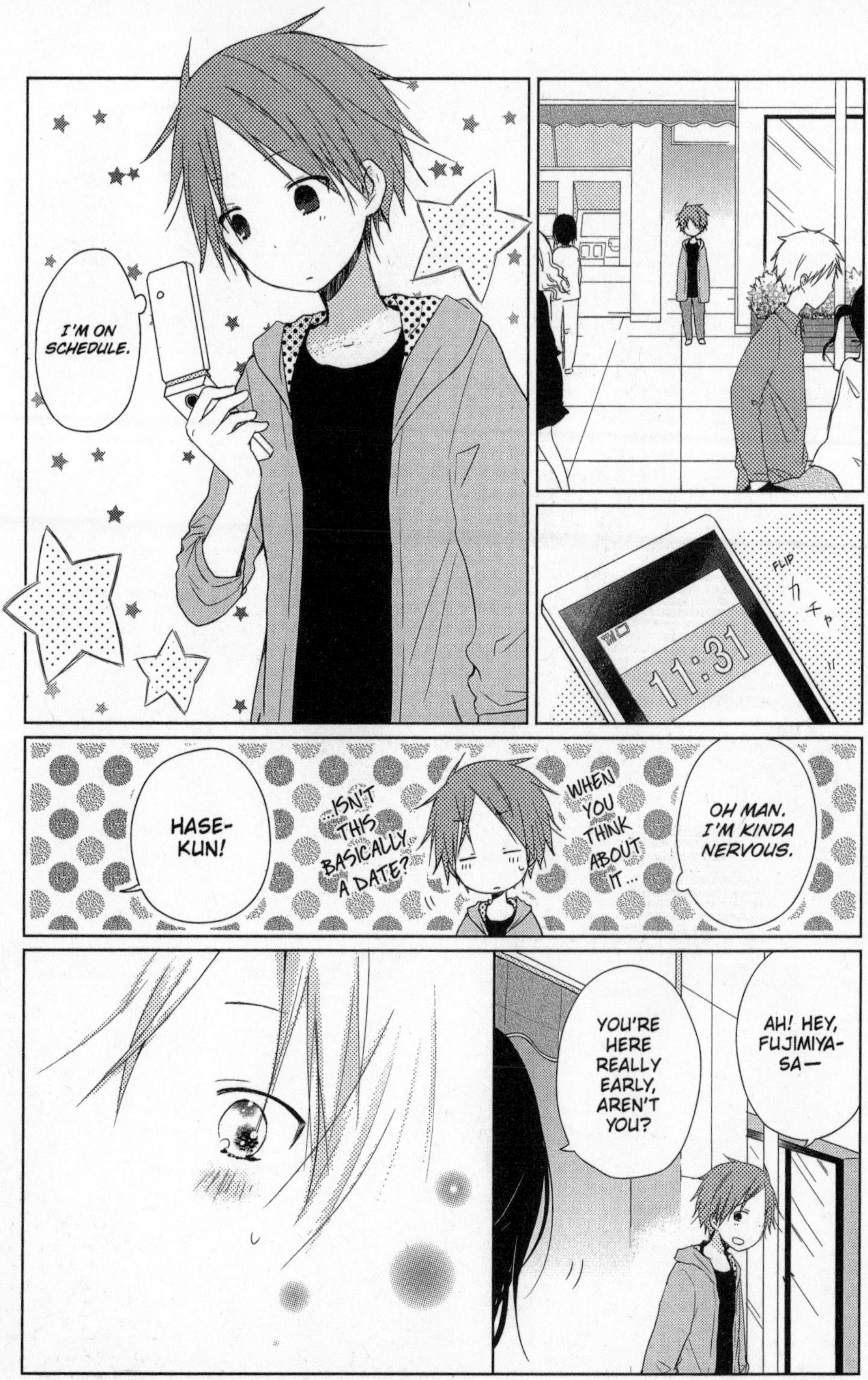
FLIP
カチャ
I'M ON SCHEDULE.
OH MAN. I'M KINDA NERVOUS.
WHEN YOU THINK ABOUT IT...
...ISN'T THIS BASICALLY A DATE?
HASE-KUN!
AH! HEY, FUJIMIYA-SA—
YOU'RE HERE REALLY EARLY, AREN'T YOU?

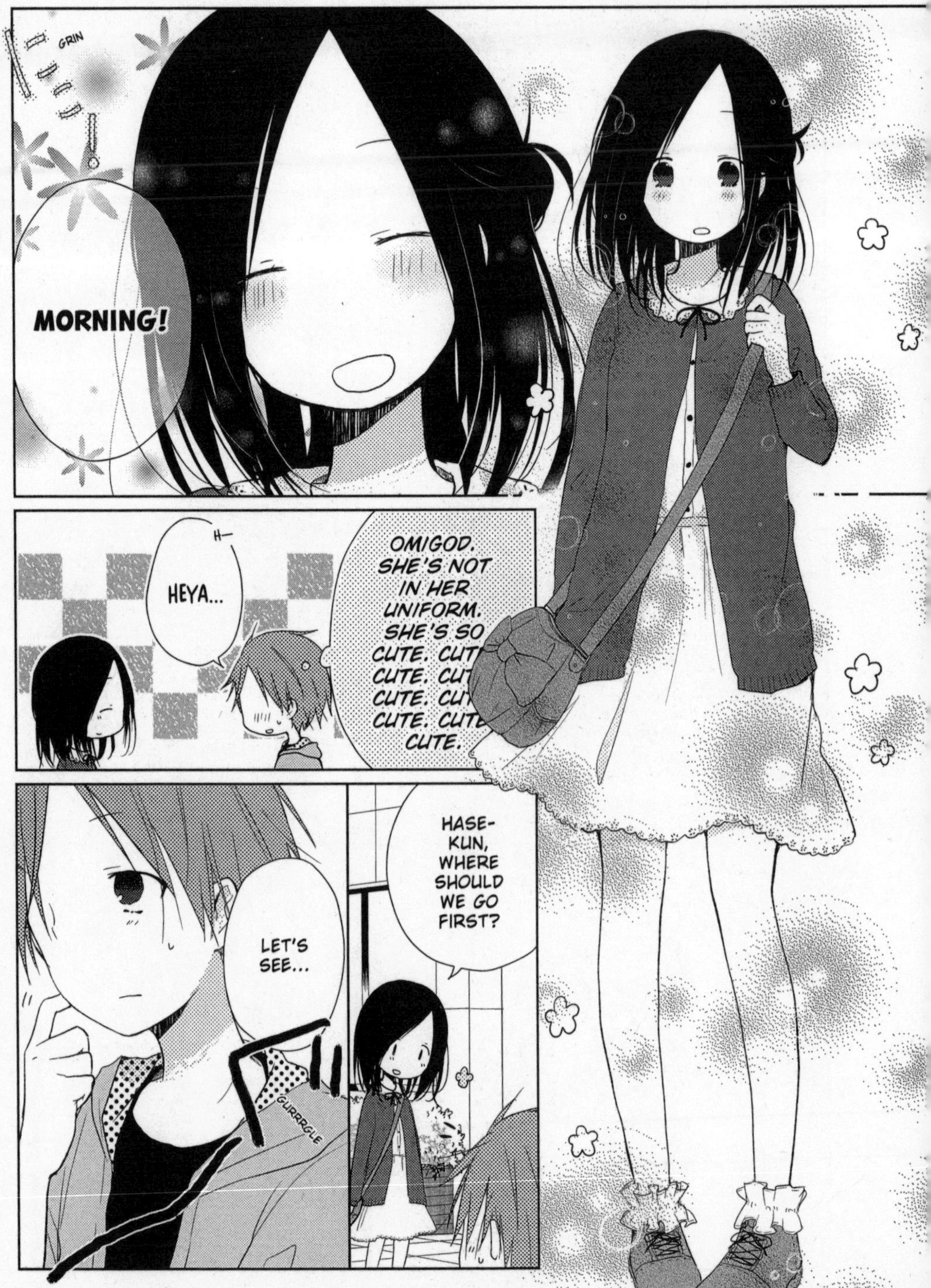
GRIN
MORNING!
OMIGOD. SHE'S NOT IN HER UNIFORM. SHE'S SO CUTE. CUT
CUTE. CUT
CUTE. CUT
CUTE. CUTE
CUTE.
H—
HEYA...
HASE-KUN, WHERE SHOULD WE GO FIRST?
LET'S SEE...
GURRRGLE

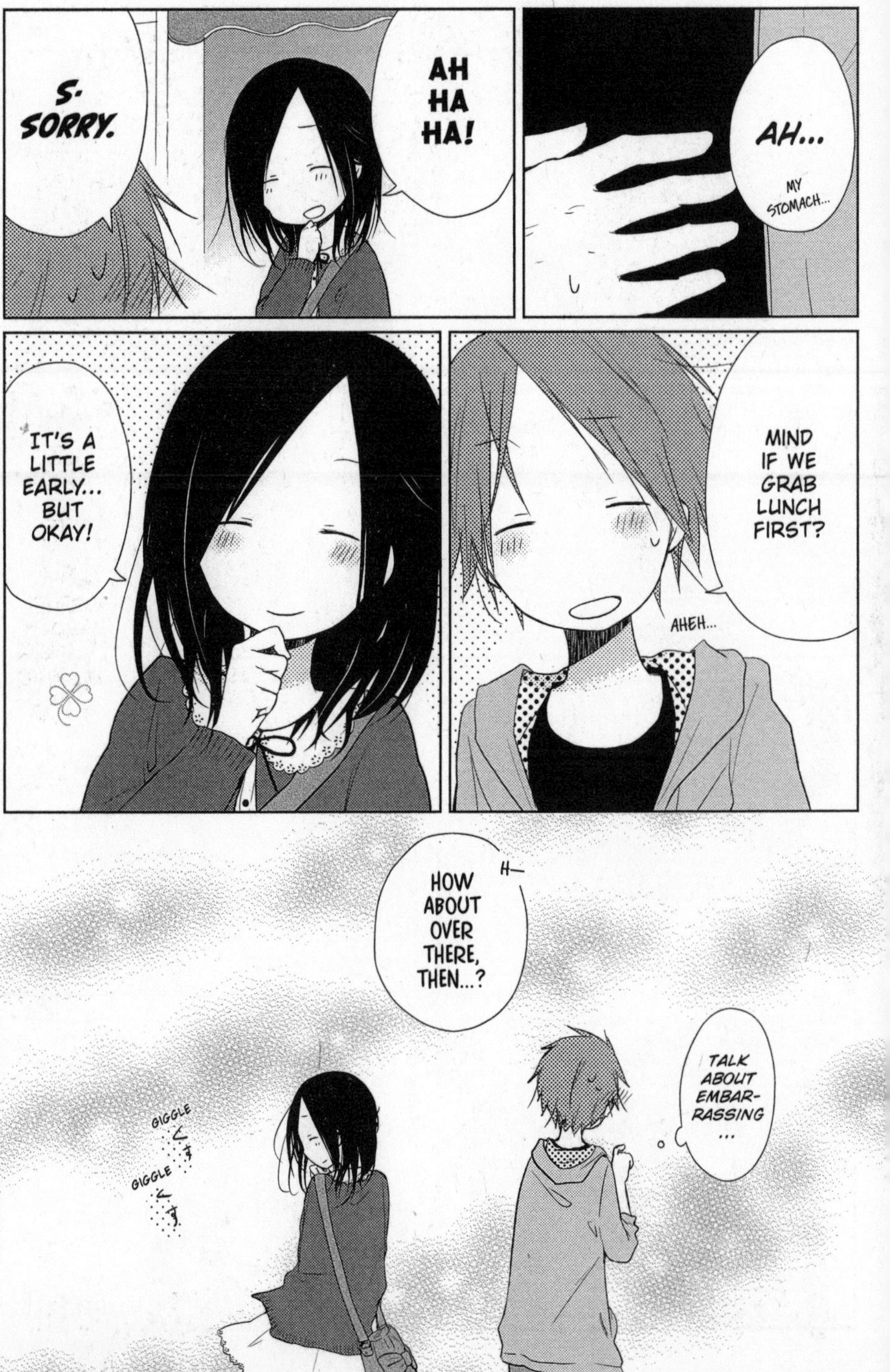
AH...
MY STOMACH...
AH HA HA!
S-SORRY.
MIND IF WE GRAB LUNCH FIRST?
AHEH...
IT'S A LITTLE EARLY... BUT OKAY!
H—
HOW ABOUT OVER THERE, THEN...?
TALK ABOUT EMBARRASSING...
GIGGLE くす
GIGGLE くす

## NERVOUS

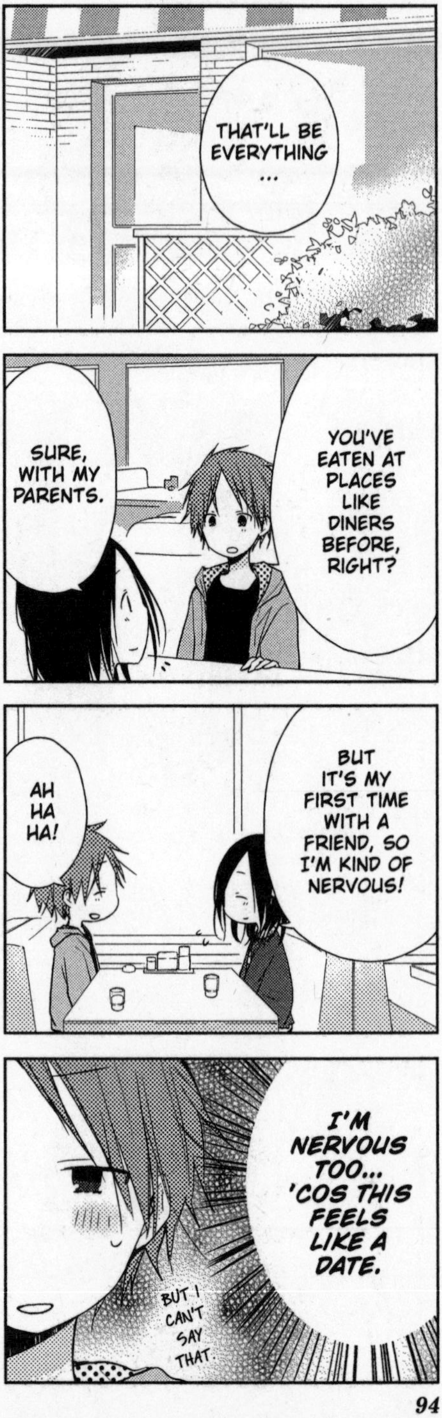
THAT'LL BE EVERYTHING ...
YOU'VE EATEN AT PLACES LIKE DINERS BEFORE, RIGHT?
SURE, WITH MY PARENTS.
BUT IT'S MY FIRST TIME WITH A FRIEND, SO I'M KIND OF NERVOUS!
AH HA HA!
I'M NERVOUS TOO... 'COS THIS FEELS LIKE A DATE.
BUT I CAN'T SAY THAT.

## MEETING UP

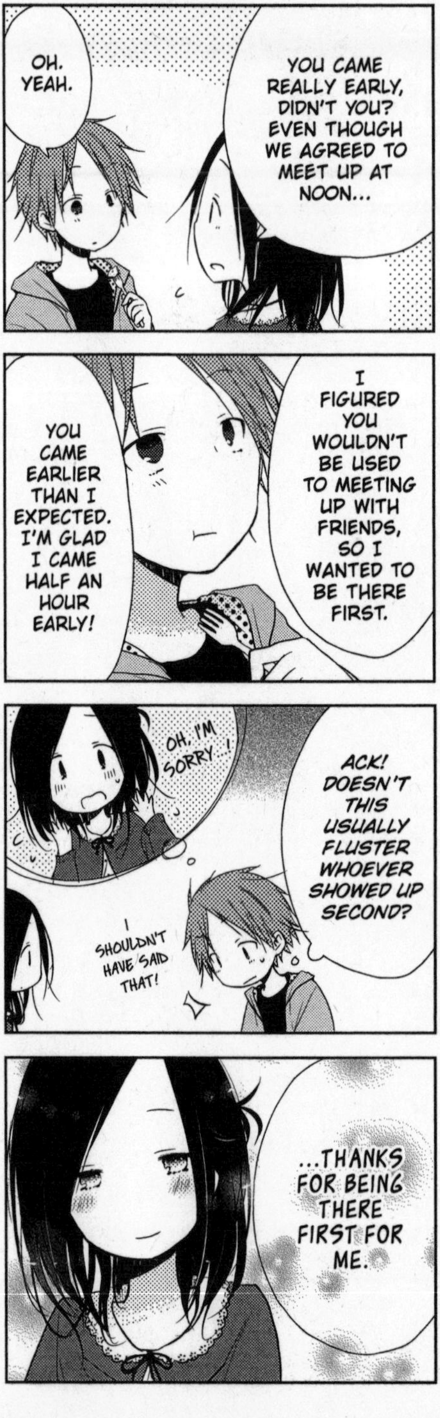
YOU CAME REALLY EARLY, DIDN'T YOU? EVEN THOUGH WE AGREED TO MEET UP AT NOON...
OH. YEAH.
I FIGURED YOU WOULDN'T BE USED TO MEETING UP WITH FRIENDS, SO I WANTED TO BE THERE FIRST.
YOU CAME EARLIER THAN I EXPECTED. I'M GLAD I CAME HALF AN HOUR EARLY!
ACK! DOESN'T THIS USUALLY FLUSTER WHOEVER SHOWED UP SECOND?
OH, I'M SORRY...!
I SHOULDN'T HAVE SAID THAT!
...THANKS FOR BEING THERE FIRST FOR ME.

## LONGING

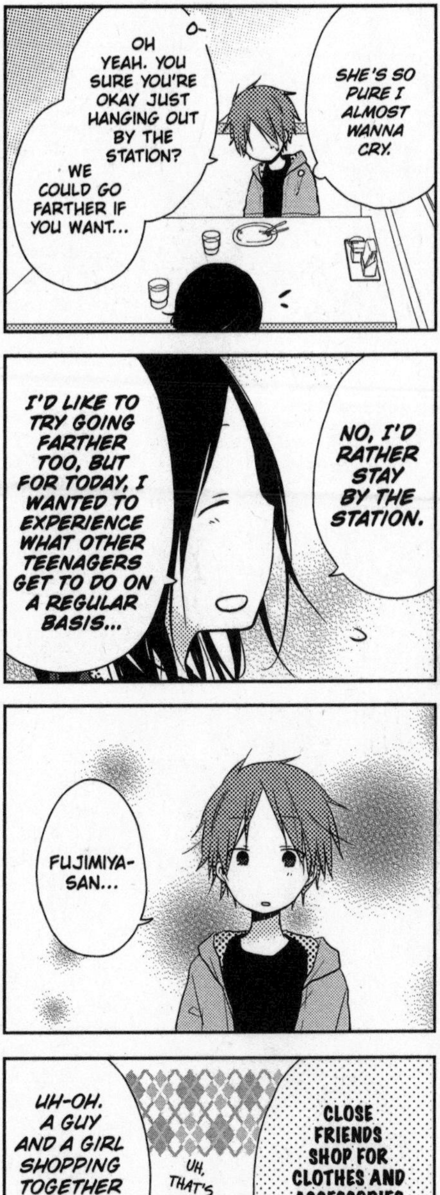

SHE'S SO PURE I ALMOST WANNA CRY.
OH YEAH. YOU SURE YOU'RE OKAY JUST HANGING OUT BY THE STATION?
WE COULD GO FARTHER IF YOU WANT...
NO, I'D RATHER STAY BY THE STATION.
I'D LIKE TO TRY GOING FARTHER TOO, BUT FOR TODAY, I WANTED TO EXPERIENCE WHAT OTHER TEENAGERS GET TO DO ON A REGULAR BASIS...
FUJIMIYA-SAN...
CLOSE FRIENDS SHOP FOR CLOTHES AND ACCESSORIES AND SO ON TOGETHER, RIGHT?
I SEE IT IN MANGA!
UH, THAT'S WITH OTHER GIRLS...
UH-OH. A GUY AND A GIRL SHOPPING TOGETHER WOULD TOTALLY LOOK LIKE A COUPLE...


## THE BILL

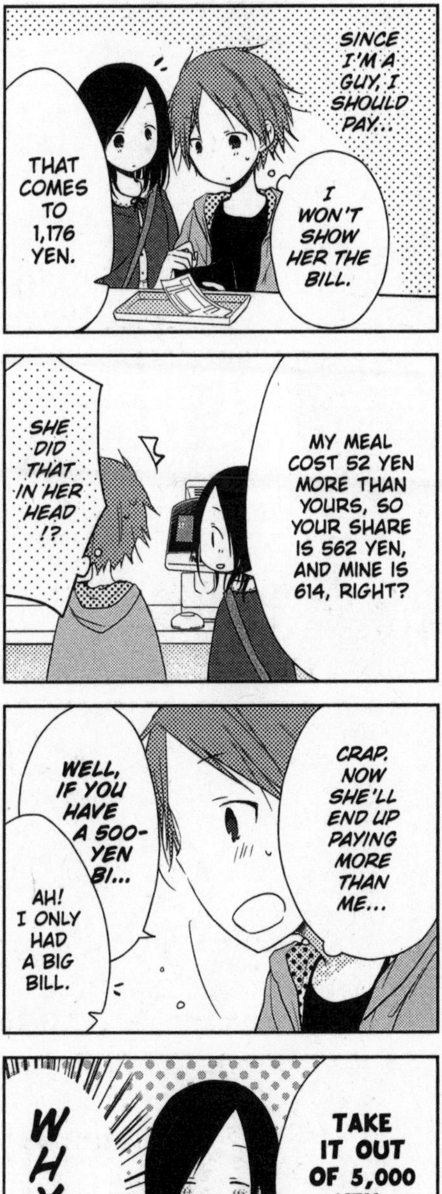

SINCE I'M A GUY, I SHOULD PAY...
I WON'T SHOW HER THE BILL.
THAT COMES TO 1,176 YEN.
MY MEAL COST 52 YEN MORE THAN YOURS, SO YOUR SHARE IS 562 YEN, AND MINE IS 614, RIGHT?
SHE DID THAT IN HER HEAD!?
CRAP. NOW SHE'LL END UP PAYING MORE THAN ME...
WELL, IF YOU HAVE A 500-YEN BI...
AH! I ONLY HAD A BIG BILL.
TAKE IT OUT OF 5,000 YEN, PLEASE.
WHYYY!?

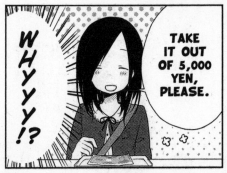

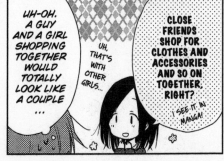

## SHOCK

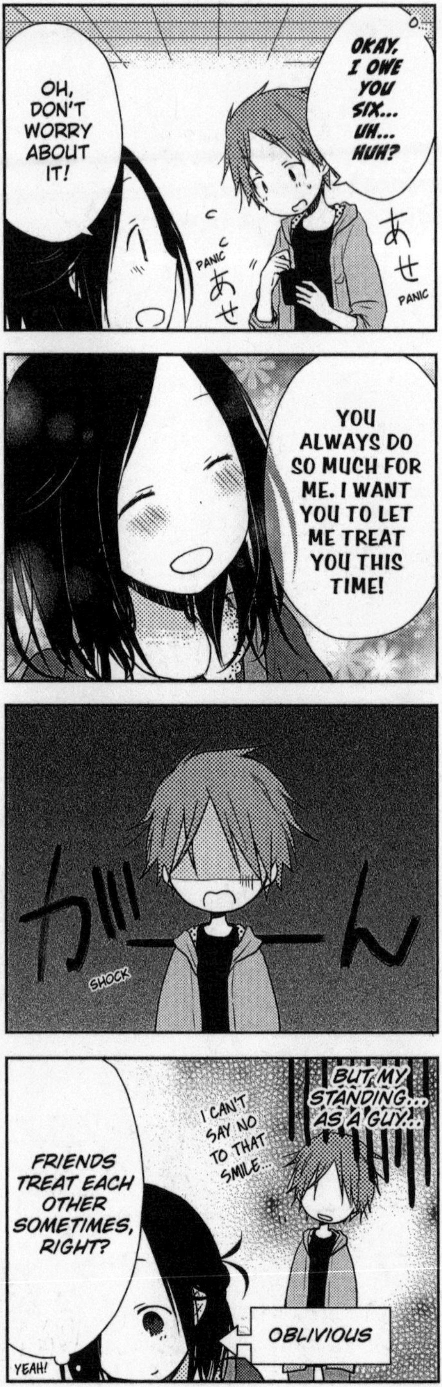
OKAY. I OWE YOU SIX... UH... HUH?
OH, DON'T WORRY ABOUT IT!
あせ PANIC
あせ PANIC
YOU ALWAYS DO SO MUCH FOR ME. I WANT YOU TO LET ME TREAT YOU THIS TIME!
がーん
SHOCK
BUT MY STANDING... AS A GUY...
I CAN'T SAY NO TO THAT SMILE...
FRIENDS TREAT EACH OTHER SOMETIMES, RIGHT?
OBLIVIOUS
YEAH!

## OPPOSITE EFFECT

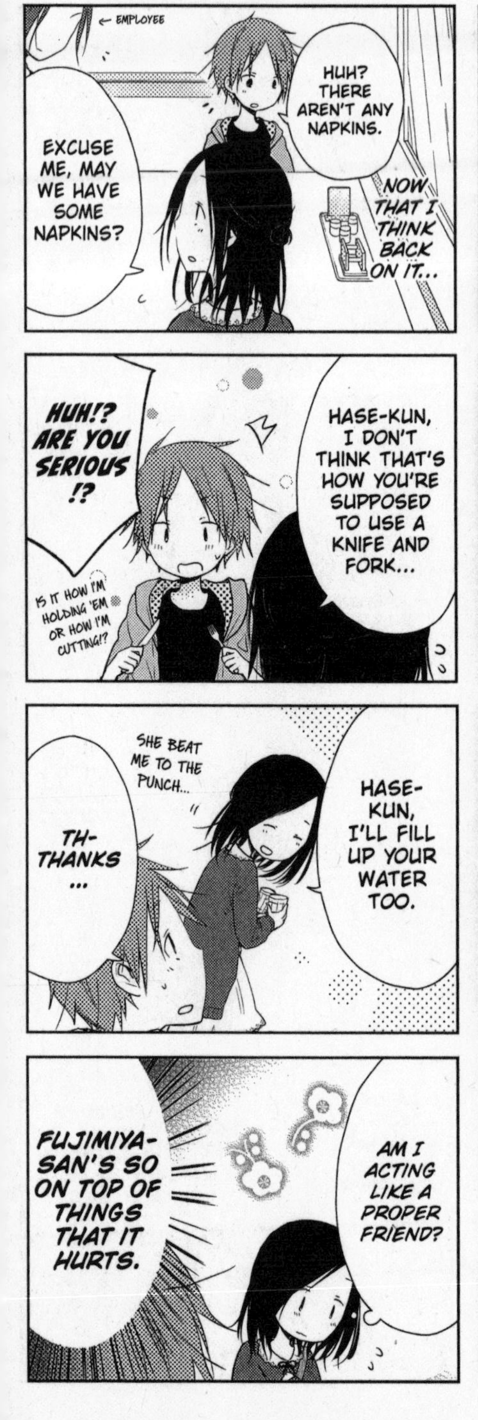
HUH? THERE AREN'T ANY NAPKINS.
NOW THAT I THINK BACK ON IT...
EMPLOYEE
EXCUSE ME, MAY WE HAVE SOME NAPKINS?
HASE-KUN, I DON'T THINK THAT'S HOW YOU'RE SUPPOSED TO USE A KNIFE AND FORK...
HUH!? ARE YOU SERIOUS!?
IS IT HOW I'M HOLDING 'EM OR HOW I'M CUTTING!?
HASE-KUN, I'LL FILL UP YOUR WATER TOO.
SHE BEAT ME TO THE PUNCH...
TH-THANKS...
AM I ACTING LIKE A PROPER FRIEND?
FUJIMIYA-SAN'S SO ON TOP OF THINGS THAT IT HURTS.

## FIRST KARAOKE

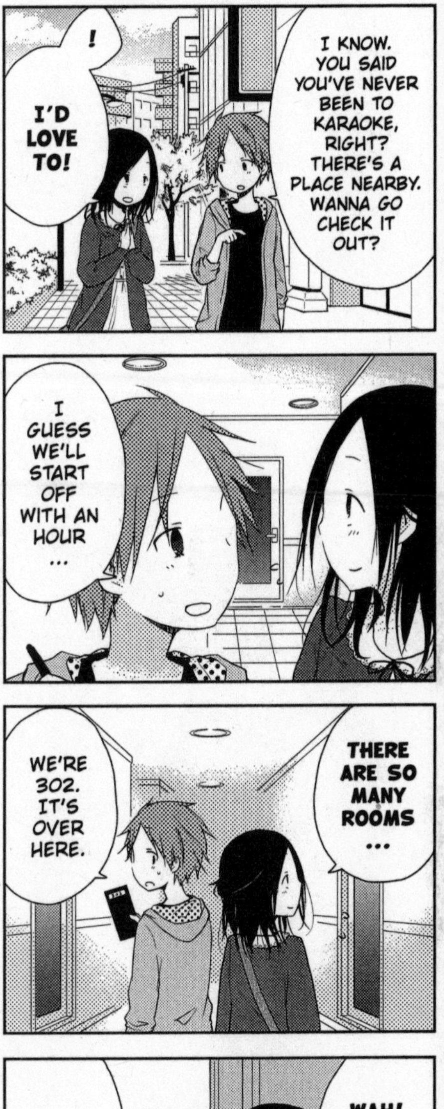
I KNOW. YOU SAID YOU'VE NEVER BEEN TO KARAOKE, RIGHT? THERE'S A PLACE NEARBY. WANNA GO CHECK IT OUT?
!
I'D LOVE TO!
I GUESS WE'LL START OFF WITH AN HOUR ...
THERE ARE SO MANY ROOMS ...
WE'RE 302. IT'S OVER HERE.
WAH! IT'S SO DARK IN HERE...!
THERE'S A LIGHT SWITCH.
SHE'S REALLY ANTSY ...

## MOVED

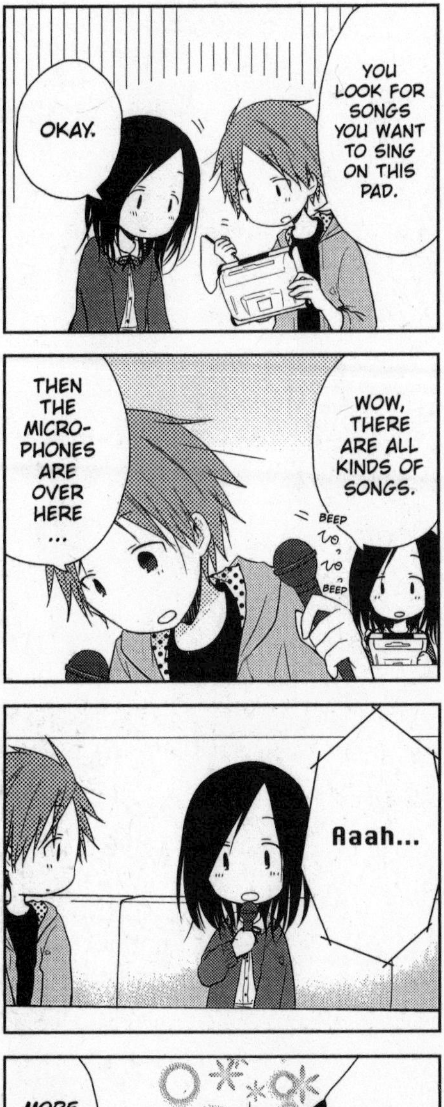
YOU LOOK FOR SONGS YOU WANT TO SING ON THIS PAD.
OKAY.
WOW, THERE ARE ALL KINDS OF SONGS.
BEEP
BEEP
THEN THE MICROPHONES ARE OVER HERE ...
Aaah...
LIKE A REAL SINGER!
MORE LIKE A LITTLE KID...
QUIVER
QUIVER

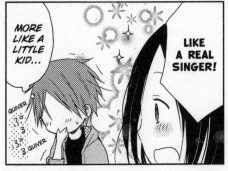

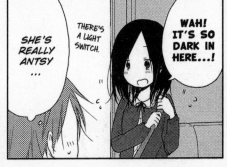

## BECAUSE SHE FOUND THEM

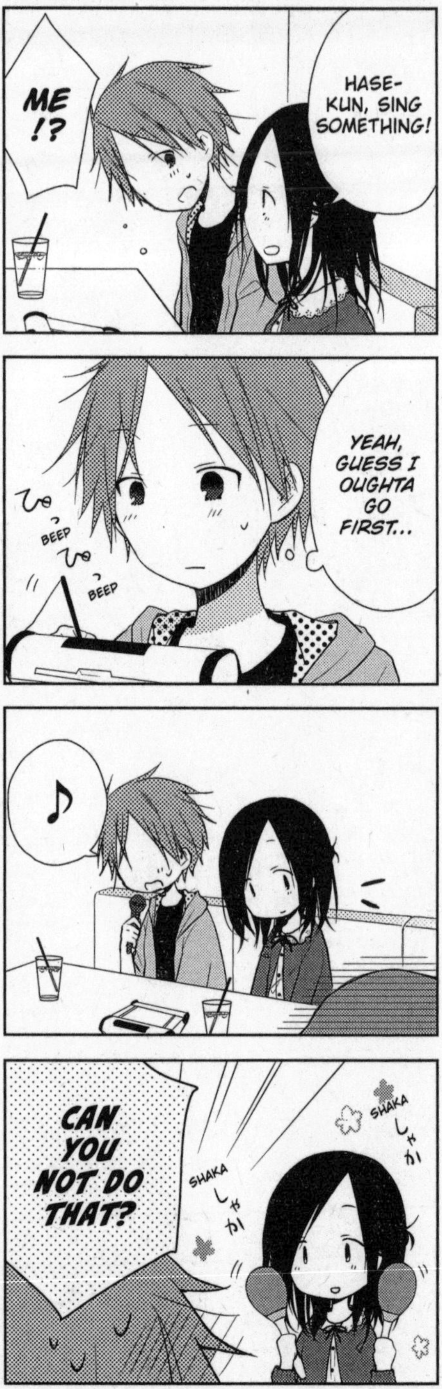
HASE-KUN, SING SOMETHING!
ME !?
YEAH, GUESS I OUGHTA GO FIRST...
BEEP
BEEP
♪
SHAKA
SHAKA
CAN YOU NOT DO THAT?

## KIND OF EMBARRASSING

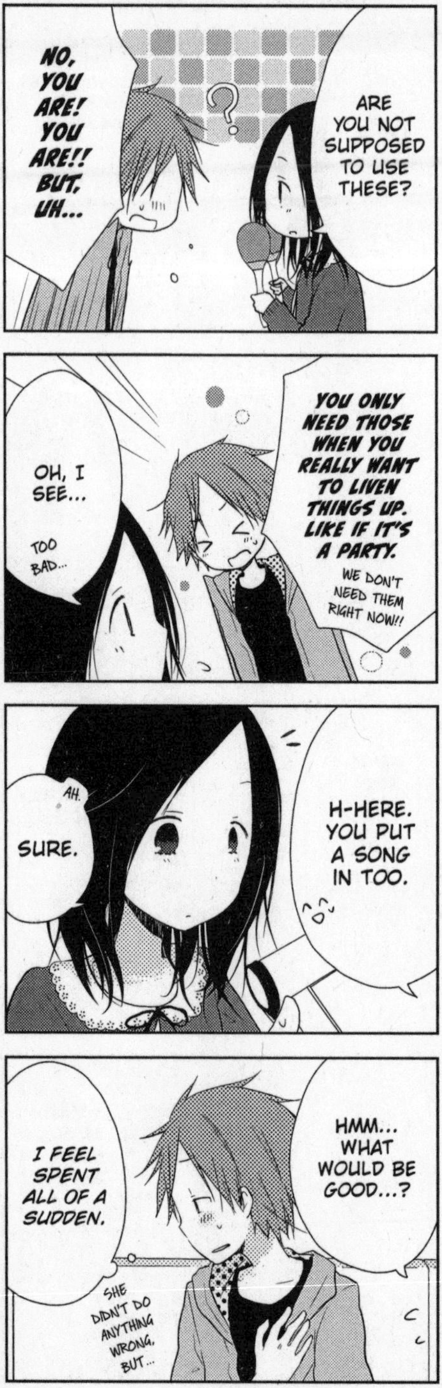
ARE YOU NOT SUPPOSED TO USE THESE?
NO, YOU ARE! YOU ARE!! BUT, UH...
YOU ONLY NEED THOSE WHEN YOU REALLY WANT TO LIVEN THINGS UP. LIKE IF IT'S A PARTY.
WE DON'T NEED THEM RIGHT NOW!!
OH, I SEE...
TOO BAD...
H-HERE. YOU PUT A SONG IN TOO.
AH.
SURE.
HMM... WHAT WOULD BE GOOD...?
I FEEL SPENT ALL OF A SUDDEN.
SHE DIDN'T DO ANYTHING WRONG, BUT...

## FIRST SONG

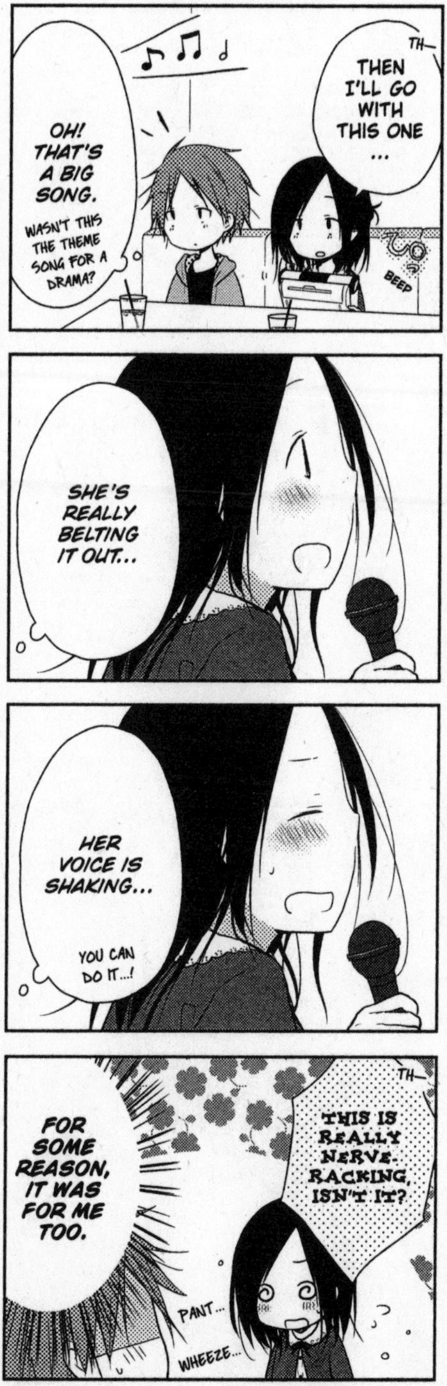
TH—
THEN I'LL GO WITH THIS ONE ...
OH! THAT'S A BIG SONG.
WASN'T THIS THE THEME SONG FOR A DRAMA?
BEEP
SHE'S REALLY BELTING IT OUT...
HER VOICE IS SHAKING...
YOU CAN DO IT...!
TH—
THIS IS REALLY NERVE-RACKING, ISN'T IT?
FOR SOME REASON, IT WAS FOR ME TOO.
PANT...
WHEEZE...

## BREAK

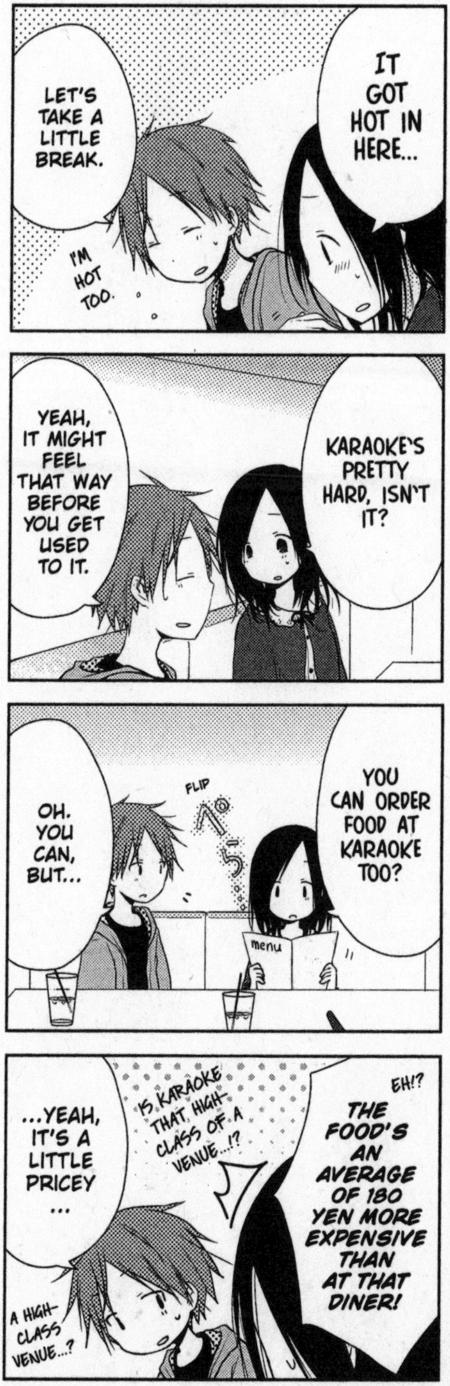
IT GOT HOT IN HERE...
LET'S TAKE A LITTLE BREAK.
I'M HOT TOO.
KARAOKE'S PRETTY HARD, ISN'T IT?
YEAH, IT MIGHT FEEL THAT WAY BEFORE YOU GET USED TO IT.
YOU CAN ORDER FOOD AT KARAOKE TOO?
FLIP
menu
OH. YOU CAN, BUT...
EH!?
THE FOOD'S AN AVERAGE OF 180 YEN MORE EXPENSIVE THAN AT THAT DINER!
IS KARAOKE THAT HIGH-CLASS OF A VENUE...!?
...YEAH, IT'S A LITTLE PRICEY ...
A HIGH-CLASS VENUE...?

## DEPARTMENT STORE

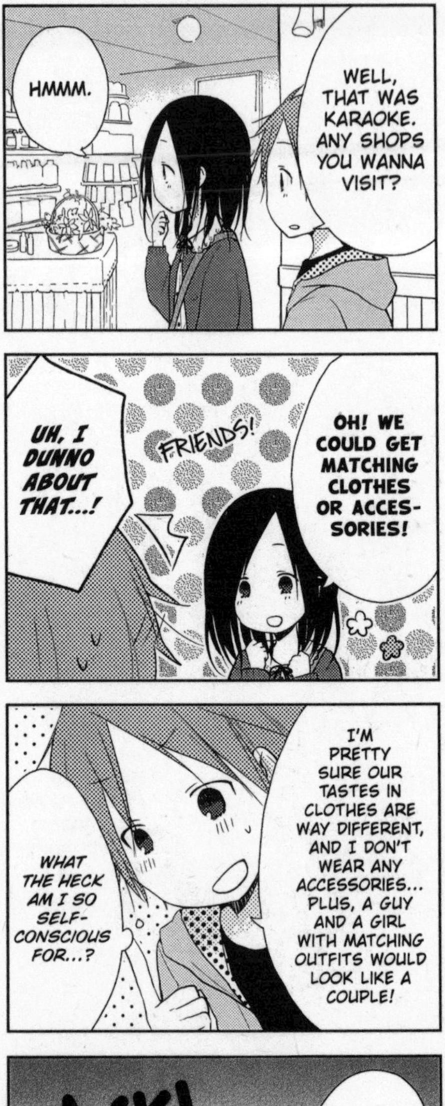
WELL, THAT WAS KARAOKE. ANY SHOPS YOU WANNA VISIT?
HMMM.
OH! WE COULD GET MATCHING CLOTHES OR ACCES-SORIES!
FRIENDS!
UH, I DUNNO ABOUT THAT...!
I'M PRETTY SURE OUR TASTES IN CLOTHES ARE WAY DIFFERENT, AND I DON'T WEAR ANY ACCESSORIES... PLUS, A GUY AND A GIRL WITH MATCHING OUTFITS WOULD LOOK LIKE A COUPLE!
WHAT THE HECK AM I SO SELF-CONSCIOUS FOR...?
...OH, I SEE...
DROOP
FRIENDS...
ACK!

## TABOO SUBJECT?

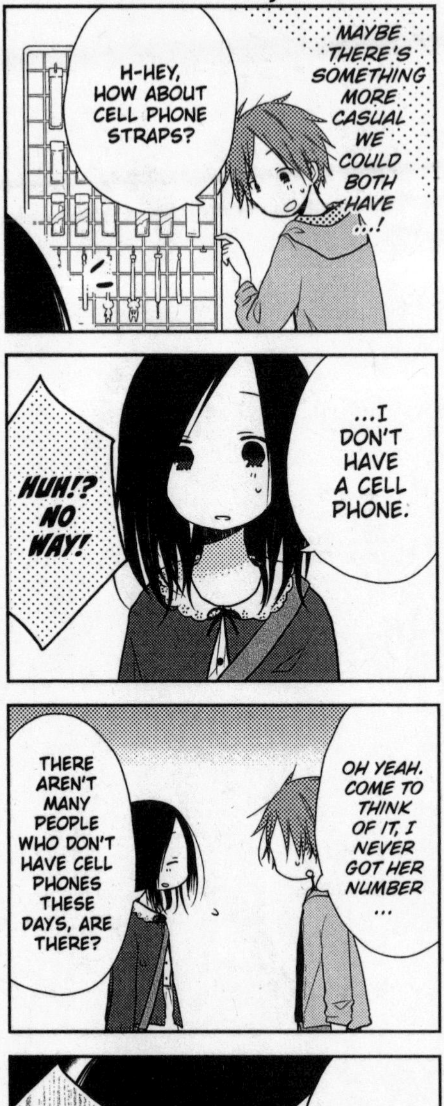
MAYBE THERE'S SOMETHING MORE CASUAL WE COULD BOTH HAVE...!
H-HEY, HOW ABOUT CELL PHONE STRAPS?
...I DON'T HAVE A CELL PHONE.
HUH!? NO WAY!
OH YEAH. COME TO THINK OF IT, I NEVER GOT HER NUMBER...
THERE AREN'T MANY PEOPLE WHO DON'T HAVE CELL PHONES THESE DAYS, ARE THERE?
BUT SINCE I DON'T HAVE ANY FRIENDS, I DON'T REALLY NEED ONE...
PLUS, I GO STRAIGHT HOME, SO...
SORRY! FORGET I BROUGHT IT UP!

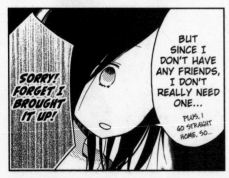

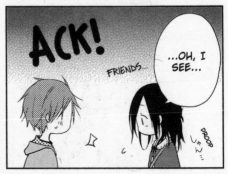

## THIS COULD WORK

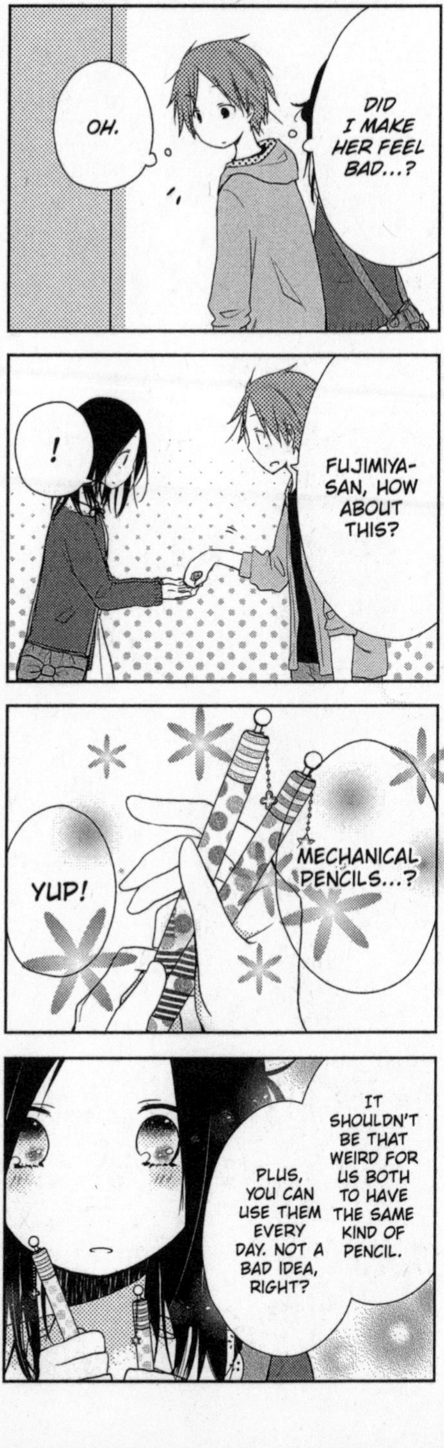
DID I MAKE HER FEEL BAD...?
OH.
FUJIMIYA-SAN, HOW ABOUT THIS?
!
MECHANICAL PENCILS...?
YUP!
IT SHOULDN'T BE THAT WEIRD FOR US BOTH TO HAVE THE SAME KIND OF PENCIL.
PLUS, YOU CAN USE THEM EVERY DAY. NOT A BAD IDEA, RIGHT?

## MATCHING

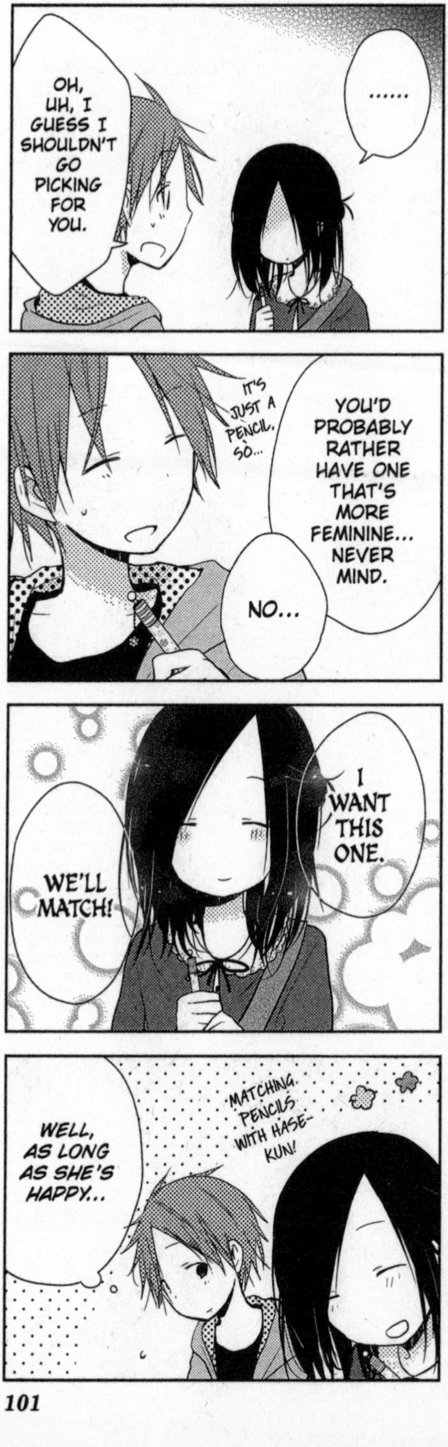
......
OH, UH, I GUESS I SHOULDN'T GO PICKING FOR YOU.
IT'S JUST A PENCIL, SO...
YOU'D PROBABLY RATHER HAVE ONE THAT'S MORE FEMININE... NEVER MIND.
NO...
I WANT THIS ONE.
WE'LL MATCH!
MATCHING PENCILS WITH HASE-KUN!
WELL, AS LONG AS SHE'S HAPPY...

## DEPARTMENT STORE BASEMENT

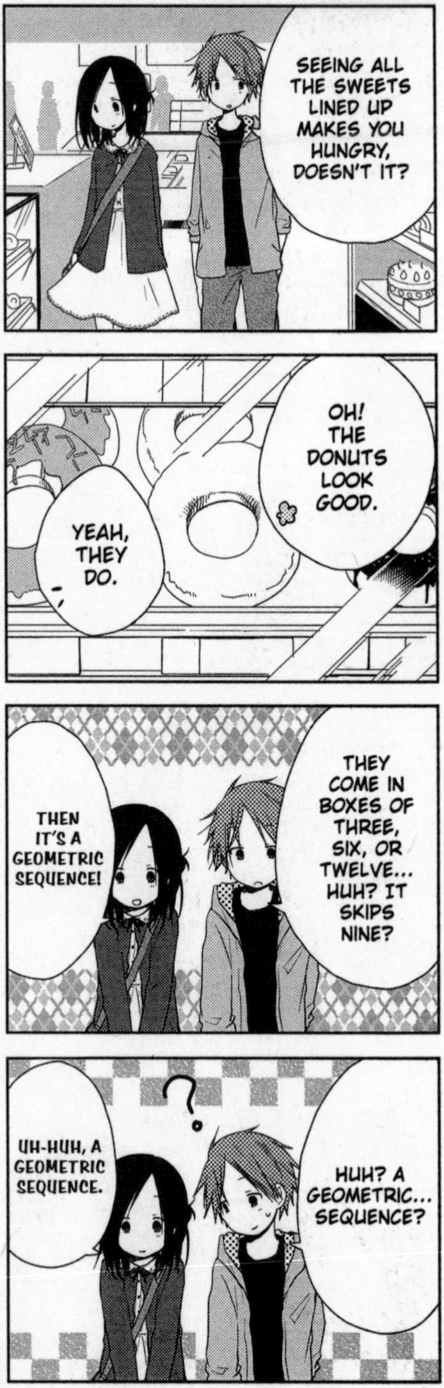
SEEING ALL THE SWEETS LINED UP MAKES YOU HUNGRY, DOESN'T IT?
OH! THE DONUTS LOOK GOOD.
YEAH, THEY DO.
THEY COME IN BOXES OF THREE, SIX, OR TWELVE... HUH? IT SKIPS NINE?
THEN IT'S A GEOMETRIC SEQUENCE!
HUH? A GEOMETRIC... SEQUENCE?
UH-HUH, A GEOMETRIC SEQUENCE.

## STUDY SESSION

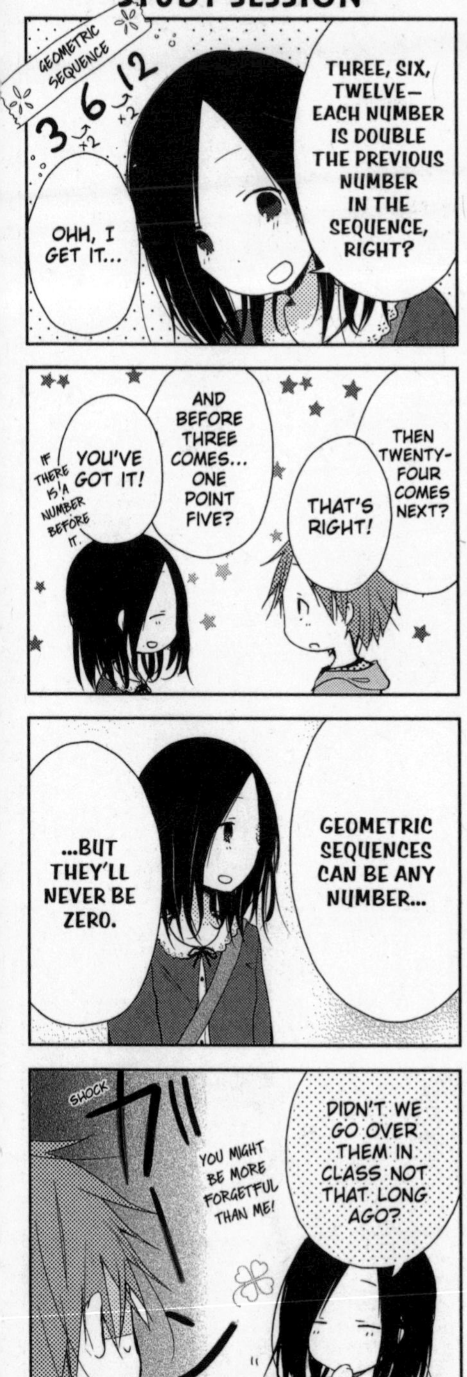
GEOMETRIC SEQUENCE
3 ×2 6 ×2 12
THREE, SIX, TWELVE— EACH NUMBER IS DOUBLE THE PREVIOUS NUMBER IN THE SEQUENCE, RIGHT?
OHH, I GET IT...
THEN TWENTY-FOUR COMES NEXT?
THAT'S RIGHT!
AND BEFORE THREE COMES... ONE POINT FIVE?
YOU'VE GOT IT!
IF THERE IS A NUMBER BEFORE IT.
GEOMETRIC SEQUENCES CAN BE ANY NUMBER...
...BUT THEY'LL NEVER BE ZERO.
DIDN'T WE GO OVER THEM IN CLASS NOT THAT LONG AGO?
YOU MIGHT BE MORE FORGETFUL THAN ME!
SHOCK

## BEFORE WE GO HOME

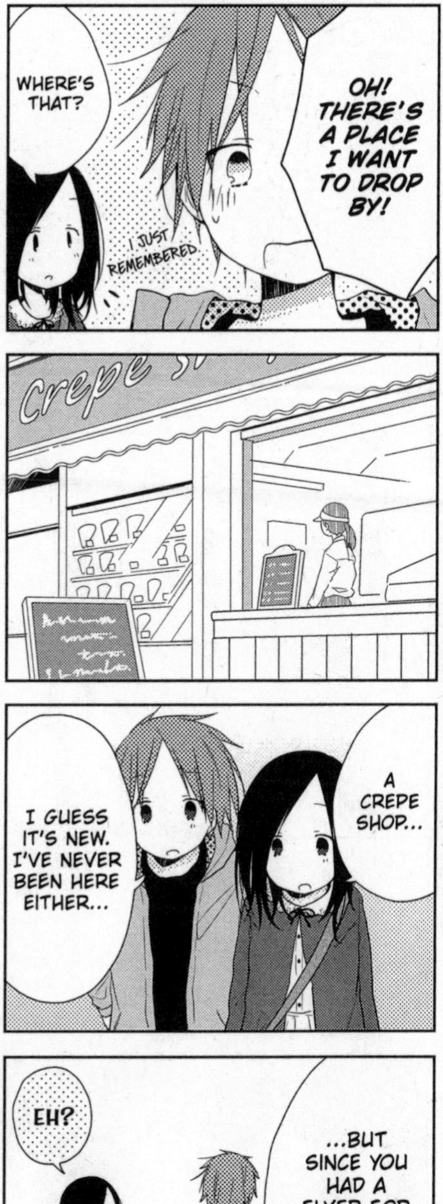
OH! THERE'S A PLACE I WANT TO DROP BY!
I JUST REMEMBERED.
WHERE'S THAT?
Crepe
A CREPE SHOP...
I GUESS IT'S NEW. I'VE NEVER BEEN HERE EITHER...
...BUT SINCE YOU HAD A FLYER FOR IT BEFORE, I KNEW WE HAD TO COME.
EH?

## DETAILED MEMORIES

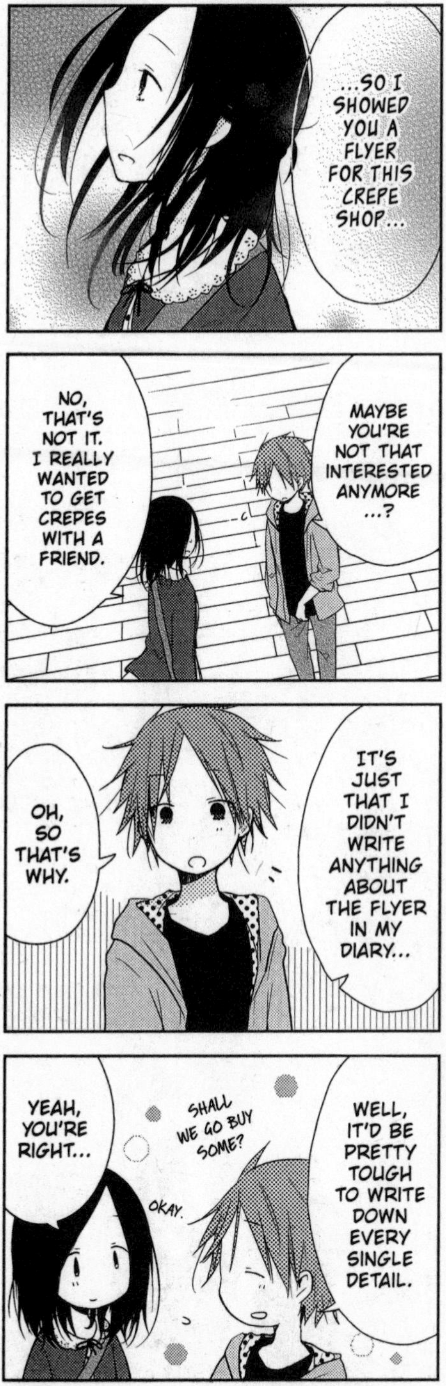
...SO I SHOWED YOU A FLYER FOR THIS CREPE SHOP...
MAYBE YOU'RE NOT THAT INTERESTED ANYMORE ...?
NO, THAT'S NOT IT. I REALLY WANTED TO GET CREPES WITH A FRIEND.
IT'S JUST THAT I DIDN'T WRITE ANYTHING ABOUT THE FLYER IN MY DIARY...
OH, SO THAT'S WHY.
WELL, IT'D BE PRETTY TOUGH TO WRITE DOWN EVERY SINGLE DETAIL.
SHALL WE GO BUY SOME?
OKAY.
YEAH, YOU'RE RIGHT...

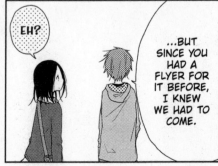

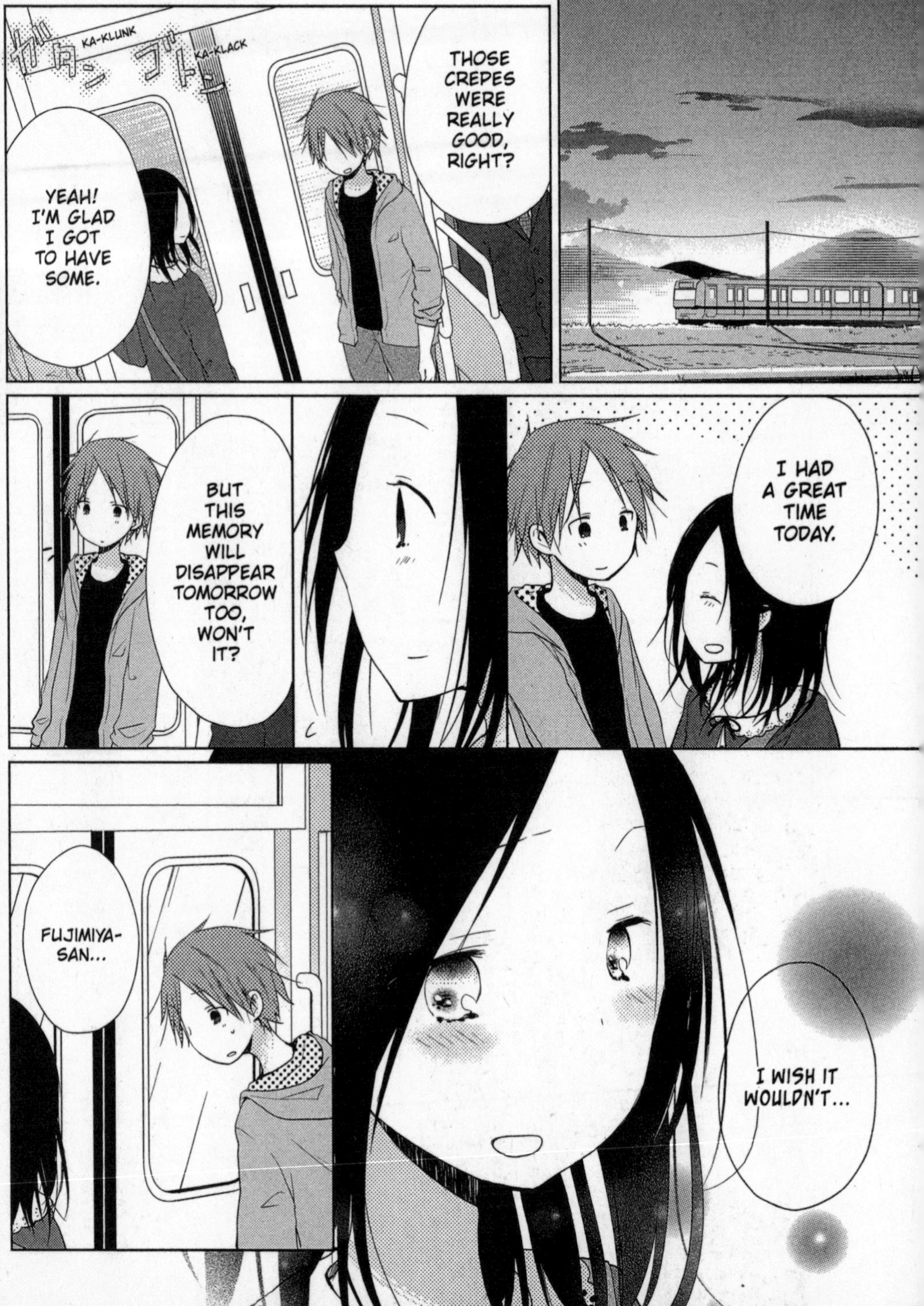
THOSE CREPES WERE REALLY GOOD, RIGHT?
KA-KLACK
KA-KLUNK
YEAH! I'M GLAD I GOT TO HAVE SOME.
I HAD A GREAT TIME TODAY.
BUT THIS MEMORY WILL DISAPPEAR TOMORROW TOO, WON'T IT?
I WISH IT WOULDN'T...
FUJIMIYA-SAN...

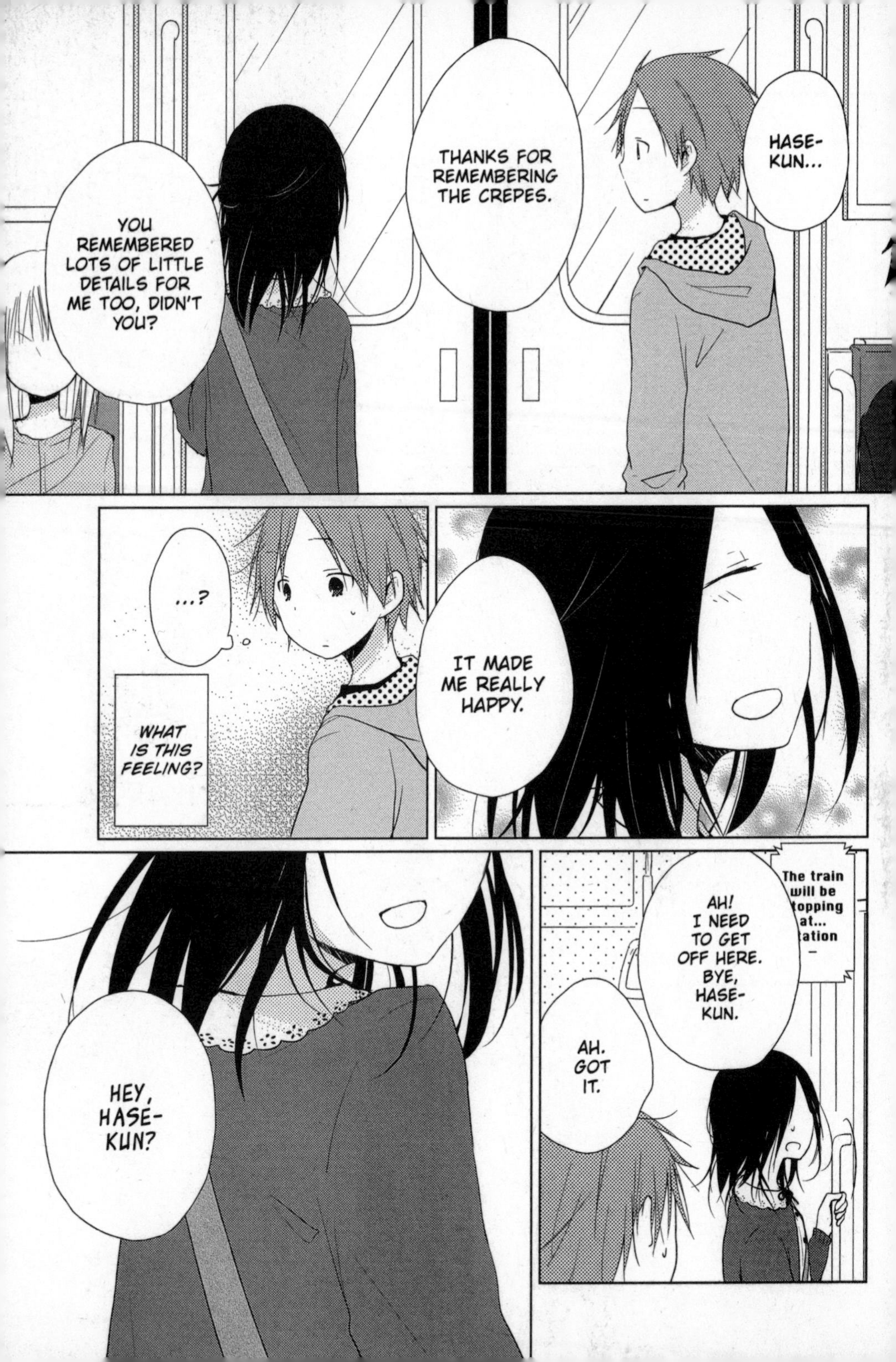
HASE-KUN...
THANKS FOR REMEMBERING THE CREPES.
YOU REMEMBERED LOTS OF LITTLE DETAILS FOR ME TOO, DIDN'T YOU?
IT MADE ME REALLY HAPPY.
...?
WHAT IS THIS FEELING?
The train will be topping at... tation —
AH! I NEED TO GET OFF HERE. BYE, HASE-KUN.
AH. GOT IT.
HEY, HASE-KUN?

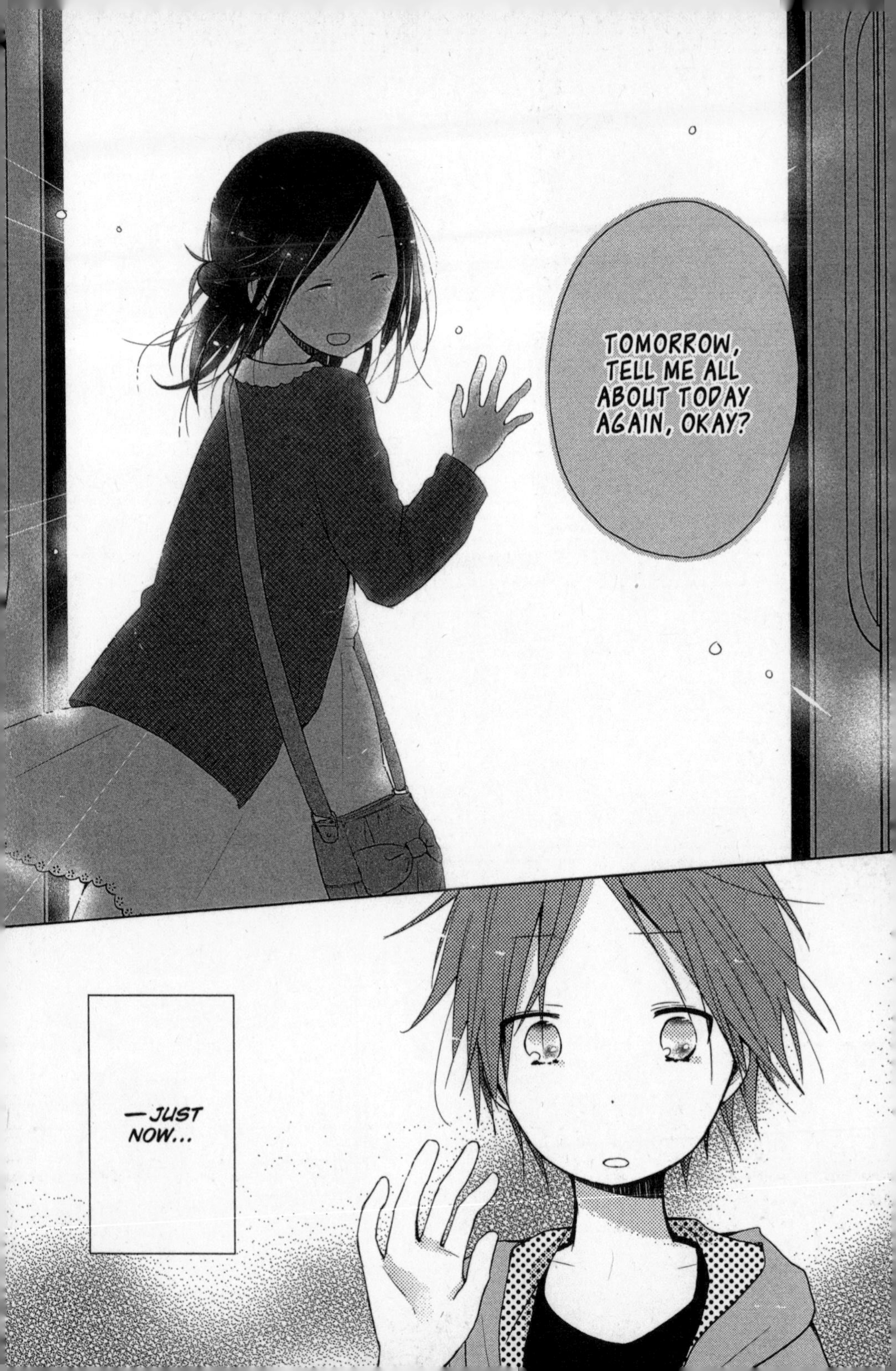
TOMORROW, TELL ME ALL ABOUT TODAY AGAIN, OKAY?
—JUST NOW...

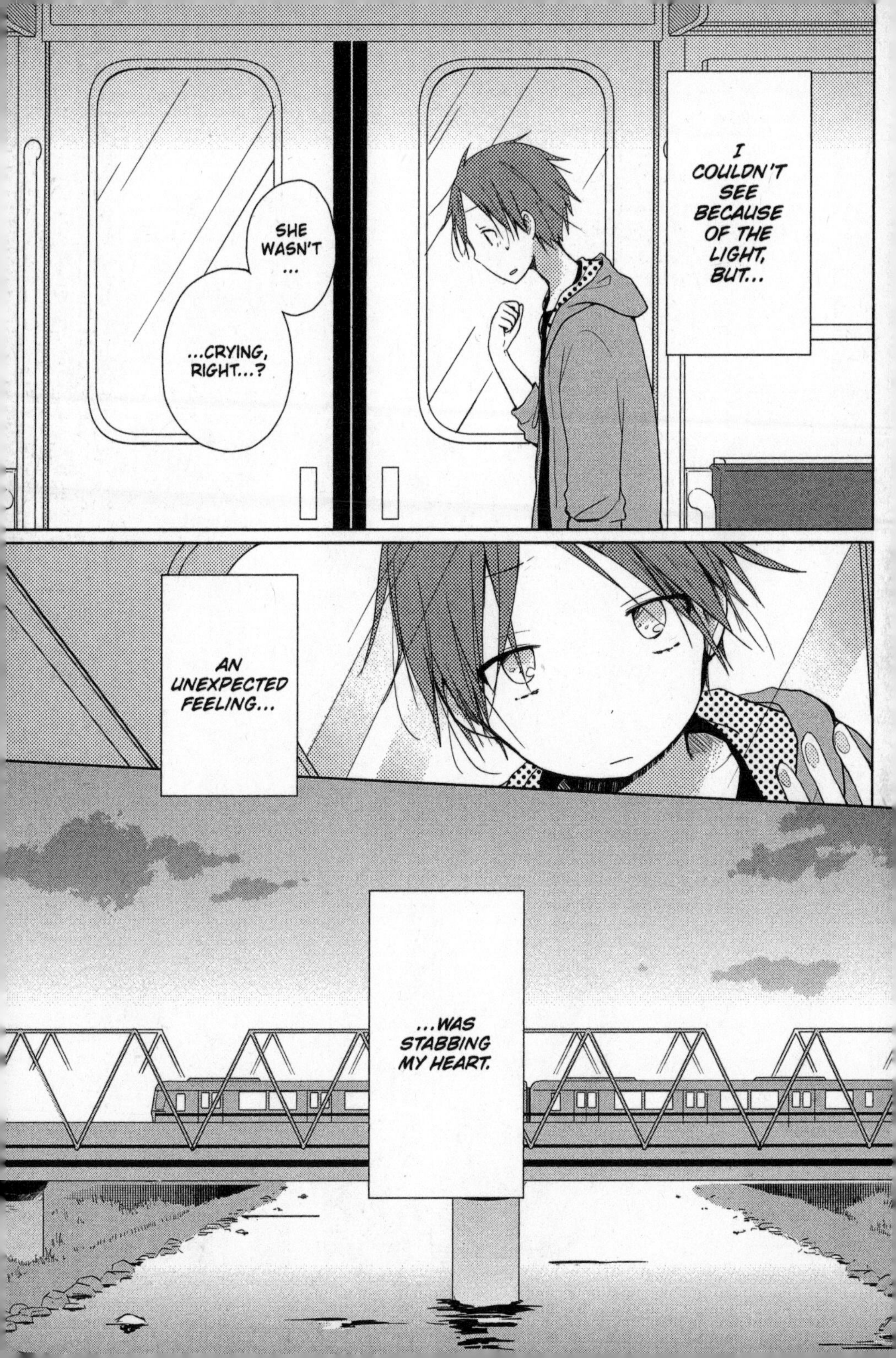
I COULDN'T SEE BECAUSE OF THE LIGHT, BUT...
SHE WASN'T ...
...CRYING, RIGHT...?
AN UNEXPECTED FEELING...
...WAS STABBING MY HEART.

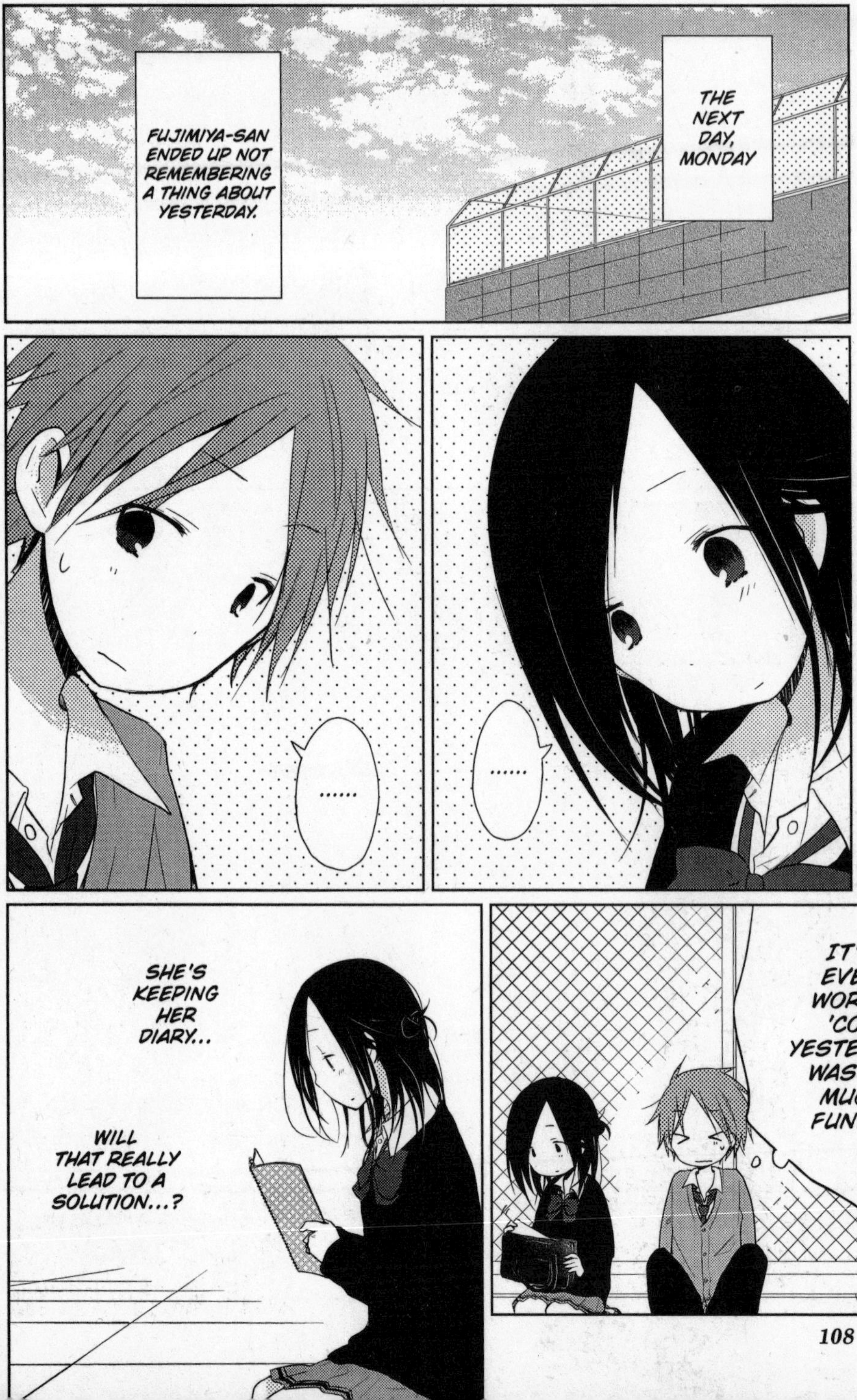
THE NEXT DAY, MONDAY
FUJIMIYA-SAN ENDED UP NOT REMEMBERING A THING ABOUT YESTERDAY.
......
......
IT'S EVEN WORSE 'COS YESTERDAY WAS SO MUCH FUN...!
SHE'S KEEPING HER DIARY...
WILL THAT REALLY LEAD TO A SOLUTION...?

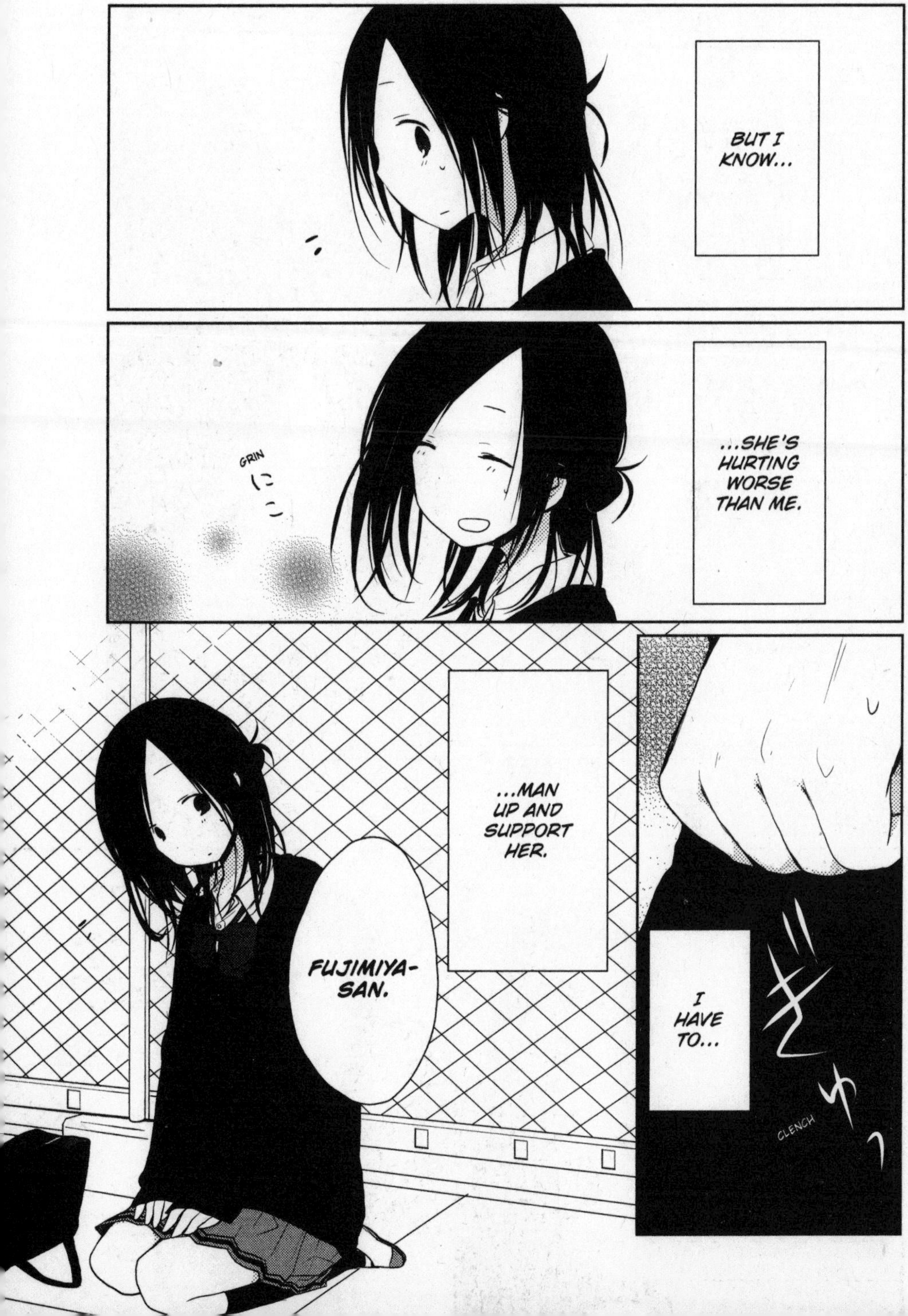
BUT I KNOW...
...SHE'S HURTING WORSE THAN ME.
GRIN
I HAVE TO...
CLENCH
...MAN UP AND SUPPORT HER.
FUJIMIYA-SAN.

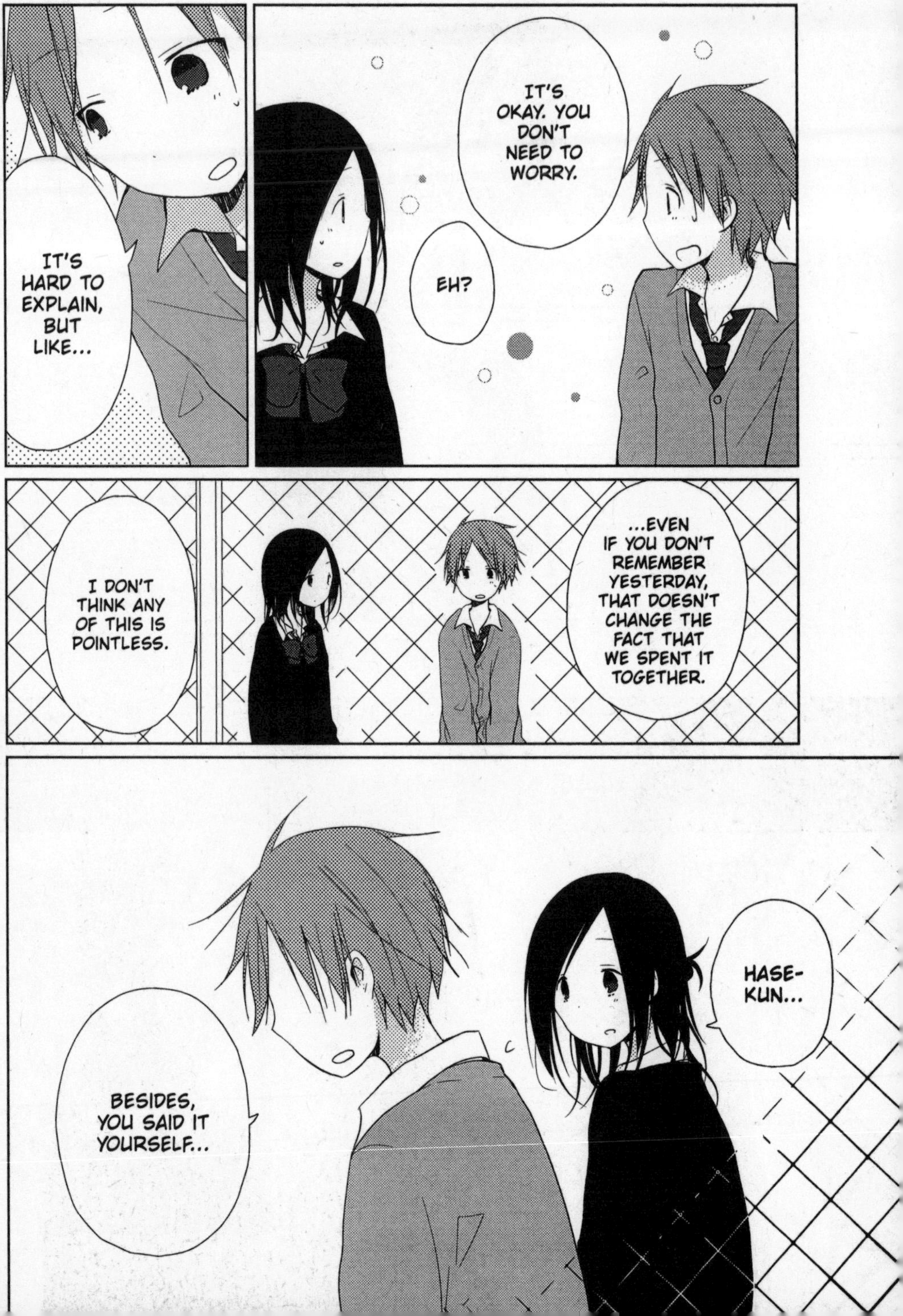
IT'S OKAY. YOU DON'T NEED TO WORRY.
EH?
IT'S HARD TO EXPLAIN, BUT LIKE...
...EVEN IF YOU DON'T REMEMBER YESTERDAY, THAT DOESN'T CHANGE THE FACT THAT WE SPENT IT TOGETHER.
I DON'T THINK ANY OF THIS IS POINTLESS.
HASE-KUN...
BESIDES, YOU SAID IT YOURSELF...

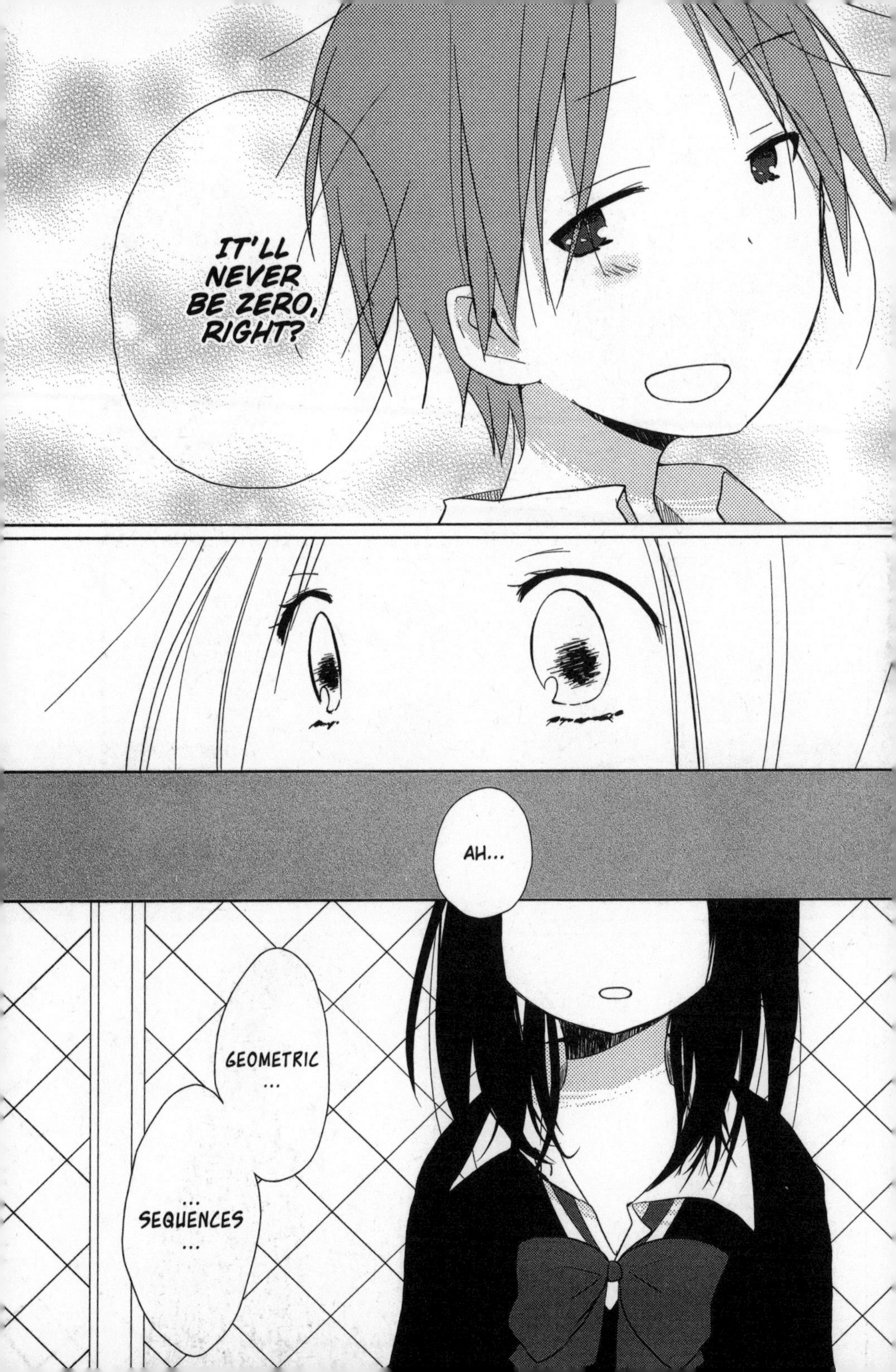
IT'LL NEVER BE ZERO, RIGHT?
AH...
GEOMETRIC ...
... SEQUENCES ...

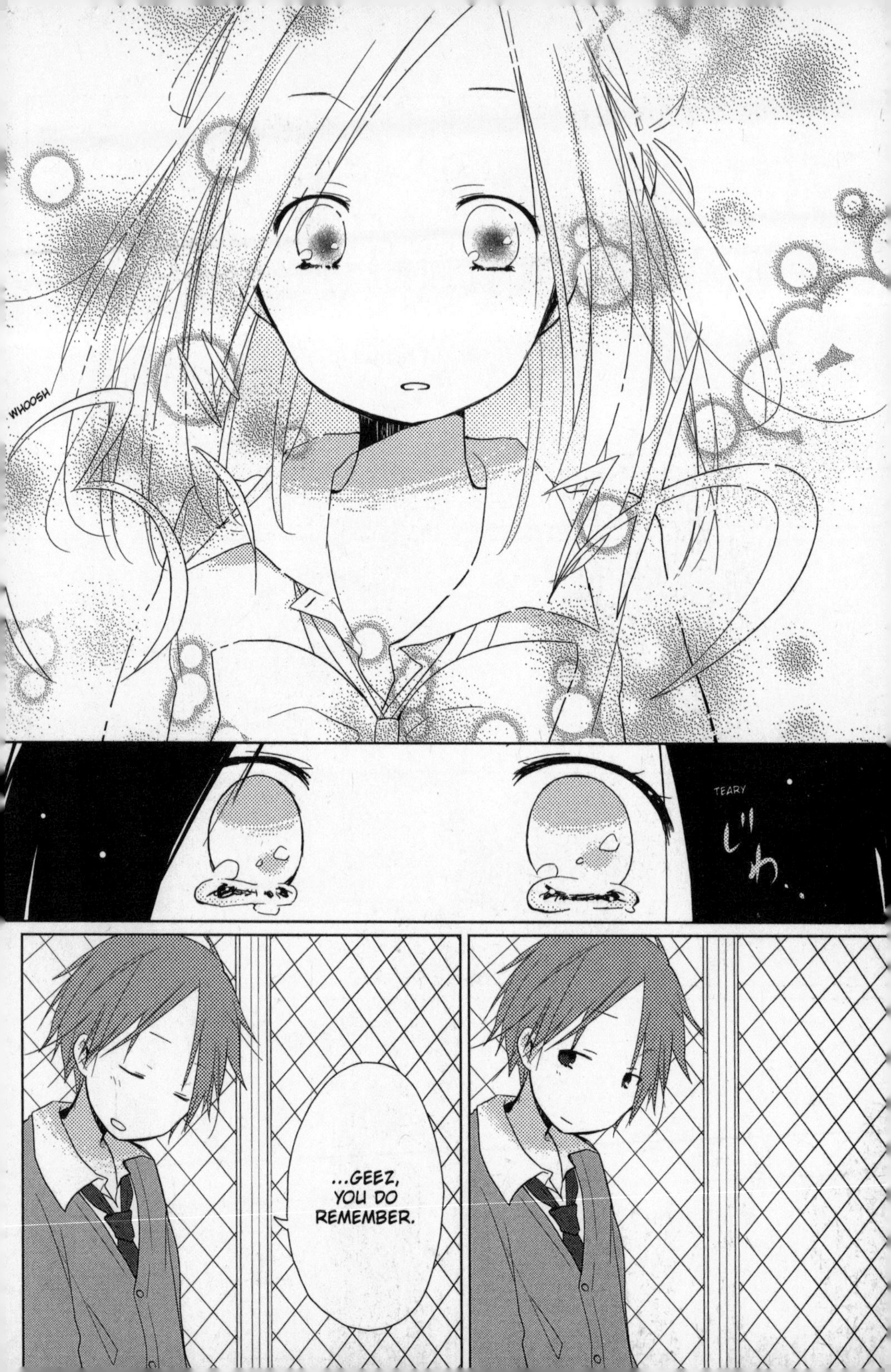
WHOOSH
TEARY
じわ..
...GEEZ, YOU DO REMEMBER.

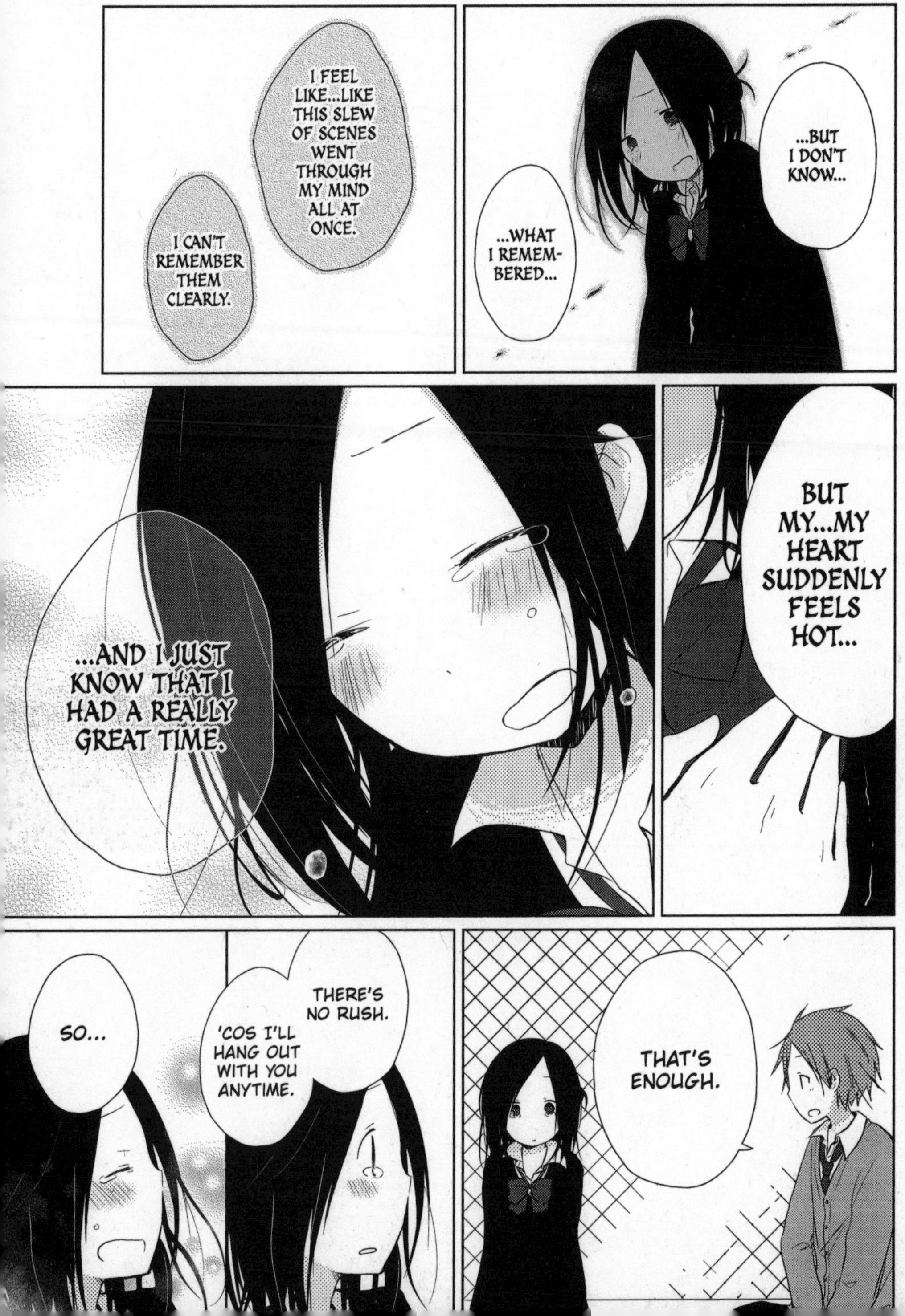
...BUT I DON'T KNOW...
...WHAT I REMEMBERED...
I FEEL LIKE...LIKE THIS SLEW OF SCENES WENT THROUGH MY MIND ALL AT ONCE.
I CAN'T REMEMBER THEM CLEARLY.
BUT MY...MY HEART SUDDENLY FEELS HOT...
...AND I JUST KNOW THAT I HAD A REALLY GREAT TIME.
THAT'S ENOUGH.
THERE'S NO RUSH.
'COS I'LL HANG OUT WITH YOU ANYTIME.
SO...

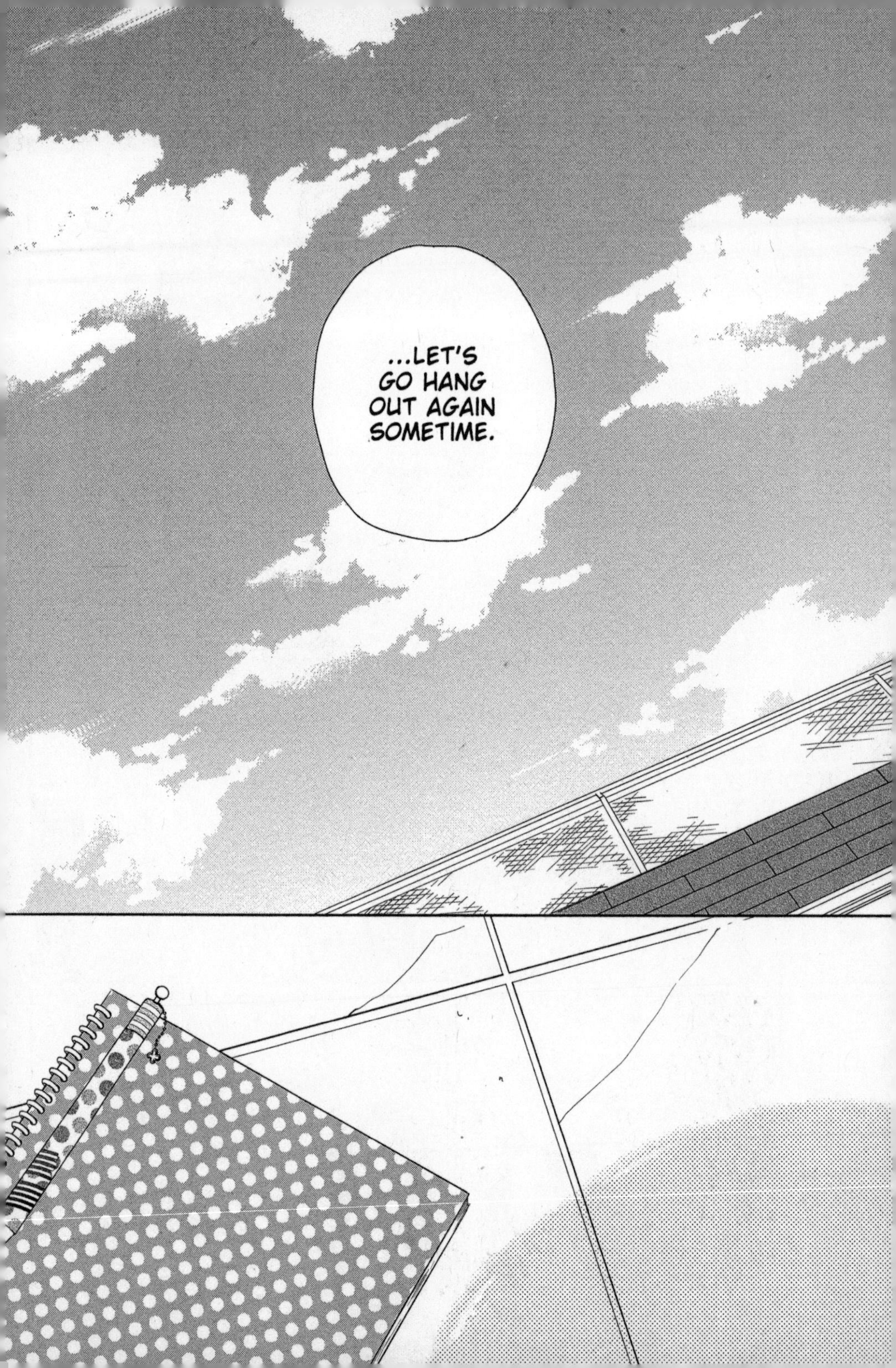
...LET'S GO HANG OUT AGAIN SOMETIME.

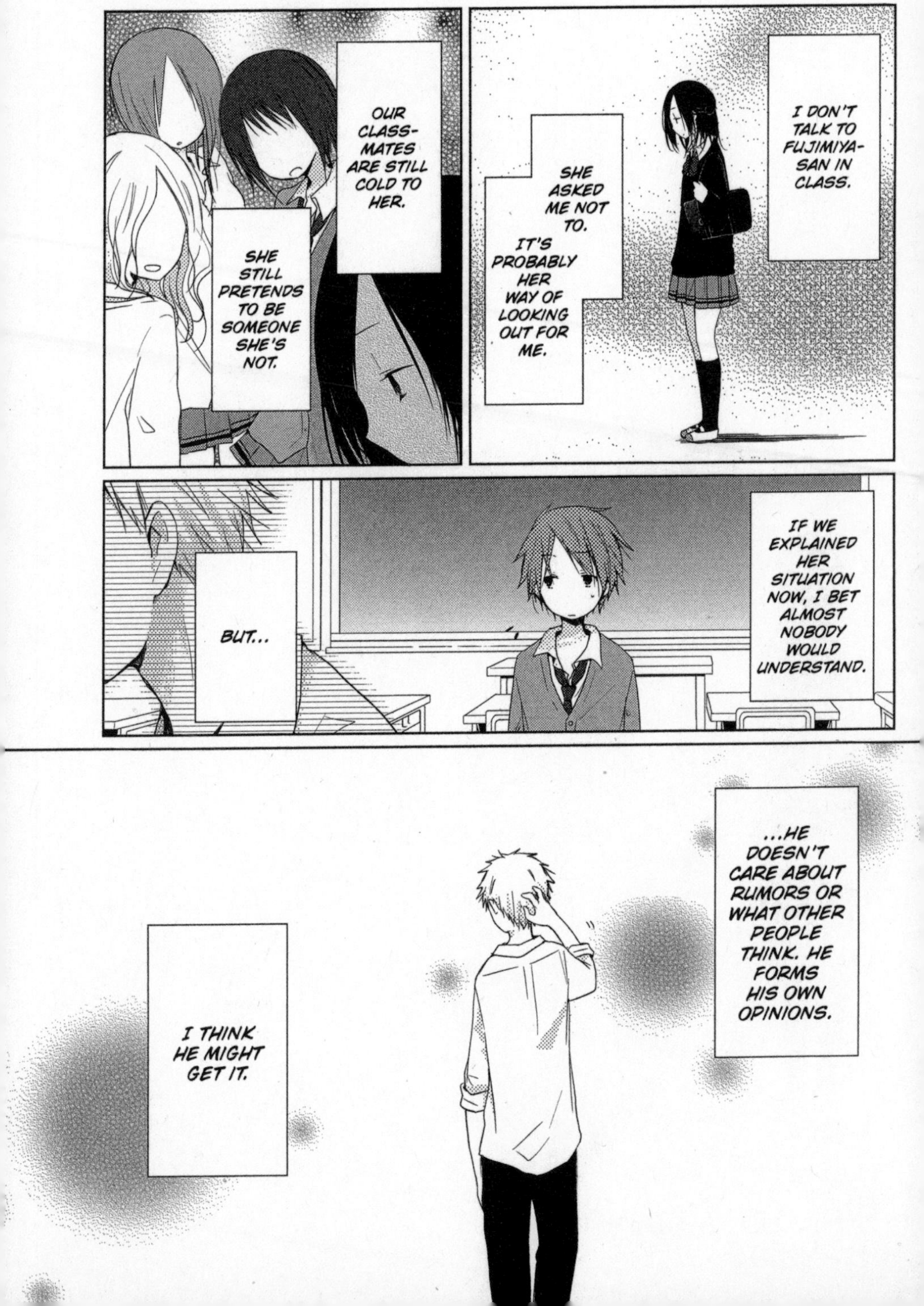
I DON'T TALK TO FUJIMIYA-SAN IN CLASS.
SHE ASKED ME NOT TO.
IT'S PROBABLY HER WAY OF LOOKING OUT FOR ME.
OUR CLASSMATES ARE STILL COLD TO HER.
SHE STILL PRETENDS TO BE SOMEONE SHE'S NOT.
IF WE EXPLAINED HER SITUATION NOW, I BET ALMOST NOBODY WOULD UNDERSTAND.
BUT...
...HE DOESN'T CARE ABOUT RUMORS OR WHAT OTHER PEOPLE THINK. HE FORMS HIS OWN OPINIONS.
I THINK HE MIGHT GET IT.

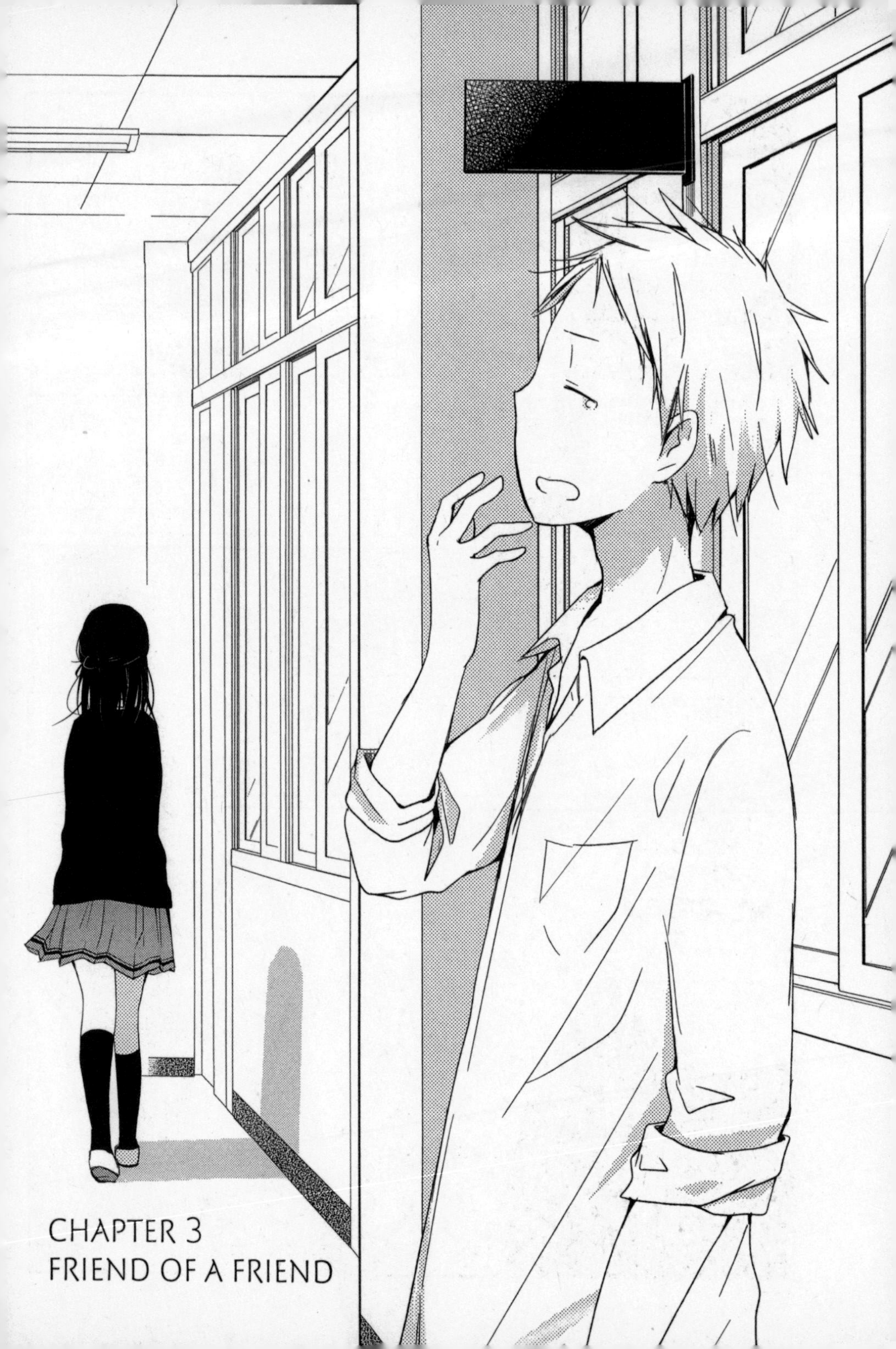

# CHAPTER 3
# FRIEND OF A FRIEND

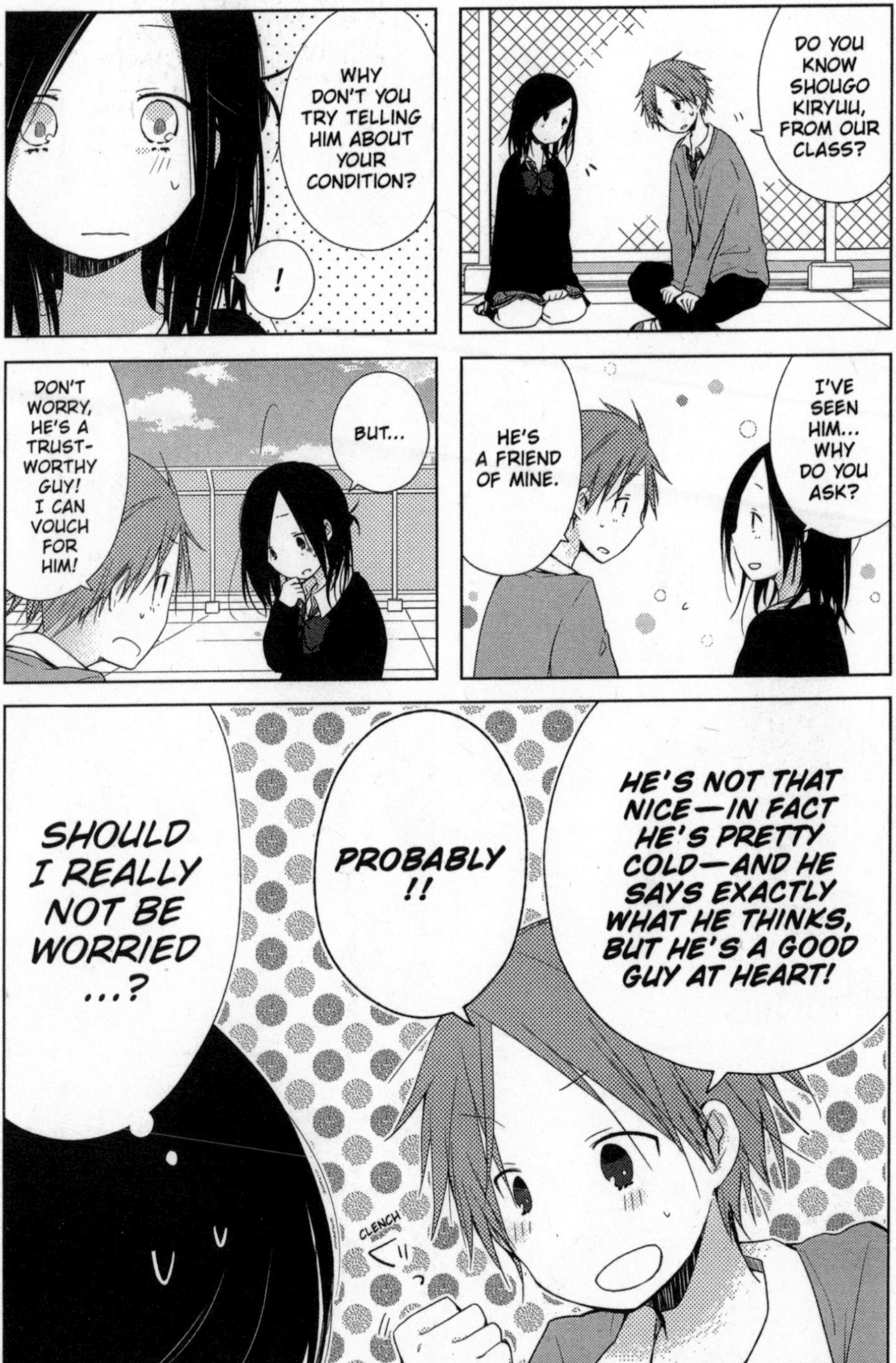
DO YOU KNOW SHOUGO KIRYUU, FROM OUR CLASS?
WHY DON'T YOU TRY TELLING HIM ABOUT YOUR CONDITION?
!
I'VE SEEN HIM... WHY DO YOU ASK?
HE'S A FRIEND OF MINE.
BUT...
DON'T WORRY, HE'S A TRUST-WORTHY GUY! I CAN VOUCH FOR HIM!
HE'S NOT THAT NICE—IN FACT HE'S PRETTY COLD—AND HE SAYS EXACTLY WHAT HE THINKS, BUT HE'S A GOOD GUY AT HEART!
PROBABLY !!
SHOULD I REALLY NOT BE WORRIED ...?
CLENCH

## FOR THE SAKE OF A SOLUTION

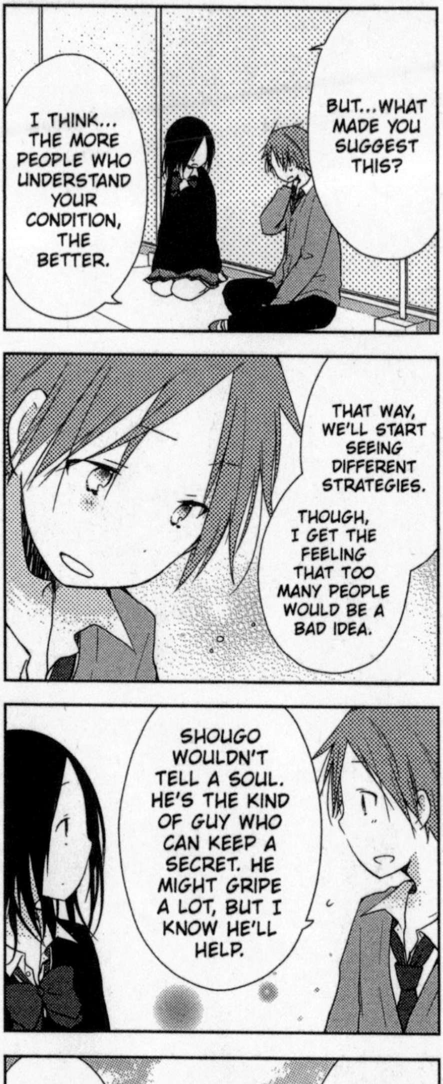
BUT...WHAT MADE YOU SUGGEST THIS?
I THINK... THE MORE PEOPLE WHO UNDERSTAND YOUR CONDITION, THE BETTER.
THAT WAY, WE'LL START SEEING DIFFERENT STRATEGIES.
THOUGH, I GET THE FEELING THAT TOO MANY PEOPLE WOULD BE A BAD IDEA.
SHOUGO WOULDN'T TELL A SOUL. HE'S THE KIND OF GUY WHO CAN KEEP A SECRET. HE MIGHT GRIPE A LOT, BUT I KNOW HE'LL HELP.
OH, I SEE! THEN IT MIGHT BE OKAY ...!
THOUGH, I'LL BE A LITTLE SAD THAT IT WON'T BE A SECRET ONLY I KNOW ANYMORE ...

## SENSING SOMETHING

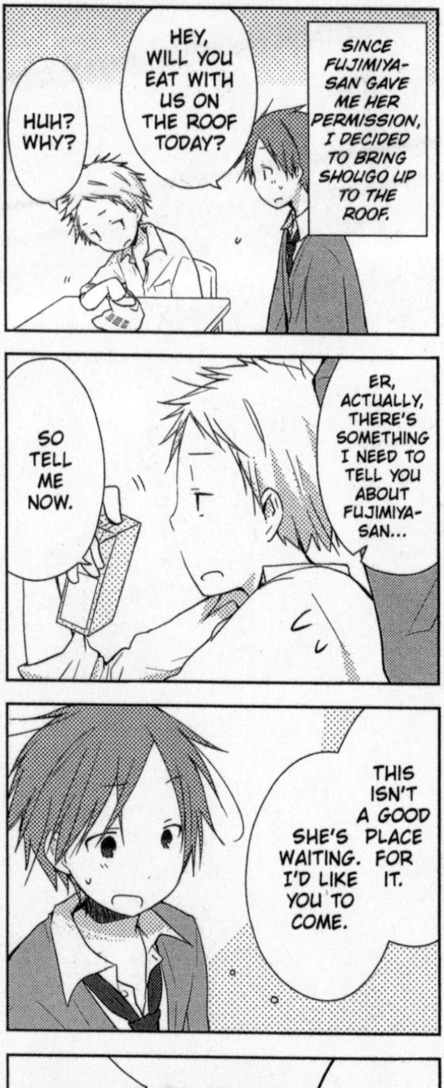
SINCE FUJIMIYA-SAN GAVE ME HER PERMISSION, I DECIDED TO BRING SHOUGO UP TO THE ROOF.
HEY, WILL YOU EAT WITH US ON THE ROOF TODAY?
HUH? WHY?
ER, ACTUALLY, THERE'S SOMETHING I NEED TO TELL YOU ABOUT FUJIMIYA-SAN...
SO TELL ME NOW.
THIS ISN'T A GOOD PLACE FOR IT.
SHE'S WAITING. I'D LIKE YOU TO COME.
THIS SOUNDS LIKE A HASSLE. I'LL PASS.
I KNEW YOU'D SAY THAT! PLEASE RECON-SIDER!
PAFF

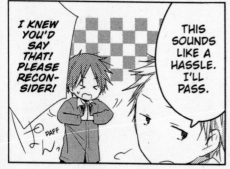

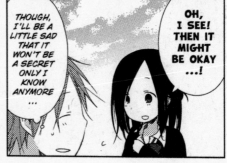

## HE'S THAT KIND OF GUY

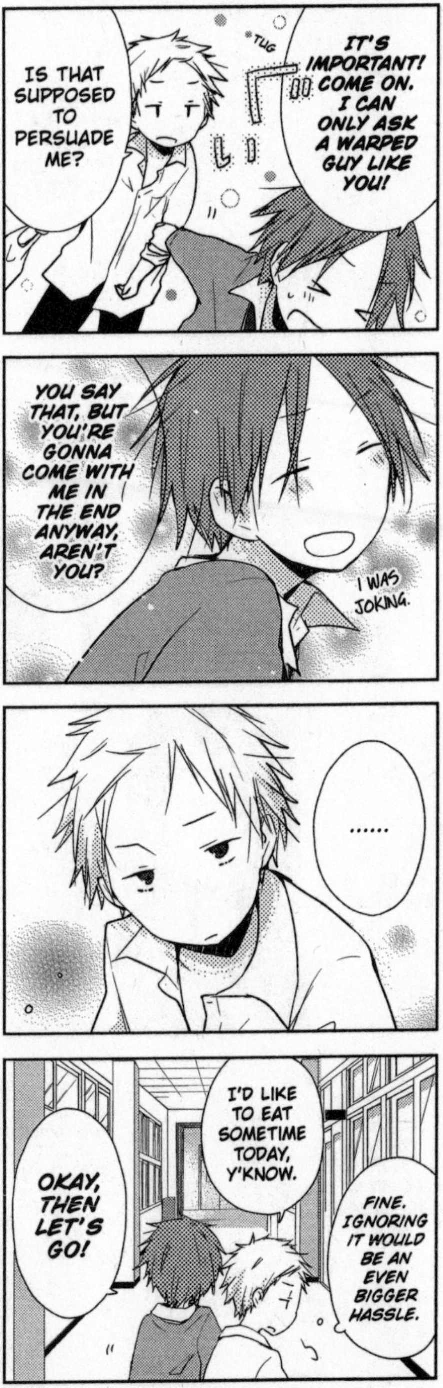
IT'S IMPORTANT! COME ON. I CAN ONLY ASK A WARPED GUY LIKE YOU!
TUG
IS THAT SUPPOSED TO PERSUADE ME?
YOU SAY THAT, BUT YOU'RE GONNA COME WITH ME IN THE END ANYWAY, AREN'T YOU?
I WAS JOKING.
......
I'D LIKE TO EAT SOMETIME TODAY, Y'KNOW.
FINE. IGNORING IT WOULD BE AN EVEN BIGGER HASSLE.
OKAY, THEN LET'S GO!

## SAYS WHAT HE THINKS

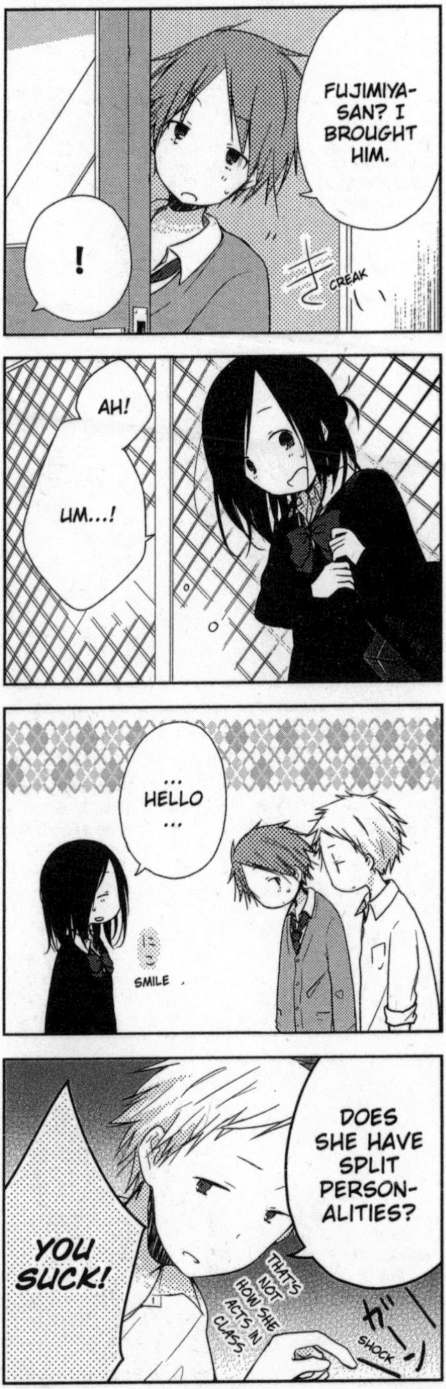
FUJIMIYA-SAN? I BROUGHT HIM.
CREAK
!
AH!
UM...!
... HELLO ...
SMILE
DOES SHE HAVE SPLIT PERSONALITIES?
THAT'S NOT HOW SHE ACTS IN CLASS
SHOCK
YOU SUCK!

## TOO HONEST

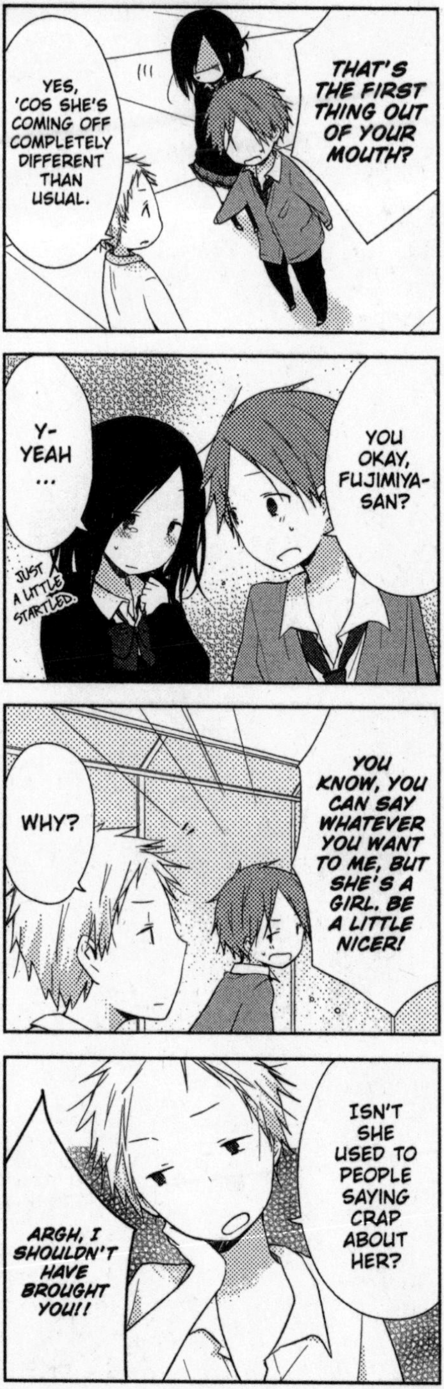
THAT'S THE FIRST THING OUT OF YOUR MOUTH?
YES, 'COS SHE'S COMING OFF COMPLETELY DIFFERENT THAN USUAL.
YOU OKAY, FUJIMIYA-SAN?
Y-YEAH...
JUST A LITTLE STARTLED.
YOU KNOW, YOU CAN SAY WHATEVER YOU WANT TO ME, BUT SHE'S A GIRL. BE A LITTLE NICER!
WHY?
ISN'T SHE USED TO PEOPLE SAYING CRAP ABOUT HER?
ARGH, I SHOULDN'T HAVE BROUGHT YOU!!

## FRESH START

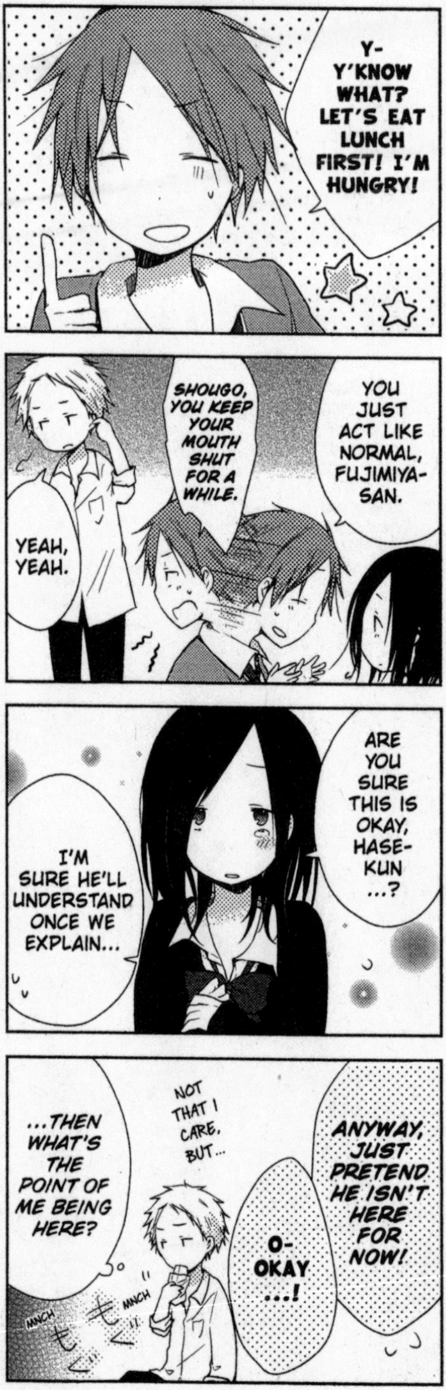
Y-Y'KNOW WHAT? LET'S EAT LUNCH FIRST! I'M HUNGRY!
YOU JUST ACT LIKE NORMAL, FUJIMIYA-SAN.
SHOUGO, YOU KEEP YOUR MOUTH SHUT FOR A WHILE.
YEAH, YEAH.
ARE YOU SURE THIS IS OKAY, HASE-KUN...?
I'M SURE HE'LL UNDERSTAND ONCE WE EXPLAIN...
ANYWAY, JUST PRETEND HE ISN'T HERE FOR NOW!
NOT THAT I CARE, BUT...
O-OKAY...!
...THEN WHAT'S THE POINT OF ME BEING HERE?
MNCH
MNCH

## SEEING FLOWERS

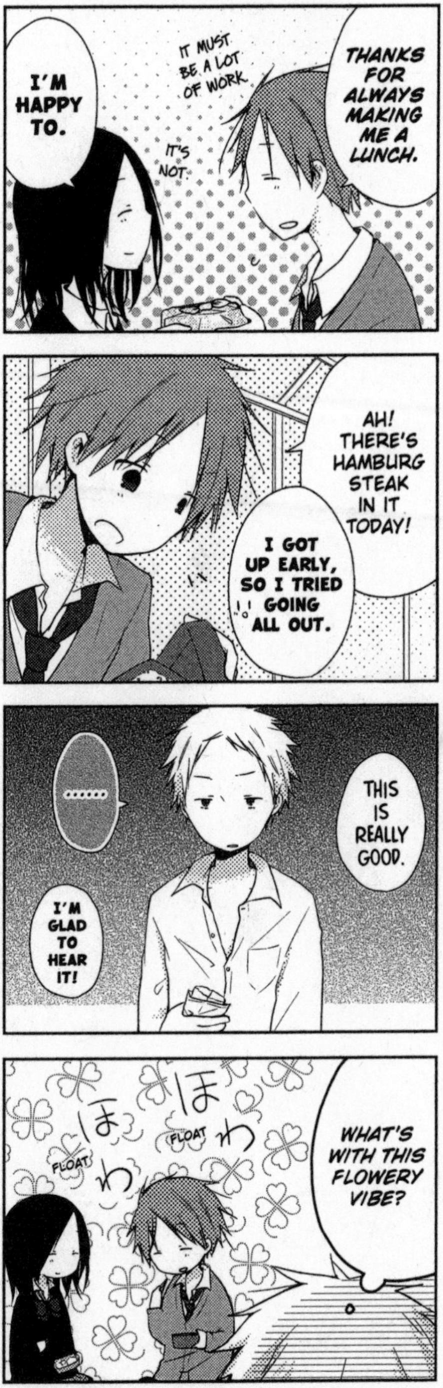
THANKS FOR ALWAYS MAKING ME A LUNCH.
IT MUST BE A LOT OF WORK.
IT'S NOT.
I'M HAPPY TO.
AH! THERE'S HAMBURG STEAK IN IT TODAY!
I GOT UP EARLY, SO I TRIED GOING ALL OUT.
THIS IS REALLY GOOD.
I'M GLAD TO HEAR IT!
......
WHAT'S WITH THIS FLOWERY VIBE?
ほわ
FLOAT
ほわ
FLOAT

## DON'T MENTION IT

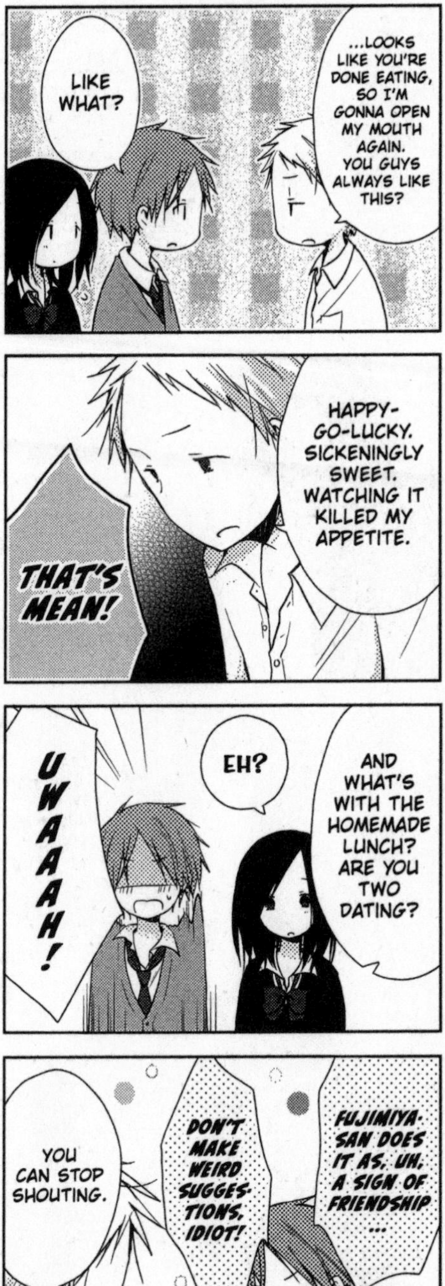
...LOOKS LIKE YOU'RE DONE EATING, SO I'M GONNA OPEN MY MOUTH AGAIN. YOU GUYS ALWAYS LIKE THIS?
LIKE WHAT?
HAPPY-GO-LUCKY. SICKENINGLY SWEET. WATCHING IT KILLED MY APPETITE.
THAT'S MEAN!
AND WHAT'S WITH THE HOMEMADE LUNCH? ARE YOU TWO DATING?
EH?
UWAAAAH!
FUJIMIYA-SAN DOES IT AS, UH, A SIGN OF FRIENDSHIP...
DON'T MAKE WEIRD SUGGESTIONS, IDIOT!
YOU CAN STOP SHOUTING.

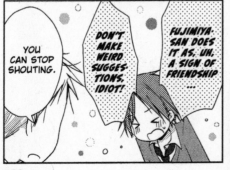

THE MAIN TOPIC

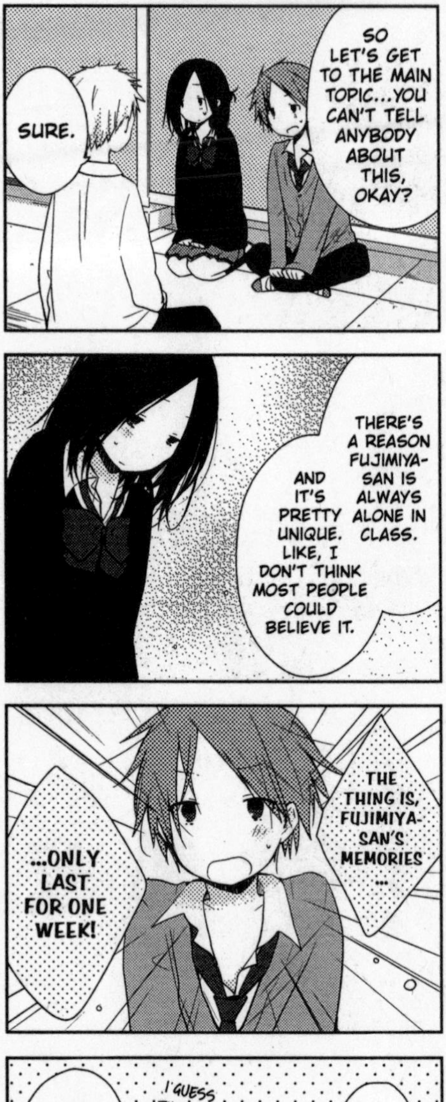
SO LET'S GET TO THE MAIN TOPIC...YOU CAN'T TELL ANYBODY ABOUT THIS, OKAY?
SURE.
THERE'S A REASON FUJIMIYA-SAN IS ALWAYS ALONE IN CLASS.
AND IT'S PRETTY UNIQUE. LIKE, I DON'T THINK MOST PEOPLE COULD BELIEVE IT.
THE THING IS, FUJIMIYA-SAN'S MEMORIES...
...ONLY LAST FOR ONE WEEK!
......?
I GUESS THAT'S A NORMAL REACTION.
UH, LET ME EXPLAIN THE FINER DETAILS.

RESULT OF EXPLAINING

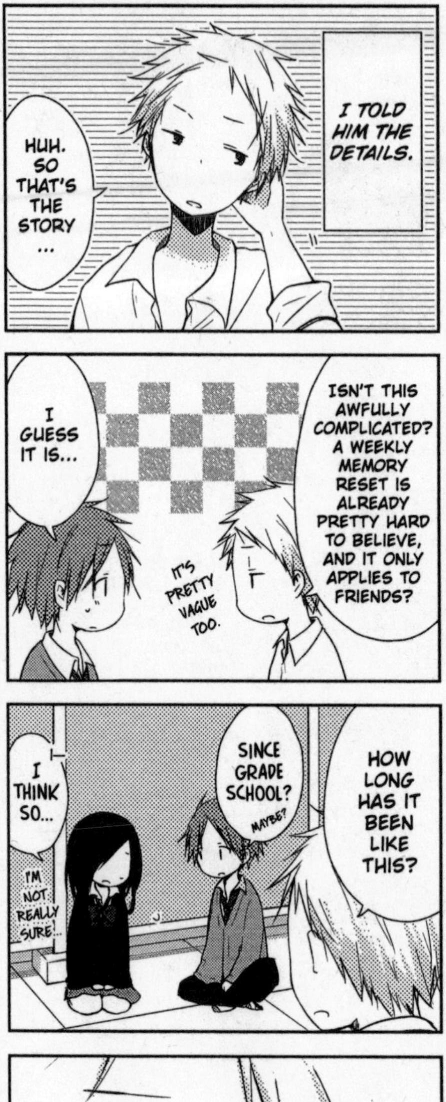
I TOLD HIM THE DETAILS.
HUH. SO THAT'S THE STORY...
ISN'T THIS AWFULLY COMPLICATED? A WEEKLY MEMORY RESET IS ALREADY PRETTY HARD TO BELIEVE, AND IT ONLY APPLIES TO FRIENDS?
IT'S PRETTY VAGUE TOO.
I GUESS IT IS...
HOW LONG HAS IT BEEN LIKE THIS?
SINCE GRADE SCHOOL?
MAYBE?
I THINK SO...
I'M NOT REALLY SURE!...
...OH, REALLY...

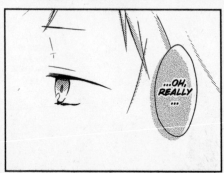

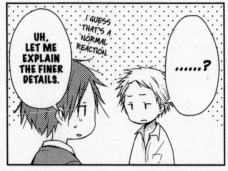

## KIRYUU'S RUNDOWN

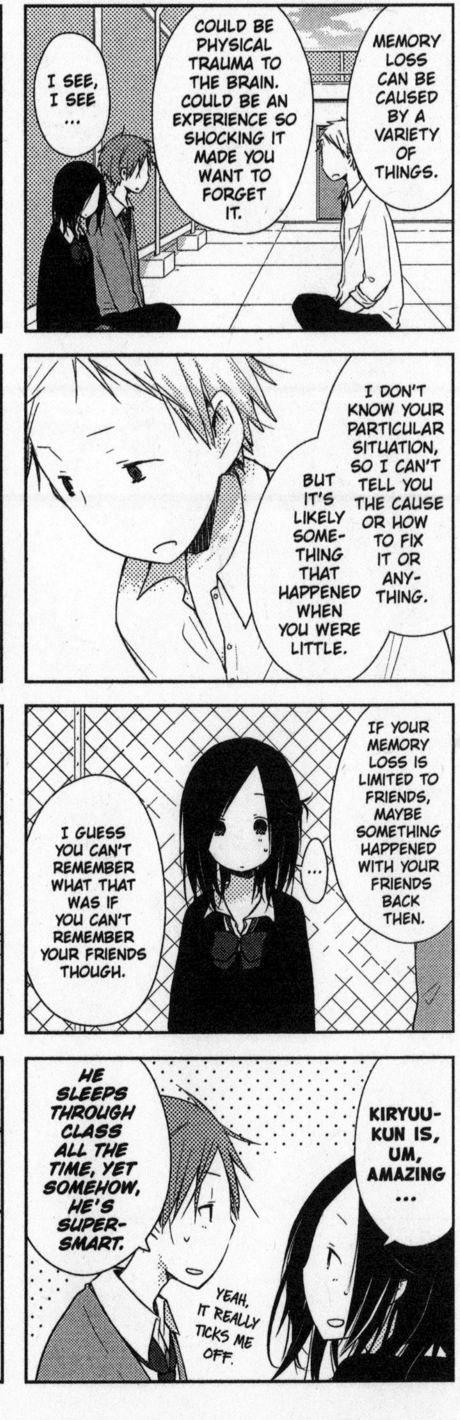
MEMORY LOSS CAN BE CAUSED BY A VARIETY OF THINGS.
COULD BE PHYSICAL TRAUMA TO THE BRAIN. COULD BE AN EXPERIENCE SO SHOCKING IT MADE YOU WANT TO FORGET IT.
I SEE, I SEE ...
I DON'T KNOW YOUR PARTICULAR SITUATION, SO I CAN'T TELL YOU THE CAUSE OR HOW TO FIX IT OR ANY-THING.
BUT IT'S LIKELY SOME-THING THAT HAPPENED WHEN YOU WERE LITTLE.
IF YOUR MEMORY LOSS IS LIMITED TO FRIENDS, MAYBE SOMETHING HAPPENED WITH YOUR FRIENDS BACK THEN.
...
I GUESS YOU CAN'T REMEMBER WHAT THAT WAS IF YOU CAN'T REMEMBER YOUR FRIENDS THOUGH.
KIRYUU-KUN IS, UM, AMAZING ...
HE SLEEPS THROUGH CLASS ALL THE TIME, YET SOMEHOW, HE'S SUPER-SMART.
YEAH, IT REALLY TICKS ME OFF.

## ONLY

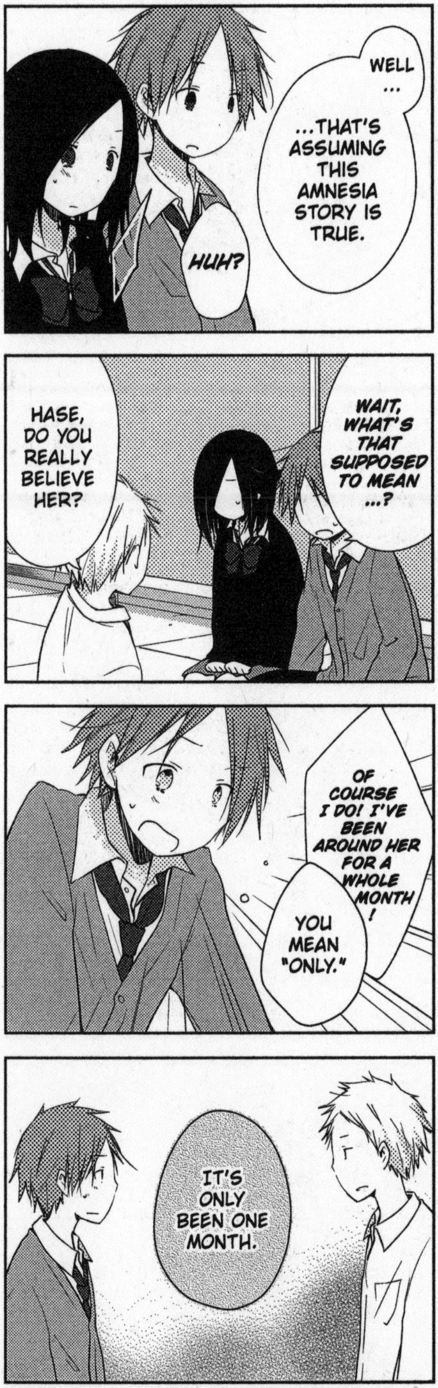
WELL ...
...THAT'S ASSUMING THIS AMNESIA STORY IS TRUE.
HUH?
WAIT, WHAT'S THAT SUPPOSED TO MEAN ...?
HASE, DO YOU REALLY BELIEVE HER?
OF COURSE I DO! I'VE BEEN AROUND HER FOR A WHOLE MONTH!
YOU MEAN "ONLY."
IT'S ONLY BEEN ONE MONTH.

## ACTING

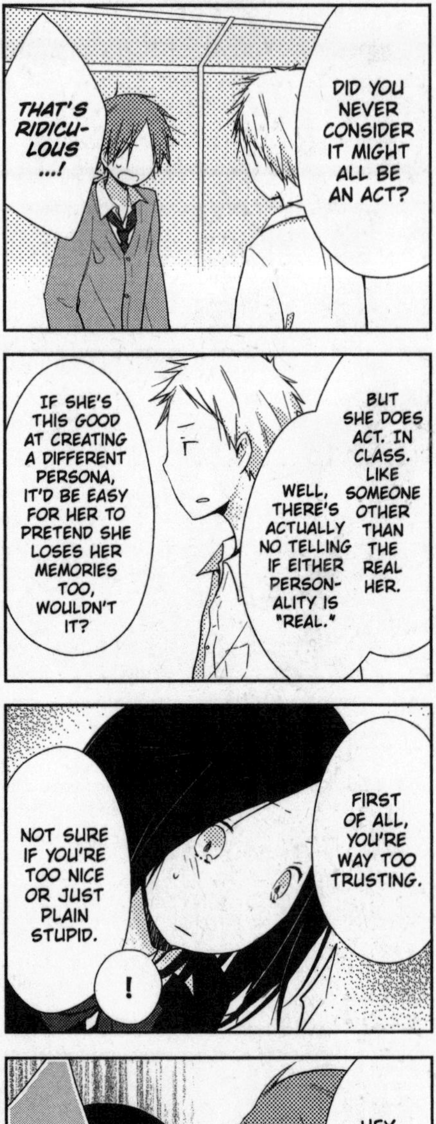
DID YOU NEVER CONSIDER IT MIGHT ALL BE AN ACT?
THAT'S RIDICULOUS ...!
BUT SHE DOES ACT. IN CLASS. LIKE SOMEONE OTHER THAN THE REAL HER. WELL, THERE'S ACTUALLY NO TELLING IF EITHER PERSONALITY IS "REAL."
IF SHE'S THIS GOOD AT CREATING A DIFFERENT PERSONA, IT'D BE EASY FOR HER TO PRETEND SHE LOSES HER MEMORIES TOO, WOULDN'T IT?
FIRST OF ALL, YOU'RE WAY TOO TRUSTING.
NOT SURE IF YOU'RE TOO NICE OR JUST PLAIN STUPID.
!
HEY, THAT'S ENOUGH ...!
STOP IT!

## COMPELLED TO SPEAK

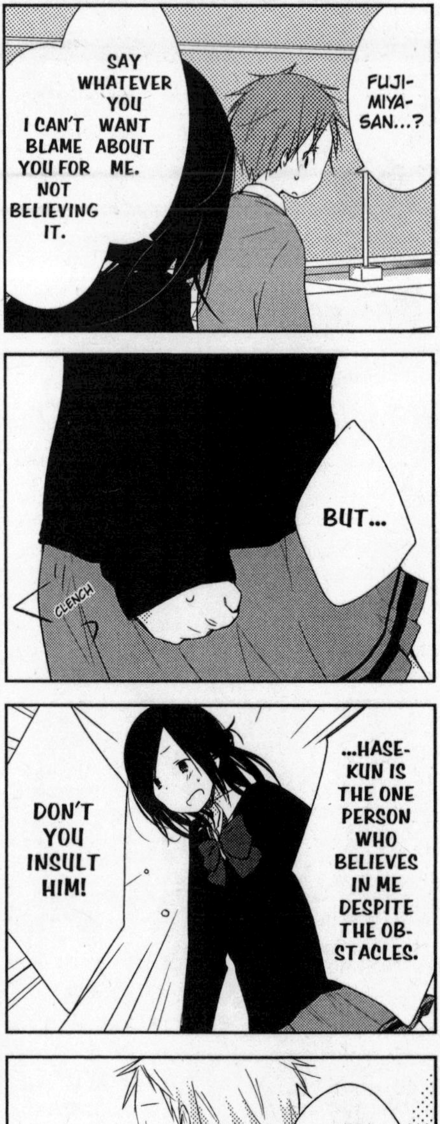
FUJI-MIYA-SAN...?
SAY WHATEVER YOU WANT ABOUT ME.
I CAN'T BLAME YOU FOR NOT BELIEVING IT.
BUT...
CLENCH
...HASE-KUN IS THE ONE PERSON WHO BELIEVES IN ME DESPITE THE OBSTACLES.
DON'T YOU INSULT HIM!
...HUH. SO YOU CAN SPEAK FOR YOURSELF AFTER ALL.
EH?

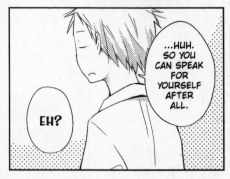

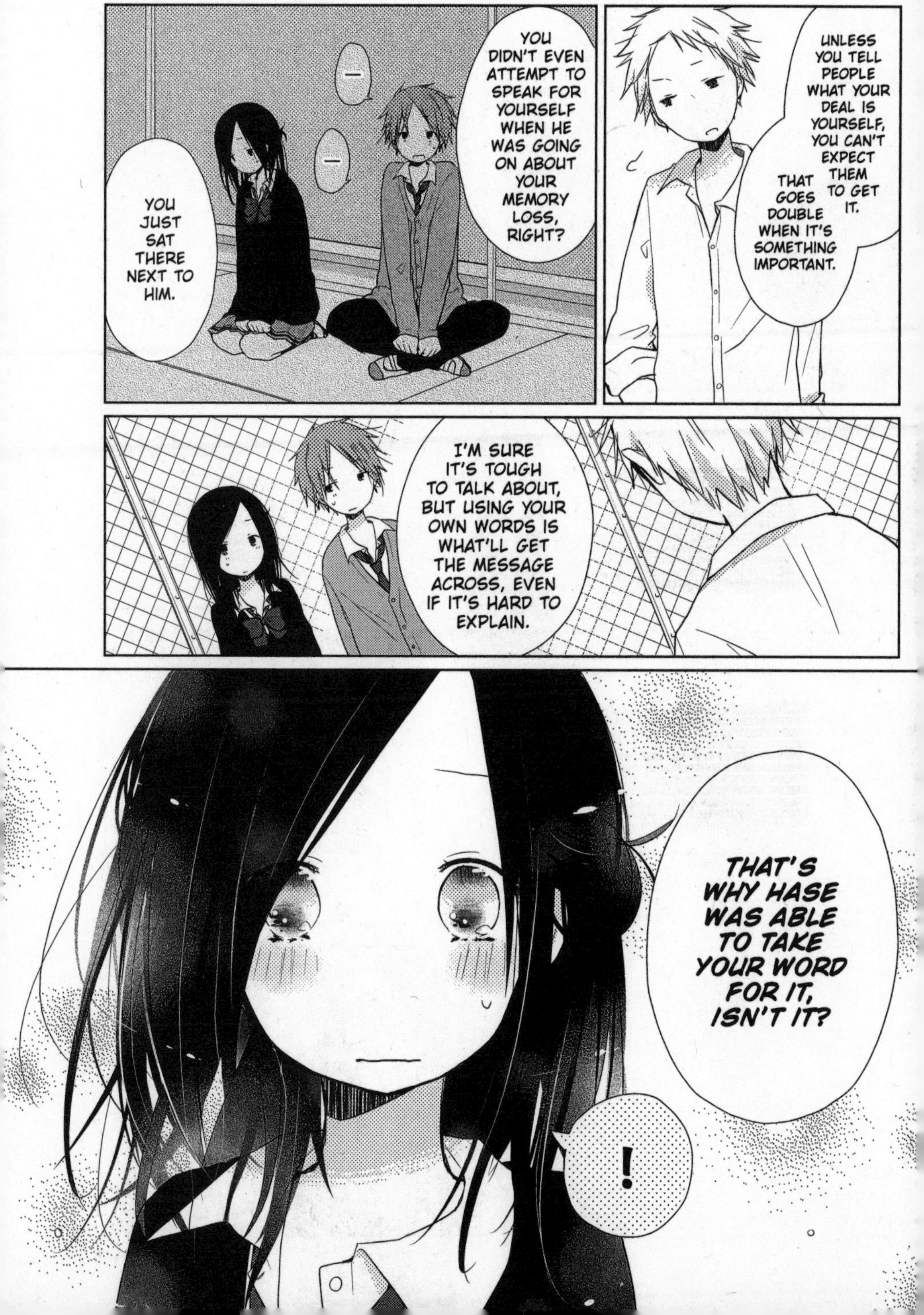
UNLESS YOU TELL PEOPLE WHAT YOUR DEAL IS YOURSELF, YOU CAN'T EXPECT THEM TO GET IT.
THAT GOES DOUBLE WHEN IT'S SOMETHING IMPORTANT.
YOU DIDN'T EVEN ATTEMPT TO SPEAK FOR YOURSELF WHEN HE WAS GOING ON ABOUT YOUR MEMORY LOSS, RIGHT?
—
—
YOU JUST SAT THERE NEXT TO HIM.
I'M SURE IT'S TOUGH TO TALK ABOUT, BUT USING YOUR OWN WORDS IS WHAT'LL GET THE MESSAGE ACROSS, EVEN IF IT'S HARD TO EXPLAIN.
THAT'S WHY HASE WAS ABLE TO TAKE YOUR WORD FOR IT, ISN'T IT?
!

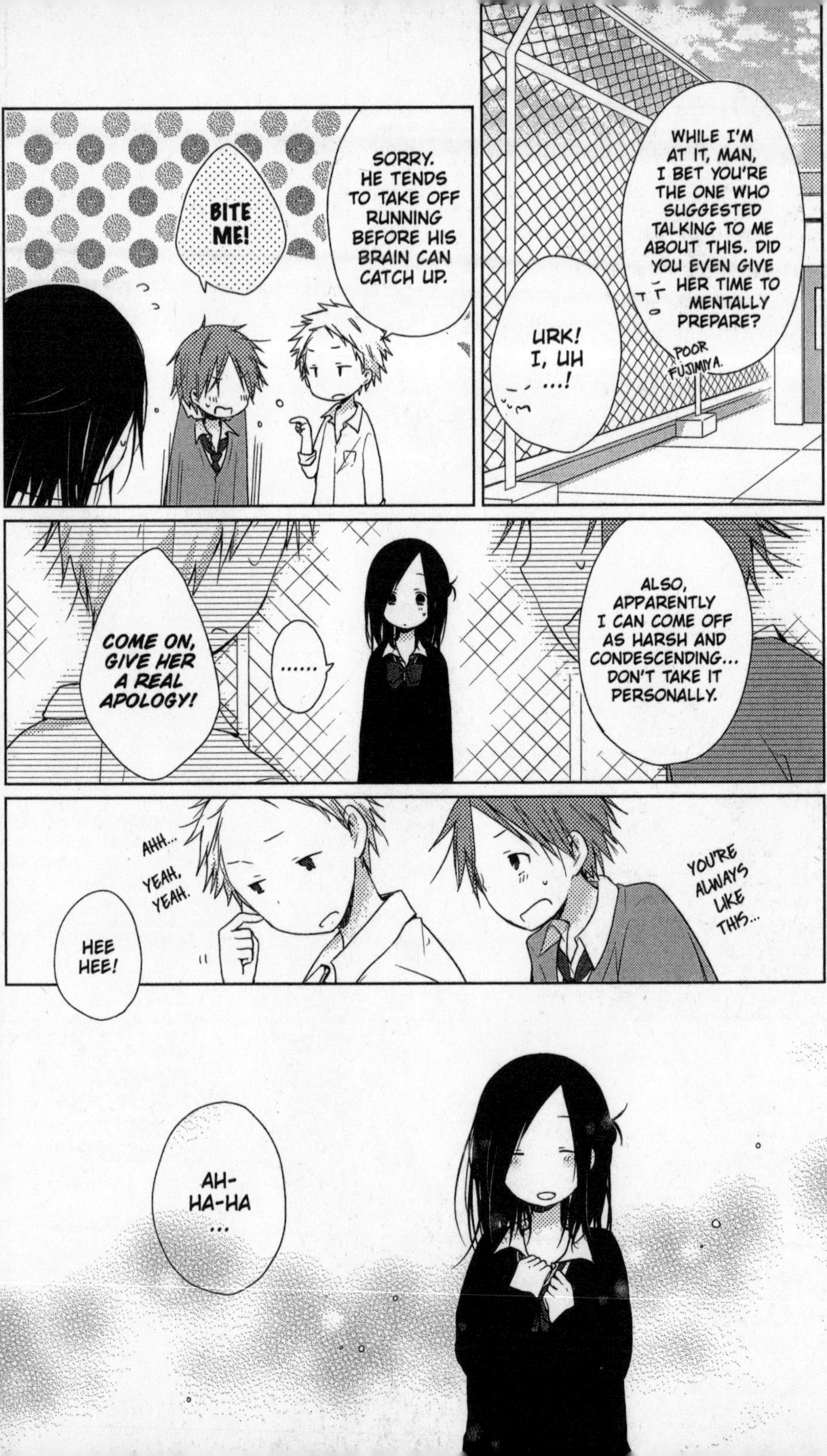
WHILE I'M AT IT, MAN, I BET YOU'RE THE ONE WHO SUGGESTED TALKING TO ME ABOUT THIS. DID YOU EVEN GIVE HER TIME TO MENTALLY PREPARE?
POOR FUJIMIYA.
URK! I, UH ...!
SORRY. HE TENDS TO TAKE OFF RUNNING BEFORE HIS BRAIN CAN CATCH UP.
BITE ME!
ALSO, APPARENTLY I CAN COME OFF AS HARSH AND CONDESCENDING... DON'T TAKE IT PERSONALLY.
......
COME ON, GIVE HER A REAL APOLOGY!
YOU'RE ALWAYS LIKE THIS...
AHH... YEAH, YEAH.
HEE HEE!
AH-HA-HA ...

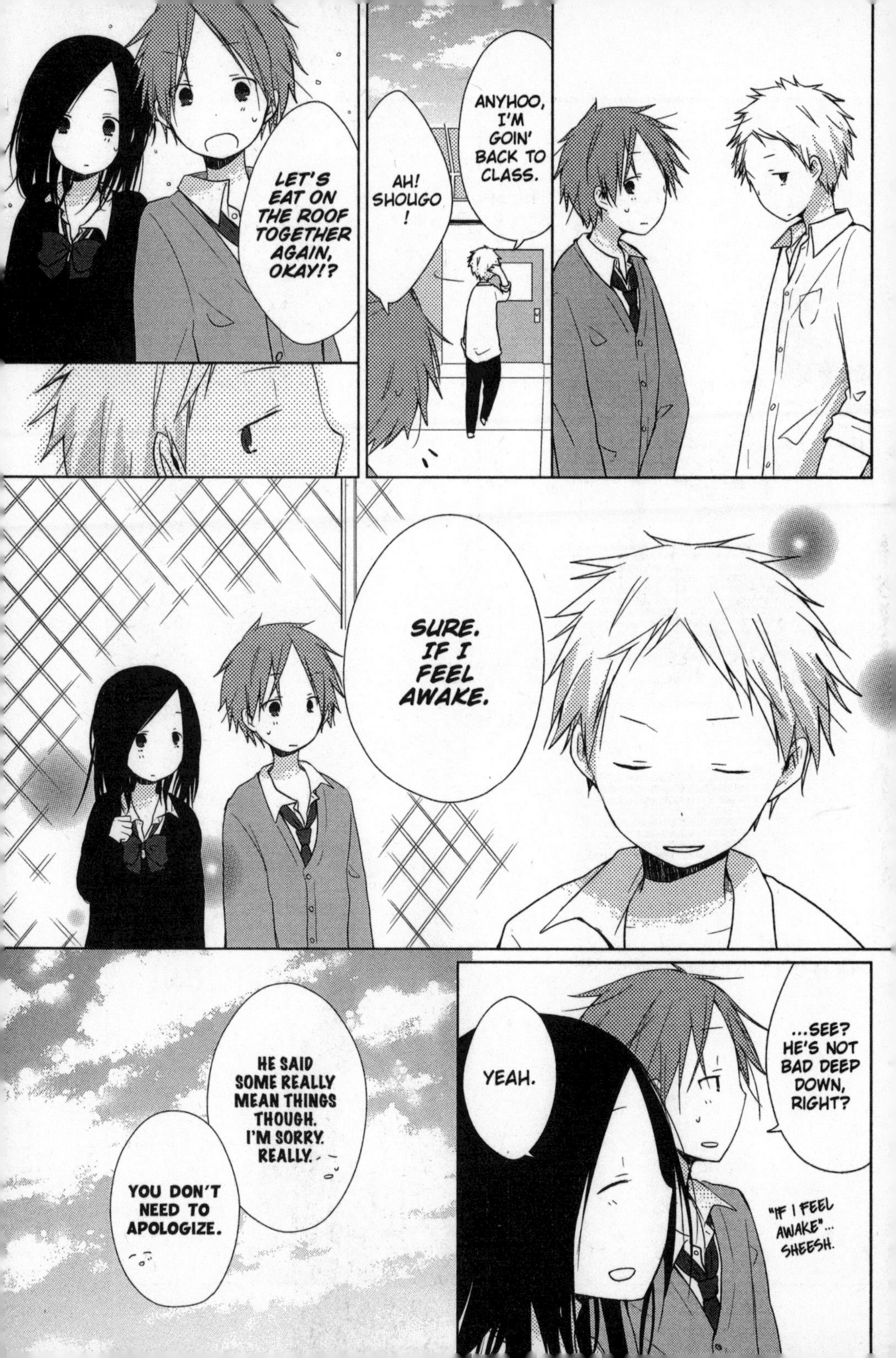

ANYHOO, I'M GOIN' BACK TO CLASS.
AH! SHOUGO!
LET'S EAT ON THE ROOF TOGETHER AGAIN, OKAY!?
SURE. IF I FEEL AWAKE.
...SEE? HE'S NOT BAD DEEP DOWN, RIGHT?
YEAH.
"IF I FEEL AWAKE"... SHEESH.
HE SAID SOME REALLY MEAN THINGS THOUGH. I'M SORRY. REALLY.
YOU DON'T NEED TO APOLOGIZE.

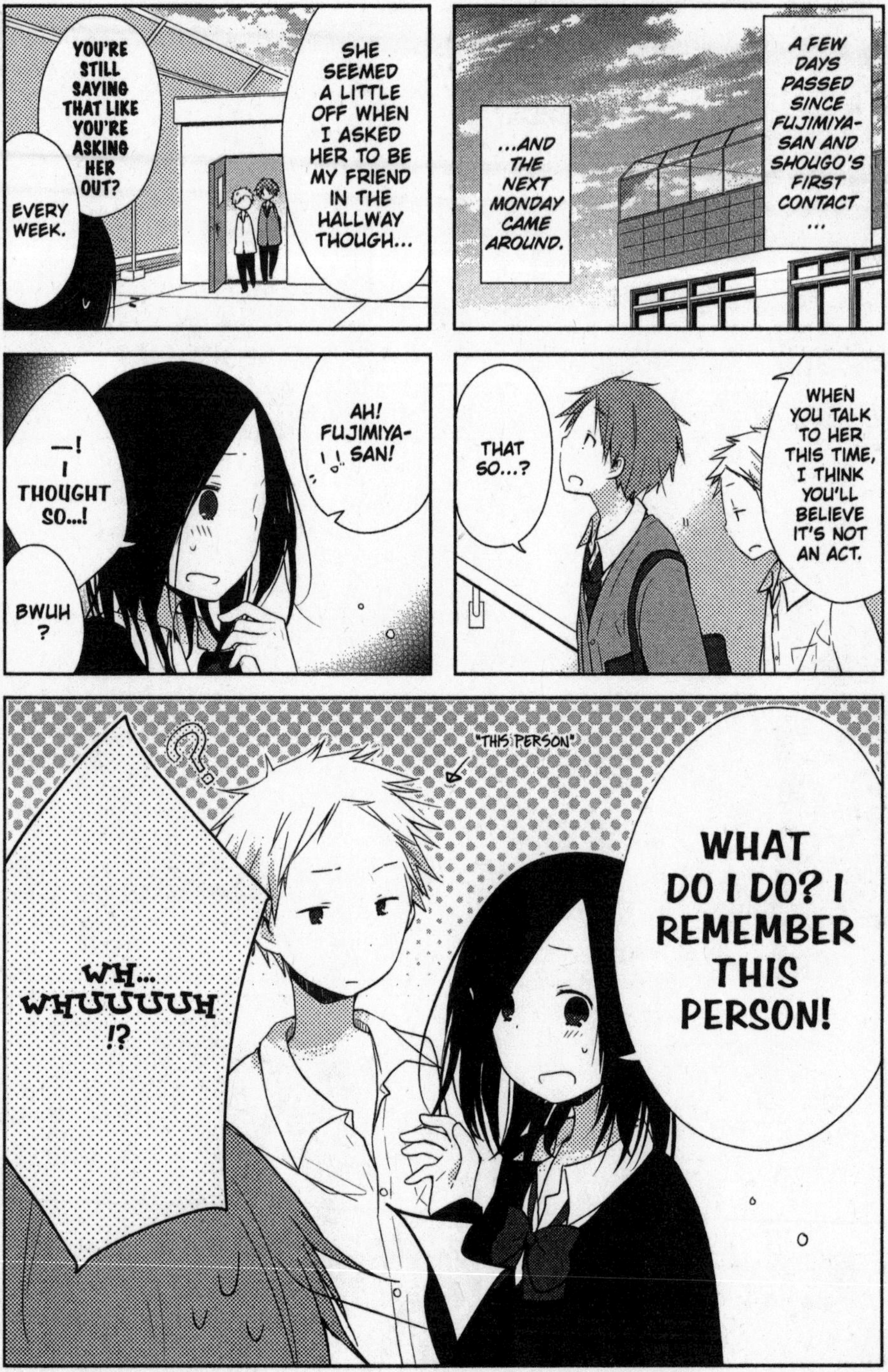
A FEW DAYS PASSED SINCE FUJIMIYA-SAN AND SHOUGO'S FIRST CONTACT ...
...AND THE NEXT MONDAY CAME AROUND.
SHE SEEMED A LITTLE OFF WHEN I ASKED HER TO BE MY FRIEND IN THE HALLWAY THOUGH...
YOU'RE STILL SAYING THAT LIKE YOU'RE ASKING HER OUT?
EVERY WEEK.
WHEN YOU TALK TO HER THIS TIME, I THINK YOU'LL BELIEVE IT'S NOT AN ACT.
THAT SO...?
AH! FUJIMIYA-SAN!
—! I THOUGHT SO...!
BWUH?
WHAT DO I DO? I REMEMBER THIS PERSON!
"THIS PERSON"
WH... WHUUUUH !?

## UNEXPECTED TWIST

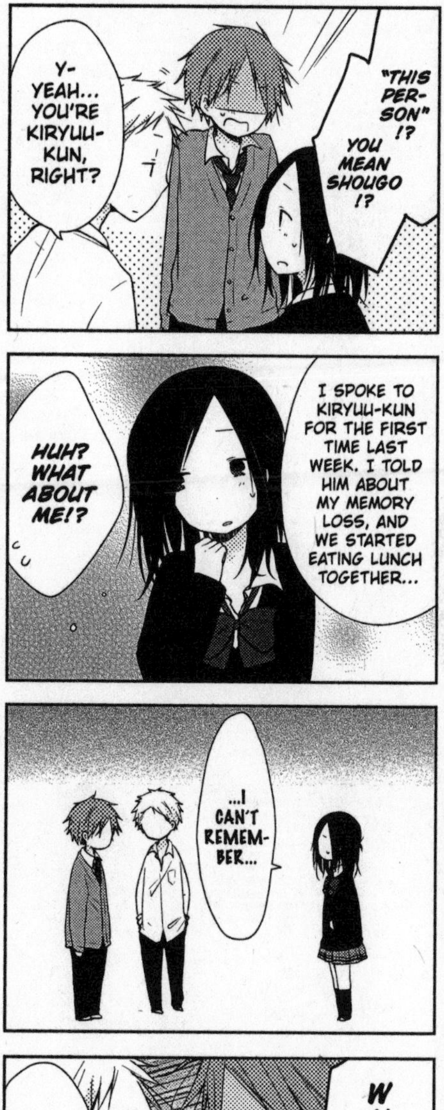
"THIS PERSON"!? YOU MEAN SHOUGO!?
Y-YEAH... YOU'RE KIRYUU-KUN, RIGHT?
I SPOKE TO KIRYUU-KUN FOR THE FIRST TIME LAST WEEK. I TOLD HIM ABOUT MY MEMORY LOSS, AND WE STARTED EATING LUNCH TOGETHER...
HUH? WHAT ABOUT ME!?
...I CAN'T REMEMBER...
WHYYYYY!?
DON'T ASK ME.

## HOW'D THIS HAPPEN?

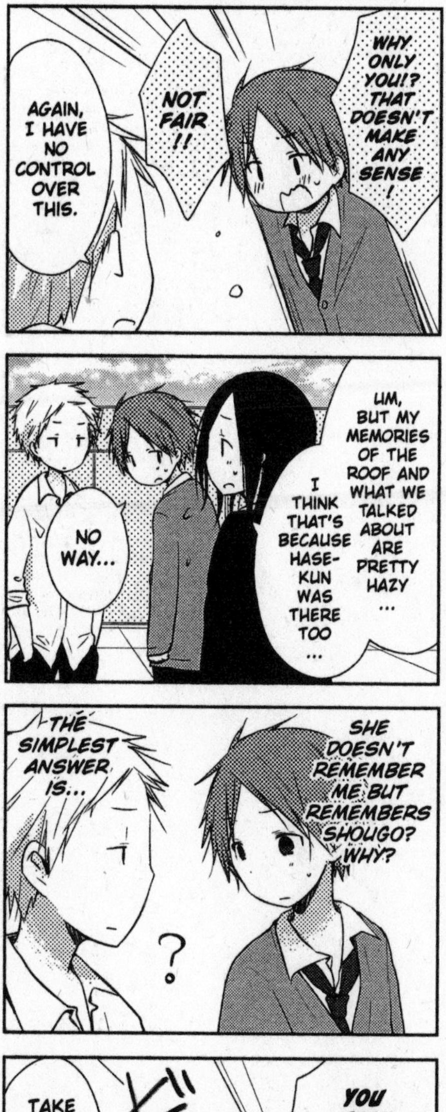
WHY ONLY YOU!? THAT DOESN'T MAKE ANY SENSE!
NOT FAIR!!
AGAIN, I HAVE NO CONTROL OVER THIS.
UM, BUT MY MEMORIES OF THE ROOF AND WHAT WE TALKED ABOUT ARE PRETTY HAZY...
I THINK THAT'S BECAUSE HASE-KUN WAS THERE TOO...
NO WAY...
SHE DOESN'T REMEMBER ME BUT REMEMBERS SHOUGO? WHY?
THE SIMPLEST ANSWER IS...
?
YOU MEAN MORE TO HER THAN ME!? IS THAT WHAT IT MEANS!?
DAAARGH
TAKE A CHILL PILL, WILL YOU?

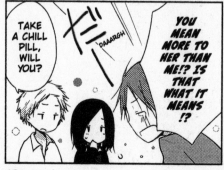

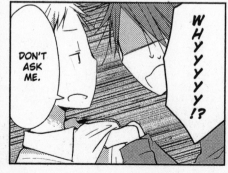

## LET'S REVIEW

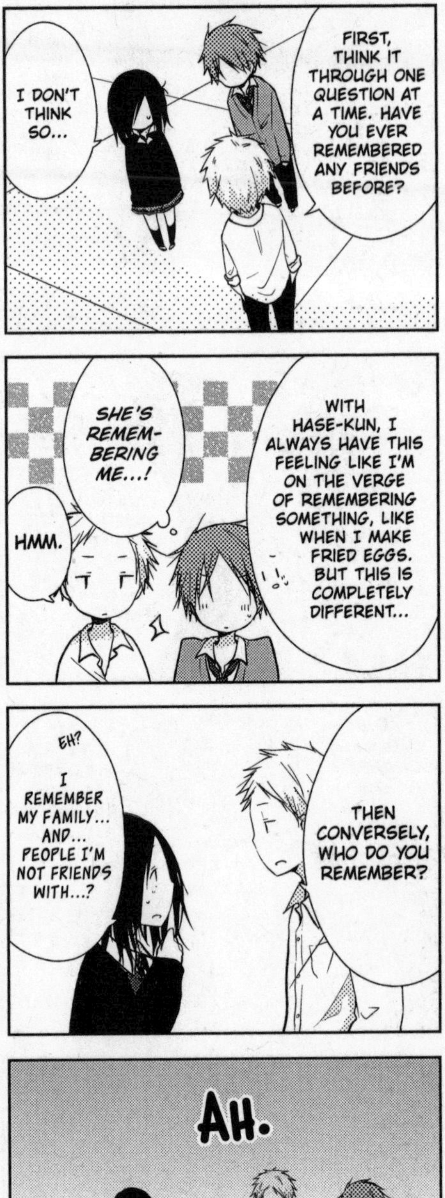
FIRST, THINK IT THROUGH ONE QUESTION AT A TIME. HAVE YOU EVER REMEMBERED ANY FRIENDS BEFORE?
I DON'T THINK SO...
WITH HASE-KUN, I ALWAYS HAVE THIS FEELING LIKE I'M ON THE VERGE OF REMEMBERING SOMETHING, LIKE WHEN I MAKE FRIED EGGS. BUT THIS IS COMPLETELY DIFFERENT...
SHE'S REMEMBERING ME...!
HMM.
THEN CONVERSELY, WHO DO YOU REMEMBER?
EH?
I REMEMBER MY FAMILY... AND... PEOPLE I'M NOT FRIENDS WITH...?
AH.

## OUCH

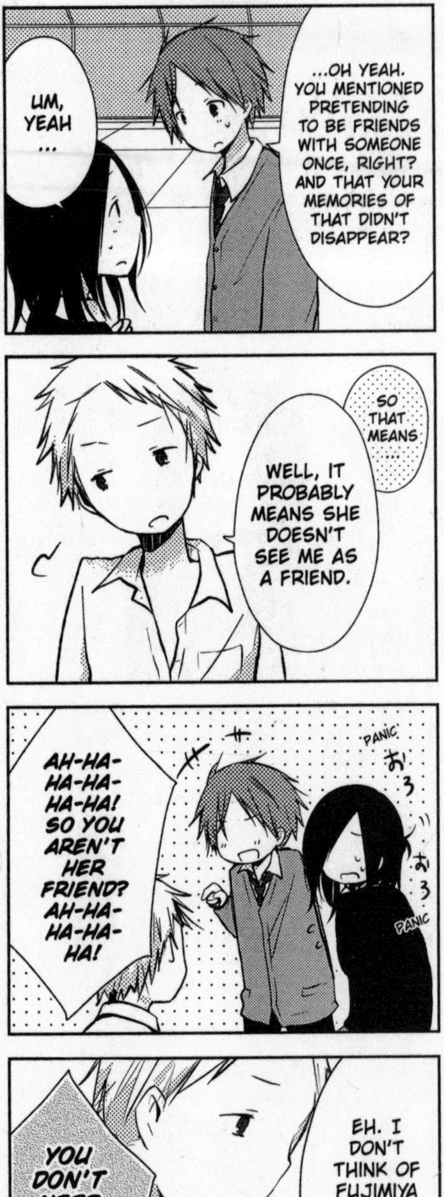
...OH YEAH. YOU MENTIONED PRETENDING TO BE FRIENDS WITH SOMEONE ONCE, RIGHT? AND THAT YOUR MEMORIES OF THAT DIDN'T DISAPPEAR?
UM, YEAH ...
SO THAT MEANS ...
WELL, IT PROBABLY MEANS SHE DOESN'T SEE ME AS A FRIEND.
PANIC
PANIC
AH-HA-HA-HA-HA-HA! SO YOU AREN'T HER FRIEND? AH-HA-HA-HA-HA-HA!
EH. I DON'T THINK OF FUJIMIYA AS A FRIEND EITHER.
SHOCK
YOU DON'T NEED TO SAY THINGS LIKE THAT!

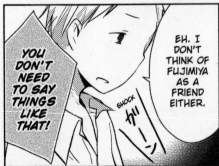

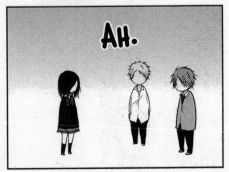

# SPECIAL SOLUTION STRATEGY

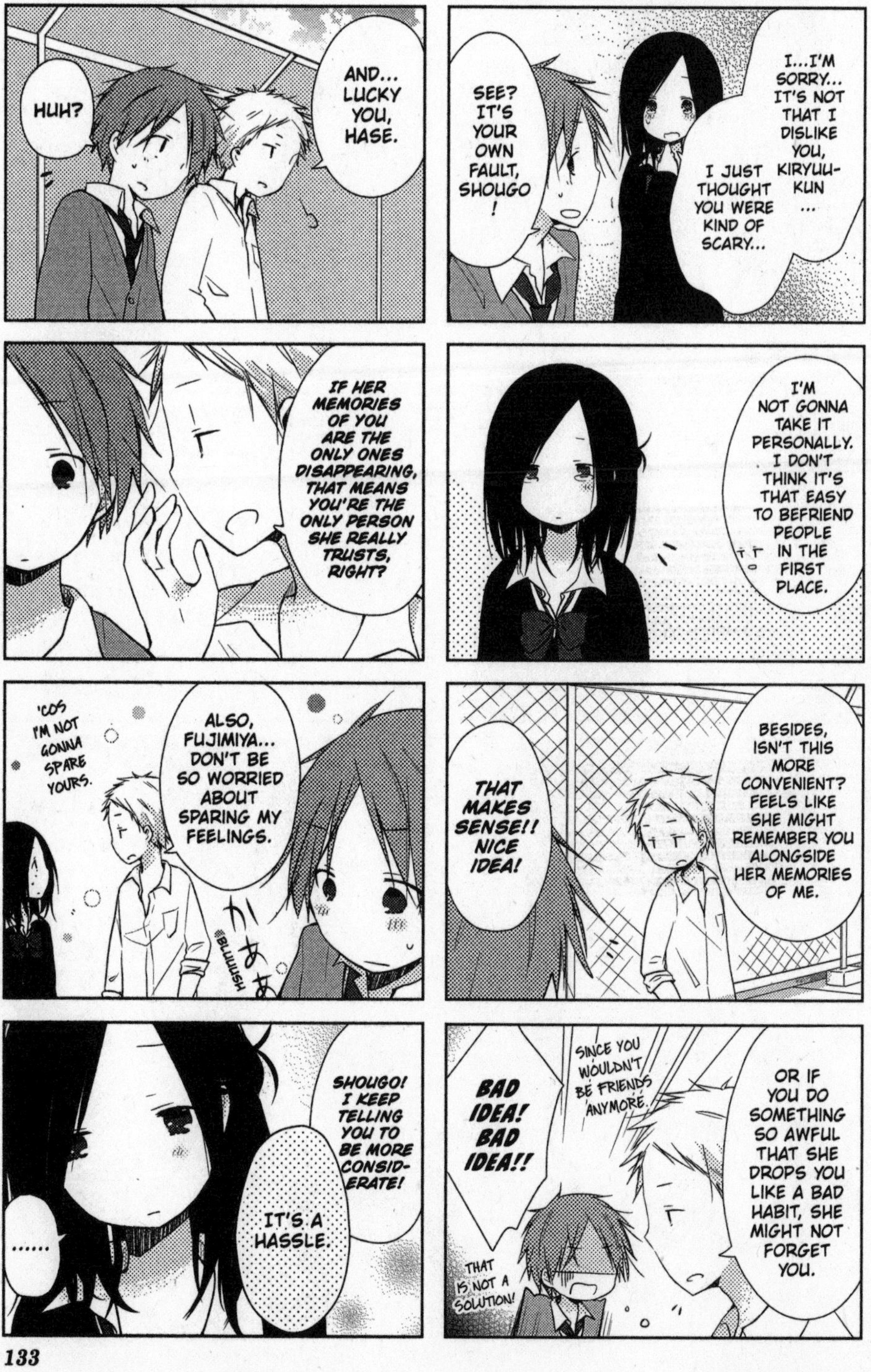

I...I'M SORRY... IT'S NOT THAT I DISLIKE YOU, KIRYUU-KUN...
I JUST THOUGHT YOU WERE KIND OF SCARY...
SEE? IT'S YOUR OWN FAULT, SHOUGO!
I'M NOT GONNA TAKE IT PERSONALLY. I DON'T THINK IT'S THAT EASY TO BEFRIEND PEOPLE IN THE FIRST PLACE.
BESIDES, ISN'T THIS MORE CONVENIENT? FEELS LIKE SHE MIGHT REMEMBER YOU ALONGSIDE HER MEMORIES OF ME.
THAT MAKES SENSE!! NICE IDEA!
OR IF YOU DO SOMETHING SO AWFUL THAT SHE DROPS YOU LIKE A BAD HABIT, SHE MIGHT NOT FORGET YOU.
SINCE YOU WOULDN'T BE FRIENDS ANYMORE.
BAD IDEA! BAD IDEA!!
THAT IS NOT A SOLUTION!
AND... LUCKY YOU, HASE.
HUH?
IF HER MEMORIES OF YOU ARE THE ONLY ONES DISAPPEARING, THAT MEANS YOU'RE THE ONLY PERSON SHE REALLY TRUSTS, RIGHT?
ALSO, FUJIMIYA... DON'T BE SO WORRIED ABOUT SPARING MY FEELINGS.
'COS I'M NOT GONNA SPARE YOURS.
BLUUUSH
SHOUGO! I KEEP TELLING YOU TO BE MORE CONSIDERATE!
IT'S A HASSLE.
......

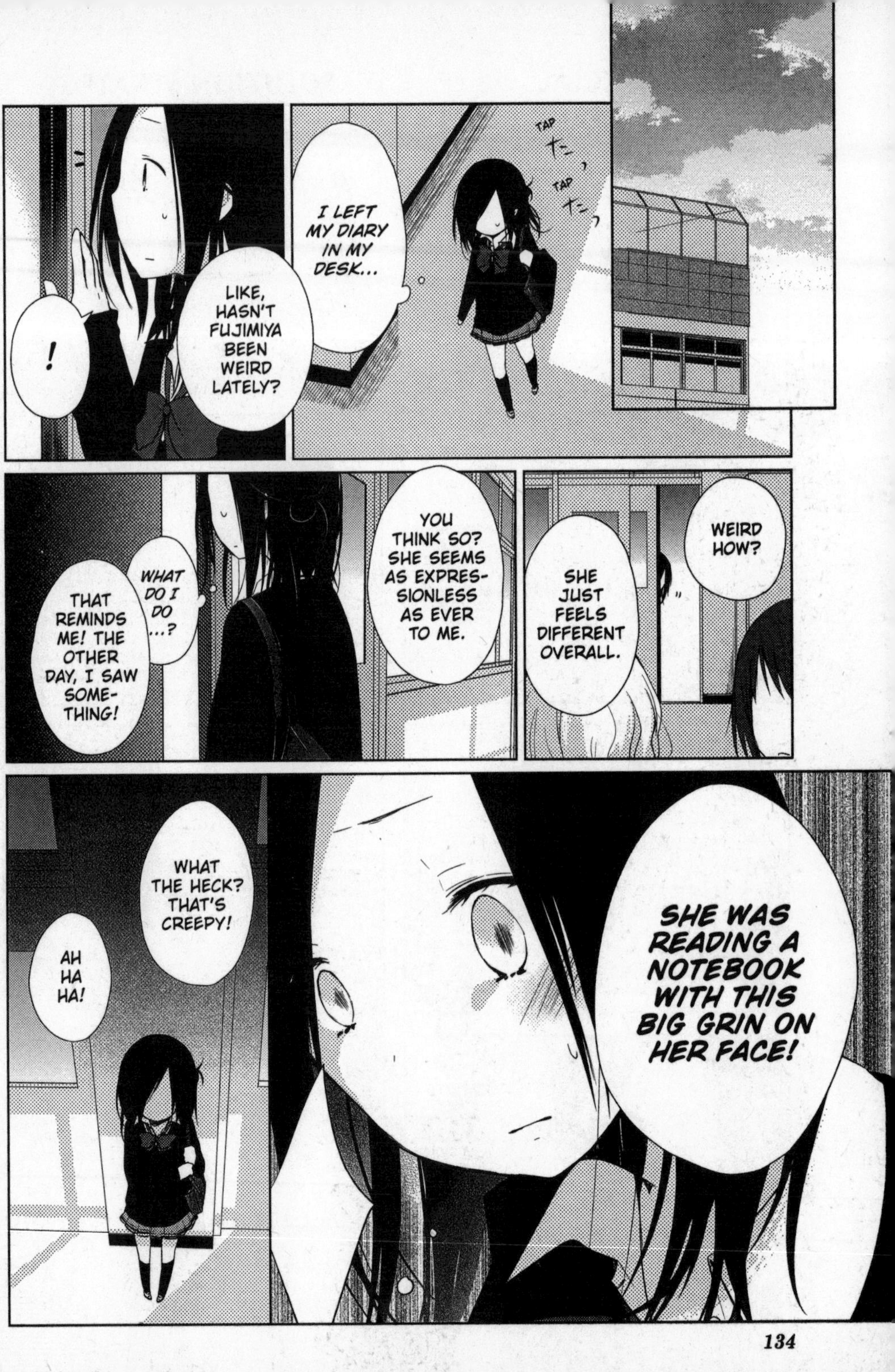
TAP
TAP
I LEFT MY DIARY IN MY DESK...
LIKE, HASN'T FUJIMIYA BEEN WEIRD LATELY?
!
WEIRD HOW?
SHE JUST FEELS DIFFERENT OVERALL.
YOU THINK SO? SHE SEEMS AS EXPRES-SIONLESS AS EVER TO ME.
WHAT DO I DO ...?
THAT REMINDS ME! THE OTHER DAY, I SAW SOME-THING!
SHE WAS READING A NOTEBOOK WITH THIS BIG GRIN ON HER FACE!
WHAT THE HECK? THAT'S CREEPY!
AH HA HA!

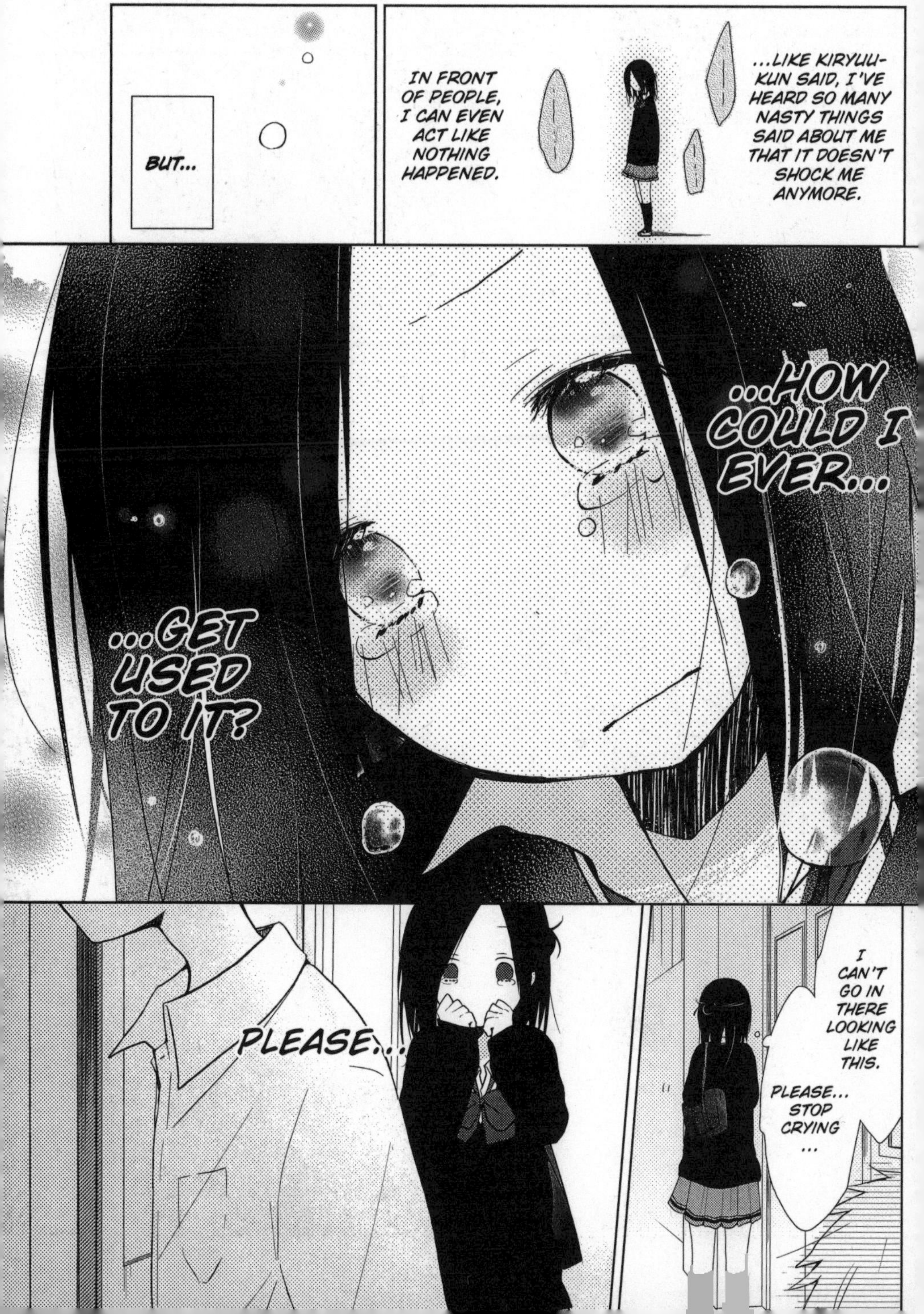
...LIKE KIRYUU-KUN SAID, I'VE HEARD SO MANY NASTY THINGS SAID ABOUT ME THAT IT DOESN'T SHOCK ME ANYMORE.
IN FRONT OF PEOPLE, I CAN EVEN ACT LIKE NOTHING HAPPENED.
BUT...
...HOW COULD I EVER...
...GET USED TO IT?
I CAN'T GO IN THERE LOOKING LIKE THIS.
PLEASE... STOP CRYING ...
PLEASE...

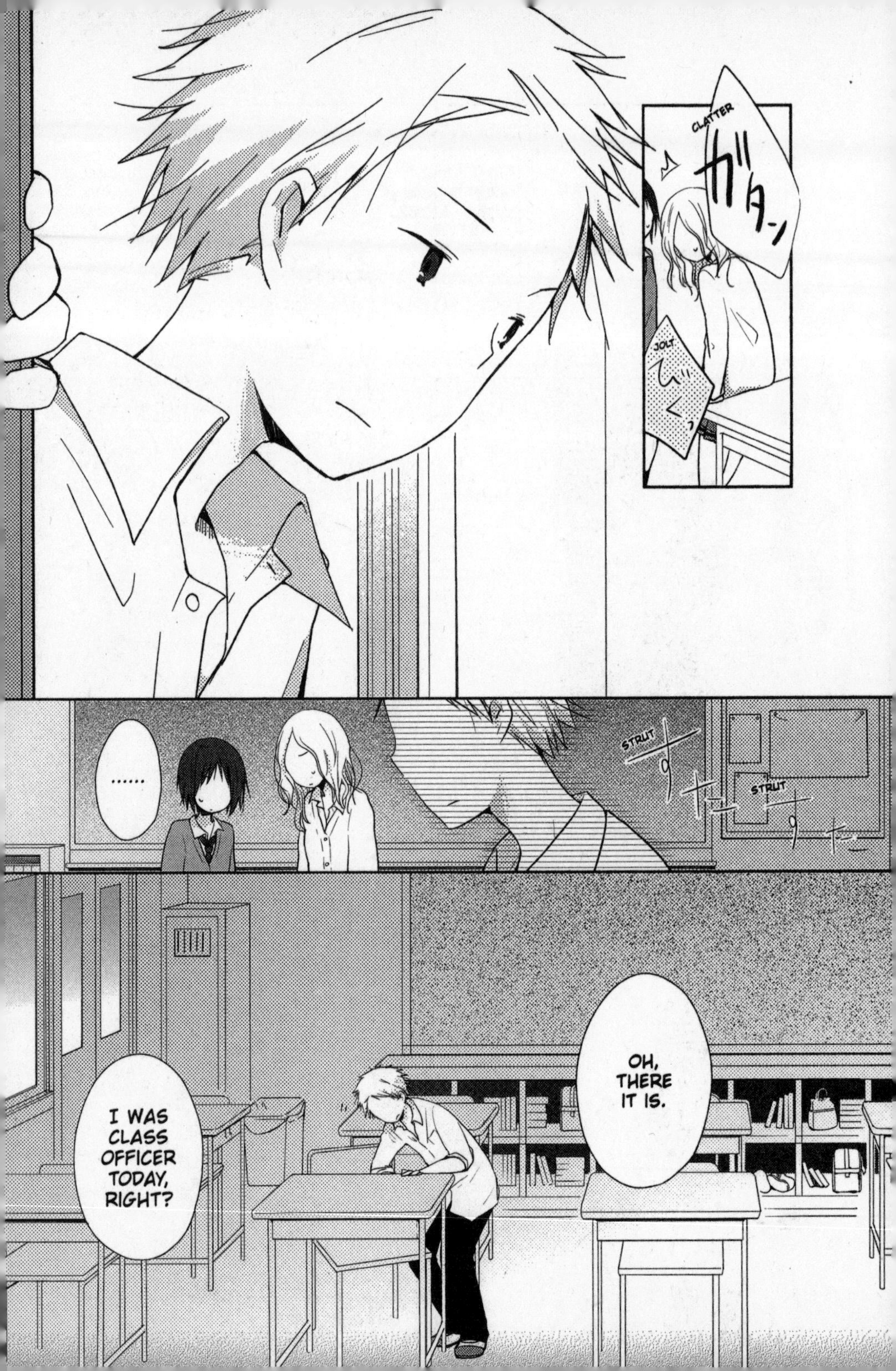
CLATTER
ガタン
JOLT
びくっ
STRUT
STRUT
......
OH, THERE IT IS.
I WAS CLASS OFFICER TODAY, RIGHT?

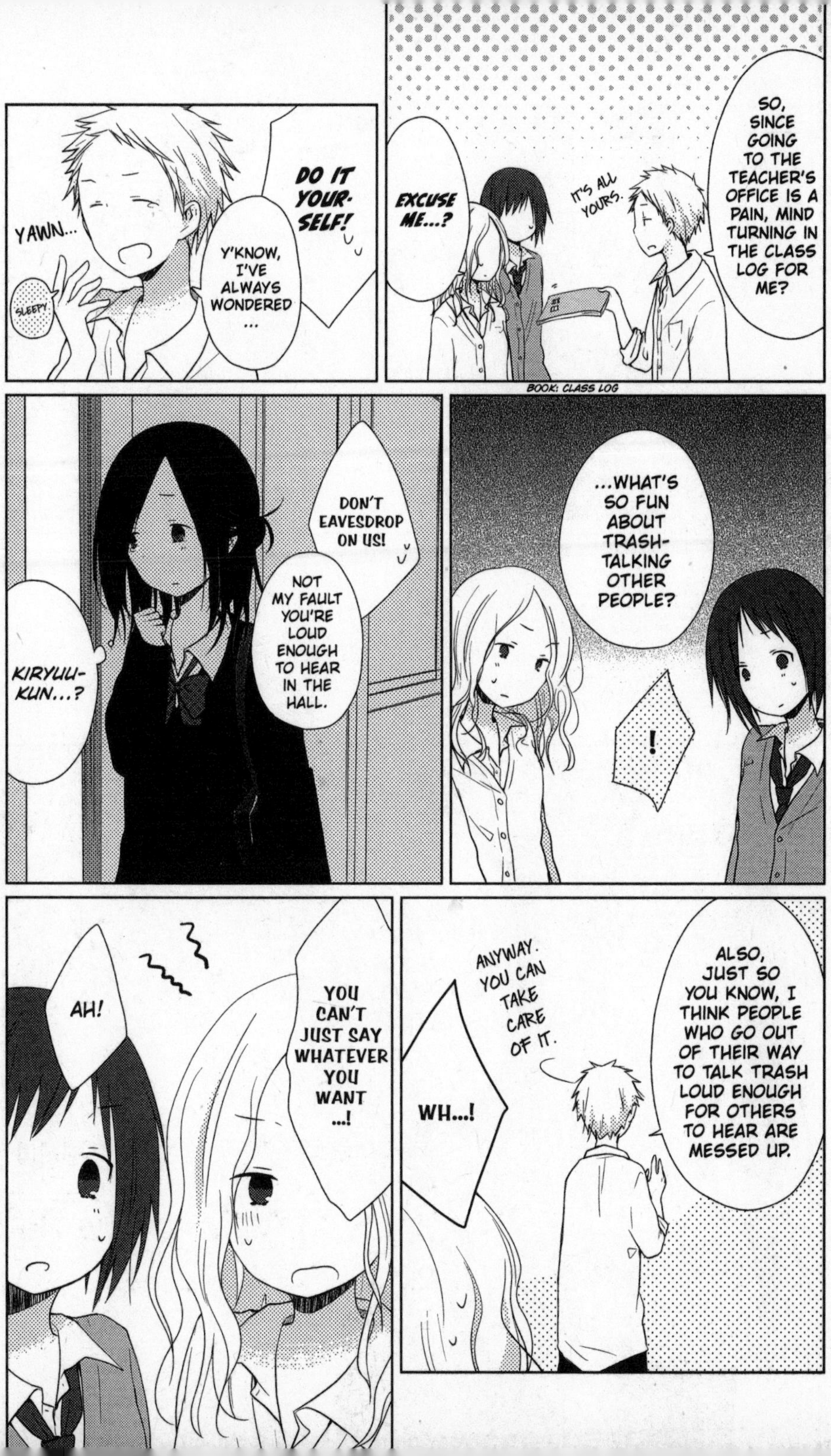
SO, SINCE GOING TO THE TEACHER'S OFFICE IS A PAIN, MIND TURNING IN THE CLASS LOG FOR ME?
IT'S ALL YOURS.
EXCUSE ME...?
BOOK: CLASS LOG
DO IT YOURSELF!
Y'KNOW, I'VE ALWAYS WONDERED...
YAWN...
SLEEPY
...WHAT'S SO FUN ABOUT TRASH-TALKING OTHER PEOPLE?
!
DON'T EAVESDROP ON US!
NOT MY FAULT YOU'RE LOUD ENOUGH TO HEAR IN THE HALL.
KIRYUU-KUN...?
ALSO, JUST SO YOU KNOW, I THINK PEOPLE WHO GO OUT OF THEIR WAY TO TALK TRASH LOUD ENOUGH FOR OTHERS TO HEAR ARE MESSED UP.
ANYWAY. YOU CAN TAKE CARE OF IT.
WH...!
YOU CAN'T JUST SAY WHATEVER YOU WANT...!
AH!

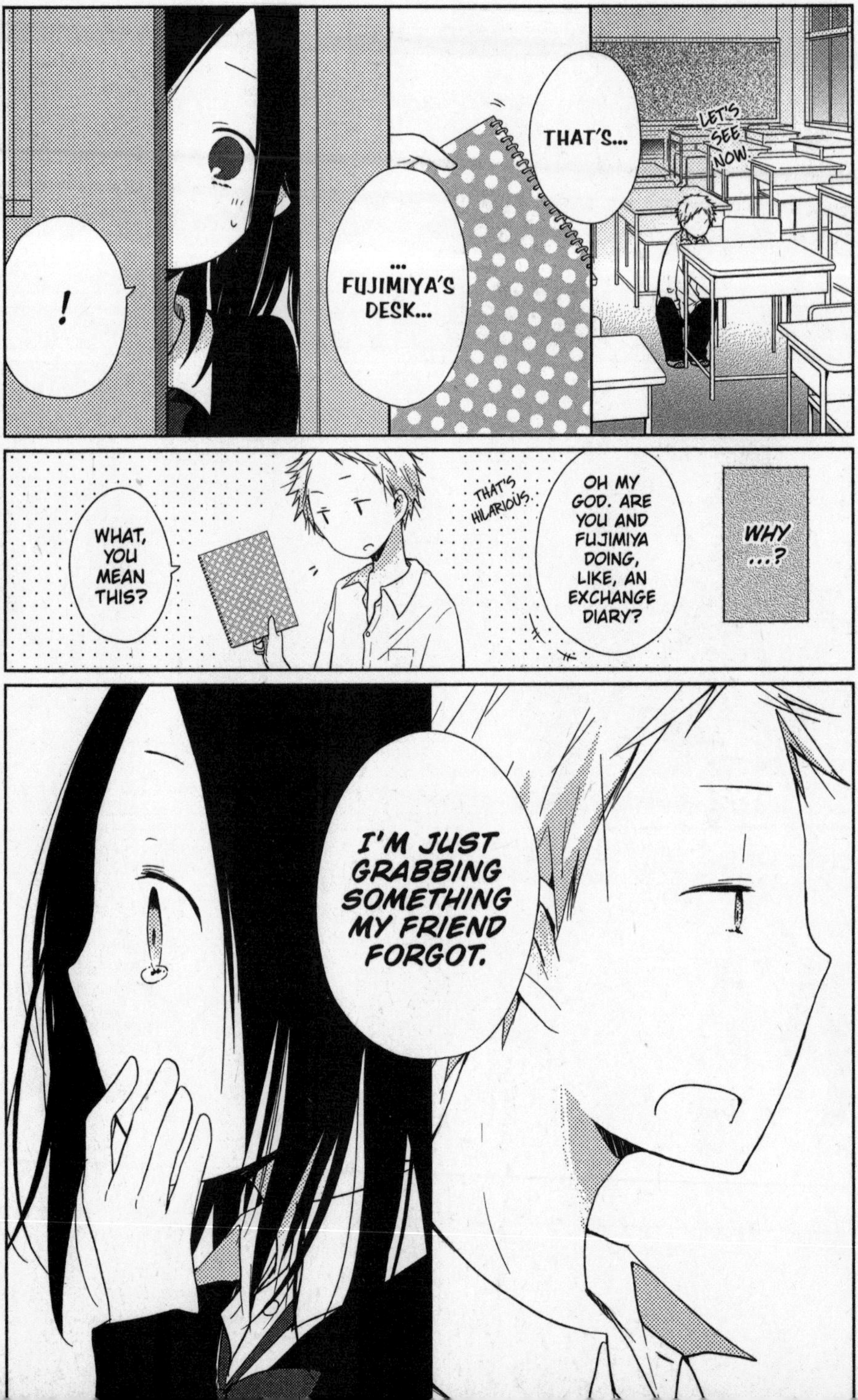
LET'S SEE NOW.
THAT'S...
...FUJIMIYA'S DESK...
!
WHY ...?
OH MY GOD. ARE YOU AND FUJIMIYA DOING, LIKE, AN EXCHANGE DIARY?
THAT'S HILARIOUS.
WHAT, YOU MEAN THIS?
I'M JUST GRABBING SOMETHING MY FRIEND FORGOT.

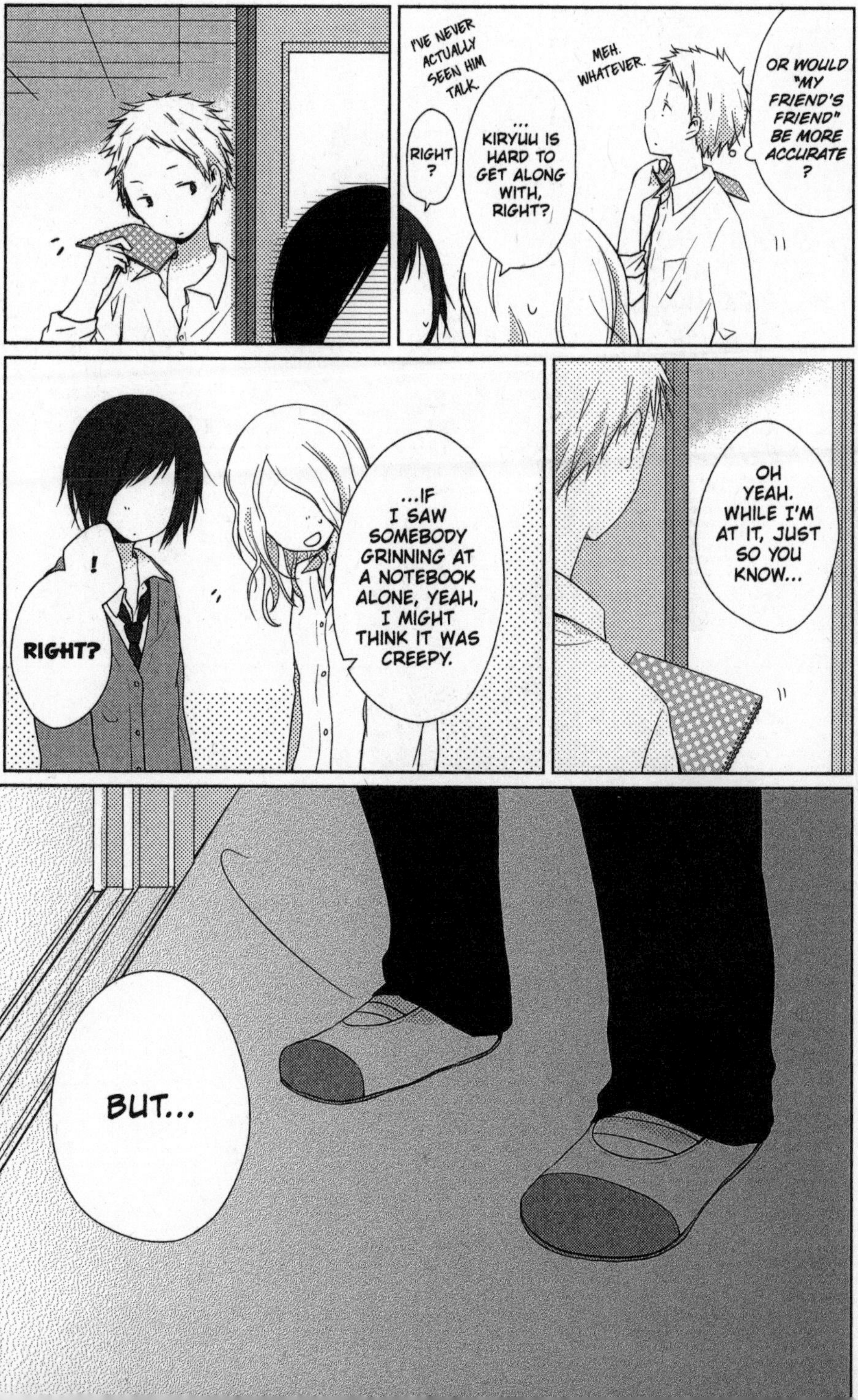
OR WOULD "MY FRIEND'S FRIEND" BE MORE ACCURATE?
MEH. WHATEVER.
... KIRYUU IS HARD TO GET ALONG WITH, RIGHT?
RIGHT?
I'VE NEVER ACTUALLY SEEN HIM TALK.
OH YEAH. WHILE I'M AT IT, JUST SO YOU KNOW...
...IF I SAW SOMEBODY GRINNING AT A NOTEBOOK ALONE, YEAH, I MIGHT THINK IT WAS CREEPY.
!
RIGHT?
BUT...

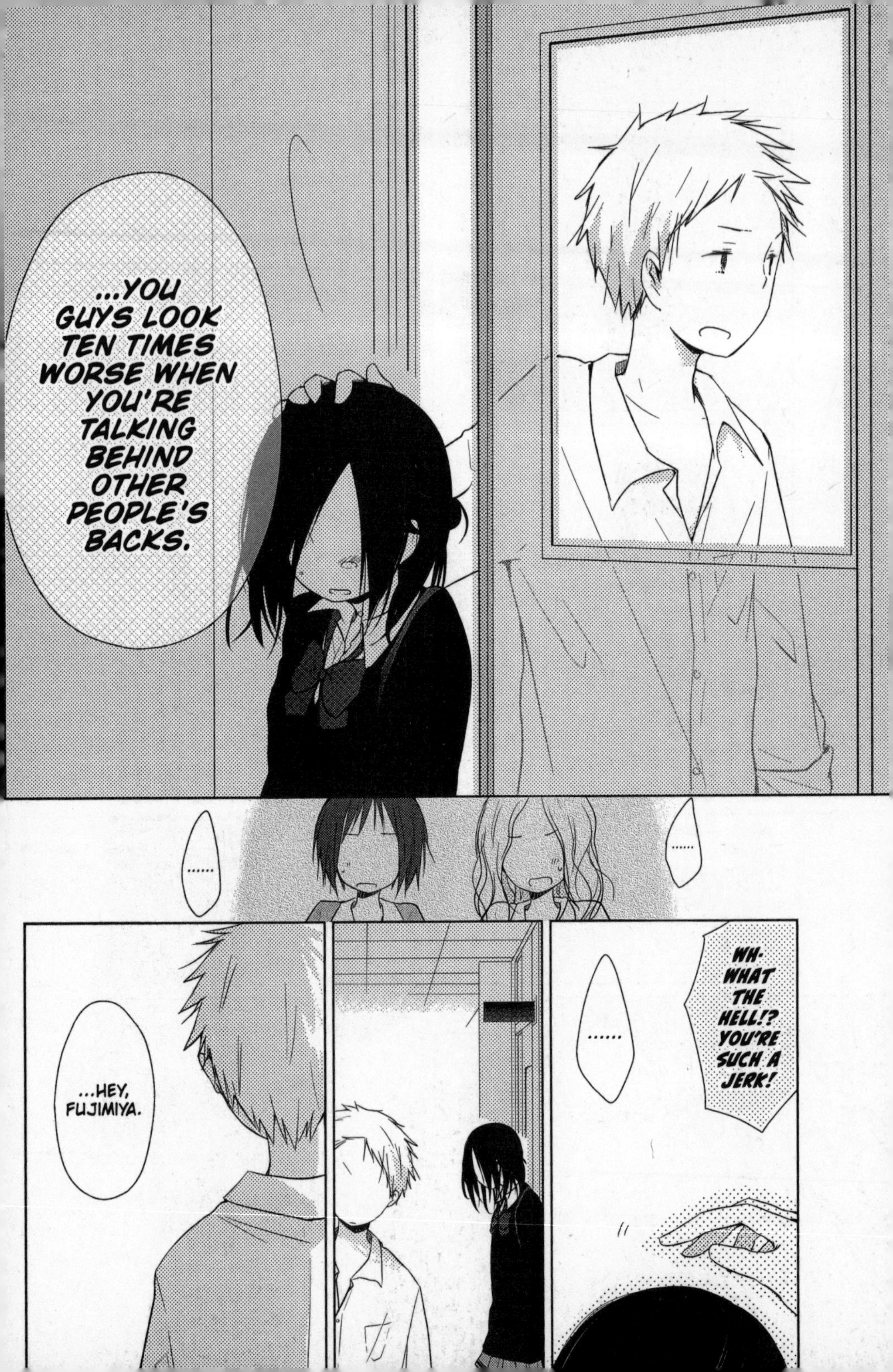
...YOU GUYS LOOK TEN TIMES WORSE WHEN YOU'RE TALKING BEHIND OTHER PEOPLE'S BACKS.
......
......
WH-WHAT THE HELL!? YOU'RE SUCH A JERK!
......
...HEY, FUJIMIYA.

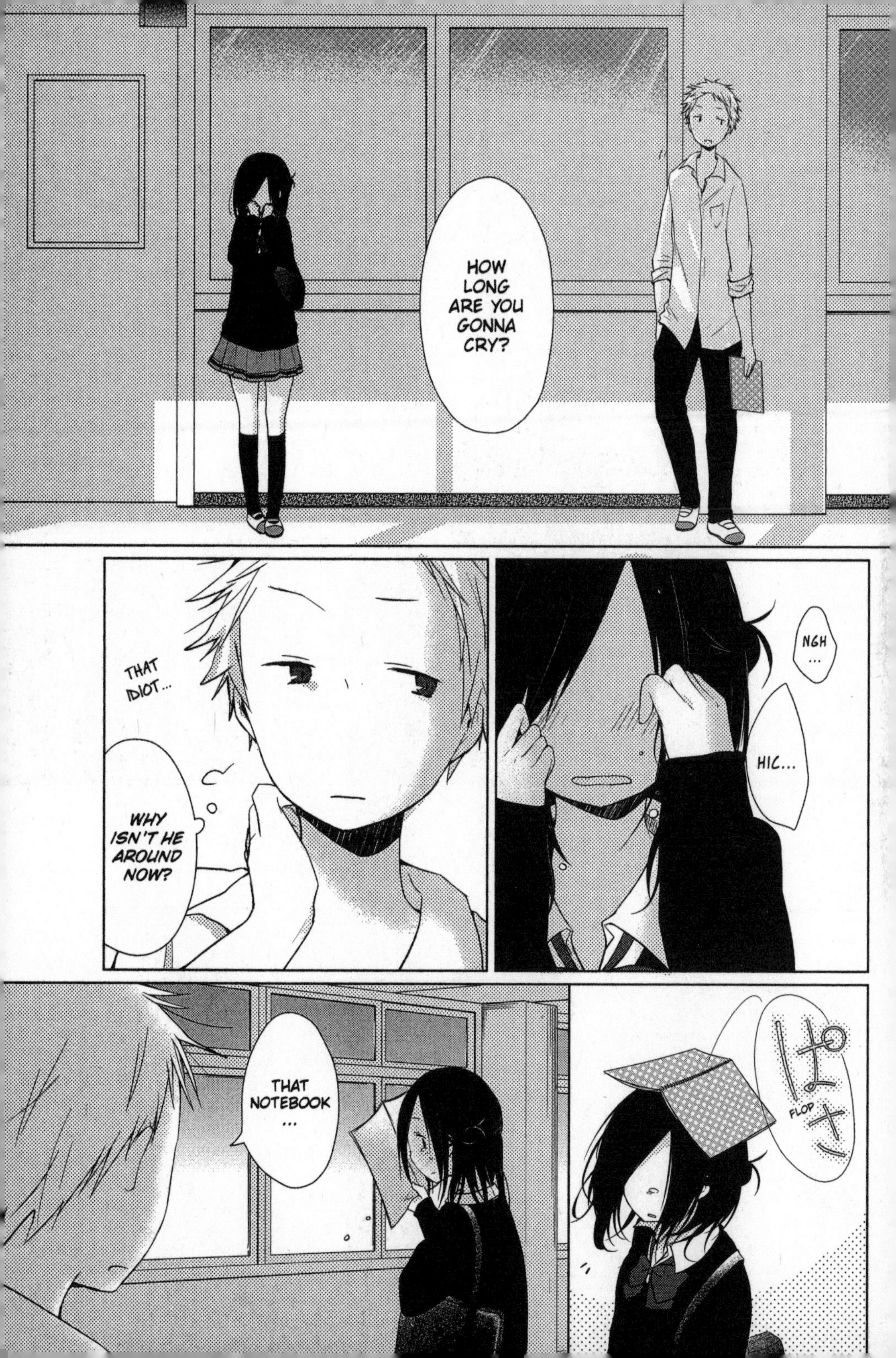
HOW LONG ARE YOU GONNA CRY?
NGH ...
HIC...
THAT IDIOT...
WHY ISN'T HE AROUND NOW?
FLOP
THAT NOTEBOOK ...

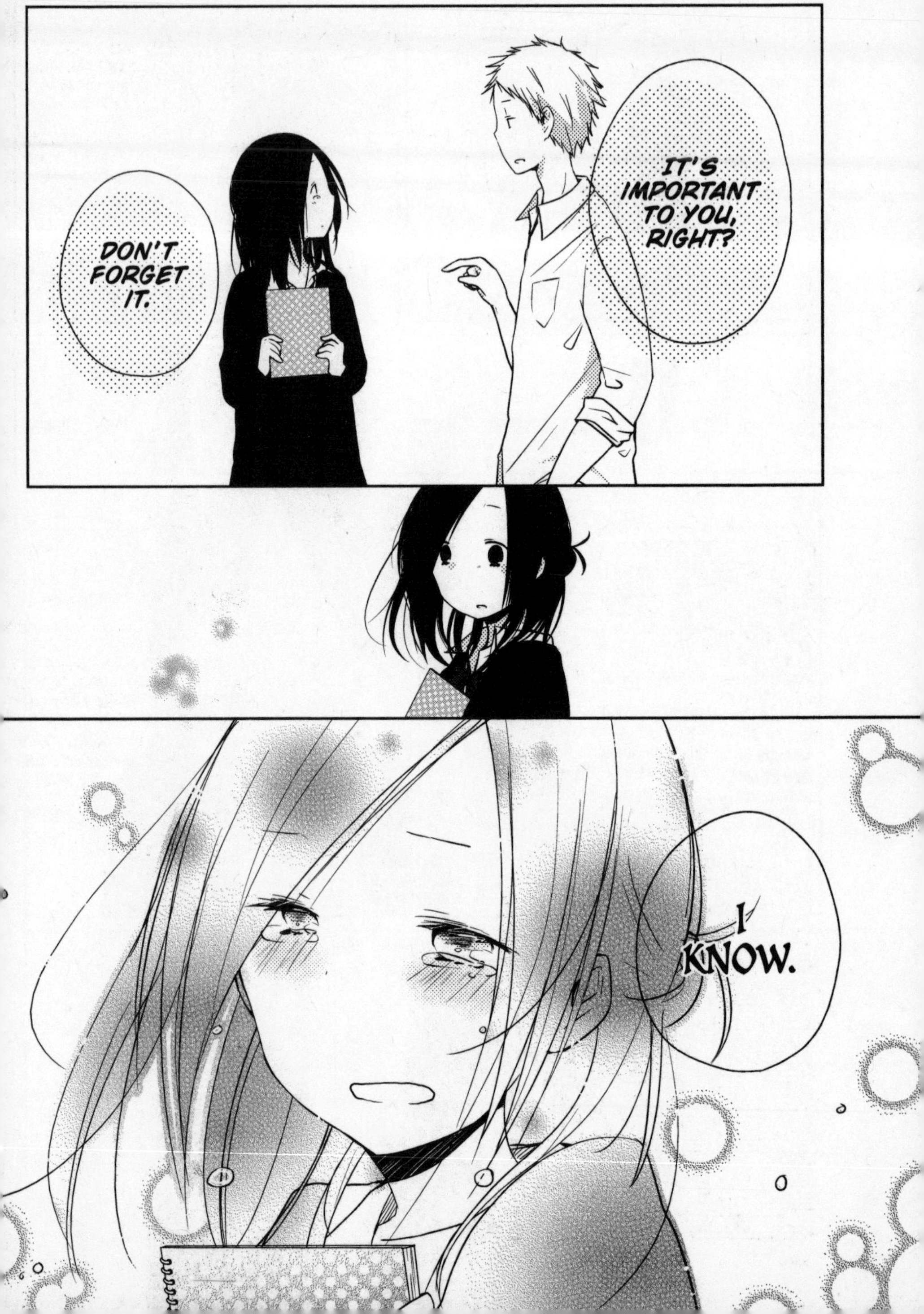
IT'S IMPORTANT TO YOU, RIGHT?
DON'T FORGET IT.
I KNOW.

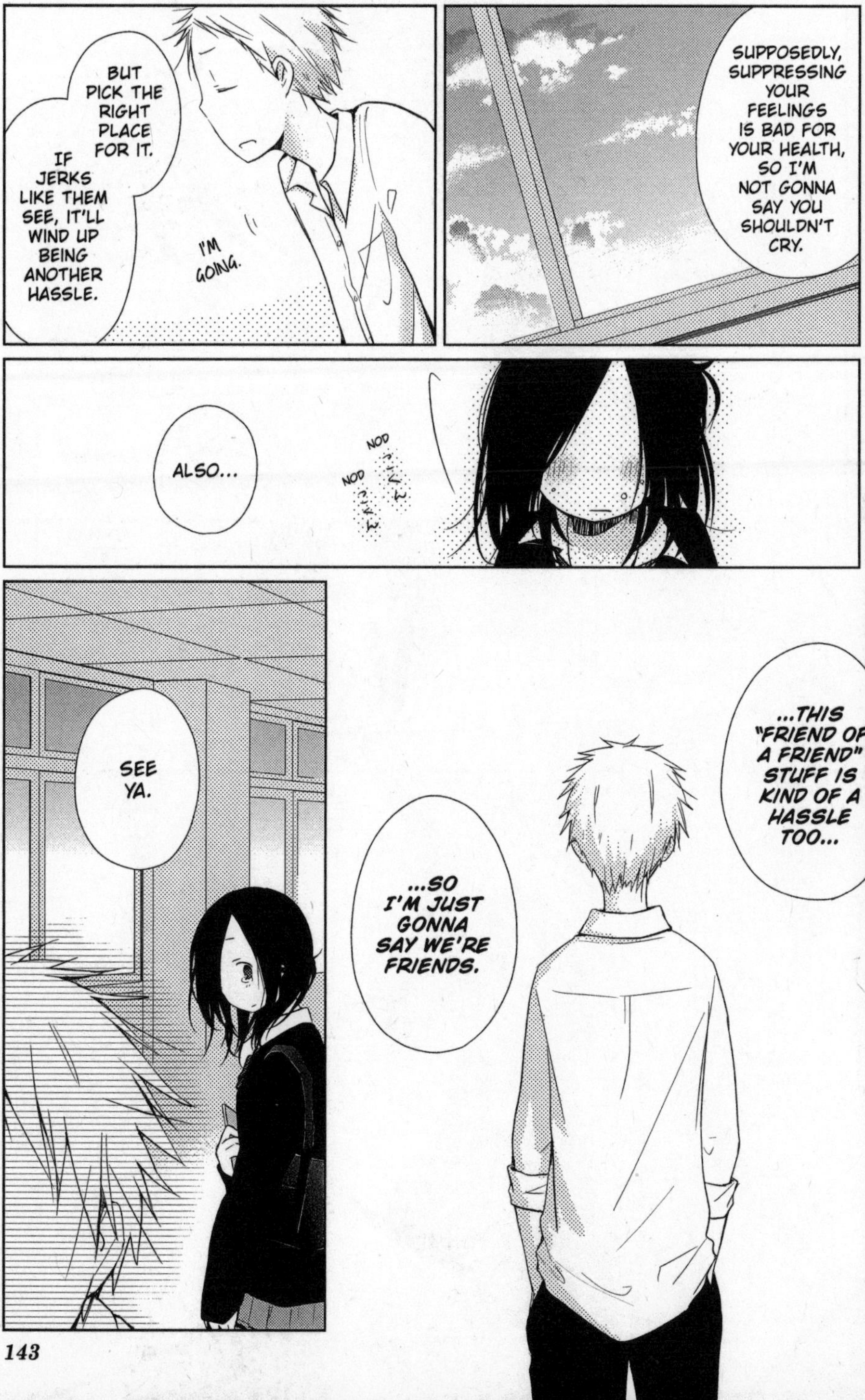
SUPPOSEDLY, SUPPRESSING YOUR FEELINGS IS BAD FOR YOUR HEALTH, SO I'M NOT GONNA SAY YOU SHOULDN'T CRY.
BUT PICK THE RIGHT PLACE FOR IT.
IF JERKS LIKE THEM SEE, IT'LL WIND UP BEING ANOTHER HASSLE.
I'M GOING.
NOD
NOD
ALSO...
...THIS "FRIEND OF A FRIEND" STUFF IS KIND OF A HASSLE TOO...
...SO I'M JUST GONNA SAY WE'RE FRIENDS.
SEE YA.

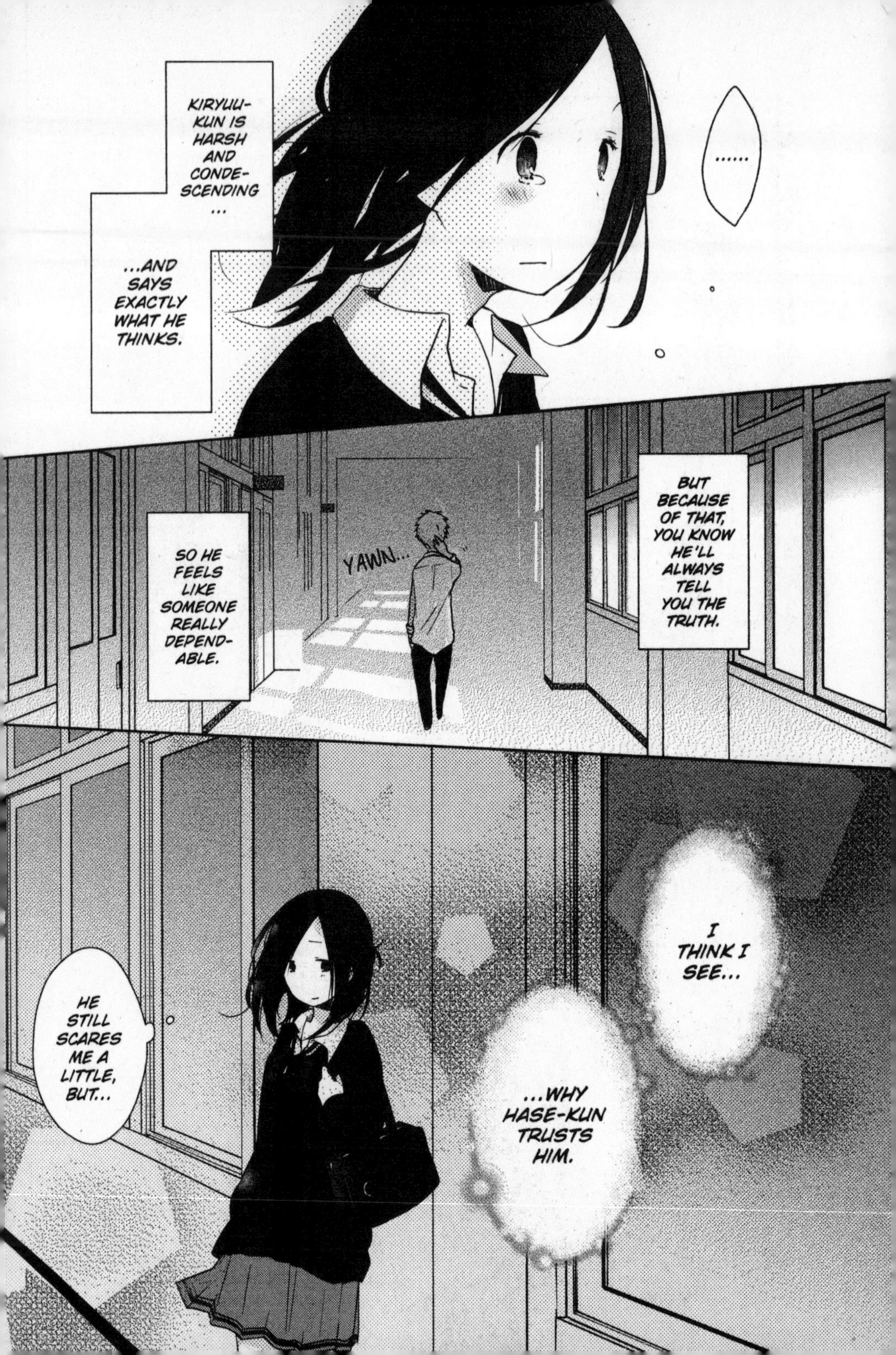
......
KIRYUU-KUN IS HARSH AND CONDE-SCENDING ...
...AND SAYS EXACTLY WHAT HE THINKS.
BUT BECAUSE OF THAT, YOU KNOW HE'LL ALWAYS TELL YOU THE TRUTH.
YAWN...
SO HE FEELS LIKE SOMEONE REALLY DEPEND-ABLE.
I THINK I SEE...
...WHY HASE-KUN TRUSTS HIM.
HE STILL SCARES ME A LITTLE, BUT...

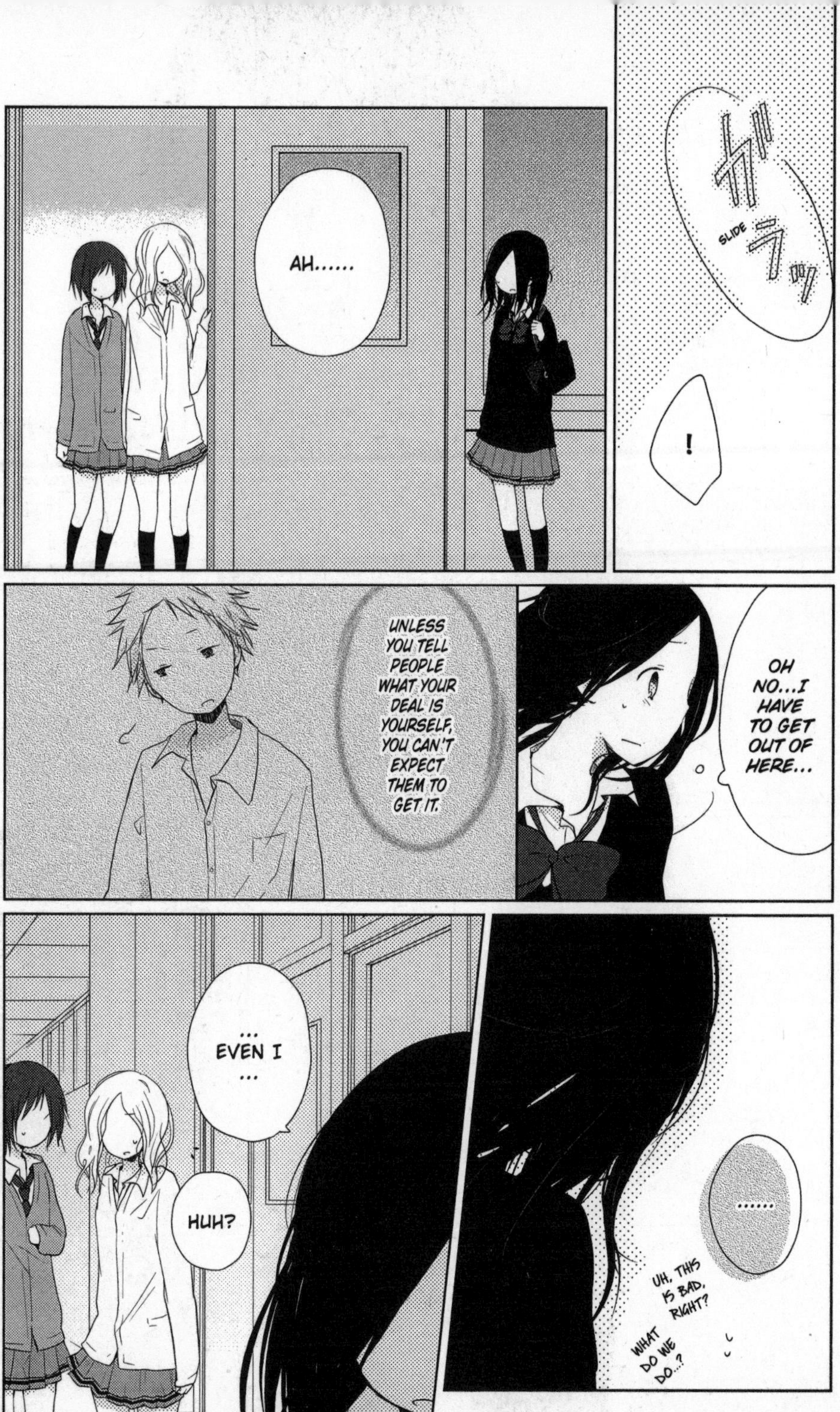
ガラッ
SLIDE
!
AH......
OH NO...I HAVE TO GET OUT OF HERE...
UNLESS YOU TELL PEOPLE WHAT YOUR DEAL IS YOURSELF, YOU CAN'T EXPECT THEM TO GET IT.
......
UH, THIS IS BAD, RIGHT?
WHAT DO WE DO..?
... EVEN I ...
HUH?

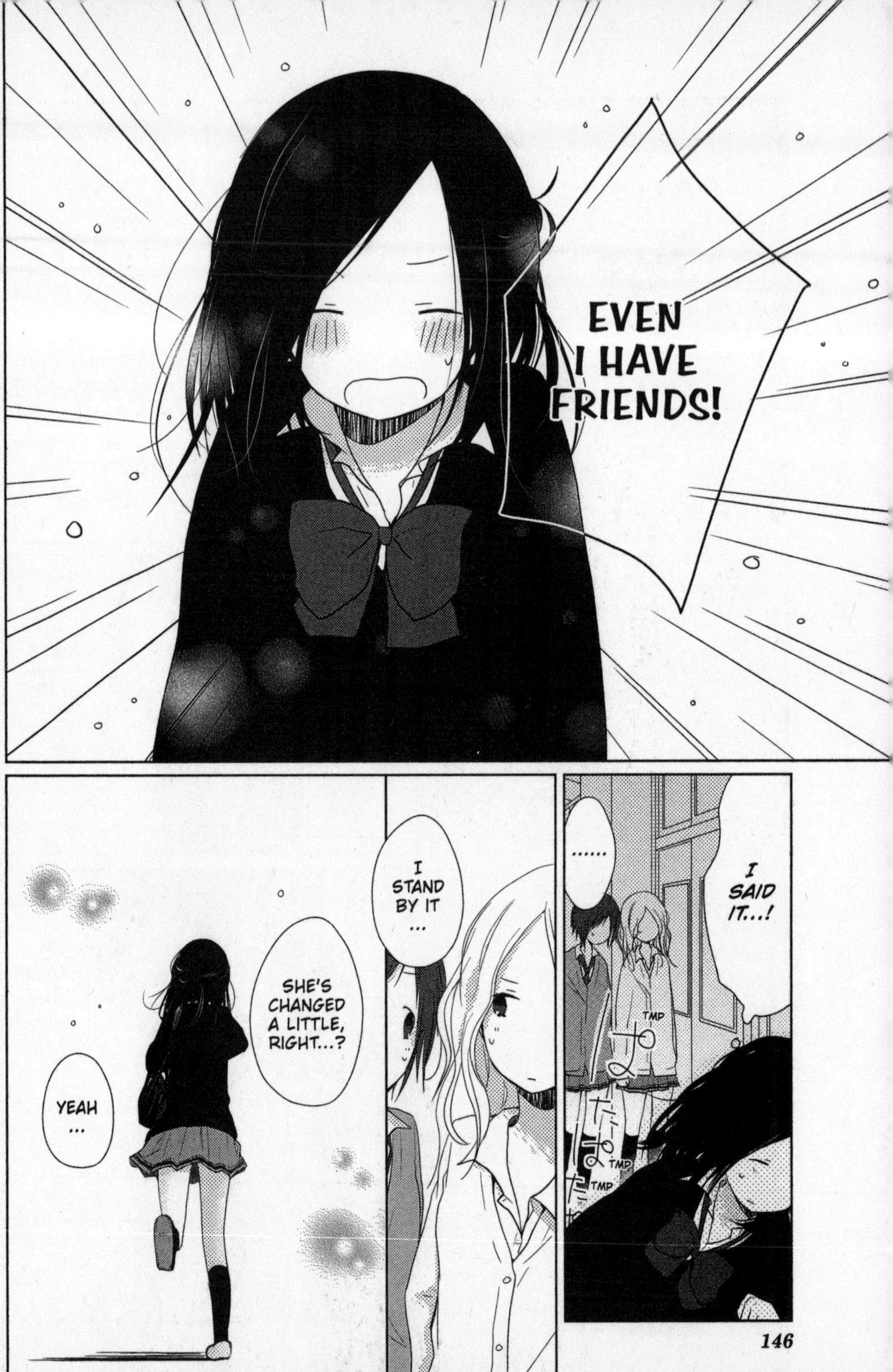

EVEN I HAVE FRIENDS!
......
I SAID IT...!
TMP
TMP
TMP
I STAND BY IT ...
SHE'S CHANGED A LITTLE, RIGHT...?
YEAH ...

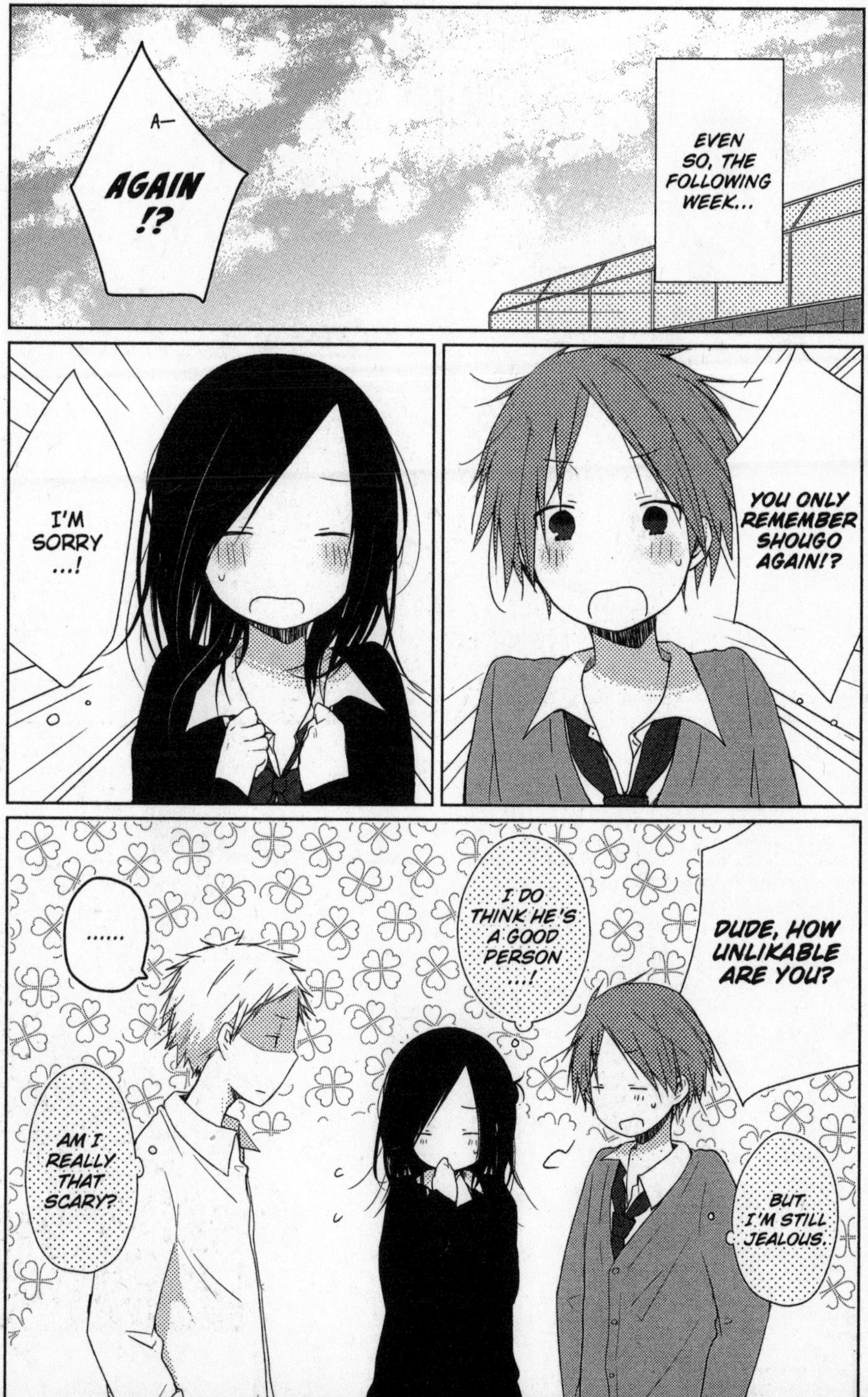
EVEN SO, THE FOLLOWING WEEK...
A— AGAIN!?
YOU ONLY REMEMBER SHOUGO AGAIN!?
I'M SORRY ...!
DUDE, HOW UNLIKABLE ARE YOU?
I DO THINK HE'S A GOOD PERSON ...!
......
BUT I'M STILL JEALOUS.
AM I REALLY THAT SCARY?

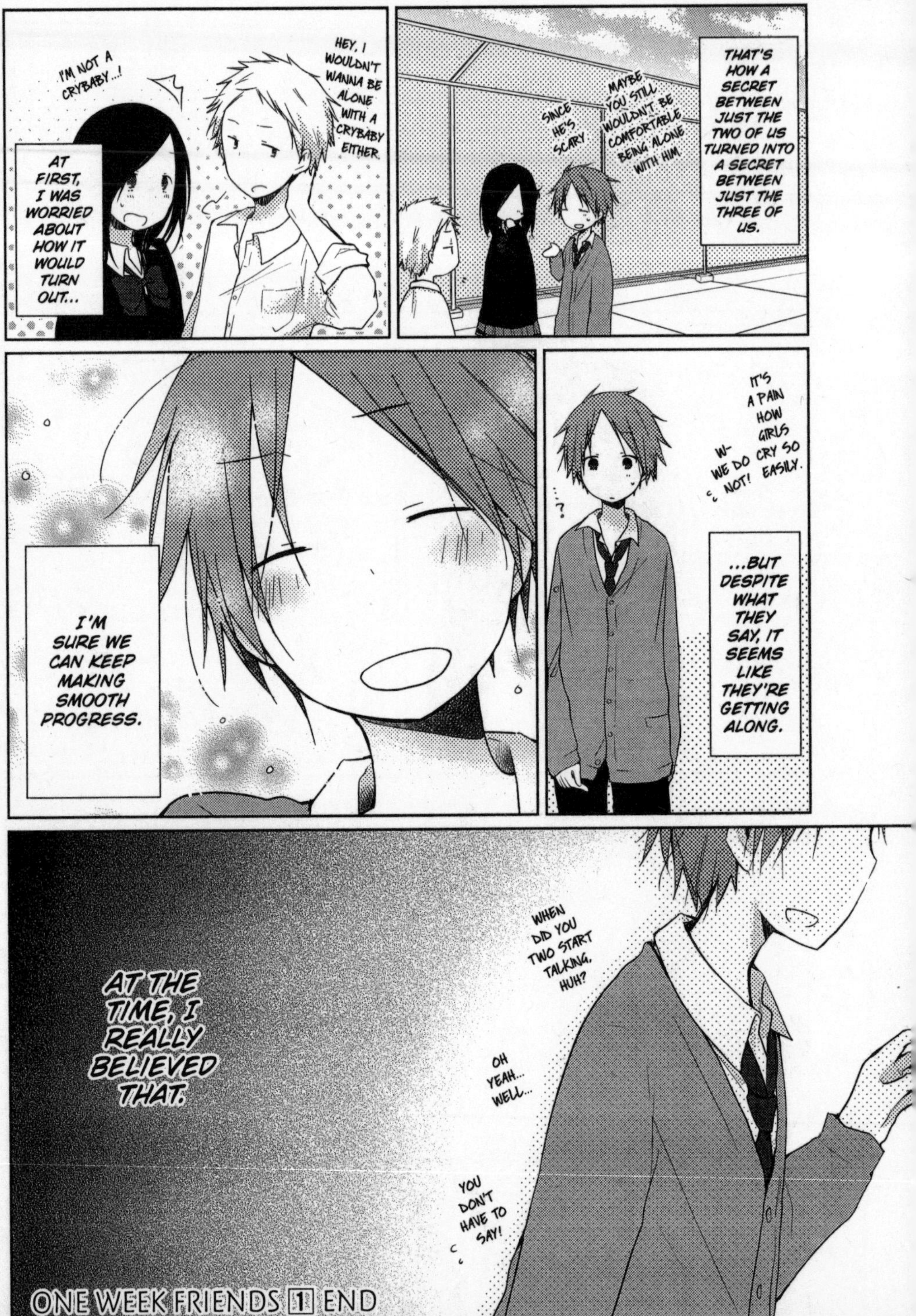
THAT'S HOW A SECRET BETWEEN JUST THE TWO OF US TURNED INTO A SECRET BETWEEN JUST THE THREE OF US.
MAYBE YOU STILL WOULDN'T BE COMFORTABLE BEING ALONE WITH HIM
SINCE HE'S SCARY
HEY, I WOULDN'T WANNA BE ALONE WITH A CRYBABY EITHER.
I'M NOT A CRYBABY...!
AT FIRST, I WAS WORRIED ABOUT HOW IT WOULD TURN OUT...
IT'S A PAIN HOW GIRLS CRY SO EASILY.
W-WE DO NOT!
...BUT DESPITE WHAT THEY SAY, IT SEEMS LIKE THEY'RE GETTING ALONG.
I'M SURE WE CAN KEEP MAKING SMOOTH PROGRESS.
WHEN DID YOU TWO START TALKING, HUH?
OH YEAH... WELL...
YOU DON'T HAVE TO SAY!
AT THE TIME, I REALLY BELIEVED THAT.
ONE WEEK FRIENDS 1 END

# ONE
# WEEK
# FRIENDS

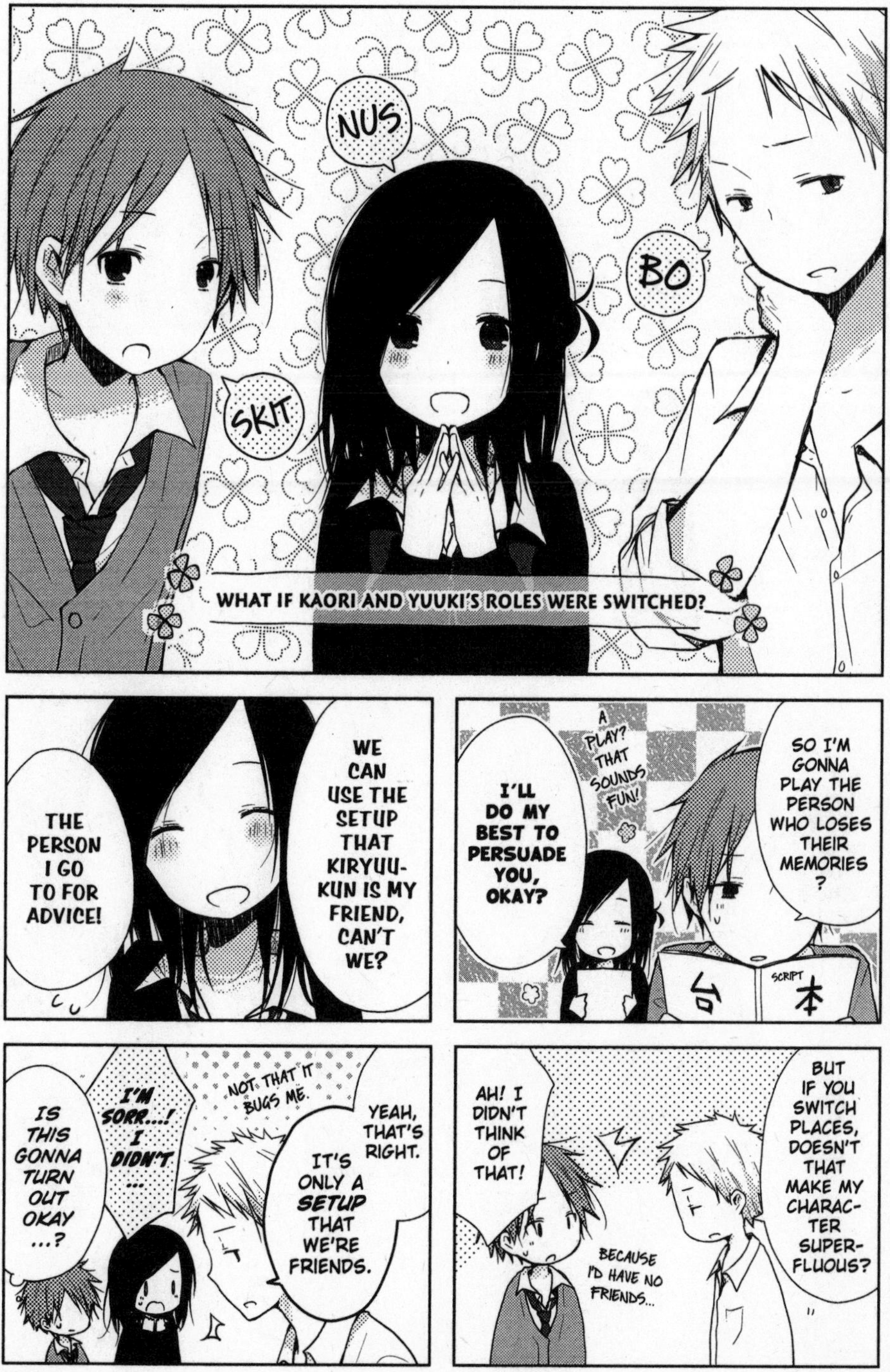
NUS
BO
SKIT
WHAT IF KAORI AND YUUKI'S ROLES WERE SWITCHED?
SO I'M GONNA PLAY THE PERSON WHO LOSES THEIR MEMORIES?
A PLAY? THAT SOUNDS FUN!
I'LL DO MY BEST TO PERSUADE YOU, OKAY?
SCRIPT
WE CAN USE THE SETUP THAT KIRYUU-KUN IS MY FRIEND, CAN'T WE?
THE PERSON I GO TO FOR ADVICE!
BUT IF YOU SWITCH PLACES, DOESN'T THAT MAKE MY CHARACTER SUPERFLUOUS?
AH! I DIDN'T THINK OF THAT!
BECAUSE I'D HAVE NO FRIENDS...
YEAH, THAT'S RIGHT.
NOT THAT IT BUGS ME.
IT'S ONLY A SETUP THAT WE'RE FRIENDS.
I'M SORR...! I DIDN'T ...
IS THIS GONNA TURN OUT OKAY ...?

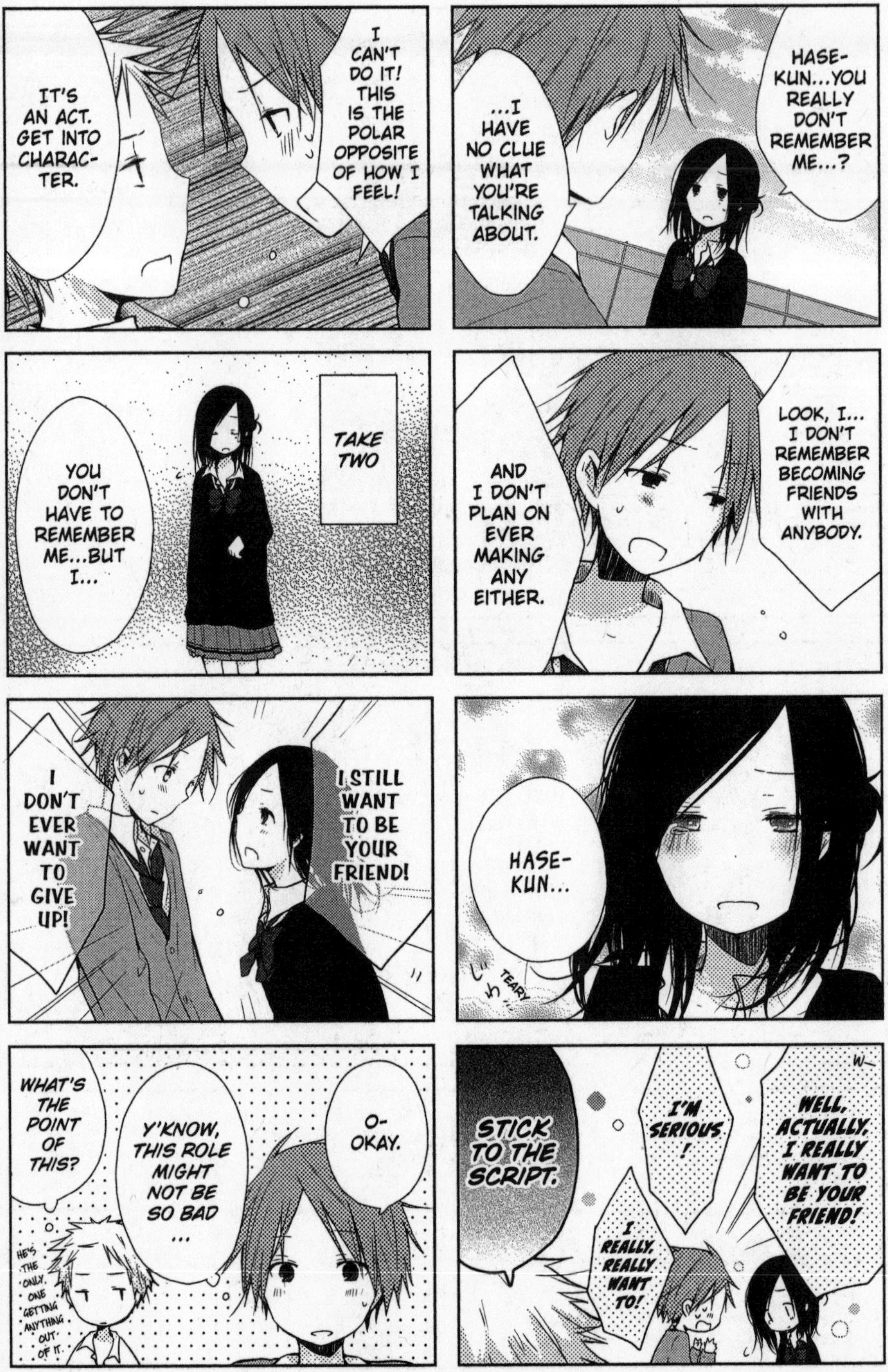
HASE-KUN...YOU REALLY DON'T REMEMBER ME...?
...I HAVE NO CLUE WHAT YOU'RE TALKING ABOUT.
I CAN'T DO IT! THIS IS THE POLAR OPPOSITE OF HOW I FEEL!
IT'S AN ACT. GET INTO CHARACTER.
LOOK, I... I DON'T REMEMBER BECOMING FRIENDS WITH ANYBODY.
AND I DON'T PLAN ON EVER MAKING ANY EITHER.
TAKE TWO
YOU DON'T HAVE TO REMEMBER ME...BUT I...
HASE-KUN...
TEARY
I STILL WANT TO BE YOUR FRIEND!
I DON'T EVER WANT TO GIVE UP!
W—
WELL, ACTUALLY, I REALLY WANT TO BE YOUR FRIEND!
I'M SERIOUS!
I REALLY, REALLY WANT TO!
STICK TO THE SCRIPT.
O-OKAY.
Y'KNOW, THIS ROLE MIGHT NOT BE SO BAD...
WHAT'S THE POINT OF THIS?
HE'S THE ONLY ONE GETTING ANYTHING OUT OF IT.

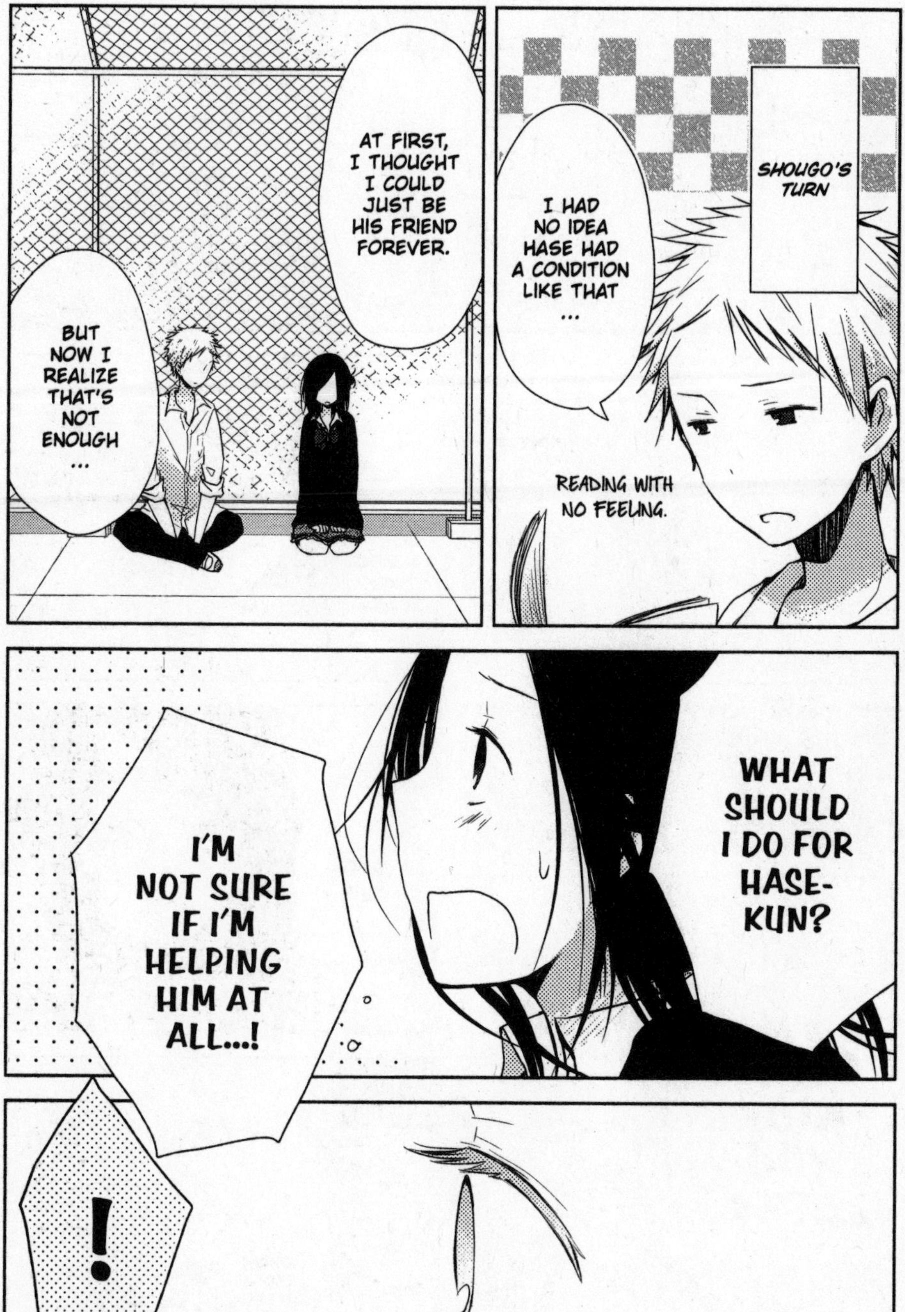
SHOUGO'S TURN
I HAD NO IDEA HASE HAD A CONDITION LIKE THAT ...
READING WITH NO FEELING.
AT FIRST, I THOUGHT I COULD JUST BE HIS FRIEND FOREVER.
BUT NOW I REALIZE THAT'S NOT ENOUGH ...
WHAT SHOULD I DO FOR HASE-KUN?
I'M NOT SURE IF I'M HELPING HIM AT ALL...!
!

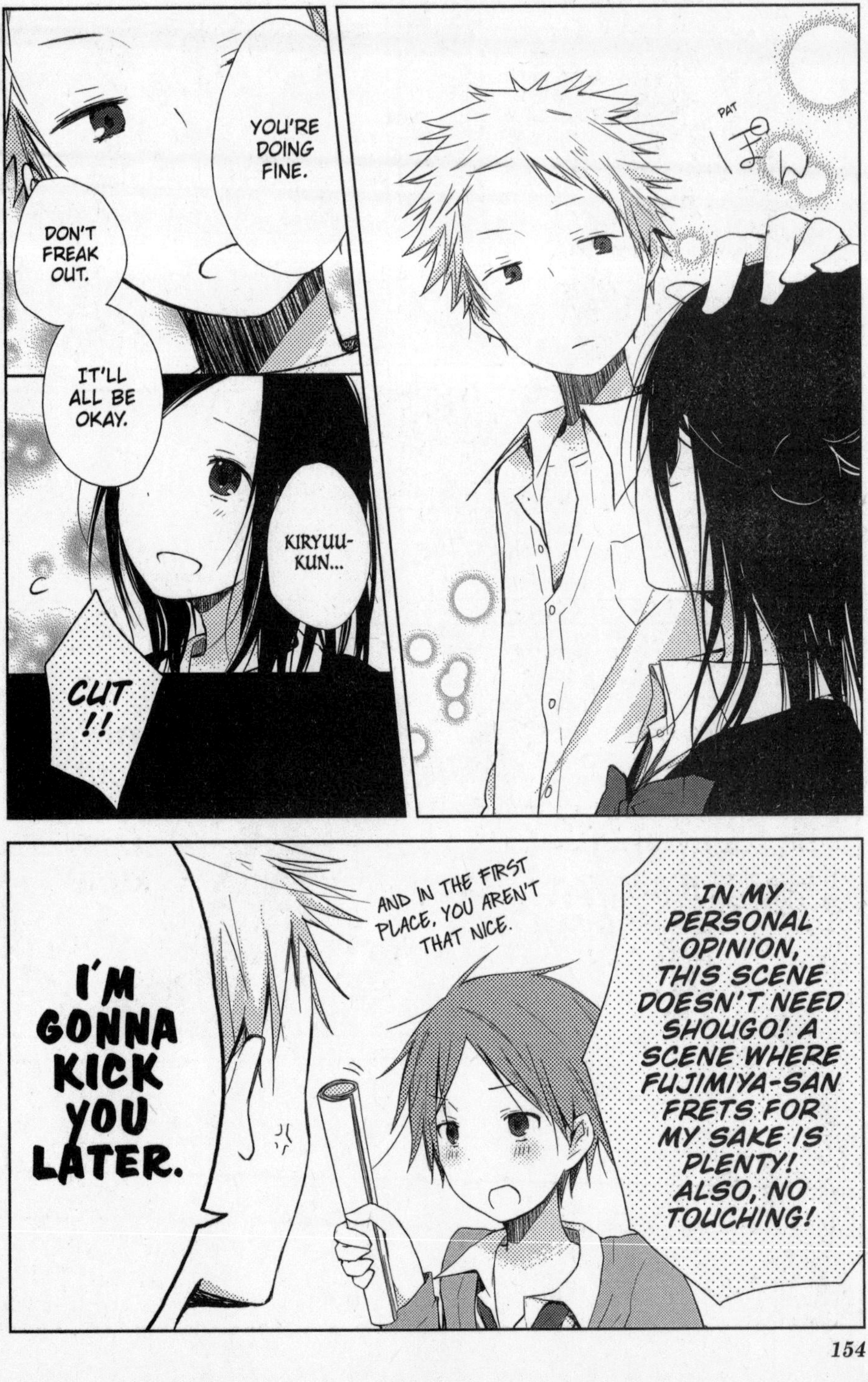
PAT
ぽん
YOU'RE DOING FINE.
DON'T FREAK OUT.
IT'LL ALL BE OKAY.
KIRYUU-KUN...
CUT!!
IN MY PERSONAL OPINION, THIS SCENE DOESN'T NEED SHOUGO! A SCENE WHERE FUJIMIYA-SAN FRETS FOR MY SAKE IS PLENTY! ALSO, NO TOUCHING!
AND IN THE FIRST PLACE, YOU AREN'T THAT NICE.
I'M GONNA KICK YOU LATER.

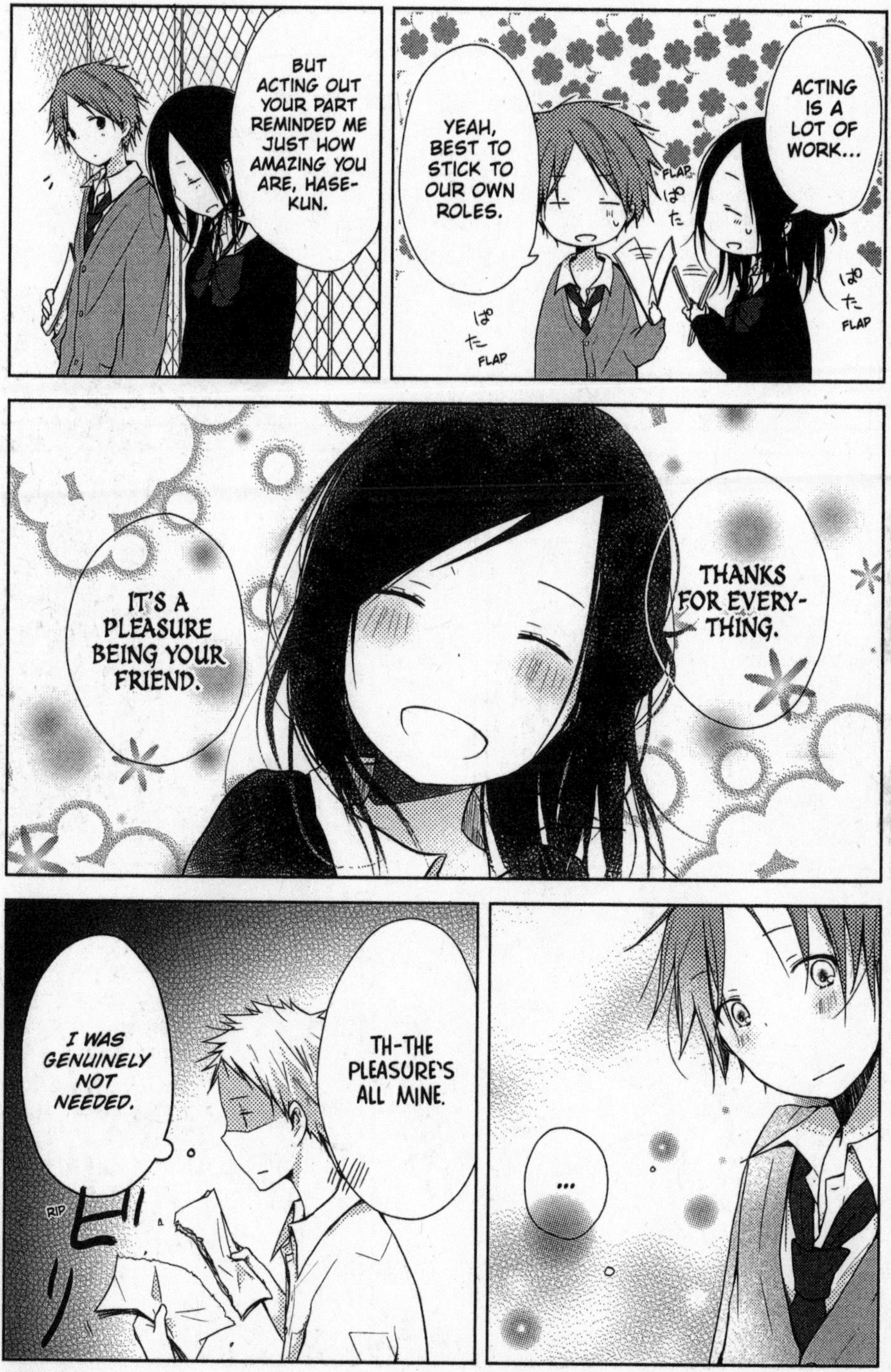
ACTING IS A LOT OF WORK...
FLAP ぱた
YEAH, BEST TO STICK TO OUR OWN ROLES.
ぱた FLAP
ぱた FLAP
BUT ACTING OUT YOUR PART REMINDED ME JUST HOW AMAZING YOU ARE, HASE-KUN.
THANKS FOR EVERY-THING.
IT'S A PLEASURE BEING YOUR FRIEND.
...
TH-THE PLEASURE'S ALL MINE.
I WAS GENUINELY NOT NEEDED.
RIP ビリ

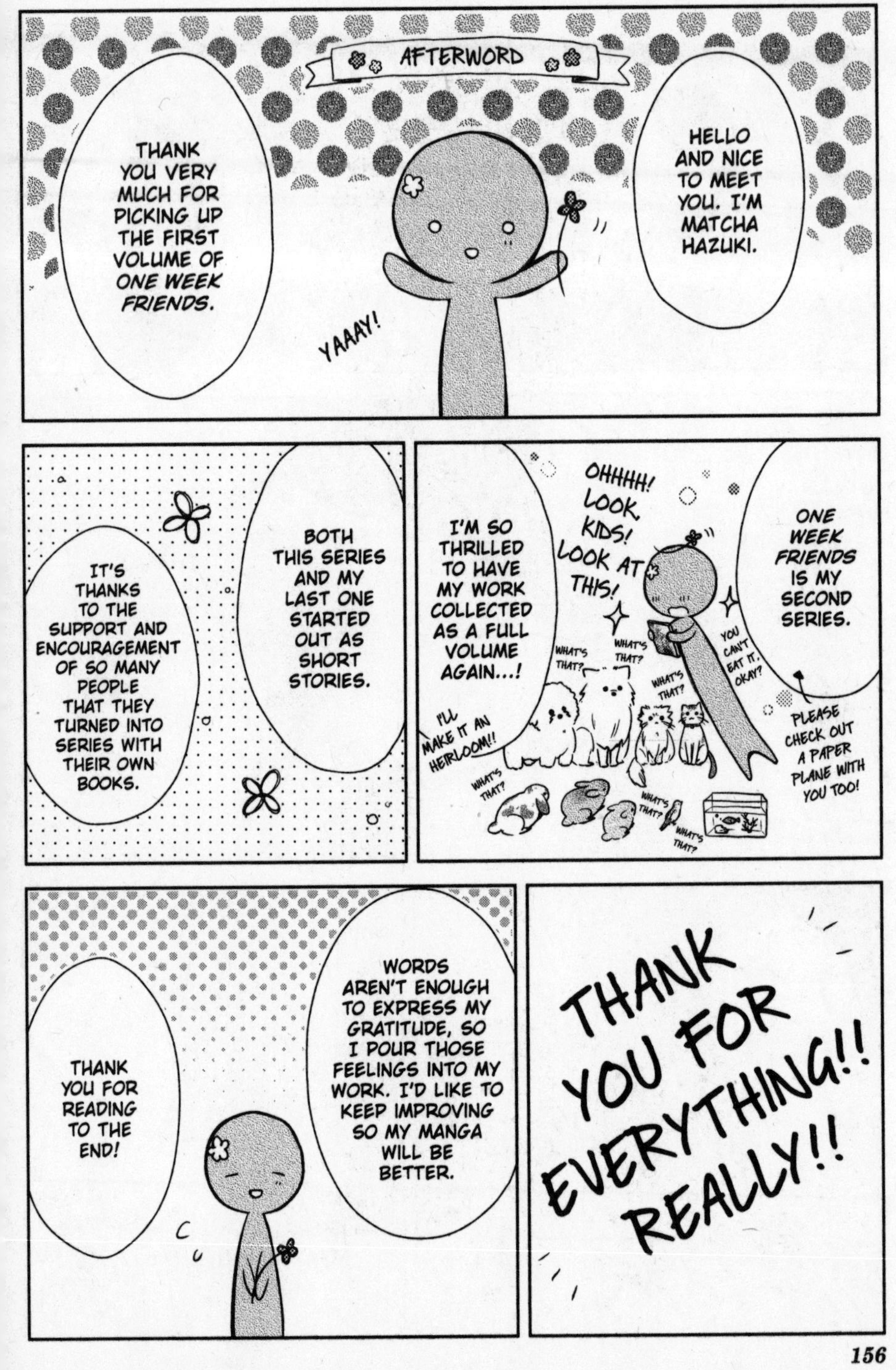
AFTERWORD
HELLO AND NICE TO MEET YOU. I'M MATCHA HAZUKI.
THANK YOU VERY MUCH FOR PICKING UP THE FIRST VOLUME OF *ONE WEEK FRIENDS*.
YAAAY!
*ONE WEEK FRIENDS* IS MY SECOND SERIES.
OHHHHH! LOOK, KIDS! LOOK AT THIS!
YOU CAN'T EAT IT, OKAY?
PLEASE CHECK OUT A PAPER PLANE WITH YOU TOO!
WHAT'S THAT?
WHAT'S THAT?
WHAT'S THAT?
WHAT'S THAT?
WHAT'S THAT?
WHAT'S THAT?
I'M SO THRILLED TO HAVE MY WORK COLLECTED AS A FULL VOLUME AGAIN...!
I'LL MAKE IT AN HEIRLOOM!!
BOTH THIS SERIES AND MY LAST ONE STARTED OUT AS SHORT STORIES.
IT'S THANKS TO THE SUPPORT AND ENCOURAGEMENT OF SO MANY PEOPLE THAT THEY TURNED INTO SERIES WITH THEIR OWN BOOKS.
THANK YOU FOR EVERYTHING!! REALLY!!
WORDS AREN'T ENOUGH TO EXPRESS MY GRATITUDE, SO I POUR THOSE FEELINGS INTO MY WORK. I'D LIKE TO KEEP IMPROVING SO MY MANGA WILL BE BETTER.
THANK YOU FOR READING TO THE END!

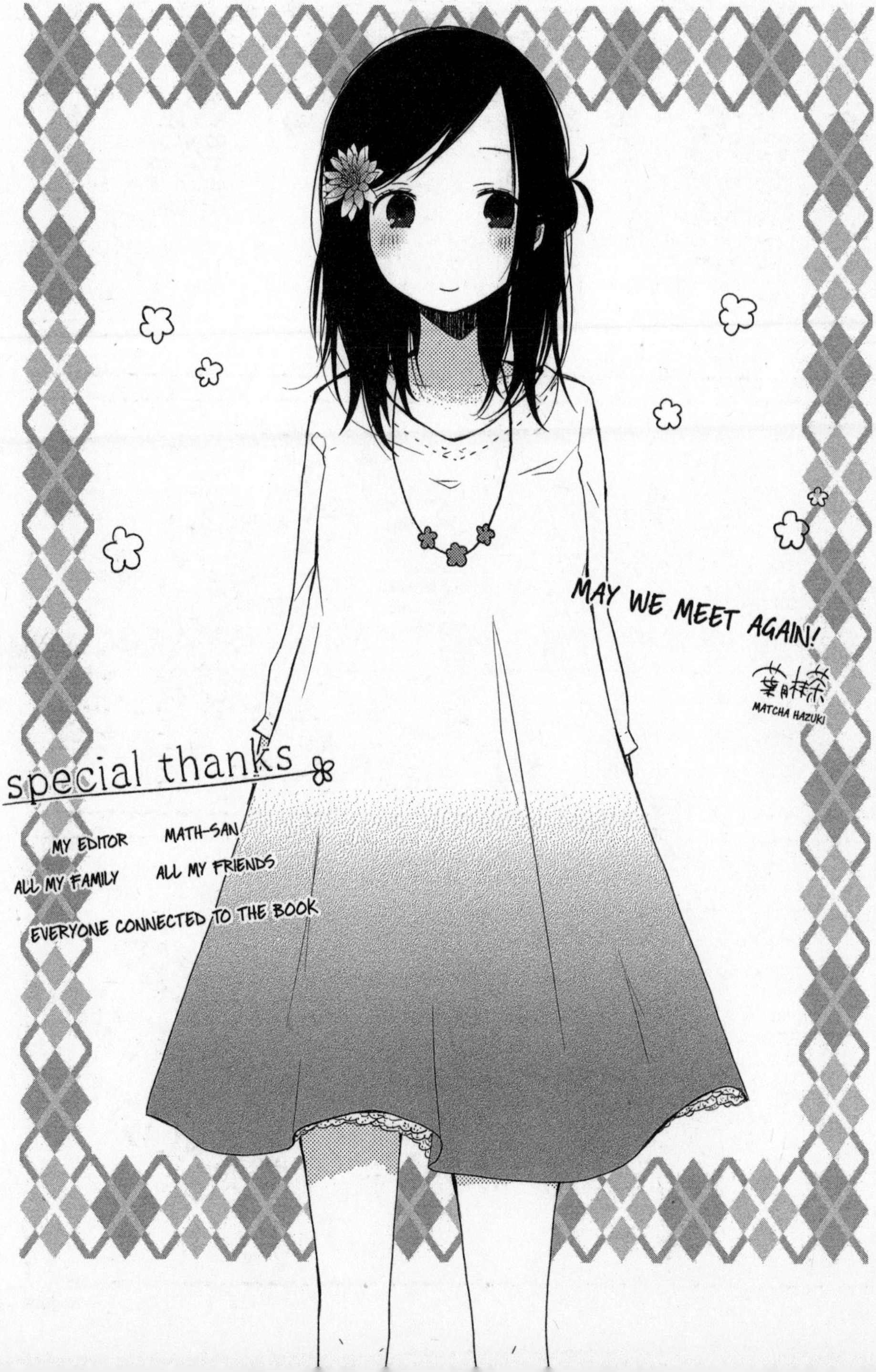
MAY WE MEET AGAIN!
葉月抹茶
MATCHA HAZUKI
special thanks
MY EDITOR
MATH-SAN
ALL MY FAMILY
ALL MY FRIENDS
EVERYONE CONNECTED TO THE BOOK

## NEXT ONE WEEK FRIENDS...

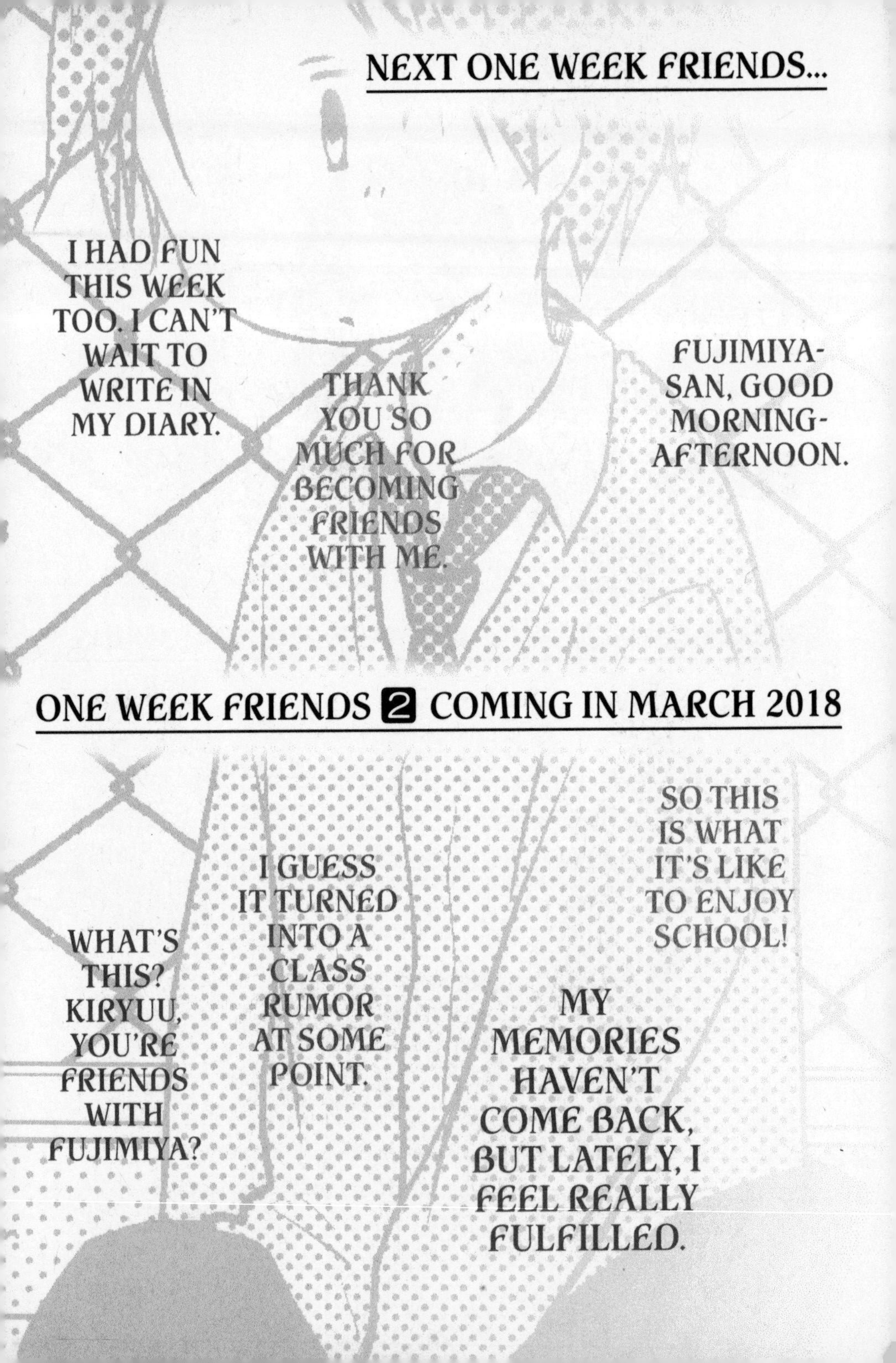
FUJIMIYA-SAN, GOOD MORNING-AFTERNOON.
THANK YOU SO MUCH FOR BECOMING FRIENDS WITH ME.
I HAD FUN THIS WEEK TOO. I CAN'T WAIT TO WRITE IN MY DIARY.
SO THIS IS WHAT IT'S LIKE TO ENJOY SCHOOL!
MY MEMORIES HAVEN'T COME BACK, BUT LATELY, I FEEL REALLY FULFILLED.
I GUESS IT TURNED INTO A CLASS RUMOR AT SOME POINT.
WHAT'S THIS? KIRYUU, YOU'RE FRIENDS WITH FUJIMIYA?

## ONE WEEK FRIENDS 2 COMING IN MARCH 2018

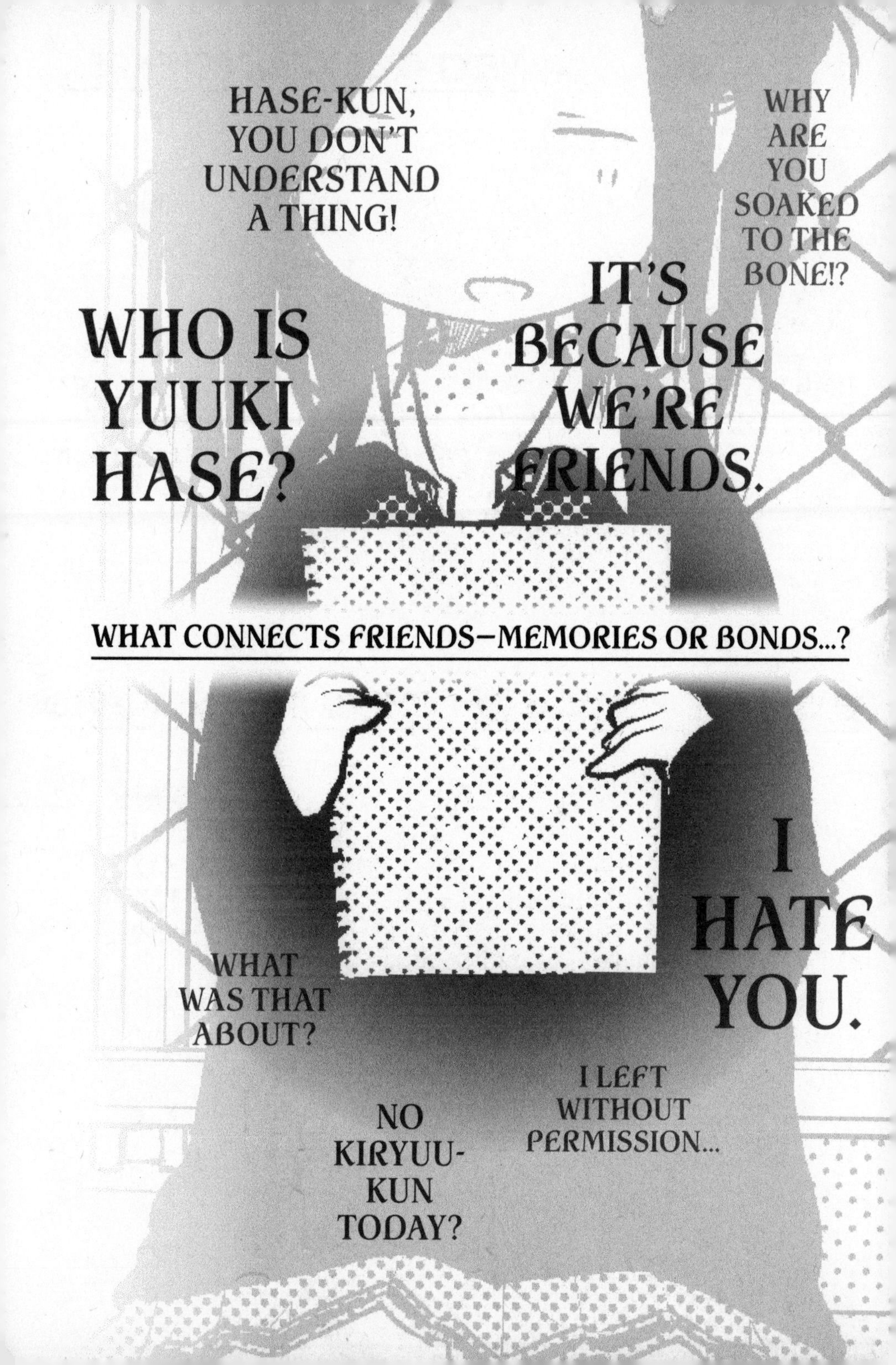
WHY ARE YOU SOAKED TO THE BONE!?
HASE-KUN, YOU DON'T UNDERSTAND A THING!
IT'S BECAUSE WE'RE FRIENDS.
WHO IS YUUKI HASE?
WHAT CONNECTS FRIENDS—MEMORIES OR BONDS...?
I HATE YOU.
WHAT WAS THAT ABOUT?
I LEFT WITHOUT PERMISSION...
NO KIRYUU-KUN TODAY?

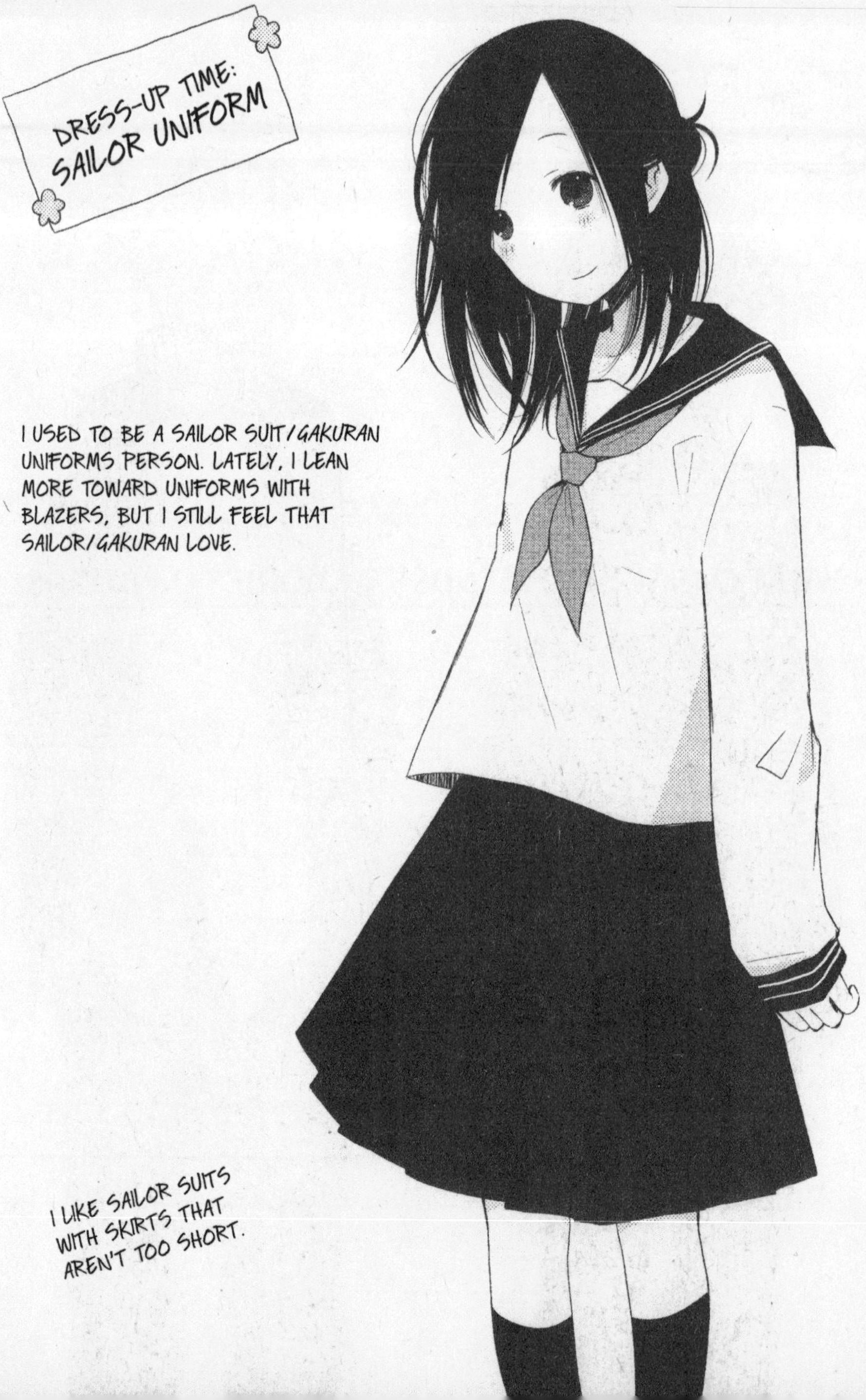
DRESS-UP TIME: SAILOR UNIFORM
I USED TO BE A SAILOR SUIT/GAKURAN UNIFORMS PERSON. LATELY, I LEAN MORE TOWARD UNIFORMS WITH BLAZERS, BUT I STILL FEEL THAT SAILOR/GAKURAN LOVE.
I LIKE SAILOR SUITS WITH SKIRTS THAT AREN'T TOO SHORT.

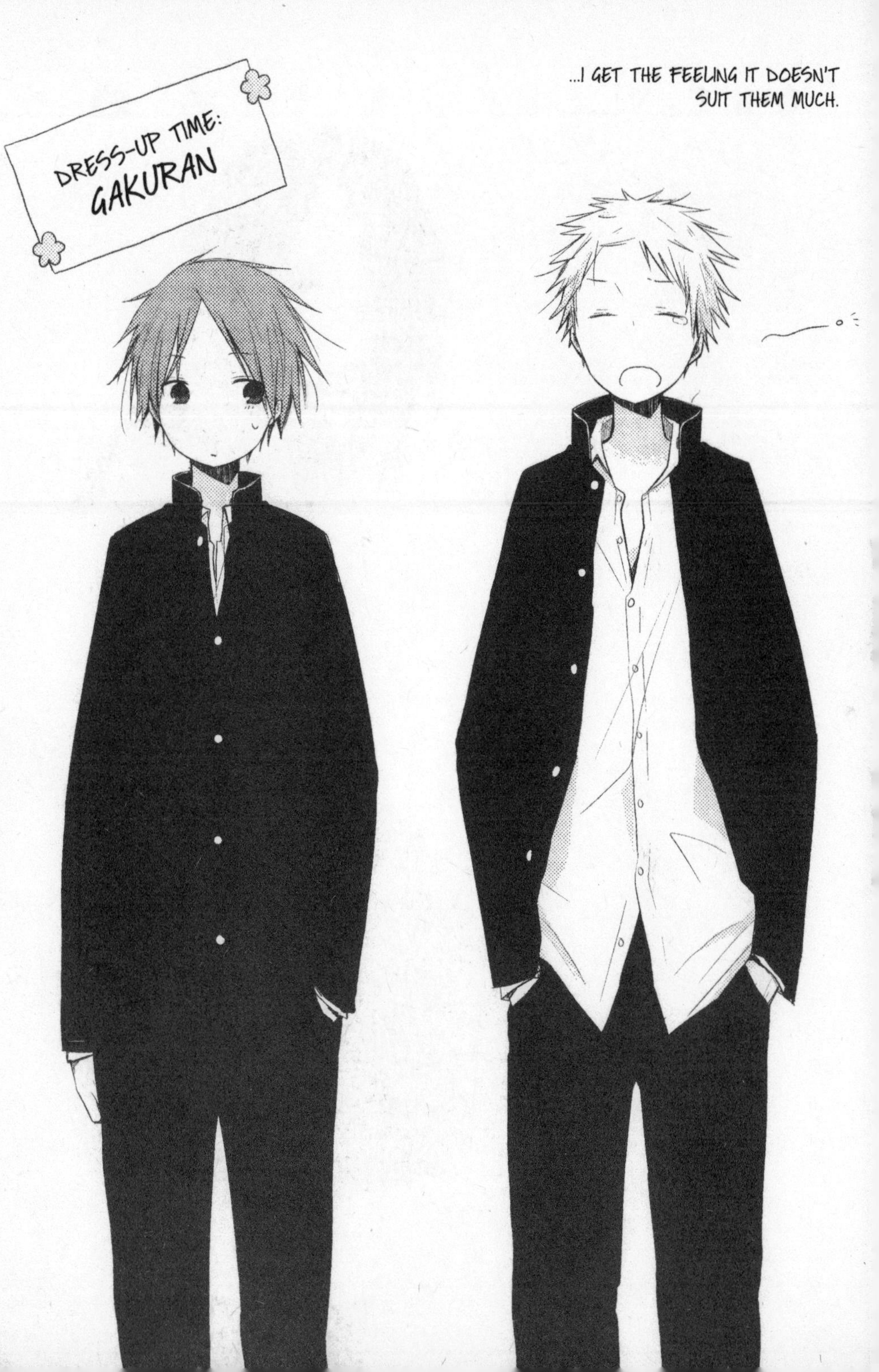
...I GET THE FEELING IT DOESN'T SUIT THEM MUCH.
DRESS-UP TIME: GAKURAN

# ONE WEEK FRIENDS 1

## MATCHA HAZUKI

Translation/Adaptation: Amanda Haley

Lettering: Bianca Pistillo

ONE WEEK FRIENDS, Volume 1 ©2012 Matcha Hazuki/
SQUARE ENIX CO., LTD. First published in Japan in 2012 by SQUARE
ENIX CO., LTD. English translation rights arranged with SQUARE
ENIX CO., LTD. and Yen Press, LLC through Tuttle-Mori Agency, Inc.

English translation © 2017 by SQUARE ENIX CO., LTD.

Yen Press
1290 Avenue of the Americas
New York, NY 10104

Visit us at yenpress.com
facebook.com/yenpress
twitter.com/yenpress
yenpress.tumblr.com
instagram.com/yenpress

First Yen Press Edition: December 2017

Yen Press is an imprint of Yen Press, LLC.
The Yen Press name and logo are trademarks of
Yen Press, LLC.

The publisher is not responsible for websites (or their
content) that are not owned by the publisher.

Library of Congress Control Number: 2017954140

ISBNs: 978-0-316-41416-6 (paperback)
       978-0-316-44734-8 (ebook)

10 9 8 7 6 5 4 3 2 1

BVG

Printed in the United States of America